Teaching Decision Making
to Adolescents

Teaching Decision Making
to Adolescents

Edited by

Jonathan Baron
University of Pennsylvania

Rex V. Brown
Decision Sciences Consortium, Inc.
Reston, VA

LEA LAWRENCE ERLBAUM ASSOCIATES, PUBLISHERS
1991 Hillsdale, New Jersey   Hove and London

Lawrence Erlbaum Associates, Inc., Publishers
365 Broadway
Hillsdale, New Jersey   07642

Library of Congress Cataloging-in-Publication Data
Teaching decision making to adolescents / edited by Jonathan Baron,
   Rex Brown.
        p.   cm.
      Includes bibliographical references (p.   ) and indexes.
      ISBN 0-8058-0497-8
      1. Decision-making—Study and teaching (Secondary)   I. Baron,
   Jonathan, 1944-   . II. Brown, Rex V.
   LB1062.5T43   1991
   658.4 '03 '0712—dc20   90-49290
                                                                     CIP

Printed in the United States of America
10 9 8 7 6 5 4 3 2 1

Contents

Chapter 3

The GOFER Course in Decision Making   **61**
Leon Mann, Ros Harmoni, and Colin Power

Chapter 4

Thinking and Decision Making   **79**
Marilyn Jager Adams and Carl E. Feehrer

Chapter 5

Toward Improved Instruction in Decision Making to Adolescents: A Conceptual Framework and Pilot Program   **95**
Jonathan Baron and Rex V. Brown

Chapter 6

Chapter 7

Chapter 8

Chapter 9

Chapter 13

Chapter 14

List of Contributors

Marilyn Jager Adams
Bolt Beranek & Newman, Inc.
Cambridge, MA

Jonathan Baron
Department of Psychology
University of Pennsylvania

Eta Berner
University of Illinois Medical Center

Ruth Beyth-Marom
Department of Decision Sciences
Carnegie Mellon University

Leslie R. Branden-Muller
Rutgers University

Rex V. Brown
Decision Science Consortium, Inc.
Reston, VA

Vincent N. Campbell
Decision Systems Inc.
Reston, VA

Maurice J. Elias
Department of Psychology
Rutgers University

Carl E. Feehrer
Bolt Beranek & Newman, Inc.
Cambridge, MA

Baruch Fischoff
Department of Decision Sciences
Carnegie Mellon University

Lita Furby
Eugene Research Institute

Greer Graumlich
Henry H. Houston Elementary School

Margaret Grier
University of Illinois Medical Center

Ros Harmoni
Department of Psychology
The Flinders University of South Australia

Marilyn Jacobs Quadrel
Department of Decision Sciences
Carnegie Mellon University

Joyce Johnson
University of Illinois Medical Center

Kathryn Blackmond Laskey
Decision Science Consortium Inc.
Reston, VA

Leon Mann
Department of Psychology
The Flinders University of South Australia

Anne W. Martin
Decision Science Consortium, Inc.
Reston, VA

Colin Power
Department of Psychology
The Flinders University of South Australia

Michael A. Sayette
Rutgers University

James Shanteau
Decision, Risk, & Management Science Program

John A. Swets
Bolt Beranek and Newman, Inc.
Cambridge, MA

Joanna P. Williams
Teachers' College, Columbia University

Daniel D. Wheeler
Department of Educational Foundations
University of Cincinnati

Prologue

Why Americans Can't Think Straight*

Jonathan Baron
University of Pennsylvania

Rex V. Brown
Decision Science Consortium, Inc.
Reston, VA

Jane, 30 and single, was living from hand to mouth as an actress and waitress when her father died and left her his life savings. The money was tied up in stock, which he had held for years because of the capital-gains tax he would have had to pay if he sold it. Jane, of course, could sell it without paying the tax, but she did not plan to do so, since the value of the stock had just gone down, and she hoped it would go back up.

A friend asked her, "If you had the money in cash instead of the stock, would you buy the stock at its current price?"

"Of course not," she replied. "I want a safe and steady income to supplement what I earn, and the stock could just as easily go down some more."

"So, if you had a choice between the stock and the cash, you'd choose the cash, right?" Jane saw that this was exactly her choice, and she sold the stock.

Jane at first exhibited a classic fallacy of decision-making called the endowment effect, an irrational tendency to favor the status quo. Yet one apt question enabled her to recognize and correct the problem.

Most Americans, however, never get that kind of help—either in school or in later life. Adolescents become involved in crime, abuse drugs, get pregnant or drop out as a result of faulty thinking. Adults make bad deci-

---

*Reproduced with permission from *The Washington Post*, August 7, 1988.

1

sions about careers, investments, marriage, insurance and medical treatment.

Nor are public officials exempt. Listen to then-senator Jeremiah Denton discussing the Tennessee-Tombigbee Waterway project in 1981: "To terminate a project in which $1.1 billion has been invested represents an unconscionable mishandling of taxpayers' dollars." This classic fallacy, the "sunk cost" effect, is also known as "throwing good money after bad." The real question, of course, is whether the benefits of future spending are sufficient to justify the expense. The money already spent is, so to speak, over the dam and irrelevant to the issue.

Even the most prestigious professions are vulnerable. Researchers have found that physicians are subject to the same sorts of defects in reasoning, which often lead to widespread misdiagnoses and failures to order treatments that produce optimal results.

Such fallacies are endemic to everyday life. They waste public and private money, make people less efficient and productive and diminish national capacity to compete abroad. But there is evidence they can be corrected. Within the past few years, a "thinking skills" movement has arisen among educators around the globe. We believe that the time has come to add a fourth "R" to the traditional three: reasoning. So does Albert Shanker, president of the American Federation of Teachers, who has endorsed the idea for years. And so do many business executives concerned about the abilities of their workers.

If schools taught children to make up their minds intelligently, more of us might avoid the above fallacies and others to which we are notoriously prone. For example:

Shortsightedness. We overweigh the immediate present. An adolescent might choose to have sex without contraception when the opportunity is at hand; but if asked the same question beforehand, would prefer not to take the chance. Governments—and the people who elect them—would rather have a budget deficit to pay off in the future than higher taxes now.

Impulsiveness. We sometimes make choices with insufficient thought or no thought at all.

Neglect of probability. Some assume that improbable events (getting pregnant, getting hooked, getting AIDS) won't happen, but, of course, they do. People also forget that choices set precedents for later choices and probabilities add up. One ride without a seatbelt is unlikely to kill you, but if it sets a precedent for thousands of rides, the chances of a serious accident *sometime* are substantial.

"My-side" bias. We defend our beliefs as if we were lawyers hired by ourselves to convince us that we were right all along.

Single-mindedness. We sometimes make decisions as though they had only a single goal, such as getting out of a bad marriage, while ignoring other relevant goals, such as raising our children well.

TEACHING DECISION MAKING

Can education help to correct these fallacies? The notion was being debated centuries before Plato and Aristotle. The Port Royal Logic—a textbook of logic and rational choice written in France in 1662—was used extensively in upper-class education in France and England. It was influenced by Pascal's ideas about decision-making, as exhibited in "Pascal's Wager," an argument for leading the Christian life: If you are not sure whether God exists or not, it is better to act as if He does, because the cost of error is too great if you act otherwise and you are wrong.

The idea of teaching people to think clearly and make careful decisions was not lost with the birth of mass education in the 20th century. Philosopher John Dewey argued that such an approach is necessary for citizens in a democracy. He believed that students should be taught to think reflectively, considering alternatives and reasons on all sides. His ideas, however, were misinterpreted as sanctioning permissiveness, and the behaviorist revolution in psychology led to a reaction against them and to an emphasis on easily measured behavior as the goal of education. (This emphasis continues today in the form of demands for "accountability," a goal that is often pursued singlemindedly, neglecting the ultimate goals of education.)

In the past few years, teachers in England, Australia, Germany and the United States have tried once again to find new ways to improve students' thinking—not by the traditional lectures on the evils of drugs or the consequences of sex without contraception, but through programs that try to teach people to reason effectively. Some of these experimental programs—in some cases beginning as early as preschool—have had measurable effects in such areas as diminished aggressive behavior and improved school performance.

One of the most thorough and successful of these programs was tested between 1980 and 1984 in Venezuela, where tests showed that it raised students' scholastic-aptitude growth rates by more than 50 percent. Inspired by Luis Alberto Machado, a Venezuelan political leader and social theorist, and jointly designed by a group at Harvard University and a Cambridge consulting firm, it was part of an ambitious national program to increase intelligence in the nation.

We are currently developing a decision-making course of our own for middle schoolers (under a grant from the National Institute of Child Health and Human Development) and piloting it in schools in the Washington and Philadelphia areas.

PERSONALIZED DECISION ANALYSIS

A major stimulus for our and others' efforts has been the emergence, over the last 20 years or so, of "personalized decision analysis" as an effective and widely used tool for professional decision makers. At the core of PDA is a sophisticated theory of rational choice. This theory can serve as a kind of standard that we should try to approximate in our everyday lives. PDA basically poses the questions: What do I want? What can I do? What might happen?

It quantifies the resulting judgments of uncertainty and subjective value as probabilities and utilities, respectively. The best choice is the one with the highest expected utility, as calculated by multiplying the probability of each outcome times its utility, and then adding the products. That is, the value of an outcome is balanced against its likelihood—if either is too low, the option is rejected.

For example, a naval captain has to decide whether to shoot down an unidentified approaching plane. He assesses a 40-percent probability that it is hostile and then considers four potential outcomes:

A. The worst case is that it is hostile and he fails to shoot. Let us call that -100 on a utility scale. B. The best case is that it is not hostile, and he does not shoot. Let us call that 0. (All utility numbers are negative in this instance.) C. If the plane is hostile and he shoots, he would assign this a utility of -20. D. Finally, if it is not hostile and he shoots, the utility is -90.

Given these values, the *expected* utility of shooting is C $(.40)(-20) +$ D$(.60)(-90)$, which comes to -62. The expected utility of *not* shooting is A $(.40)(-100) +$ B$(.60)(0)$, or -40. Therefore, not shooting is not as bad as shooting, and he ought not to shoot. By the same kind of analysis, if the probability of the plane being hostile were 90 percent, the expected utility would be -27 for shooting and -90 for not shooting, and he ought to shoot.

So far, PDA has proven most popular in such fields as business, government and medicine, where the costs of an error are high enough to justify substantial effort and expenditure. PDA has been applied to decisions involving such matters as location of nuclear waste, investments and diversification, surgical alternatives, and options in undertaking military missions. PDA is now taught routinely to business students, medical students and other professionals—and to undergraduates in elective courses—as a technique to be deliberately applied in such high-profile cases.

In principle, PDA can correct the fallacies we noted earlier. Students who understand the underlying theory of rational choice will be able to comprehend why these fallacies need to be corrected. In practice, such an understanding needs to be buttressed by practical rules of thumb: examine arguments on the other side; think about the future; ignore the past (sunk coat) except for its effect on the future; consider other goals; and so on. These rules protect people against the fallacies.

But we believe that even ordinary decisions, in the personal, professional and civic lives of ordinary people, can be improved by teaching the principles of good decision-making. Instruction beginning in adolescence or before can prevent the development of poor reasoning habits and, with enough practice, instill better habits.

It is not enough, we think, just to walk students through the steps of making a decision unless we show them what missteps they might make. Students make decisions all the time. The paramount issue is that they do not always make them well.

Our approach is to teach decision-making as an academic subject, but anchored firmly to issues that have immediate significance for the students. The core unit consists of eight lessons to develop basic concepts: qualitative exposition of the principles of rational choice and the fallacies that interfere with it; formal PDA techniques to correct those fallacies (with exercises and computer aids); and application of formal and informal methods to real cases. In one such lesson—based on a real-life case—students discuss how to counsel a youth who skips school to practice basketball four hours a day and explains, "I want to become a pro and earn a million dollars a year like Dr. J." The kid is short and fat.

Follow-on modules are adapted to specific regular courses:

Biology or health—making health related decisions (e.g., sex, drugs and diet)

Civics—analyzing public policy decisions (such as whether nuclear energy should be banned or whether teachers should get merit pay).

Math—solving computationally intensive problems (such as whether a maintenance contract is worth its cost).

History—analyzing epic decisions (such as Queen Isabella's decision to bankroll Columbus, or President Truman's decision to drop the atomic bomb) through the eyes of the decision-maker.

English—analyzing decisions made by characters in fiction, or writing essays in which alternative courses of action are fairly considered;

Counseling program—making career decisions.

THE REFLECTIVE SELF

The teaching of decision-making in schools is part of a larger movement to make schooling more thoughtful. In our case, we ask students to reflect on their own thinking, analyze it and compare it to certain standards. Other programs place more emphasis on social and emotional aspects. It may turn out that different approaches are suited to different periods in students' development.

The time is ripe for a major national and international effort to include thinking and decision-making in school curricula. (To imagine what material could most readily be cut to make room, think about what you learned in school but then forgot because you never used it.) Of course, change takes time. Most teachers, after all, never studied this field. They, too, are subject to the endowment effect and biased toward the status quo. A new curriculum will have to prove itself by standards that will never be applied to plane geometry or trigonometry. In addition, many school officials are reluctant to embrace such a program because of anticipated objections by fundamentalist parents.

Thinking clearly and having the intellectual tools to make good decisions will not solve all the problems of human behavior. We may understand what we should do and still lack the will to do it.

What is needed is a concerted effort by teachers, spurred if necessary by parental and public pressure, to apply this technology in the schools. If successful and generally adopted, such a program could significantly raise our useful intelligence—and thereby, perhaps, the quality of our lives.

The Wizard of Oz may have been only slightly ahead of his time when he conferred a diploma of "Thinkology" on the Scarecrow.

Chapter 1

Introduction

Jonathan Baron
University of Pennsylvania

Rex V. Brown
Decision Science Consortium, Inc.
Reston, VA

SCOPE OF BOOK

Motivation

It is easy to find decisions that turn out badly. Teenagers get pregnant, couples enter into marriages that end in divorce or physical conflict, national leaders promulgate policies that drive their own (or other) countries into ruin, citizens vote for leaders who do this, and we all waste time and money in countless ways.

The chapters in this book assume that bad outcomes often result from poorly made decisions. By teaching people to make better decisions, we can improve their lives. By teaching decision making to adolescents, we have a chance to influence the decision making of a much broader range of citizens than those who attend college. We also have a chance to influence decision making before many bad decisions are made.

The chapters here are concerned with methods of instruction in decision making that could be used with adolescents. The book is directed primarily to those who want to attempt such instruction, either as new curriculum, as enrichment of traditional curriculum, or as research. It is thus directed to teachers, teachers in training, educational researchers, and research students. The book attempts to answer several questions about decision making suggested by an old saw: Is it broke? Can we fix it? What will it take?

7

How can we tell if it's fixed? The bulk of the discussion concerns the "What will it take?" question.

Structure of Chapters

The book begins with a wide-ranging chapter (Beyth-Marom, Fischhoff, Jacobs, & Furby) that reviews literature in the field and previous teaching efforts (some of which are described elsewhere in the book).

This is followed by reports on two of the most significant courses yet developed. Mann, Harmoni, and Power report on GOFER, an Australia-based 50-hour course, which may be the most extensive effort to date dedicated solely to teaching decision skills to children. Adams and Feehrer report on the decision component of ODYSSEY, an ambitious thinking skills program developed as an experiment in Venezuela and now widely adopted elsewhere.

Three chapters then describe a teaching program developed under a grant to Decision Science Consortium,Inc. (see Acknowledgments), which we call the DSC project. These chapters comprise a conceptual framework of pedagogy and evaluation (Baron & Brown), and a description and appraisal of pilot courses (Laskey & Campbell; Baron & Graumlich).

The next five chapters report on distinctive supplementary approaches to instruction. Elias, Branden-Muller, and Sayette complements the normative–cognitive orientation of the above courses with attention to the role of emotions in decision. Shanteau, Grier, Johnson, and Berner focus on training anchored to realistic familiar choices. Martin and Brown explore the use of balance beams and Williams the use of stories as pedagogical devices. Swets proposes a statistical (Bayesian) inference approach to the uncertainty element of decisions. Campbell and Laskey address the issue of implementing a decision-making program in the schools. Finally, Wheeler, in addition to describing his own pioneering effort, provides a provocative perspective on the whole enterprise.

The chapters overlap considerably in the issues they address, but they represent a fairly rich variety of perspectives on these issues. Following is an overview of some of the main themes.

ADOLESCENT DECISION MAKING: IS IT DEFICIENT AND, IF SO, HOW?

All authors subscribe to the view, propounded by the Post article in the Prologue, that deficient decision making is a serious problem throughout society at large and that the problem needs addressing in childhood or adolescence.

Beyth-Marom and colleagues, Baron and Brown, and Shanteau and colleagues cite evidence from laboratory experiments in decision making as well as evidence of apparent poor decisions in the real world.

Shanteau and colleagues focus on some specific problems of nurses in training. They had found that nurses, when making decisions, tended to gather too much information, to overestimate the risk of drug addiction when medicating patients for pain, and to use habitual, inflexible heuristics rather than responding to the particulars of a case when making a decision.

Mann and colleagues discuss certain faulty coping patterns: unthinking adherence to an ongoing course of action; unthinking change to a new course of action; defensive avoidance of making choices; and hypervigilance ("panic"). Elias and colleagues also focus on the role of emotions, assuming that children need to be taught to recognize the emotions they experience and the effects of these emotions on their decisions.

Baron and Brown point to the lack of "actively open-minded thinking" as a fundamental problem in decision making.

To a considerable extent, these various views of the problem are not in conflict. Instead, they represent different levels of description of the same phenomena, or attempts to flesh out a simple explanation. The faulty coping mechanisms described by Mann and colleagues for example, are possible causes of failure to think with active open-mindedness, and the errors discussed by Shanteau and colleagues could result from such failure in particular areas.

HOW SHOULD DEFICIENCIES IN DECISION MAKING BE CORRECTED?

Most of the approaches described in this book try to teach, at least implicitly, normative models of decision making. These are idealized methods of analysis. They are similar to methods of formal analysis used by professionals and taught in business schools and medical schools (e.g., Brown, Kahr, & Peterson, 1974; von Winterfeldt & Edwards, 1986; Watson & Buede, 1987). In the main, courses (including DSC's) emphasize the qualitative consideration of the underlying factors of goals, options, and uncertainty.

Several programs (DSC; Adams & Feehrer; Mann et al.; Shanteau et al.) emphasize the analysis of decisions into multiattribute tables, in which each of several options is evaluated on each of several attributes or dimensions. The value of each option on each attribute can be represented by a number or by some other symbol such as + or + + +. Use of such tables in decision making requires (explicit or implicit) assignment of weights to various attributes. Multiattribute tables are closely related to the decisional balance sheet, a technique invented by Benjamin Franklin, revived by Janis and

Mann (1977), and used by Mann and colleagues and Wheeler in their chapters here.

If multiattribute tables are to be used in the analysis of everyday decisions, students must be able to apply the concepts of outcome, attribute, and importance to the sorts of verbal descriptions of decisions that they would naturally provide themselves. Williams addresses the construction of hypothetical scenarios that can be used as examples, and the way in which students understand those scenarios. Most of the programs described here use such scenarios for both instruction and testing, and they are often presented in printed form. Many students have difficulty comprehending such scenarios whether they are presented in text or speech. Williams examines these comprehension difficulties, and she reports on a training program designed to overcome these difficulties by training students to recognize a general problem-solving schema. She also makes suggestions that will be useful to those who want to integrate the teaching of decision making into "language arts."

Multiattribute tables are analogous to tables analyzing decisions into options and uncertain events, as used by the DSC group and Shanteau and colleagues. If options are listed in the columns, then the rows consist of uncertain events that could affect the outcome, such as whether the weather will be sun, rain, or snow. An outcome is placed in each cell of the table, and a utility value can be assigned to that outcome.

Martin and Brown explore the use of an analog representation of two-option decisions, the balance beam, which can represent both multiattribute and probabilistic decisions. The critical idea here is that of the weighted sum. For probabilistic decisions, the utility of each outcome is represented by the distance of the weight from the center, and the probability is represented by the numerical weight. The force pulling down on each side is a weighted sum. For multiattribute tables, the numerical weights can correspond to the importance of each attribute, and the distances can correspond to the utility of an option on the attribute in question.

Adams and Feehrer's decision-making program is part of a larger course in thinking called ODYSSEY. One general theme of the course is the value of analysis, and the decision-making component is no exception. Like other chapters, this one emphasizes the relation between decision making and thinking in general.

Swets describes some ways in which certain formal approaches to inference, as an element of decision making, can be incorporated into a high-school math course. These exercises serve two purposes. First, they help to directly counter a variety of errors that people make in situations that involve repeated decisions. For example, Peterson and Uhela (1964) found that subjects asked to guess which of two events will occur will not always guess the most likely event, but will instead tend to match the frequency of their guesses to the frequency of the events, even when the events are obviously unpredictable. Swets's classroom exercises will directly demonstrate the futility of such a strategy. More generally, it will demonstrate that using probability as a guide to action is often the best we can do.

The second purpose of the exercises is to introduce students to the Bayesian approach to probability and statistics as branches of mathematics. Here, the materials are not very relevant to students' everyday lives, but they are highly relevant to those students who go on to study mathematics in college and to those who enter various professions. The Bayesian approach is becoming more important and more widely recognized in medicine, science, and even law (e.g., Tillers & Green, 1988).

Shanteau and his colleagues review their efforts to train nurses to overcome certain specific errors in decision making. This project, like most others reviewed here, tries to identify problems before correcting them. Although the teaching was done with trainee nurses, it is a sort of instruction, and a sort of approach, that could be applied much earlier.

One method that is common to most programs is the use of a general heuristic framework for thinking about decisions. This is not a formal analytic method, but a set of things to consider when faced with a decision. Mann and colleagues use the acronym GOFER to remind students to consider "goals, options, facts, effects, and review." The DSC project used GOOP to stand for "goals, options, outcomes, and probabilities." Individual lessons can focus on different aspects of the framework, but students can be reminded that the whole framework is always potentially worth thinking about.

Other approaches focus more on the emotional impediments to good decision making. The chapter by Maurice Elias and his colleagues represents an important tradition that we might call "social problem solving," which is concerned with development and with problems that begin in childhood, such as poor relationships with peers. In addition to the works Elias cites, Spivack and Shure (1985) are important advocates of this tradition. Its origins go back to John Dewey, but it has been developed by clinical psychologists, so along the way it has come to be more concerned with emotional factors than Dewey would have been (although he did not neglect the emotions). The approach is related to various schools of "cognitive behavior therapy" or just "cognitive therapy" for individuals, but the goal of Elias's program is prevention as well as treatment.

What this tradition has in common with other approaches represented in this book is its emphasis on thinking about decisions that come up, by considering alternative options, possible consequences of those options, and values. (Here, the values are often emotional.) The common assumption is that children, adolescents, and adults too often fail to "stop and think." The tradition differs from some other approaches in its emphasis on emotions. Children are taught to recognize and describe their feelings in social situations as an early and important part of training in decision making.

Emotions are seen as important indicators that there is a problem to be solved.

The approach taken by Mann and colleagues also emphasizes explicit instruction about social and emotional effects on decision making and how to avoid them, for unthinking adherence to a course of action can result from social influence, and hypervigilance can result from fear.

Like Mann and colleagues, Wheeler was inspired in part by the work of Janis and Mann (1977). Although Wheeler's efforts were the earliest of those described, his chapter comes at the end because it provides a reflective overview of the whole field, comparing the problem-solving and decision-making perspectives with other "metaphors" that might on occasion be just as useful as views of the world.

A unique feature of the Elias and colleagues approach is the use of role-taking exercises in which students practice putting themselves in the position of another person or even an object. This is an implicit recognition of the moral aspects of decision making. (Another recognition in the same program is the emphasis on considering feelings of others as well as one-self.) Other attempts to incorporate moral elements of decision making are found in the DSC lesson concerned with "Self and others," (see Laskey & Campbell) and in the decisional balance sheet used by Mann and colleagues and by Wheeler, which explicitly asks the student to consider intangible consequences and consequences for others as well as tangible consequences for the self. The incorporation of moral components into decision-making instruction is, we believe, a rich field for further research.

EVALUATING SUCCESS

Most of the approaches described in this book have been subjected to some degree of evaluation, but almost none have got very far toward testing for, much less demonstrating, beneficial impact on the quality of real-world decision-making. That is the objective we are primarily concerned with.

It would not be surprising, nor particularly discouraging, if, in fact, these pioneering, typically short, courses did not produce much improvement in how their graduates made significant choices in their lives. After all, only one of them, GOFER, had more than about a dozen class units devoted specifically to the decision process. (Other skills of arguably comparable significance to a youngster's development, such as English, are taught to them daily throughout their school careers.)

Not much can therefore be expected by way of efforts to measure such improvement, given the difficulty (discussed in Baron & Brown) of establishing decision quality and attributing any of it to one among many determinants—in this case an introductory decision skills course.

Formal Evaluations of Teaching Effects

Nevertheless, it is not unreasonable to expect progress toward this goal in measurable respects. Several attempts have been made to formally compare treatment and control groups in some of these respects, for courses discussed in this book. The tests vary greatly in their ambitiousness and therefore in the interest of their findings.

Reproduction of Course Material. The weakest, but most straightforward and prevalent, evaluations basically called for verbal self-reports from students on how they made decisions. Typically, and perhaps inevitably, these implicitly tested, in varying degrees, student mastery of course content (including terminology). Not surprisingly they fared well in comparison with untaught control groups. This approach figured as a major part of course evaluations reported in this book (Laskey & Campbell, Shanteau et al., Mann et al.) and elsewhere (courses reviewed by Beyth-Marom et al.).

Mastery of Cognitive Processes. A more demanding test is that subjects are able to apply techniques they have learned to novel decision problems presented verbally. For example, students are given problems in which making the decision on the basis of "the most important attribute" leads to one option but a full multiattribute analysis leads to another. The importance of the various attributes to the decision maker must be clear from the problem.

This technique is also used by programs, particularly Laskey and Campbell, and Williams and colleagues. Martin and Brown evaluated skill in a specific set of formal operations (intuiting expected, or probability weighted, utility). Of course, this approach is similar to the first approach, in that some of the training concerns the analysis of such verbal problems, but the difference is that no technical terms are used in the problems. We can therefore use such problems as appropriate ways of comparing experimental and control groups, for the problems are just as meaningful to the control groups.

Formal evaluation is one source of evidence that a course is useful and effective. It is especially useful in establishing that the course has been sufficiently intensive, and at an appropriate level for the students. If students do not learn what they are taught, something needs to be fixed.

Quality of Hypothetical Choices. At a still more demanding level, subjects can be evaluated in terms of whether they choose the correct option in a hypothetical case. Here, the attributes are not necessarily provided, nor is their relative importance stated in the scenario given to the student. The criterion for a "correct" answer is expert judgment rather than application of the content of the course.

Shanteau and colleagues find that their course improved the decisions of nursing students on written cases that had also been given to expert nursing professors. Although this material was chosen for a particular preprofessional group, the course was general, of a sort that could be given to high-school students. Evaluation of a course for students enrolled in a general high-school program might focus on other types of decisions that could be evaluated by experts, such as consumer purchases or decisions about education.

Effect on Real Decisions.   Ideally, as we noted earlier, decision-making courses should be evaluated in terms of their effects on real decisions, for that is the purpose of teaching them. A common approach to measuring these effects is to see to what extent observable decisions conform to the evaluator's conception of a sound choice (e.g., not taking drugs, having premarital sex, or dropping out of school). Two "life-skills" courses reviewed in Beyth-Marom and colleagues showed significant effects of this kind, but not necessarily attributable to the decision process component of the courses. A similar approach has been taken by Larrick, Morgan, and Nisbett (1989). The Adams and Feehrer decision-making course was part of a larger program that was evaluated in a variety of ways. In general, the entire course was effective in increasing general cognitive abilities as well as the specific abilities taught in each segment.

Potential for More Definitive Evaluations.   Given the early stage of development and adoption of decision skills courses for adolescents, it is probably inappropriate to devote too many resources to the definitive evaluation of their impact on the quality of real decisions. To the best of our knowledge, such an evaluation has never been attempted. However, applied to an extensive and thoroughly developed intervention, it could provide useful evidence of the effectiveness of instruction. Baron and Brown propose a general paradigm for this purpose which involves a battery of complementary and potentially conflicting measures to be reconciled.

Informal Evaluation

But formal evaluation is not, in our view, an especially important source of evidence for the purpose of deciding whether a course should be instituted. In this context, Wheeler contrasts architecture and modern physical medicine as applied disciplines. Medicine is driven by outcome studies. Every procedure must prove its value in well-controlled experiments. Methods of architecture are rarely evaluated in this way. Architects and builders have relied more heavily on case studies, on tinkering as they were building, on mini-experiments carried out during a single project (e.g., the invention of buttresses for cathedrals), and most recently on a well worked-out theory (Gordon, 1978).

Is education more like medicine or more like architecture? Some of the things that make it more like architecture are the difficulty of exactly replicating a method in different sites, and the possibility of obtaining rich data during the development of a process. In medicine, it is also easy to measure the important outcomes. In architecture as in education, the most important outcomes occur years after the "treatment" and cannot easily be measured in time to be of use.

In architecture, we are concerned at a minimum with whether the structure falls down immediately or not, and in education, we are likewise minimally concerned with whether the students learn what they are taught. But if the structure stays up and if the students learn, the more important questions seem to be those of values, unlike medicine, where the values are usually obvious. We believe, following Silberman (1970) that education needs to concern itself more with purposes, with the theory of what it is trying to do and why. When this is clarified, the methods for achieving these purposes will be discovered mostly through research in practice.

It is unlikely that the teaching of decision making is impossible once we figure out what we want to do and set our minds to doing it. We can very likely make faster progress by spending more time tinkering and developing and less time evaluating. Evaluation induces conservatism: once something works, we are loath to change it.

INSTITUTIONALIZING TEACHING IN THE SCHOOLS

All our fine efforts to develop and validate pedagogy for teaching decision skills to adolescents will be for naught if it is not adopted in the school system, and effectively incorporated into the curriculum. Indeed, the latter is a necessary, if not sufficient, condition of the former.

Incorporation Into the Curriculum

Below the college level, decision making is not a traditional subject (and even in college, it is at best optional). In principle, decision-making instruction could, and perhaps should, occur in many traditional subjects—social studies, history, literature, mathematics, and science (see Swartz & Perkins, 1989, for examples)—as well as nontraditional "extras" such as health, family life, and what used to be called home economics.

The strategy embodied in the DSC project was to develop a 6–8 unit core-course that could be inserted into any of several host courses (and was in fact offered as part of regular English, science, and social studies courses). Follow-on modules were then planned for specific regular courses, adapted to their distinctive requirements and orientation. For example, the work with balance beams as an analog for expected utility and other weighted sum operations was taught as a four-unit segment of an eighth grade science course, immediately following instruction in the physics of torque.

The Swets article describes part of a mathematics course that teaches some aspects of decision theory. All the other programs described here, however, were experiments outside of the regular curriculum.

Adams and Feehrer were part of a team (headed by Adams) that was asked by the Venezuelan government to develop a model program for the purpose of raising the effective intelligence of eighth-grade students. The experimental course was taught to eighth graders over the period of a year. Other courses described here were experiments, although the one described by Elias and colleagues has attained a kind of stability in the schools where it was developed.

Stand-alone vs. Assimilated Teaching.   Although integration of decision-making instruction into the whole curriculum is an important long-term goal, we think that the development of stand-alone courses, of the sort described here, is important for two reasons. First, it may be helpful and efficient to include such courses in the curriculum as an introduction to material that will be covered in later courses in the traditional subjects. Many schools already have segments on decision making covered under "health" or "family life" programs. Many of the courses described here are not much more extensive than those that already exist.

The second reason for developing stand-alone courses is for research. Although most of the chapters in this volume do not emphasize control groups, statistics, and Persian counterbalancing, we see them all as a very important kind of research. We might call it "research in practice." This kind of research is necessary in the development of any application. It is an accepted kind of inquiry in such applied fields as computer science and architecture, but it is a necessary part of any applied field. These chapters will, we think, teach the reader a lot about the problems of teaching decision making in general, and their possible solutions.

Getting Instruction Institutionalized

Campbell and Laskey point to four tasks that must be covered if a decision skills course is to be successfully implemented in the schools. First, the material taught must be appropriate to the student population and the institutional setting. In particular a home must be found in a crowded curriculum. Second, the material must be taught in a way that engages the students' interest and is appropriate to their skill level and developmental stage. Third, enthusiastic teacher support and commitment is required. Finally, outreach to community and parents is required for long-term success and broader dissemination.

Several of the chapters in this book support these observations. For example, *The Washington Post* article in the Prologue, and a number of TV and radio interviews that followed, gave the DSC project a visibility and credibility, which certainly made easier a fifth essential task: enlisting the support of critical players in the educational establishment, broadly defined.

Most of the teaching reported consisted of pilot courses. These required the participation, not only of teachers prepared to make available precious time in established courses to host decision skills teaching, but also school principals, school area and district supervisors, and interested staff and funding agencies. To move beyond localized pilot teaching into routine, or at least widespread, adoption, a new level of support has to be enlisted such as publishers, teacher training staff, National Education Association, state education authorities, legislators, and the ever-indispensable funding agencies. The most successful in this respect is no doubt the ODYSSEY program (Adams & Feehrer), which had the vigorous support of a minister in the Venezuelan government, Luis Machado.

Decision training outside the schools has not been explicitly addressed in this book, partly because so little seems to have been done. A public television series on career decisions, called "Whadya wanna be?", aired a few years back, but has not apparently been built upon; except that some career decision aiding computer programs are currently available, the most notable of which is SIGI PLUS, put out by the Educational Testing Service in Princeton, NJ. (The Children's Television Workshop, of "Sesame Street" fame, has expressed some interest in developing decision skills material for their "1-2-3 Contact" or "Electric Company" programs.)

SHOULD DECISION MAKING BE TAUGHT?

Given the inconclusive nature of available evaluations, are we justified in acting on the basis of the tentative prescriptions described in this book? We think that we are.

We face a decision ourselves, which, in its simplest form, is whether to teach decision making as best we know how, or not to teach it. The consequences of not teaching it are that students go on making decisions as they have done. The consequences of teaching are that students change toward what we think are better ways of making decisions (with some probability, of course, since we cannot be sure that our teaching will have an effect). The fact that one of these outcomes is the status quo should not in itself determine our decision.

Of course, we must also consider the cost of teaching decision making, both in the direct effort expended and the time taken away from other worthwhile activities. We should also consider the risk of failure and the effect of such failure on the willingness of those in the future to try new ideas. In some schools, these costs are low, because decision making is already being "taught," or at least students are being walked through various hypothetical decisions with the purpose of improving their decision making.

We hope that the chapters in this book inspire more attempts to teach decision making as part of traditional courses, more efforts to develop materials that could be used as part of district-wide courses, and more research.

ACKNOWLEDGMENTS

The editing of this book and the research described in several of the papers in it were supported by a Small Business Innovation Research grant, #2-R44-HD23071-02, to Decision Science Consortium, Inc. from the Child Development Branch of the National Institute of Child Health and Human Developments, *A formal approach to teaching children decision-making.* We thank Dr. Kathryn B. Laskey for comments on this Introduction.

REFERENCES

Brown, R. V., Kahr, A. S., & Peterson, C. R. (1974). *Decision analysis for the manager.* New York: Holt, Rinehart, & Winston.

Gordon, J. E. (1978). *Structures, or Why things don't fall down.* Harmondsworth: Penguin.

Janis, I. L., & Mann, L. (1977). *Decision making: A psychological analysis of conflict, choice, and commitment.* New York: Free Press.

Larrick, R. P., Morgan, J. N., & Nisbett, R. E. (1989). *Who uses the normative rules of choice.* Unpublished manuscript, Department of Psychology, University of Michigan, Ann Arbor.

Peterson, C. R., & Uhela, Z. J. (1964). Uncertainty, inference difficulty, and probability learning. *Journal of Experimental Psychology, 67,* 523–530.

Swartz, R. J., & Perkins, D. N. (1989). *Teaching thinking: Issues and approaches.* Pacific Grove, CA: Midwest Publications.

Spivack, G., & Shure, M. B. (1985). ICPS and beyond: Centripetal and centrifugal forces. *American Journal of Community Psychology, 13,* 226–243.

Silberman, C. E. (1970). *Crisis in the classroom: The remaking of American education.* New York: Random House.

Tillers, P., & Green, E. D. (Eds.). (1988). *Probability and inference in the law of evidence: The uses and limits of Bayesianism.* Dordrecht: Kluwer Academic Publishers.

von Winterfeldt, D., & Edwards, W. (1986). *Decision analysis and behavioral research.* Cambridge, England: Cambridge University Press.

Watson, S. R., & Buede, D. M. (1987). *Decision synthesis: The principles and practice of decision analysis.* Cambridge, England: Cambridge University Press.

Chapter **2**

Teaching Decision Making to Adolescents: A Critical Review

Ruth Beyth-Marom
Baruch Fischhoff
Marilyn Jacobs Quadrel
Carnegie Mellon University

Lita Furby
Eugene Research Institute, Eugene, OR

INTRODUCTION

"Problem solving and comprehension," "The complete problem solver," "A decision-making approach to sex education," "Decision skills curriculum," "A curriculum for thinking," "Personal decision making," "Decisions and outcomes," "The decision-making book for children," "Learning to think and choose," "Power and choice'—all are curricula aimed at improving young people's decision-making skills. Moreover, these are just a small subset of the many programs now on the market. Some teach only decision making, whereas others teach decision making as one of many general thinking skills. Some teach decision-making skills in general, while others teach decision making in specific contexts. Their target age varies from kindergarten to college, with a few concentrating on adults.

This proliferation of programs is one response to a widely perceived need to improve higher-order thinking skills in general and decision-making skills in particular, so that adolescents can meet the challenges of today's world (Resnick, 1987). Here, we take a step back and look critically at the products of this enterprise.

Our review begins by defining decision making in terms of normative approaches describing what constitutes adequate performance. We then review the reasons that have been advanced for teaching decision making. The following section offers a set of criteria for evaluating programs, which

19

is then applied to several of the better evaluated ones. We end with conclusions and recommendations.

As mentioned, there are many decision-making programs. The best-known ones usually owe their recognition to publications in which they are described and sometimes evaluated. They typically have been developed by academics, sensitive to the need for publication and evaluation. Other programs have been developed by practitioners, in response to such specific needs as inducing adolescents not to smoke or drink. These programs are seldom evaluated in any systematic way or mentioned in the scientific literature. In the course of assembling materials for this review, we quickly realized that there is no way to identify all potentially relevant programs, much less to secure copies of them. Many practitioners are not organized for disseminating materials; some seemed not eager to have outsiders examine their hard-earned experience. As a result, we decided to concentrate on those programs for which we had access to curricular materials and evaluation reports. We further constrained our focus to programs directed at adolescents. Obviously, this strategy may lead to overlooking as-yet-untested programs that are superior to those that have been evaluated, as well as programs directed at other ages that might be usefully adapted to adolescents.

DECISION MAKING: DEFINITION AND NORMATIVE MODELS

Decision theorists define decision making as the process of making choices among competing courses of actions (Raiffa, 1968; von Winterfeldt & Edwards, 1986). For the developers of curricula, the expression "problem solving" often accompanies, or even replaces, "decision making" (as can be seen in the list of titles opening this article). In the psychological literature, however, the two have somewhat different definitions.

A "problem" is a task whose solution is not immediately perceived. Problem solving is identifying a course of action that closes the gap between the present situation and a desired future one (Newell & Simon, 1972). That process requires being able to tell whether the gap has been closed, that is, whether the solution that one currently favors is acceptable. Decision makers must also identify a solution. However, they often face conflicting objectives, whose relative importance must be weighed before the relative adequacy of different possible solutions can be determined. As a result, one must often compare alternative solutions with regard to how well they maximize one's goals, rather than being able to stop once an adequate solution has been found. In addition, many decisions are made under conditions of uncertainty, so that decision makers cannot tell exactly which consequences will follow from their choices. Observers should, in principle, be able to tell whether a proposed solution meets the constraints of a problem. Observers of decisions face the additional challenges of having to discern what goals decision makers were trying to achieve or what role fortune and misfortune play in what happens to them. As a result, the "normative" theory of decision making is couched in terms of the processes that people should follow in order to have the best chance of reaching their goal. The most widely accepted normative models of optimal decision making were developed by philosophers and economists and then adopted by psychologists for the descriptive study of human decision making (Coombs, Dawes, & Tversky, 1970; Edwards, 1954). These models prescribe the rules that people should follow when making decisions, given their beliefs and values.

According to the most general normative model, a person facing a decision should (a) list relevant action alternatives, (b) identify possible consequences of those actions, (c) assess the probability of each consequence occurring (if each action were undertaken), (d) establish the relative importance (value or utility) of each consequence, and (e) integrate these values and probabilities to identify the most attractive course of action, following a defensible decision rule. People who follow these steps are said to behave in a *rational* way. People who do so effectively (e.g., they have accurate probability estimates, they get good courses of action into their list of possibilities) are said to behave *optimally*. Thus, if one does not execute these steps optimally, one can be rational without being very effective at getting what one wants.

Why Train for Decision Making?

Cognitive psychologists have studied decision making for some 30 years, revealing a mixture of strengths and weaknesses in people's performances (Abelson & Levi, 1985; Fischhoff, 1988; Fischhoff, Svenson, & Slovic, 1987; Slovic, Lichtenstein, & Fischhoff, 1988). The identification of systematic biases has spurred an interest in "debiasing" techniques of the sort that could be incorporated in training programs for decision making (Fischhoff, 1982; Kahneman, Slovic, & Tversky, 1982; Nisbett, Krantz, Jepsen, & Kunda, 1983).

In many ways, the decision-making literature echoes general themes of contemporary psychology. One such theme, introduced by White (1959), is the concept of "competence," defined as "an organism's capacity to interact effectively with its environment." Guilford (1959) talked about "social intelligence," believing that socially intelligent people were more "fluent" in thinking about the behavior of others and more flexible in analyzing human problems. A common view (e.g., D'Zurilla & Goldfried, 1971) is that interpersonal competence requires active problem-solving and decision-making behavior, whereby one defines a problematic situation, searches for possible alternative solutions, selects the best alternative, and then verifies its suitability by observing the consequences of its implementation. This approach relies heavily on Bandura's (1977) social learning theory, according to which people who experience social difficulties are less able to set appropriate goals in social situations and to generate possible ways to achieve those goals (Argyle, 1969). The social learning approach holds, however, that these competencies can be acquired through counseling or training. For example: "Life Skills counseling equips adolescents to handle current problems, anticipate and prevent future ones and advance their mental health, social functioning, economic welfare and physical well-being" (Schinke & Gilchrist, 1984, p. 13).

In addition to social-learning theory's concern with competent behavior, various professions (e.g., clinical and counseling psychology, social work) have been concerned with the cognitive and social processes leading to deviant behavior. Such behaviors could be viewed either as the result of social incompetence or as the competent pursuit of socially unacceptable goals. Jessor and Jessor's (1977) problem behavior theory provides a cognitive psychosocial approach to reducing the incidence of socially undesirable behavior. Its advocates attempt to improve personal and interpersonal functioning through training in social and thinking skills in general and in decision making in particular.

Jahoda (1958) was among the first to emphasize the relationship of effective interpersonal problem solving to social and emotional adjustment. In one early study advancing this position, Spivack and Shure (1974) found that both more aggressive and more inhibited youths are less competent in solving problems and making decisions. Delinquents appear to be particularly deficient in social problem-solving skills (Kennedy, 1984; Little & Kendall, 1979), although it is unclear to what extent delinquency is caused by the lack of these skills and to what extent it keeps youths from acquiring them.

In education, the field of instructional psychology (Glaser, 1982) promotes cognitive competence, usually conceptualized as engineering the transition between learners' current skill states and that desired by educators (Lochhead & Clement, 1979). This emphasis on thinking skills has focused research on *how* children think, rather than on *what* they know. Focal topics have included the intuitive understanding of physical concepts, such as movement (e.g., McCloskey, Caramazza, & Green, 1980), energy (Solomone, 1983), time (Levine, 1983) and density (Strauss, Globerson, & Minz, 1983); of statistical concepts, such as the arithmetic average (Strauss & Bichler, 1988) and probability (e.g., Kahneman & Tversky, 1973); of biological concepts such as natural selection (Brumby, 1984); and of deductive reasoning (e.g., Evans, 1983). In each case, the goal has been to identify cognitive deficiencies that might be corrected through instruction. This concern for intuitive thought processes reflects a belief that education must consider where children are coming from, cognitively, as well as where one wants them to be.

No explicit training is needed, of course, if a skill develops by itself to its full potential at a reasonable pace. Thus, speaking need not be taught to a hearing child who has the normal chances to practice that skill. For many years, thinking and decision making were perceived as skills that did not have to be taught. It was assumed that "mental competence" develops like language skills through biological maturation, social interaction, and conventional learning. However, various evaluations (e.g., National Assessment of Education Progress, 1983) have found that many students fail to develop basic thinking skills. A number of investigators concluded that high school students often could not deal effectively with problems requiring abstract thinking (e.g., Renner & Stafford, 1972) and that as many as 50% of incoming college students operate below Piaget's level of formal thinking (Gray, 1979). These results, too, suggested that thinking skills have to be taught.

In addition to the growth of cognitive psychology, and, with it, the more precise ability to measure thinking skills, increased sensitivity to the changing nature of modern society has also prompted interest in teaching thinking skills. In a world full of novel situations (Chen & Novik, 1984; Ellul, 1963) and information overload (Bell, 1978; Carroll, 1971), one cannot teach just facts. By the time students have mastered one set of facts, it may be outdated by new developments. Such rapid changes require people to think for themselves and by themselves, and educators to provide these general skills (Fletcher & Wooddell, 1981; Simon, 1980). The comparable change in counselors' roles has been to emphasize personal responsibility and maturity in decision making (Wrenn, 1962), that is, counselors should be helping clients learn how to make better decisions (Gelatt, 1962).

As expressed by Nickerson, Perkins, and Smith (1985, p.4), "Most of us who live in developed countries in the free world have a much greater range of options than did our grandparents, whether we are choosing what to have for dinner, what to do for entertainment, where to go for a vacation, or how to spend a life. It seems reasonable to expect this freedom of choice to continue to increase. But options imply the burden of making decisions and living with them; and the ability to choose wisely assumes the ability to assess the alternatives in a reasonable way." Accordingly, Lewis (1983) argued that it is necessary to teach students to "analyze information, synthesize it and apply it in a value-oriented way."

Cassidy and Kurfman (1977) specifically advocated teaching decision-making in the social studies curriculum, claiming that: "Decision making as an educational goal derives its justification from two values which underlie our American social–political system. One of these is belief in popular rule, and the other is respect for the individual. From the democratic value of popular rule comes support for developing skill in making decisions about public issues. From the value of individual dignity comes support for making sound decisions about personal problems" (p. 3).

In addition to the general challenges of living in a modern society, adolescents face particular challenges, placing severe demands on their decision-making abilities. Adolescence is characterized by rapid physical, cognitive, affective, and social development. As they become more autonomous, adolescents must make more decisions about their lives. In doing so, they must cope with the often conflicting demands of parents, schools, peers, and jobs (Hartup, 1970; Utech & Hoving, 1969).

One significant category of such decisions are those involving risk-taking behaviors, such as smoking cigarettes, drug use, school dropout, and sexual activity. The long-term consequences of the behavioral choices made here, for both individual youths and society as a whole, are well known. Rather less is known about the processes leading to them. Although incurring these risks may reflect ineffective decision making, it may also represent a deliberate choice, say, to let the short-term benefits of conforming to peer pressure dominate the long-term health risks of smoking. Awareness of the complexity of the decisions that youths face has led to statements like, ". . . knee jerk prescriptions such as just say no, while perhaps appropriate developmentally speaking for the 5–10 year old . . . are unlikely to fortify developing early adolescents against unhealthy behavior, nor give him the tools to function autonomously . . . the just say no approach fails to respect the child as an active processor of experience . . ." (Zamansky-Shorin, Selman, & Richmond, 1988, p. 15). (See also Duryea, 1986; Mahoney & Thoreson, 1972.)

With so many advocates and so many reasons for training in decision making, it is not surprising that much effort has been directed at developing such programs.

Decision-Making Training: A Classification

Programs that provide decision-making training can be classified according to: (a) their focus: social or cognitive, and (b) their scope: general or specific (where scope is defined somewhat differently for the two foci).

General social programs teach skills for solving interpersonal problems, such as coping strategies, assertiveness techniques, and decision-making methods. *Specific social programs* focus on particular problems like smoking, peer and family relationships, sexuality, physical and psychological health, vocational and career goals, or societal adaptation. Many are designed for particular populations as well. Proponents of these latter approaches argue that general cognitive abilities are necessary, but not sufficient for dealing with social problems. Rather, adolescents need substantive social knowledge as well as the interpersonal skills needed to deal effectively with others, what are often called "life skills."

In cognitive programs, thinking skills are the focus of interest and not just mediating variables. *General cognitive programs* teach decision making as one of many thinking skills; *specific cognitive programs* teach decision making per se.

Evaluation

Following Nickerson's (1975) example, we will distinguish between "effectiveness" and "logical soundness," as criteria for evaluating decision-making (and, hence, the impact of decision-making curricula). A decision-making process is "effective" to the extent that it produces desired outcomes. That is usually determined easily after the fact. Decisions are "logically sound" to the extent that the decision makers' choices are consistent both with their values and with the information available to them at the time of decision.

Although logical soundness is much more difficult to evaluate than effectiveness, it is also a more essential criterion. The outcome of a decision is often determined by factors outside the decision maker's control, whereas a logically sound decision is one that makes the best of a situation. Over the long run, logically sound decisions ought to be more effective. However, that assumption need not hold in any particular instance, so that a sound decision may have an unhappy outcome.

Nonetheless, it appears temptingly simple to evaluate decision makers by how well individual decisions worked out. Not only do people have a fascination with such effectiveness (Baron & Hershey, 1988), but it seems so easy to evaluate. By contrast, assessing logical soundness requires answering such difficult questions as, What information was available to decision makers at the time of the decision? What were their preferences? What were their subjective probabilities? How did they combine that information to reach a decision? (Blackshaw & Fischhoff, 1988). Rather than addressing all these features, attempts to evaluate logical soundness have typically concentrated on just one or two components (e.g., how people list alternatives, how they estimate probabilities).

Whatever criterion is used, it should be assessed through detailed observation of the processes followed in actual decisions. As might be expected from the difficulty of such research, few such efforts have been mounted. A more modest (and more common) evaluative criterion is that participants in a program learn principles of good decision-making, under the assumption that such conscious knowledge is necessary for better behavior. An even more modest criterion is that a program at least teach these principles. This criterion can be applied to any curriculum, regardless of what data have been collected. Decision theory's normative rules are described in the following section.

Of course, merely presenting the principles of good decision-making carries no assurance that they have been learned. A pedagogically sound curriculum should be built on available scientific knowledge regarding how people make decisions and how they can be helped to improve their decision making. A brief summary of these descriptive results follows.

Normative Principles

As mentioned, philosophers and economists have developed various normative models of optimal decision making (Raiffa, 1968). All these models, whatever their complexity, include some basic steps that any decision maker should follow (e.g., listing alternatives), as well as some steps that are specific to particular circumstances (e.g., evaluating probabilities in uncertain situations).

Table 2.1 offers one characterization of the normatively prescribed steps that a decision maker should follow (and that a decision-making curriculum should teach if they do not come naturally). These are:

1. Distinguishing between decision calling for different decision-making models (e.g., decisions under certainty, risk, and uncertainty)
2. Identifying and defining a decision-making situation
3. Listing action alternatives
4. Identifying criteria for comparing the alternatives and the possible consequences of each alternative
5. Assessing the probability of possible consequences (when necessary)
6. Assessing the utilities of possible consequences (when necessary)
7. Evaluating each alternative in terms of its attractiveness and probability
8. Assessing the value of collecting additional information
9. Evaluating the decision-making process

Descriptive Principles

Choosing what to teach and how to convey it requires an understanding of what students know already and how they intuitively approach decision-making tasks. Without such understanding, one is imposing a foreign perspective, rather than taking students from their current state to a more sophisticated one.

The professional literature contains many assertions like "adolescents are risk takers," "adolescents' decision making is all emotion," or "adolescents have a limited time perspective." However, these statements seem to be grounded primarily in anecdotal observation. As a result, even if they are accurate, they provide little insight regarding the details of adolescents' psychological processes. In the absence of systematic evidence, the most rel-

TABLE 2.1
Curricula's Content

Decision-making Skills	GOFER	Personal Decision Making	Odyssey	Life Skills— Schinke et al.	Life Skills— Botvin	Decision Skills Curricula
Distinguishing between different decision situations			X			
Defining & identifying decision-making situations	X		X	X	X	X
Listing action alteratives	X	X	X	X	X	X
Identifying criteria for comparing alternatives	X	X	X	X	X	X
Assessing probabilities (when necessary)			X			
Assessing utilities (when necessary)		X	X			
Assessing alternatives	X	X	X	X	X	X
Assessing the value of information						
Evaluating decision process	X	X	X			X

evant empirical basis for training adolescents may be research with adults. This approach is supported by Harmoni, Mann, and Power's (1987) literature review finding no demonstrated differences between the decision-making processes of older adolescents and adults, and only a few differences between younger adolescents and adults. The latter include Rowe's (1984) finding that 14-year-olds generated fewer potential alternatives than did 18-year-olds when asked to structure decision problems, and Lewis's (1981) findings that 12th graders produced both more possible future consequences of their actions and a higher portion of negative items than did 7th graders. Contrasted with younger children (grades K to 4), adolescents have been found to have a "reflective tempo" which is better suited to cognitive tasks than the more "impulsive tempo" of younger children (Eska & Black, 1971; Kagan, 1965, 1967; Mann 1973; Yando & Kagan, 1970). Other investigators have found that greater anxiety leads to shorter and less effective decision processes (Keinan, 1987; Keinan, Friedland, & Ben-Porat, 1987; Messer, 1970). The stresses of adolescence might make this threat particularly great. Ironically, drinking and drugs, common ways to reduce stress, distort decision-making processes in their own way (Wills, 1985).

Even though the research base with adolescents is limited, most steps in the decision-making process have been studied some with adults. These studies reveal something about how people approach these tasks, how well they do, and what difficulties they face. Systematic overviews can be found in Abelson and Levi (1985), Fischhoff (1988), Fischhoff, Svenson, and Slovic (1987), Slovic, Lichtenstein, and Fischhoff (1988), and von Winterfeldt and Edwards (1986).

Two examples might suggest the implications of such research for curriculum development:

1. Uncertainty is a basic element of many decisions. Research with adults has found a common tendency to underestimate the uncertainty in situations, reflecting, among other things, failure to realize how complex they are (Fischhoff, Slovic, & Lichtenstein, 1977; Lichtenstein, Fischhoff, & Phillips, 1982). If, as is often claimed, children have simplistic views about many things, then their thinking, too, should be characterized by unwarranted certainty (Sieber, Clark, Smith, & Sanders, 1978). As a result, uncertainty ought to be a main concept in curricula, touching topics like what is uncertainty, what are the different kinds of uncertainty, and what is the relationship between uncertainty and amount of information.

2. The starting point for any decision is the definition of its basic components (the alternatives, consequences, sources of uncertainty). Observers have hypothesized that adolescents often behave as if they have no choices, meaning that their definitions of decision situations have no alternatives (or the single, simple alternative of resignation to fate). A related result with adults is the inability to generate alternative courses of action, or to realize how adequate (or impoverished) one's source of alternatives is (Fischhoff, Slovic, & Lichtenstein, 1978; Gettys, Mehle, & Fisher, 1986; Mehle, Gettys, Manning, Baca, & Fisher, 1981). If this is the case, then curricula must teach students to consider multiple alternatives and to specify those alternatives clearly enough that they can be evaluated. To that end, they should be taught generic techniques for generating options and generic options such as delaying decisions and seeking help.

Similar analyses must be made for each step of the decision-making process, beginning with the curricular implications of the existing behavioral literature. In the absence of relevant research, curricula can at best be treated as informed guesses at how to teach these skills. A detailed analysis will raise additional design questions, such as:

1. At which age should various decision-making skills be taught?
2. What lower-order skills constitute the building blocks on which higher-order decision-making skills are based?
3. To what extent are there general decision-making skills, as opposed to skills related to specific contexts? Studies of problem solving strongly indicate that expertise reflects domain-specific schemata (Larkin, 1983; Simon & Chase, 1973). Others, however, believe that there are some basic cognitive skills (Baron, 1985).
4. How can transfer of training be maximized? According to Sternberg (1983), for example, transfer is more likely when students experience decision making rather than just learn about it. According to Brown, Campione, and Day (1981), an understanding of what a program does, how it does it, and why is also necessary (also Vye, Delclos, Burns, & Bransford, 1988).

Review of Programs: An Overview

Our review of programs begins with a description of each program's goals and approach. We then focus on whatever attempts have been made to evaluate it. Evaluating a curriculum manipulation is like evaluating any other behavioral intervention. Its impact must be compared to that of no manipulation at all (i.e., letting education take its natural course) or to that of alternative curricula. Ideally, such comparisons would involve random assignment to treatment groups and appropriate pre- and post-treatment measurement of the dependent variables (Campbell & Stanley, 1963). Even though some evaluation has been performed for every study discussed here, none approaches these ideal standards. As a result, we must evaluate the evaluations, focusing on the nature of each manipulation and the behavioral measures used to assess its impact.

The Curriculum Manipulations. Unless a curriculum is clearly defined and faithfully applied, any improvement can be attributed to other causes, and any failure can be attributed to the curriculum having been improperly implemented. Thus, evaluating a curriculum requires asking questions like: Was it clear what was training in decision making and what was training for other abilities? Do we really know what was done during the training (i.e., how structured was the training? how much control did the experimenter have over how it proceeded?)?

Analogous questions must be asked about any comparison groups. One must also ask whether the non-instructional aspects of their treatments were equivalent to those of the curriculum group. For example, did they re-

TABLE 2.2
Evaluation Studies

		Curriculum				
Feature	GOFER	Personal Decision Making	Odyssey	Life Skills— Schinke et al.	Life Skills— Botvin	Decision Skills Curriculum
Manipulation						
Structure	high	high	high	low	high	intermediate
Duration (hours)[a]	(16–20)	(10)	56(5)	8(2)	10–20(2)	8(2)
Groups[b]	M,NM	M,NM	M,NM	M,NM M,OM	M,NM	M,NM
Decision Making Measures						
	Flinders ADM questionnaire	Decision-making test	Ability tests	Perspective taking Means–end thinking	Decision-making autonomy	Decision-making questionnaire
	Virgil questionnaire		TAT	Anticipating consequences	Confidence in problem solving	
	Decision knowledge questionnaire					
Time of Testing	Immed.	Immed.	Immed.	Immed.	Immed.	Immed. & 10 months later

[a]The number in brackets specifies the number of hours devoted to decision making.
[b]M = group receiving focal curriculum; NM = control group receiving no treatment; OM = group receiving another curriculum.

ceive as much attention and motivational encouragement? As a result, the top half of Table 2.2 characterizes evaluation studies according to each curriculum's degree of structure, its duration (in hours of instruction in decision making), and the nature of the control groups. We distinguish three levels of structure. Counseling programs typically are relatively unstructured, whereas programs with a student textbook and a detailed teacher's manual usually are highly structured.

The Behavioral Measures.   The ultimate goal of decision-making curricula is improving decision-making skills. As a result, changes in those skills provide the appropriate measure of a curriculum's effectiveness. However, for life skills and social skills curricula, decision-making skills are intervening variables. Their ultimate goal is changing some behavior, like cigarette smoking.

Whatever variables interest the creators of a curriculum, evaluation is possible only if they can be defined operationally. Because of the difficulty of measuring actual behavior, most curricula have focused on verbal expressions, such as expressed attitudes toward smoking or knowledge about the stages of sound decision making. Unfortunately, knowing what to say on a knowledge or attitude test need not mean accepting those responses as personal beliefs nor implementing them in one's personal life. Several thoughtful reviews exist for the impact of social and life skills programs on behaviors like smoking and drinking (Biglan & Ary 1985; Cook, 1985; Glasgow & McCaul, 1985). This review focuses on measures of decision making. The second half of Table 2.2 characterizes each evaluation study in terms of what decision-making measures were used and how soon after the training they were administered. We had planned to classify the measures along two dimensions—what was measured (knowledge, attitudes, or behavior) and how it was measured (by observed behavior or verbal reports in questionnaires). However, we found that all measures were verbal reports of either knowledge or attitudes.

Other Issues.   In addition to these specific measurement issues, the studies reviewed here face the routine methodological issues of any curriculum evaluation. These include how subjects are sampled, how they are assigned to conditions, and how results are analyzed. Particular criticism has been leveled at evaluations that have used pupils as their unit of analysis when it is actually whole classes that have been assigned to treatments (Cook, 1985). There is also constant concern over generalizing results beyond the kinds of classes that have been studied. Acknowledging the practical problems facing evaluators, reviewers typically call for identifying common trends among a set of imperfect studies, rather than demanding a single perfect study. The present review constitutes such a search for overall patterns.

We begin our review with programs focused on decision-making skills alone, proceed to the decision-making portion of programs devoted to thinking skills in general, and then consider that aspect of social and life skills programs. Table 2.1 characterizes the content of each program in terms of how it treats nine normative issues (reflecting the steps a good decision maker should take). We had planned to indicate here the attention paid by each curriculum to the descriptive literature regarding how people intuitively perform each step. However, such attention proved so infrequent that there was little to indicate.

PROGRAMS FOCUSED ON DECISION-MAKING SKILLS

Decision-Making Curricula

GOFER: A High-School Course on Decision Making (see ch. 3)

Goal: This course, which was developed by Mann, Harmoni, and Power (1988a, 1988b), is based on Janis and Mann's (1977) conflict theory of decision making under stress. That theory identifies several distinctive responses to difficult decision situations, such as vigilance (careful appraisal of options and consequences), hypervigilance (rapid and impulsive choice), defensive avoidance, and complacency (e.g., adherence to simple courses of action). It offers a comprehensive account of the requirements for good decision making, as well as a coherent explanation for poor decision habits. GOFER embodies this theory in a general course in decision making intended to reinforce students for applying appropriate decision-making skills to a wide range of problems in their lives, including vocational and curriculum choice.

Level: The course is designed for 15-year-olds whom the authors claim want and are able to learn decision-making skills (Harmoni, Mann, & Power, 1987).

Duration: GOFER provides a program of readings and exercises designed to be taught in 40–50 hours over at least a year.

Course content: GOFER stands for five steps of sound decision making: *G*oals clarification, *O*ption generation, *F*act finding, consideration of *E*ffects, *R*eview and implementation. According to Mann, Harmoni, and Power (1988a):

> The course materials consist of two books: "Basic principles of decision making" and "Decision making in practice." The first book contains three parts: "What is decision making?" deals with the concept of decision making and how decision tasks change according to age, the GOFER strategy as a sequence of steps to follow for making sound decisions, and the consequences of missing a step on the quality of decisions. "Understanding how decisions work" explains the relationship between self esteem and decision making; the concept of a "batting average" in decision making; poor patterns of decision making (known as "Goofers") such as "drift on," "follow the leader," "cop out" and "panic"; and how to recognize tendencies to use "Goofers" and what to do about them. "Making decisions work for you" discusses techniques to assist each step of sound decision making. Students learn how to recognize and define decision problems; how to clarify the goals and values involved in major choices; how to generate options; how to check the reliability of information; how to assess risks; how to compare options; and how to "hatch" decisions, including announcement, selling the decision, implemen-

tation, fine tuning and, if necessary, undoing mistakes. In the second book, "Decision making in practice," principles of decision making are applied to several problem areas of importance to adolescents. There are five parts: Decision making in groups, Friendships and decision making, Subject choice, Money! Money! and Beyond GOFER. (p.6)

The two books are supplemented by student workbooks with exercises and a teacher's manual.

As indicated in Table 2.1, GOFER addresses most of the main steps of decision making. Of all the programs we have reviewed, GOFER builds most explicitly on results from descriptive research. This empirical base is drawn from Janis and Mann's (1977) research on affective barriers to effective decision making. The behavioral decision theory literature on cognitive barriers to sound decision making apparently did not play a role in GOFER's formulation. These barriers tend to affect people's ability to execute particular stages in the decision-making processes, unlike the affective barriers that affect people's ability to make deliberate decisions at all.

Evaluation: GOFER has been evaluated in two studies. The first had 40 experimental subjects and 51 controls who received no treatment at all. Both were tested only after the course had been taught to the experimental subjects. In the second study, the 152 experimental subjects were also pretested, but not the 220 control subjects. Instruction lasted 16 to 20 hours, so that less than half of the full course was taught. Three questionnaires were used as dependent variables.

1. The Flinders Adolescent Decision Making Questionnaire contains 30 Likert-type items, anchored at "almost always true" and "not at all true for me." Six items refer to each of five topics: Decision Self-Esteem (e.g., "The decisions I make turn out well"), Vigilance (e.g., "I like to think about a decision before I make it"), Panic (e.g., "I can't think straight if I have to make a decision in a hurry"), Cop Out (e.g., "I don't like to take responsibility for making decisions"), and Complacency (e.g., "When faced with a decision, I go along with what others suggest").

2. The Virgil Questionnaire attempts to measure competence in GOFER's five steps of good decision making. For each of 20 pairs of hypothetical individuals, students are asked "which kind of person are you most like" (e.g., "a person who goes through with plans to get to know some people better" or "a person who doesn't go through with plans to get to know some people better").

3. The Decision Knowledge Questionnaire contains 24 multiple-choice and 6 open-ended questions related to knowledge about three aspects of decision-making: person knowledge (e.g., what makes someone a really good decision maker?), task knowledge (e.g., what is the difference between a simple decision and a thinking decision?), and strategy knowledge (e.g.,

you want to teach a younger student how to make a decision; what advice could you give the younger student?)

As expected, treatment subjects reported engaging in more appropriate behavior for all five topics in the first questionnaire. There were, however, no differences in self descriptions on the second questionnaire, which measured competence in GOFER. The third questionnaire revealed differences in a "strategy knowledge subscale," but only for the first study.

In summarizing their results, Mann, Harmoni, Power, Geswick, and Ormond (1988) claimed that the course appears to improve adolescent decision making in the 12–16-year-old age range because students report using vigilance as a decision strategy. They further claimed that the course is acceptable to most students and increases their self-esteem as decision makers. They admitted, however, that the absence of differences in competence on the five steps of vigilance is problematic. They blamed the measure, because "all other measures suggest that the course produced changes."

Evaluating the evaluation: As noted in Table 2.2, one critical limitation to this evaluation is the fact that the control group received no treatment at all. As a result, improvement in measures such as reported self-esteem might just reflect the greater attention paid to the treatment group (Battjes & Bell, 1985). A second limit is that all the measures involved questionnaires regarding knowledge of the course material. The authors themselves note that reliance on questionnaires leaves open the question of the course's impact on behavior. Thus, the program's apparent success may simply reflect students having learned the right answers to the self-report questions. For example, a student who has seen 16–20 hours of coursework ought to know the "right" choice between, "I like to think about a decision before I make it" and "When faced with a decision, I go along with what others suggest."

One aspect of the knowledge conveyed in GOFER (and other curricula) is the meaning of specific terms about decision making. Youths in the control condition, who had not learned those terms, might fail the test even if they understood the underlying concept. Indeed, Mann et al. reported that 50% of the control subjects in the first study did not attempt the task and strategy knowledge items. They concluded that "These findings are of interest as they suggest that about one in two control students may have lacked the knowledge to attempt the task and strategy items, and they also suggest that the obtained group difference might have been greater if more control students had attempted the items" (p. 12). An alternative speculation is that the difference between groups might have been much less had more accessible phrasing been used in questions like, "What is the difference between a simple decision and a thinking decision?" A course's ability to teach terms is much less interesting that its ability to teach concepts or, ultimately, to affect behavior. However, understanding of terms is an important condition for the success of any course.

Finally, one might be concerned by the fact that the course's greatest impact was in increasing students' confidence in their decision making (whether this refers to process or outcome is hard to know from the report). Although the authors cited this as a sign of success, it might be a sign of failure if confidence was increased without a corresponding increase in competence (especially if people are overconfident to begin with) (Lichtenstein & Fischhoff, 1977; Oskamp, 1962). On the other hand, Mann (personal communication) suggests that increased confidence might encourage many adolescents to think about decisions actively, to avoid "drift on."

Personal Decision Making

Goal: Personal Decision Making (Ross, 1981a) conceives of the decision-making process as involving five steps: (a) identifying a set of alternative courses of action, (b) identifying appropriate criteria, (c) evaluating alternatives by these criteria, (d) summarizing information about alternatives, and (e) self-evaluation. The program is based on an explicit descriptive theory of how untrained individuals approximate the skills used by sophisticated decision makers, identifying five developmental stages for each of these five steps (Ross, 1981b). For example, the five stages for identifying alternatives were: single alternative, a small list of alternatives, brainstorming alternatives, constructing alternatives by classification, and constructing alternatives using criteria. The program then offers a sequence of exercises for traversing these stages.

Level: A condensed version of the program has been prepared for seventh-grade students and an advanced version for eighth-grade students (Ross, Boutillier, Gutteridge, & North, n.d.-a, n.d.-b).

Duration: The instructional package contained 10 lessons, each requiring about 1 hour of class time.

Course content: Detailed, virtually scripted lesson plans were constructed containing directions for teachers and students. "The first lesson consisted of a pretest and a teacher-directed analysis of a typical problem designed to identify the five steps of decision making. Two lessons were devoted to each of the first three [steps] and one lesson was given to each of the remaining [steps]. The ninth and tenth lessons consisted of a review of the five [steps] and posttest" (Ross, 1981a, p. 288).

As summarized in Table 2.1, this program covered many of the elements of decision making, but did not mention probability, utility, or value of information. Although some of the example problems involved uncertainty, that topic was not treated directly. The program relies heavily on descriptive studies claiming to show that unskilled decision making is but a simple version of skilled decision making (Ross, 1981a). Instead of listing all possible alternative courses of action, for example, unskilled individuals list but one or two. This theoretical orientation is at odds with the claim that unskilled performance is fundamentally different from that of experts.

Evaluation: The curriculum was assessed in three studies in which treatment students were pretested and posttested on an instrument involving one forced-choice test for each of the five decision-making steps. The five possible answers corresponded to Ross's five skill levels. Two sets of items were prepared, one for smoking decisions, and one for a career choice decision. The first served as a pretest, whereas the second was a posttest.[1]

The first study involved experimental and control classes in the same school, with the latter receiving no treatment at all. The second study had no explicit control group, using instead pretest norms established in the same school system 1 year earlier. The third study involved one teacher with four classes which constituted a Solomon Four-Group Design (Campbell & Stanley, 1963). This design crosses whether groups receive the treatment and whether they receive a pretest (or just a posttest) (Solomon, 1949).

Findings from the three studies were very consistent. The program substantially improved students' performance on the skills of identifying alternatives, assessing alternatives, and summarizing information. More modest improvements occurred for the skill of self-evaluation. The program actually appeared to leave students less capable of selecting criteria.

Evaluating the evaluation: Ross's measures are noteworthy for their sophistication. Nonetheless, they, too, test primarily whether subjects have learned the right answers to questions. They, too, reward knowledge of specific terms taught in the course.[2] A problem more specific to Ross's mea-

---

[1]For example, to test the skill level for identifying alternatives, subjects were told: Sarah is a student in a school where a lot of students smoke cigarettes. She is trying to make up her mind about smoking. The first thing she does is to try to make up a list of all the choices about smoking that she could make. Directions: Here are some things that Sarah could do to find out what choices she could make. If you were Sarah, what would you do? Circle the letter of your answer.

1. Sarah should make up a list of all the choices that are possible by asking her friends in school, her adult friends, and her relatives. [level 3, brainstorming]

2. Sarah should make up a list of all choices that she can think of. [level 2, small list]

3. Sarah should think about this problem very carefully, then she should write down what is the best thing to do. [level 1, single alternative]

4. Sarah should make up a list of all the choices she can think of. She should divide this list into groups. Then Sarah should think of new choices that could go in each group. She should add these to her list. [level 4, classifying]

5. Sarah should make up a list of all the choices she can think of. Then she should add new choices by thinking about the things to consider when making up her mind. [level 5, using criteria]

[2]For example, the level 5 item of the skill "summarizing the information" is: You gave a weight to each consideration that showed how important it is. Then you multiplied the value of each choice by the weight of each consideration. You added up the total points for each choice. You picked "never smoke" because it had the highest total score.

sures is forcing subjects to choose the correct answers from sets of alternatives that are not mutually exclusive.[3] Ross himself expressed dissatisfaction with these measures and, in a recent paper (Ross, 1988), used open-ended items requiring subjects to solve decision problems and describe their strategies. These were then coded in terms of the levels for each step.

General Thinking Skills Curricula

Introduction

In their review of approaches and programs to teach thinking skills, Nickerson, Perkins, and Smith (1985) divided programs into five broad categories:

1. those that focus on basic cognitive skills held to be essential to intellectual competence (e.g., Feuerstein, Rand, Hoffman, & Miller's [1980] Instrumental Enrichment Program)
2. those that emphasize explicit methods, like problem-solving heuristics, that are presumably applicable to a variety of cognitive tasks (e.g., Whimbey & Lochhead's [1979] Problem Solving and Comprehension)
3. those that promote formal operational thinking within conventional subject matter courses (e.g., Schermerhorn, Williams, & Dickison's [1982] COMPAS - Consortium for Operating and Managing Programs for the Advancement of Skills)
4. those that emphasize symbol manipulation skills (e.g., Feurzeig, Papert, Bloom, Grant, & Solomon's [1969] Logo computer language)
5. thinking about thinking approaches (e.g., Lipman, Sharp, & Oscanyan's [1980] Philosophy for Children).

Although there are many programs devoted to thinking skills, very few have a decision-making component. Possibly, decision making is perceived as a higher-order, complex thinking skill that can be taught only after the more fundamental, lower-order skills have been acquired. Beyth-Marom, Novik, and Sloan (1987) analyzed the normative decision-making process from an instructional point of view, showing the numerous cognitive abilities and educational objectives upon which it is based. This might explain why the few examples of decision-making units within thinking skills programs are in curricula aimed at college students (e.g., Hayes, 1981; Wheeler

---

[3]In the example of footnote 1, although brainstorming is only an intermediate level, it is not a wrong strategy when done along with more sophisticated ones.

& Dember, 1979). The one program that we found for adolescents is Odyssey—A Curriculum for Thinking.

Odyssey—A Curriculum for Thinking

Goal: The program was initiated by the Venezuelan government and created by researchers at Harvard University and Bolt Beranek and Newman, Inc. Odyssey attempts to improve students' performance in a wide variety of intellectually demanding tasks.

Level: The course materials were developed for Venezuelan 7th-grade students and have been translated into English (Adams, 1986).

Duration: There are approximately 100 45-minute lessons, making for 75 hours of direct instruction.

Course content: The course's teacher's manual contains six series of lessons, each treating a different topic: the foundations of reasoning, understanding language, verbal reasoning, problem solving, decision making, and inventive thinking. Each lesson has its rationale for inclusion, its objectives, target abilities (for students to acquire), products, materials, and classroom procedures.

The decision-making section has three units, each divided into several lessons, for a total of 10 lessons:

- Unit 1—Introduction to Decision Making: Decision Situations, Anticipating Outcomes, and Alternatives with Unknown Outcomes.
- Unit 2—Gathering and Evaluating Information to Reduce Uncertainty: Assessing the Likelihood of Outcomes, Deciding Whether Information Is Relevant, Deciding Whether Information Is Consistent, Deciding Whether Information Is Credible, and the Importance of Double Checking Information.
- Unit 3—Analyzing Complex Decision Situations: Expressing Preferences and Weighting Dimensions.

This curriculum is very structured, with a detailed teacher's manual including guidelines as to what the teacher might say and how students might react. There is also a student guide. The 10 lessons devoted to decision-making cover 8 of the 9 topics in Table 2.1. They present uncertain situations and the concept of probability. They deal with preferences and how to weight them. Three lessons deal with properties of information: credibility, relevance, consistency. There is, however, little direct reference to any descriptive literature regarding intuitive decision-making processes.

Evaluation: Three matched pairs of Venezuelan schools participated in the experiment, with four classes in each school. Twelve of the classes (463 students) were experimental classes, and 12 (432 students) were control classes. The experimental classes met 4 days a week during an entire academic year, whereas the control classes had their normal curriculum. Only 56 of the 100 lessons (5 out of the 10 in decision making) were taught because of time constraints. They were chosen to represent the full set of 100. A variety of standard ability tests were administered to all students before the beginning of the course, after its completion, and, in some cases, at various points during the year. In addition, six Target Abilities Tests (TATs) (one for each unit) were created to test for the abilities that the lessons were intended to teach. Detailed results appear in the project's Final Report (Harvard University, 1983) and in Herrnstein, Nickerson, Sanchez, and Swets (1986). Both experimental students and control students showed some improvement in test scores over the year of the experiment. In most cases, students in the experimental group showed greater gains than those in the control group. Not surprisingly, differences were much greater in the TATs than in the general ability tests. No specific effects on decision making were reported.

Evaluating the evaluation: Herrnstein and colleagues (1986) summarized their evaluation by pointing to some major unresolved issues: (a) only short-term results are available at present. It is unclear whether the effects will fade without additional training, and (b) it is difficult to know whether beneficial effects were due to specific aspects of the course or simply to the motivational effects of receiving such great attention. To these concerns, we would add the possibility that the TAT tests (which showed the greatest impact) measure primarily the acquisition of specific terms and facts. These tests are particularly vulnerable to charges of training to the criterion because the explicit objectives of many study units were to enhance the comprehension and use of terms used in the test questions.

PROGRAMS TEACHING SOCIAL AND LIFE SKILLS

Both social skills and life skills programs are based on the same theoretical orientations: Bandura's (1977) social-learning theory and Jessor and Jessor's problem behavior theory (1977). According to these approaches, personal and social competence depend on two main factors: people's general cognitive skills and their ability to interact effectively with their social environment.

"Life skills counseling equips adolescents to handle current problems, anticipate and prevent future ones and advance their mental health, social functioning, economic welfare and physical well being" (Schinke & Gilchrist, 1984, p. 13). Typically, courses attempt to achieve these very broad goals through improving certain (behavioral) skills relating to a specific problem in a predetermined target group. Hence, there are life skills programs designed to prevent smoking, drug abuse, alcohol abuse, and early pregnancy, as well as to improve adolescents' peer and family relationships, to help them cope with stress, et cetera. By contrast, social skills programs attempt to improve social behavior in general. In practice, though, every life-skills program has some social component. Nonetheless, we will follow the distinction made by curriculum developers. We look only at those curricula that address decision making explicitly. There is, of course, the theoretical possibility that improved decision making will be a by-product of training for other skills.

Life Skills Programs

Life Skills Counseling

Goal: According to Schinke and Gilchrist (1984), personal and social competence can be acquired through life skills counseling. This counseling involves six components:

1. Giving accurate and relevant *information.*
2. Building internal control by *"self-instruction* counseling through modeling and rehearsal."
3. Teaching adaptive *coping* techniques.
4. Shaping effective *communication* schemas.
5. Encouraging the building of "cognitive interpersonal and environmental *systems of support."*
6. Improving the process of decision making.

These interventions are called "counseling" rather than programs, reflecting a flexible, less structured process. No structured curricula have been published.

Level: Schinke and his colleagues have worked with a wide range of ages, including elementary school children preparing for junior high school, sixth-grade students concerned about smoking, and high school students dealing with their sexuality and the risk of pregnancy.

Duration: The substance abuse prevention programs consist of 8 twice-weekly sessions. The program preparing students for junior high school lasted for 8 hours over 2 months, as did an intervention for stress management (Schinke, Schilling, & Snow, 1987). The decision-making component of these programs takes only an hour or two of the total time.

Course content: Generally, Schinke and his collaborators' counseling is directed at specific problems such as interpersonal relationships (e.g., Schinke & Rose, 1976), preventing teenage pregnancy (Schinke, 1982), preventing the use of alcohol, cigarettes, and drugs, and reducing unemployment (e.g., Schinke & Blythe, 1981), or preparing students for junior high school (Snow, Gilchrist, Schilling, Schinke, & Kelso, 1986).

Problem solving is the component of these programs that is the most relevant to decision making. Schinke's general instructions to counselors usually describe the following steps to good decision making: define the problem, generate solutions, evaluate the solution, select the best one, and plan to implement it. Examples from students' personal experience are used to teach these various steps. Students are encouraged to pose questions like: What's the problem? Who's got the problem? What happens if the problem goes on? How did you get into this mess? Who can get out of it? What can you do to solve the problem? Can you order your options from the most to the least attractive solutions? Can you tell what will happen if you use each solution? Students are also taught assertive communication skills through role playing designed to provide them with practice in sticking to tough decisions, dealing with risky situations (and influential people), and exercising self-control. A combination of modeling, feedback, reinforcement, and coaching are utilized to teach these skills. Homework assignments provide additional practice.

Evaluation: Many of these life skills interventions have undergone some evaluation, typically involving pretest and posttest evaluations with experimental and control groups. Botvin and Wills (1985) and Botvin (in press) have reviewed the impact of these programs on substance abuse; Snow, Gilchrist, and Schinke (1985) have done so for smoking prevention. These evaluations have often shown significant changes in these focal behaviors. Schinke and Gilchrist (1983) reported, for example, a 79% reduction in experimental smoking. The occasional attempts to measure social and cognitive mediating processes have produced less clear-cut results.

Evaluating the evaluations: A general problem in evaluating counseling interventions is operationalizing the independent variable. As life skills training is not structured, it is very difficult to know exactly what is done and, hence, what aspects of a program cause any observed changes in behavior. In only one case (Schinke & Gilchrist, 1986) has an attempt been made to vary the features of programs across experimental groups.

Schinke and his colleagues have been concerned about the validity of their behavioral measures. Early studies often used self-reports as their dependent measures, running the risk that subjects will report what they believe to be desired answers, rather than their actual attitudes or behavior. More recent studies have collected saliva or breath samples prior to collecting self-report data.

Unfortunately, these evaluations have produced little reliable information regarding cognitive and social variables (such as assertiveness, locus of control, social anxiety, decision making, and problem solving), hypothesized to have mediated these changes. Some evaluation studies ignore these mediating cognitive skills (e.g., Schinke & Gilchrist, 1986; Snow, Gilchrist, Schilling, Schinke, & Kelso, 1986). Others mention that general problem-solving ability was measured, but provided few details how this was done beyond general references to skills such as perspective taking, means–end thinking, and anticipation of consequences (e.g., Schinke & Gilchrist, 1985; Schinke, Gilchrist, Snow, & Schilling, 1985). Schinke and Gilchrist (1984) described two of these measures. With regard to means–end thinking, "counselors supply adolescents with the beginning and the end of a social situation and youths must detail what happens in the middle. Youths' responses are scored for realism, interpersonal sensitivity, recognition of possible obstacles and for how well and how directly they are able to link the beginning to the end" (p. 30). With regard to anticipating consequences, "A written or verbal prompt from the counselor outlines a situation containing a temptation. Adolescents are asked to list everything that might be going through their minds while they decide what to do, what they choose to do, and what happens" (p. 30). The reliability of the scoring for these tasks and their relevance to specific decision-making skills is unclear.

Botvin's Life Skills Training—A Self-Improvement Approach to Substance Abuse Prevention

Goal: To prevent tobacco, alcohol, and drug abuse through the development of general coping skills, as well as skills and knowledge specifically related to resisting social influences. A central feature of the program is teaching cognitive skills for enhancing self-esteem (e.g., goal setting), resisting persuasive appeals (e.g., formulating counterarguments), coping with anxiety (e.g., relaxation techniques), and improving communication and decision making.

Level: The program is aimed at middle or junior high school students.

Duration: The full course takes about 15 hours.

Course content: Compared to Schinke's counseling program, this training program has the markings of a curriculum. There is a structured guide, as well as a detailed teacher's manual. The curriculum is taught using a combination of instruction, modeling, rehearsal, feedback and reinforcement, and practice through homework assignments.

The curriculum contains 5 major components (Botvin, 1983):

1. A cognitive component intended to present information concerning the short- and long-term consequences of substance use, prevalence rates and social acceptability, and the process of becoming dependent on tobacco, alcohol, or marijuana.

2. A decision-making component intended to foster the development of critical thinking and responsible decision making.

3. A component intended to provide students with techniques for coping with anxiety.

4. A social skills training component, including both general coping skills and assertiveness techniques that can be used to resist direct peer pressure to smoke, drink, and use drugs.
5. A self-improvement project designed to provide students with techniques for changing specific personal skills or behaviors.

Each component contains two to six lessons. Each lesson is divided into 12 units, containing a major goal, measurable student objectives, content, and classroom activities.

The decision-making unit (two lessons) is called "Decision making and independent thinking." The goal of the unit is that "Students will gain understanding of how group pressures and persuasive tactics influence their decisions." Its objectives are (a) identify everyday decisions, (b) describe how important decisions are made, (c) present a 5-step normative model for making decisions, (d) demonstrate how decisions are influenced by group pressures, (e) discuss reasons why people are influenced by group members, (f) identify persuasive tactics (flattery, appeal to authority), (g) identify ways of resisting persuasive tactics (Botvin, 1983). Thus, five of Table 2.1's nine decision-making skills are taught. Descriptive behavioral research is reflected in only one social aspect of the program, how group pressure affects decision making.

Evaluation: Five studies are reported in the literature and several more are underway (Botvin, Baker, Renick, Botvin, Fillazola, & Millman, 1984; Botvin, Baker, Renick, Fillazola, & Botvin, 1984; Botvin & Eng, 1980; Botvin & Eng, 1982; Botvin, Eng, & Williams, 1980; Botvin, Renick, & Baker, 1983). Each involves an experimental and a control group, receiving pre- and posttests. The test questionnaire asks for self-reported smoking status, knowledge about cigarette smoking, assertiveness, psychosocial knowledge, locus of control, coping strategies, self-esteem, social anxiety, attitudes toward smoking, personal efficacy, interpersonal control, academic confidence, decision-making autonomy, problem-solving confidence and need for group acceptance. It has been administered in studies varying implementation schedule (5 to 15 weeks, with or without "boosters"), implementers (staff members, peer leaders, regular teachers), and length of follow up (from 1 to 24 months). All studies show a decrease in the number of new smokers in the experimental group and a decrease in regular smokers when subjects are tested again after a year or two. Furthermore, experimental subjects were found to have greater knowledge about substances, psychosocial processes, and advertising. They also reported greater decision-making autonomy.

Evaluating the evaluations: Botvin is quite self-critical about his evaluations, even incorporating a manipulation check to see whether the implementation was proper. Recognizing the weakness of self-report measures of the dependent variable (smoking or other substance use), he added a saliva sample in later studies.

Botvin and his collaborators measure social and cognitive mediating variables with 112 forced-choice questions, mostly of the Likert type. Seven relate to decision making (e.g., "I think about the different choices that exist before I take any action," "I think about which of the alternatives is best"), and eight relate to confidence in solving problems (e.g., "Many of the problems that I face are too hard to solve," "I have the ability to solve most problems even though at first it looks as if there's no solution"). As elsewhere, one must ask whether these questions encompass the full set of skills that the program attempts to teach and whether the behavior reported in them is actually adopted or is just a learned "right answer."

Spitzhoff, Stephen, and Wills' Decision Skills Curriculum

Goal: This program (Spitzhoff, Ramirez, & Wills, 1982) is based on a theoretical orientation, supported by empirical evidence, that views addictive behavior as a stress-reducing factor (Shiffman & Wills, 1985). However, as such, addictive behavior is a *destructive* coping pattern. Wills (1985) showed that *constructive* coping patterns (such as decision making and cognitive coping) are negatively correlated with substance use. They presumably act to increase resistance to internal and external pressures to engage in destructive behaviors. The program was designed to affect mediating coping variables presumed relevant to deterring smoking initiation, specifically, decision-making ability, internal locus of control, knowledge about the negative consequences of smoking, and assertiveness skills.

Level: The curriculum is taught to seventh-grade students.

Duration: The full program takes 2 weeks.

Course content: The program has an intermediate level of structure. It contains eight modules and includes teachers' worksheets, slides, role-playing exercises, and video cassettes which teachers are apparently free to use in different ways. There is no student textbook.

Its eight modules are:

1. A values clarification exercise that focuses on leisure activities.
2. Decision making: Students are encouraged to bring up many decisions and are introduced to six normative steps of decision making.
3. Social influences through the media: Students consider the effects of the media on their health behavior, particularly on the onset of smoking.
4. Social influences through peer pressure and how to counteract those influences.
5. Assertiveness training.

6. Stress management: a four-step process to deal with stress.
7. Stress management: how to incorporate stress management techniques into one's life style, focusing on progressive muscle relaxation.
8. Health consequences of smoking.

The decision-making module includes two lessons. They introduce the topic, provide examples, describe six steps of normative decision making, and present practice on hypothetical situations.

Evaluation: An intervention program that was conducted with the entire seventh grade in three junior high schools initially showed similar levels of reported smoking. The two schools in the experimental condition received the full smoking prevention program that year and a follow-up program the next year. Evaluation data were obtained with a simple questionnaire which was administered in school classrooms by project staff at the beginning and end of each school year. The items were divided into 11 factors (by previous factors analyses): decision making, adult social support, cognitive coping, peer social support, substance use, physical exercise, aggression, social entertainment, individual relaxation, parental support, and prayer. The decision-making portion of the questionnaire contained nine items beginning, "When I have a problem, I . . ." and ending with one of nine completions: think about which information is necessary, think about choices before taking any action, get information needed to deal with the problem, think about which alternative is best, think about risks in different ways, think about possible consequences of alternatives, compromise to get something positive from a situation, change an attitude that contributes to the problem, change behavior that contributes to the problem. The five-point response scale was anchored at "never" and "usually."

In one of the two experimental schools, the program increased decision-making skills and internal health locus of control, while decreasing stress and smoking initiation. In the other experimental school, however, there was no effect on any variables, dependent or mediating. Wills (1985) described some aspects of the latter school's atmosphere that may have blunted the treatment.

Evaluating the evaluation: The control group received no treatment at all, but the treatment program was relatively structured, raising the risk of attentional effects. There is also the risk of training to the criterion in the self-reports of decision making. The study was unique in testing long-term impacts on the mediating variables.

Social Skills Programs

Pellegrini and Urbain (1985) evaluated 19 training programs aimed at improving "interpersonal problem-solving skills," perhaps the most systematic and comprehensive of which were developed by Myrna Shure, George

Spivack, and their colleagues at the Hahnemann Medical College in Phila-delphia (e.g., Shure & Spivack, 1971; Spivack & Shure, 1974). Details on the content, duration, and level of these programs can be found in Pelle-grini and Urbain's review, which also provides an instructive summary of potential methodological problems.

Shure and Spivack concentrated on developing and integrating three skills:

1. Alternative thinking: the ability to generate multiple solutions to in-terpersonal problems.
2. Consequential thinking: the ability to foresee both short-term and long-range consequences of different alternatives.
3. Means–ends thinking: the ability to develop a plan of specific actions to attain one's goals, anticipating and overcoming potential obstacles.

The program uses a sequential series of scripted games and group exercises.

Although they are potentially relevant to improving the decision-making skills of adolescents in general, the social skills programs covered by Pelle-grini and Urbain's review were all directed either at preadolescent children or at special populations, such as delinquent or aggressive/impulsive youths (Zahavi & Asher, 1978). In addition, there was no specific measurement of decision-making abilities. Therefore, we will not summarize this review.

SUMMARY AND CONCLUSIONS

Content

As shown in Table 2.1, most of the programs reviewed here provide training in four to six elements of the normative process of decision making. The Odyssey program is exceptionally comprehensive. It alone teaches how to distinguish among different decision situations and conveys ideas about probability and utility. However, there is more to decision making than even these steps.

Most of the curricula that we have reviewed are equally incomplete in their treatment of the research literature regarding decision-making pro-cesses. Although GOFER and Personal Decision Making are significant ex-ceptions, each has a fairly narrow perspective. GOFER builds on research regarding the obstacles that stress poses to cognitive functioning in general and to decision making in particular. The importance of those factors is suggested by Zakay and Wooler's (1984) finding that the improvement gen-erated by a training program for adults disappeared when decisions had to be made under time pressure (which reduced the performance of trained and untrained subjects to the same low level). By contrast, Personal Decision Making is based on research that claims to show that intuitive decision-making processes are only a simplified version of the normatively correct ones. Neither of these programs considers the research central to the other. Neither they nor any of the other thinking and decision-making curricula are sensitive to the research on peer pressures and socialization that is central to the life and social skills programs. Finally, none of these programs demonstrate more than a passing familiarity with the cognitive literature of behavioral decision theory. Studies there provide some insight into how people intuitively perform each component of the decision-making process, where they need the most help, and what interventions are most effective (e.g., Fischhoff, 1982).

Educational programs ought to reflect all that we know about how people behave. Thus, the content of decision-making programs must be faulted unless it either incorporates this literature or demonstrates its irrelevance (just as behavioral decision-making researchers might be faulted for not having translated their results with adults into programs for adolescents). A legitimate claim can be made that no program has enough time to teach everything. However, that is no excuse for not making what is taught sensitive to research regarding those topics.

Evaluation Studies

An evaluation is meaningless unless one knows just what has been done. Unfortunately, defining the manipulation or treatment is a recurring problem with most of the life and social skills programs, much more so than with the more structured thinking skills and decision-making programs. Where the exact procedures can be discerned, they often appear to be somewhat at odds with the programs' proclaimed goals of improving decision-making and problem-solving skills. Namely, "many programs in this area teach students how to behave as opposed to how to think. That is, alternative ways of responding to interpersonal problem situations are often modeled by the teachers or therapists and then children are often coached and given social reinforcement for their behavior. The problem this creates is that it becomes difficult to separate out the effects of the cognitive aspects of the training from the effects of role modeling, coaching and social reinforcement" (Adsit, 1988, p. 28).

The brevity of most programs (line 2, Table 2.2) must raise some doubts about the possibilities for changing anything so fundamental as general decision-making skills. It would be hard to expect such changes from students who bring with them no bad habits, much less from students who already have inappropriate intuitions that must be unlearned. The relatively short duration of these interventions could be contrasted with the much greater class time invested in teaching a skill like addition, where it is much easier to give clear-cut feedback. The last row of Table 2.2 shows the absence of long-term follow-up studies. Considering the modest size of the present interventions, we suspect, regrettably, that such studies would show little effect on decision-making abilities. We would be similarly reserved about the prospects for showing generalization beyond the context within which tests were made (Glasgow & McCaul, 1985).

In almost all cases, training programs were compared to control groups receiving no treatment at all. Where present, control groups typically received no attention at all (or even negative attention, if they knew that other classes in their school were receiving special treatment). An attention manipulation is particularly important considering the exhortation to work hard that is part of most curricula (e.g., list many alternatives, think about many criteria). That pressure might by itself produce improvement on test tasks, regardless of the other features of a curriculum. This may be particularly true when, as was typically the case, the test was no more than a self-report. It is relatively straightforward to tell teachers what they want to hear about one's behavior. Learning right answers may be a necessary condition for better decision making. However, it is clearly not sufficient. All too often, whatever support can be found for a curriculum may reflect no more than training to the criterion. Moreover, even that learning may be somewhat illusory where a significant part of the training involves teaching a special vocabulary—so that test questions may only be meaningful to course takers. Thus, control group subjects might behave similarly but simply not recognize the terms in which behavior is described. Some of those problems can be avoided. Where the critical kind of behavior is a form of overt "risk taking," like smoking, then it may be possible to take supplementary measures like urine or saliva samples. Where decision-making processes are the dependent variable, direct observation is much more difficult. A final source of concern is that despite teaching relatively similar steps of decision making (Table 2.1), every program studied uses its own set of dependent measures (Table 2.2, middle section), with no cross-referencing or psychometric studies. Thus, this critical aspect of evaluation is quite undeveloped.

One particularly suspect measure used in several evaluation studies was confidence in personal decision-making capabilities. For example, GOFER students responded to statements like "the decisions I make turn out well." Botvin's students responded to "I have the ability to solve most problems even though at first it looks as if there is no solution." Improvements in this sort of confidence might even be undesirable if it represented an increase in confidence (and in overconfidence) without a corresponding increase in competence. In this respect, the GOFER question would be especially troubling. Botvin's question asks more about perceived ability to do something constructive (instead of panic, delay a decision, etc.), whereas the GOFER statement represents faith that things will work out.

Despite this inconclusive evidence regarding changes in decision-making behavior, some programs do seem to have demonstrably reduced risky behaviors, like smoking and drug abuse. There is, however, simply no way of knowing why they work and what is the specific contribution of their decision-making component. Conceivably, they do not teach decision-making at all. Rather, the decision-making component just serves to give students a feeling that they are being trusted to make their own choices. That, in turn, makes it easier for them to accept the strong persuasive messages in the rest of the program materials, telling them *what* to decide about sex, drugs, smoking, and so forth, under the guise of telling them *how* to go about deciding.

Decision Making about Decision-Making Curricula

Reviewing the experience with existing curricula raises several general questions regarding future programs and their evaluations:

What are the Aims of the Program?

"Improving decision-making skills" is too general a goal for designing or evaluating a curriculum. We have already mentioned the difference between knowledge about decision-making principles, attitudes toward decision-making procedures, and actual decision-making behavior. To the extent that appropriate knowledge and attitudes are necessary conditions for behavior change, they should also be goals of training. However, learning the right answers to knowledge questions provides no guarantee of wanting or being able to implement them in practice. Thus, behavior change should also be measured—recognizing the difficulties of doing so.

What Theoretical Approach Guides a Curriculum?

As Sternberg (1983) noted, any training program should be based on a theory of intellectual performance. We have argued that the theoretical bases for decision-making curricula should be a normative theory of how decisions should be made and a descriptive theory of how they are made. That descriptive account should include not only intellectual aspects of decision making, but also its emotional, motivational, and social aspects. There is an extensive literature regarding these aspects, at least for adult behavior, but it is as yet neglected. It should be supplemented by the more general literature of instructional psychology which emphasizes lessons like the importance of explicating the appropriate problem-solving structure, procedures, and strategies, and of allowing problems to arise naturally, in order to address them and replace them with new behaviors.

The normative content of decision-making curricula also requires further thought. The model implicit to most existing programs is that the expert decision maker is an industrious person, going over all decision-making stages, quantifying every step, and integrating it effectively, unaffected by any bias. There is little discussion of the possibility that good decision making may also involve knowing how to make efficient short cuts, or having "canned" decisions available for some situations. If "an important aspect of intelligence is deciding just how one's resources and especially attentional resources should be allocated" (Sternberg, 1986), then that also ought to be an important aspect of good decision making. An expert decision maker might know, for example, when the transaction costs and expected yield of a full-blown decision-making process are not worth the effort. Decision-making expertise might mean having a set of general decision schemata and being able to match them to specific decision situations.

How Should We Evaluate a Decision-Making Program?

A comprehensive answer to this question (like the others) requires an article of its own. Clearly, a set of evaluative criteria ought to be in place before a program is undertaken. These should include criteria of internal validity such as the fidelity of the program to the normative and descriptive literatures on decision making. They should include criteria of external validity such as changes in behavior, emphasizing generalizability and durability.

Should Decision Making Be Taught in a Specific Domain or in Its Own Right?

Our review covered two kinds of program: life- and social-skills programs, which taught decision making for the purpose of influencing specific behaviors (e.g., smoking, drinking), and decision-making programs, aimed at improving decision making per se. This contrast in approaches is a special case of the general issue regarding the generality and specificity of intellectual processes. This conflict has long been a controversial topic in the educational and psychological literature.

Those who advocate the specific approach (e.g., Glaser, 1984) claim that one cannot separate knowledge from processes:

> High aptitude individuals appear to be skillful reasoners because of the level of their content knowledge as well as because of their knowledge of the procedural constraints of a particular problem form . . . Thus, improvement in the skills of learning . . . takes place through the exercise of conceptual and procedural knowledge in the context of specific knowledge domains. Learning and reasoning skills develop not as abstract mechanisms of heuristic

search and memory processing. Rather, they develop as the content and concepts of a knowledge domain are attained in learning situations that constrain this knowledge to serve certain purposes and goals (p. 99).

From this perspective, it seems best to teach such skills as problem solving and decision making in terms of familiar knowledge domains. Summarizing the literature, Glaser and Bassok (1989) concluded, "Useful knowledge is not acquired as a set of general propositions, but by active application during problem solving in the context of specific goals".

According to the general approach (Sternberg, 1985), "processes of various degrees of domain generality are critical to the acquisition and utilization of domain-specific knowledge, just as domain-specific knowledge is critical to the acquisition and utilization of further domain-specific knowledge" (p. 572). Those who hold this belief recognize the value of using familiar materials in teaching, but view it as a vehicle for conveying general skills. They argue, however, that it is more efficient overall to seek such general understanding, rather than having to address decision making in every domain separately.

How Can We Get Good Transfer?

The relative efficiency of general and specific approaches is one aspect of the transferability of training. "Transfer" is change in the performance of one task as a result of the prior performance of a different task (Gick & Holyoak, 1987). Typically, the amount of transfer depends on the degree of similarity between the two tasks. Thus, more transfer would be expected to decision problems in life that are similar to those considered in the training period. Although the principle of similarity is well established, the definition of similarity must be determined for particular tasks. The role-playing exercises in many curricula seem to represent attempts to capture as much as possible of the setting in which actual decisions will be made, including their emotional and social pressures. Although this appears to be a reasonable strategy, a more comprehensive account is needed. For example, if we successfully teach six basic steps of decision making for every decision, then that is probably what will happen in real-life situations that cue lessons from the course. However, real-life situations often involve time pressure, making such thoroughness a luxury. Thus, even if there are strong commonalities to decision making in different contexts, a program might still have to provide the special decision-making skills needed for specific situations.

Several other principles of training are worth remembering: (a) More training improves transfer; 2 to 8 hours of decision-making training is obviously not enough for such a complex skill; (b) Transfer is best with varied training problems; (c) Transfer is best if an abstract rule or explanation accompanies the specific solutions (Gick & Holyoak, 1983; Glaser & Bassok, in press).

When Shall We Teach What?

No doubt, adolescence raises serious decisions. Although that raises an urgent need to teach decision making, that effort may be useless unless adolescents have already acquired the necessary basic cognitive skills. Beyth-Marom and colleagues (1987) provide such task analysis for decision-making under certainty. Matched with an analysis of cognitive development (Keating, 1980; 1988; Kuhn, Amsel, & O'Loughlin, 1988), it could provide the basis for timing and sequencing the learning of these skills.

How Much Teaching Is Needed?

If decision making requires many higher-order thinking skills, much time is clearly needed. The only sustained improvement in general thinking skills reported in the literature involved 2 years of graduate training (Lehman, Lempert, & Nisbett, 1988).

What Are the Opportunity Costs?

Students participating in a curriculum are doing that rather than something else. One must, therefore, ask what they are giving up. We suspect that decision making can be taught and that it is worth the investment of significant class time. However, a much stronger evidentiary base is needed if that claim is to be made on the basis of scientific results rather than scientists' impressions.

ACKNOWLEDGMENT

Preparation of this report was sponsored by Carnegie Corporation of New York. It is gratefully acknowledged. The opinions expressed are those of the authors.

REFERENCES

Abelson, R., & Levi, A. (1985). Decision making. In W. Gardner & G. Lindzey (Eds.), *Handbook of social psychology* (pp. 231–309). Reading, MA: Addison-Wesley.

Adams, M. J. (Coordinator). (1986). *Odyssey: A curriculum for thinking.* Watertown, MA: Mastery Education Corp.

Adsit, J. D. (1988). *Training in decision making.* Unpublished manuscript, University of Minnesota, Minneapolis, MN.

Argyle, M. (1969). *Social interaction.* London: Methuen.

Bandura, A. (1977). *Social learning theory.* Englewood Cliffs, NJ: Prentice-Hall.

Baron, J. (1985). What kinds of intelligence components are fundamental? In S. F. Chipman, J. W. Segal, & R. Glaser (Eds.), *Thinking and learning skills, Vol. 2: Research and open questions* (pp. 365–390). Hillsdale, NJ: Lawrence Erlbaum Associates.

Baron, J., & Hershey, J. (1988). Outcome bias in decision evaluation. *Journal of Personality and Social Psychology, 54*(4), 569–579.

Battjes, R. J., & Bell, C. S. (1985). Future directions in drug abuse prevention research. In C. S. Bell & R. Battjes (Eds.), *Prevention research: Deterring drug abuse among children and adolescents* (pp. 221–228). (NIDA Research Monograph 63. Department of Health and Human Services Publication No. ADM87-1334.) Washington, DC: US Government Printing Office.

Bell, D. (1978). The social framework of the information society. In M. L. Dertouzos & J. Moses (Eds.), *The computer age: A twenty-year view.* (pp. 163–211) Boston: MIT Press.

Beyth-Marom, R., Novik, R., & Sloan, M. (1987). Enhancing children's thinking skills: An instructional model for decision making under certainty. *Instructional Science, 16,* 215–231.

Biglan, A., & Ary, D. V. (1985). Methodological issues in research on smoking prevention. In C. S. Bell & R. Battjes, (Eds.), *Prevention Research: Deterring drug abuse among children & adolescents.* (pp. 170–195). (NIDA Research Monograph 63. Department of Health and Human Services Publication No. ADM87-1334). Washington, DC: Government Printing Office 170–195).

Blackshaw, L., & Fischhoff, B. (1988). Decision making in online search. *Journal of American Society for Information Sciences, 39*(6), 369–389.

Botvin, G. J. (1983). *Life Skills Training: A self-improvement approach to substance abuse prevention. Teacher's Manual.* New York: Smithfield Press.

Botvin, G. J. (1988). Substance abuse prevention: Theory, practice and effectiveness. In N. Morris & M. Tonry (Eds.), *Crime and justice.* Chicago: University of Chicago.

Botvin, G. J., Baker, E., Renick, N. L., Botvin, E. M., Filazzola, A. D., & Millman, R. B. (1984). Alcohol abuse prevention through the development of personal and social competence: A pilot study. *Journal of Studies on Alcohol, 45,* 550–552.

Botvin, G. J., Baker, E., Renick, N. L., Filazzola, A. D., & Botvin, E. M. (1984). A cognitive behavioral approach to substance abuse prevention. *Addictive Behaviors, 9,* 137–147.

Botvin, G. J., & Eng, A. (1980). A comprehensive school-based smoking prevention program. *Journal of School Health, 50,* 209–213.

Botvin, G. J., & Eng, A. (1982). Efficacy of a multicomponent approach to the prevention of cigarette smoking. *Preventive Medicine, 11,* 199–211.

Botvin, G. J., Eng, A. M., & Williams, C. L. (1980). Preventing the onset of cigarette smoking through Life Skills Training. *Preventive Medicine, 9,* 135–143.

Botvin, G. J., Renick, N., & Baker, E. (1983). The effects of scheduling format and booster sessions on a broad spectrum psychosocial approach to smoking prevention. *Journal of Behavioral Medicine, 6,* 359–379.

Botvin, G. J., & Wills, T. A. (1985). Personal and Social Skills Training: Cognitive behavioral approaches to substance abuse prevention. In C. S. Bell, & R. Battjes (Eds), *Prevention research: Deterring drug abuse among children and adolescents.* (pp. 8–49). (NIDA Research Monograph Series No. 63. Department of Health and Human Services Publication No. ADM87-1334). Washington, DC: U.S. Government Printing Office.

Brown, A. L., Campione, J. C., & Day, J. D. (1981). Learning to learn: On training students to learn from text. *Educational Researcher, 10,* 14–21.

Brumby, M. N. (1984). Misconceptions about the concept of natural selection by medical biology students. *Science Education, 68*(4), 493–503.

Campbell, D. T., & Stanley, J. C. (1963). Experimental and quasi-experimental designs for research on teaching. In N. L. Gage (Ed.), *Handbook for research on teaching* (pp. 171–246). Skokie, IL: Rand McNally.

Carroll, J. (1971). Participatory technology. *Science, 171*(19), 647–653.

Cassidy, E. W., & Kurfman, D. G. (1977). Decision making as purpose and process. In D. G. Kurfman (Ed.), *Developing decision making skills.* Arlington, VA: National Council for the Social Studies.

Chen, D., & Novik, R. (1984). Scientific and technological education in an information society. *Science Education, 68,* 421–426.

Cook, T. D. (1985). Priorities in research in smoking prevention. In C. S. Bell & R. Battjes (Eds.), *Prevention research: Deterring drug abuse among children & adolescents* (pp. 196–220). (NIDA Research Monograph 63. Department of Health and Human Services Publication No. ADM87-1334.) Washington, DC: U.S. Government Printing Office.

Coombs, C. H., Dawes, R. M. & Tversky, A. (1970). *Mathematical psychology.* Englewood Cliffs, NJ: Prentice-Hall.

Duryea, E. J. (1986). Introducing conceptual tempo: An attempt to refocus health decision making in youth. *Adolescence, 21,* 737–741.

D'Zurilla, T. J., & Goldfried, M. R. (1971). Problem solving and behavior modification. *Journal of Abnormal Psychology, 78,* 107–126.

Edwards, W. (1954). The theory of decision making. *Psychological Bulletin, 51,* 380–417.

Ellul, J. (1963). *Propaganda.* New York: Knopf.

Eska, B., & Black, K. (1971). Conceptual tempo in young grade school children. *Child Development, 42,* 505–516.

Evans, J. St. B. T. (1983). *The psychology of deductive reasoning.* London: Routledge & Kegan Paul.

Feuerstein, R., Rand, Y., Hoffman, M., & Miller, R. (1980). *Instrumental enrichment.* Baltimore: University Park Press.

Feurzeig, W., Papert, S., Bloom, M., Grant, R., & Solomon, C. (November 1969). *Programming-language as a conceptual framework for teaching mathematics* (Report No. 1889). Cambridge, MA: Bolt, Beranek & Newman, Inc.

Fischhoff, B. (1982). Debiasing. In D. Kahneman, P. Slovic, & A. Tversky, (Eds.), *Judgment under uncertainty: Heuristics and biases.* (pp. 422–444). New York: Cambridge University Press.

Fischhoff, B. (1988). Judgment and decision making. In R. J. Sternberg & E. E. Smith (Eds.), *The psychology of human thought* (pp. 153–187). New York: Cambridge.

Fischhoff, B., Slovic, P., & Lichtenstein, S. (1977). Knowing with certainty: The appropriateness of extreme confidence. *Journal of Experimental Psychology: Human Perception and Performance, 3,* 552–564.

Fischhoff, B., Slovic, P., & Lichtenstein, S. (1978). Fault trees: Sensitivity of assessed failure probabilities to problem presentation. *Journal of Experimental Psychology: Human Perception and Performance, 4,* 330–344.

Fischhoff, B., Svenson, O., & Slovic, P. (1987). Active responses to environmental hazards. In D. Stokols & I. Altman (Eds.), *Handbook of environmental psychology.* (pp. 1089–1133) New York: Wiley.

Fletcher, B. H., & Wooddell, G. (1981). Education for a changing world. *Journal of Thought, 16*(3), 21–32.

Gelatt, H. B. (1962). Decision making: A conceptual frame of reference for counseling. *Journal of Counseling Psychology, 9*(6), 240–242.

Gettys, C. F., Mehle, T., & Fisher, S. (1986). Plausibility assessment in hypothesis generation. *Organizational Behavior and Human Decision Process, 37,* 14–33.

Gick, M. L., & Holyoak, K. J. (1983). Schema induction and analogical transfer. *Cognitive Psychology, 15,* 1–38.

Gick, M. L., & Holyoak, K. J. (1987). The cognitive basis of knowledge transfer. In S. M. Cormier & J. D. Hagman (Eds.), *Transfer of learning: Contemporary research and application.* New York: Academic Press.

Glaser, R. (1982). Instructional psychology: Past, present and future. *American Psychologist, 37,* 292–305.

Glaser, R. (1984). Education and thinking: The role of knowledge. *American Psychologist, 39,* 93–104.

Glaser, R., & Bassok, M. (1989). Learning theory and the study of instruction. *Annual Review of Psychology, 40,* 631–666.

Glasgow, R. E., & McCaul, K. D. (1985). Social and personal skills training programs for smoking prevention: Critiques and directions for future research. In C. S. Bell & R. Battjes (Eds.), *Prevention research: Deterring drug abuses among children and adolescents* (pp. 50–66). (NIDA Research Monograph 63. Department of Health and Human Services Publication No. ADM87-1334.) Washington, DC: U.S. Government Printing Office.

Gray, R. L. (1979). Toward observing that which is not directly observable. In J. Lochhead & J. Clement (Eds.), *Cognitive process instruction.* (pp. 217–228) Philadelphia: Franklin Institute Press.

Guilford, J. P. (1959). *Personality.* New York: McGraw-Hill.

Harmoni, R., Mann, L., & Power, C. (1987). *Adolescent decision making: The development of competence.* Unpublished manuscript. Woden, ACT: Flinders University of South Australia.

Hartup, W. (1970). Peer interaction and social organization. In P. Mussen (Ed.), *Carmichael's Manual of Child Psychology* (3rd ed.). (Vol. 2; pp. 361–456). New York: Wiley.

Harvard University. (1983). *Project Intelligence: The development of procedures to enhance thinking skills.* Final Report, submitted to the Minister for the Development of Human Intelligence, Republic of Venezuela.

Hayes, J. R. (1981). *The complete problem solver.* Philadelphia: Franklin Institute Press.

Herrnstein, R. J., Nickerson, R. S., Sanchez, M., & Swets, J. A. (1986). Teaching thinking skills. *American Psychologist, 41,* 1279–1289.

Jahoda, M. (1958). *Current concepts of positive mental health.* New York: Basic Books.

Janis, I. L., & Mann, L. (1977). *Decision making: A psychological analysis of conflict, choice and commitment.* New York: Free Press.

Jessor, R., & Jessor, S. L. (1977). *Problem behavior and psychosocial development. A longitudinal study of youth.* New York: Academy Press.

Kagan, J. (1965). Individual differences in the resolution of response uncertainty. *Journal of Personality and Social Psychology, 2,* 154–160.

Kagan, J. (1967). Developmental studies in reflection and analysis. In A. H. Kidd & J. L. Riviore (Eds.), *Perceptual and conceptual development in the child.* New York: International University Press. 487–522.

Kahneman, D., Slovic, P., & Tversky, A. (Eds.). (1982). *Judgment under uncertainty: Heuristics and biases.* New York: Cambridge University Press.

Kahneman, D., & Tversky, A. (1973). On the psychology of prediction. *Psychological Review, 80,* 237–251.

Keating, D. P. (1980). Thinking processes in adolescence. In J. Adelson (Eds.), *Handbook of adolescent psychology* (pp. 211–246). New York: Wiley.

Keating, D. P. (1988). *Cognitive processes in adolescent.* Toronto: Ontario Institute for Studies in Education.

Keinan, G. (1987). Decision making under stress: Scanning of alternatives under controllable and uncontrollable threats. *Journal of Personality and Social Psychology, 52,* 639–644.

Keinan, G., Friedland, N., & Ben-Porat, Y. (1987). Decision making under stress: Scanning of alternatives under physical threat. *Acta Psychologica, 64,* 219–228.

Kennedy, R. E. (1984). Cognitive behavioral interventions with delinquents. In A. W. Meyers & W. E. Craighead (Eds.), *Cognitive behavior therapy with children.* (pp. 351–376) New York: Plenum Press.

Kuhn, D., Amsel, E., & O'Loughlin, M. (1988). *The development of scientific thinking skills*. San Diego, CA: Academic Press.

Larkin, J. H. (1983). The role of problem representation in physics. In D. Gentner & A. S. Stevens (Eds.), *Mental models*. Hillsdale, NJ: Lawrence Erlbaum Associates.

Lehman, D. R., Lempert, R. O., & Nisbett, R. E. (1988). The effects of graduate training on reasoning: Formal discipline and thinking about everyday life events. *American Psychologist, 43,* 431–442.

Levine, I. (1983). The nature and development of time concepts in children: The effects of interfering cues. In W. J. Friedman (Ed.), *The developmental psychology of time*. New York: Academic Press.

Lewis, A. J. (1983). Education for the 21st Century. *Educational Leadership, 41,* 9–10.

Lewis, C. C. (1981). How adolescents approach decisions: Changes over grades seven to twelve and policy implications. *Child Development, 52,* 538–544.

Lichtenstein, S., & Fischhoff, B. (1977). Do those who know more also know more about how much they know? The calibration of probability judgments. *Organizational Behavior and Human Performance, 20,* 159–183.

Lichtenstein, S., Fischhoff, B., & Phillips, L. D. (1982). Calibration of probabilities: State of the art to 1980. In D. Kahneman, P. Slovic, & A. Tversky (Eds.), *Judgment under uncertainty: Heuristics and biases* (pp. 306–344). New York: Cambridge University Press.

Lipman, M., Sharp, A. M., & Oscanyon, F. S. (1980). Philosophy in the classroom (2nd ed.). Philadelphia: Temple University Press.

Little, V. L., & Kendall, P. C. (1979). Cognitive behavioral interventions with delinquents: Problem solving, role taking, and self control. In P. C. Kendall & S. D. Hollon, (Eds.), *Cognitive behavioral interventions: Theory, research and procedures.* (pp. 81–115) New York: Academic Press.

Lochhead, J., & Clement, J. (Eds.). (1979). *Cognitive process instruction*. Philadelphia: Franklin Institute Press.

Mahoney, M. J., & Thoreson, C. E. (1972). Behavioral self control: Power to the person. *Educational Researcher, 1,* 5–8.

Mann, L. (1973). Differences between reflective and impulsive children in tempo and quality of decision making. *Child Development, 44,* 272–279.

Mann, L., Harmoni, R., & Power, C. N. (1988a). *GOFER: Basic principles of decision making*. Woden, ACT: Curriculum Development Centre.

Mann, L., Harmoni, R., & Power, C. N. (1988b). *GOFER: Decision making in practice*. Woden, ACT: Curriculum Development Centre.

Mann, L., Harmoni, R., Power, C., Geswick, G., & Ormond, C. (1988). Effectiveness of the GOFER course in decision making for high school students. *Journal of Behavioral Decision Making, 1,* 159–168.

McCloskey, M., Caramazza, A., & Green, B. (1980). Curvilinear motion in the absence of external forces: Naive beliefs about the motion of objects. *Science, 210,* 1139–1141.

Mehle, T., Gettys, C. F., Manning, C., Baca, S., & Fisher, S. (1981). The availability explanation of excessive plausibility assessments. *Acta Psychologica, 49,* 127–140.

Messer, S. (1970). The effect of anxiety over intellectual performance on reflection impulsivity in children. *Child Development, 41,* 723–735.

National Assessment of Educational Progress. (1983). *The Third National Mathematics Assessment: Results, trends and issues* (13-MA-01). Denver, CO: Educational Commission of the States.

Newell, A., & Simon, H. A. (1972). *Human problem solving*. Englewood Cliffs, NJ: Prentice-Hall.

Nickerson, R. S. (1975). *Decision making and training: A review of theoretical and empirical studies of decision making and their implications for the training of decision makers*. Cambridge, MA: Bolt, Beranek & Newman, Inc.

Nickerson, P. S., Perkins, D. N., & Smith, E. E. (1985). *The teaching of thinking.* Hillsdale, NJ: Lawrence Erlbaum Associates.

Nisbett, R. E., Krantz, D. H., Jepsen, C., & Kunda, Z. (1983). The use of statistical heuristics in everyday inductive reasoning. *Psychological Review, 90,* 339–363.

Oskamp, S. (1962). The relationship of clinical experience and training methods to several criteria of clinical prediction. *Psychological Monographs, 76* (Whole No. 547).

Pellegrini, D. S., & Urbain, E. S. (1985). An evaluation of interpersonal cognitive problem solving training with children. *Journal of Child Psychology and Psychiatry, 26*(1), 17–41.

Raiffa, H. (1968). *Decision analysis. Introductory lectures on choices under uncertainty.* Reading, MA: Addison Wesley.

Renner, J. W., & Stafford, D. G. (1972). *Teaching science in the secondary school.* New York: Harper & Row.

Resnick, L. (1987). *Education & learning to think.* Washington, DC: National Research Council.

Ross, J. A. (1981a). Improving adolescent decision-making skills. *Curriculum Inquiry, 11*(3) 279–295.

Ross, J. A. (1981b). The measurement of student progress in a decision-making approach to values education. *Alberta Journal of Educational Research, 27,* 1–15.

Ross, J. A. (1988). *Improving social environmental studies problem solving through cooperative learning.* Unpublished manuscript. OISE Trent Valley Centre, Peterborough, Ontario.

Ross, J. A., Boutilier, D., Gutteridge, S., & North, (n.d. -a). *Personal decision-making. Condensed version, Grade 7 Guidance Unit.* Unpublished manuscript. OISE Trent Valley Centre, Peterborough, Ontario.

Ross, J. A., Boutilier, D., Gutteridge, S., & North (n.d. -b). *Personal decision-making. Advanced version, Grade 8 Guidance Unit.* Unpublished manuscript. OISE Trent Valley Centre, Peterborough, Ontario.

Rowe, K. L. (1984, August). *Adolescent contraceptive use: The role of cognitive factors.* Paper presented at the meeting of the American Psychological Association, Toronto, Canada.

Schermerhorn, L. L., Williams, L. D., & Dickison, A. K. (1982). *Project COMPAS. A design for change.* Stanford, FL: Seminole Community College.

Schinke, S. P. (1982). School-based model for preventing teenage pregnancy. *Social Work in Education, 5,* 34–42.

Schinke, S. P., & Blythe, B. J. (1981). Cognitive behavioral prevention of children's smoking. *Child Behavior Therapy, 3,* 25–42.

Schinke, S. P., & Gilchrist, L. D. (1983). Primary prevention of tobacco smoking. *Journal of School Health, 53,* 416–419.

Schinke, S. P., & Gilchrist, L. D. (1984). *Life skills counseling with adolescents.* Austin, TX: Pro-ed Publishers.

Schinke, S. P., & Gilchrist, L. S. (1985). Preventing substance abuse with children and adolescents. *Journal of Consulting and Clinical Psychology, 53,* 596–602.

Schinke, S. P., & Gilchrist, L. D. (1986). Preventing tobacco use among young people. *Health and Social Work, 11,* 59–65.

Schinke, S. P., Gilchrist, L. E., Snow, W. H., & Schilling, R. J. (1985). Skills building methods to prevent smoking by adolescents. *Journal of Adolescent Health Care, 6,* 439–444.

Schinke, S. P., & Rose, S. D. (1976). Interpersonal skill training in groups. *Journal of Counseling Psychology, 23,* 442–448.

Schinke, S. P., Schilling, R. F., & Snow, W. H. (1987). Stress management with adolescents at the junior high transition: An outcome evaluation of coping skills intervention. *Journal of Human Stress, 31,* 16–22.

Shiffman, S., & Wills, T. (1985). *Coping and substance use.* New York: Academic Press.

Shure, M. B., & Spivack, G. (1971). *Solving interpersonal problems: A program for 4-year-old nursery school children: Training script.* Philadelphia: Department of Mental Health Science, Hahnemann Medical College.

Sieber, J. E., Clark, R. E., Smith, H. H., & Sanders, N. (1978). Warranted uncertainty and students' knowledge and use of drugs. *Contemporary Educational Psychology, 3,* 246–264.

Simon, H. A. (1980). Problem solving and education. In D. T. Tuma & R. Reif (Eds.), *Problem solving and education: Issues in teaching and research.* Hillsdale, NJ: Lawrence Erlbaum Associates.

Simon, H. A., & Chase, W. (1973). Skill in chess. *American Scientist, 61,* 394–403.

Slovic, P., Lichtenstein, S., & Fischhoff, B. (1988). Decision making. In R. C. Atkinson, R. J. Herrnstein, G. Lindzey, & R. D. Luce (Eds.), *Stevens' Handbook of Experimental Psychology* (2nd ed.; pp. 673–738). New York: Wiley.

Snow, W. H., Gilchrist, L., Schilling, R. J., Schinke, S. P., & Kelso, C. (1986). Preparing students for junior high school. *Journal of Early Adolescence, 6,* 127–137.

Snow, W. H., Gilchrist, L. D., & Schinke, S. P. (1985). A critique of progress in adolescent smoking prevention. *Children and Youth Services Review, 7,* 1–19.

Solomon, R. L. (1949). An extension of control group design. *Psychological Bulletin, 46,* 137–150.

Solomone, J. (1983). Learning about energy: How pupils think in two dimensions. *European Journal of Science Education, 5,* 49–59.

Spitzhoff, D., Ramirez, S., & Wills, T. A. (1982). *The Decision Skills Curriculum: A program for primary prevention of substance abuse.* Unpublished manuscript. New York: American Health Foundation.

Spivack, G., & Shure, M. B. (1974). *Social adjustment of young children: A cognitive approach to solving real-life problems.* San Francisco: Jossey-Bass.

Sternberg, R. J. (1983). Criteria for intellectual skills training. *Educational Researcher, 12,* 6–13.

Sternberg, R. J. (1985). All's well that ends well, but it's a sad tale that begins at the end: A reply to Glaser. *American Psychologist, 40,* 571–573.

Sternberg, R. J. (1986). Inside intelligence. *American Scientist, 74,* 137–144.

Strauss, S., & Bichler, E. (1988). The development of children's concepts of the arithmetic average. *Journal of Research in Mathematics Education, 19,* 64–80.

Strauss, S., Globerson, T., & Minz, R. (1983). The influence of training for the atomistic schema of the development of the density concept among gifted and ungifted children. *Journal of Applied Developmental Psychology, 4,* 125–147.

Thelen, J. J. (1983). Values and valuing in science. *Science Education, 67,* 185–192.

Utech, D., & Hoving, K. L. (1969). Parents and peers as competing influences in the decisions of children of differing ages. *Journal of Social Psychology, 78,* 267–274.

von Winterfeldt, D,. & Edwards, W. (1986). *Decision analysis and behavioral research.* New York: Cambridge University Press.

Vye, N. J., Delclos, V. R., Burns, M. S., & Bransford, J. D. (1988). Teaching thinking and problem solving: Illustrations and issues. In R. J. Sternberg & E. E. Smith (Eds.), *The psychology of human thought* (pp. 337–362). New York: Cambridge University Press.

Wheeler, D. D., & Dember, W. N. (Eds.). (1979). *A practicum in thinking.* Cincinnati: University of Cincinnati, Department of Psychology.

Whimbey, A., & Lochhead, J. (1979). *Problem solving and comprehension: A short course in analytic reasoning.* Philadelphia: Franklin Institute Press.

White, R. W. (1959). Motivation reconsidered: The concept of competence. *Psychological Review, 66,* 297–333.

Wills, T. A. (1985). Stress and coping related to smoking and alcohol use in early adolescence. In S. Shiffman & T. A. Wills (Eds.), *Coping and substance use.* New York: Academic Press.

Wrenn, C. G. (1962). *The counselor in a changing world.* Washington, DC: American Personnel & Guidance Association.

Yando, R., & Kagan, J. (1970). The effect of task complexity on reflection–impulsivity. *Cognitive Psychology, 1,* 192–200.

Zahavi, S., & Asher, S. R. (1978). The effect of verbal instructions on preschool children's aggressive behavior. *Journal of School Psychology, 16,* 146–153.

Zakay, D., & Wooler, S. (1984). Time pressure, training and decision effectiveness. *Ergonomics, 27,* 273–284.

Zamansky-Shorin, M., Selman, R. L., & Richmond, J. B. (1988). *A developmental approach to the investigation of links between knowledge and action in the domain of children's healthful behavior.* A position paper prepared for the Carnegie Council in Adolescent Development Workshop. Washington, DC: Carnegie Council on Adolescent Development, Carnegie Corporation of New York.

Chapter **3**

The GOFER Course
in Decision Making

Leon Mann
Ros Harmoni
Colin Power
The Flinders University of South Australia

The activity of decision making involves cognitive processes, such as information search and evaluation, judgment, and problem solving, as well as
responses to a set of motivational forces that determine the manner in
which decisions are made. Motivational forces that shape decision making
activity include such elements as reluctance to recognize that there is an opportunity or threat (and that it is therefore imperative to make a decision);
tendencies to show resistance and reactance in the face of unwarranted social pressure to choose a particular alternative (Brehm & Brehm, 1981); the
disruptive and sometimes energizing effects of psychological stress on processing of information relating to choice alternatives (cf. Janis & Mann,
1977); tendencies to use the no-choice or procrastination option (Corbin,
1980); tendencies to become trapped in commitment to an outworn decision (cf. Kiesler, 1971) and post-decisional tendencies to resolve cognitive
dissonance by idealizing chosen alternatives and derogating unchosen ones
(Festinger, 1957). The study of decision making would be incomplete without recognition that these motivational elements form an integral part of
decision-making activity.

The approach we take in the GOFER course is founded upon an analysis
of cognitive and motivational factors involved in decision making. Thus,
the course instructs students in the steps of high quality information processing in decision making—how to clarify goals, how to compare options

with the aid of a decisional balance sheet[1], how to check the reliability of so-called facts, how to take account of the riskiness of options. The course also instructs students in how to take control over and responsibility for their choices, how to recognize the effects of their self-esteem and confidence in decision making, how to deal with unwarranted social pressures to choose a less preferred option, and how to reinforce decision commitment by such devices as decision contracts.

We are fond of saying that during adolescence, promoting the youngster's confidence in making decisions is nearly as important as teaching competence in making decisions, on the assumption that if the adolescent is unwilling to even attempt a choice, he or she is also unlikely to learn how to make decisions and cope when something turns out wrong. In sum, GOFER builds upon cognitive and motivational factors, and both are given their due in the course.

THE ORIGIN OF GOFER

It is pertinent to say something about the origins of GOFER. The materials of the GOFER course (Mann, Harmoni, & Power, 1988) consist of two books: *Basic principles of decision making* and *Decision making in practice*. The cover of the first book depicts a cartoon dog holding a stack of books in the manner of a studious high school sophomore. The cover of the second features the same dog, this time wearing a hard hat, sleeves rolled up and ready for work. The cartoon character, Gofer, grows during the course of these two books from a rather error-prone pooch into a competent canine with increasingly human qualities and features. We chose to

---

[1]The decisional balance sheet dates back at least two centuries (Benjamin Franklin advocated their use back in 1772). In its modern incarnation (Janis & Mann, 1977), the balance sheet is intended to provide a record of the pros and cons of each option (to assist in making comparisons) and to identify gaps in thinking. For example, when considering options, people often tend to concentrate on material gains and approval from others at the expense of losses in self-esteem. Accordingly, to ensure that a wider set of considerations is considered, the decisional balance sheet is set out as an 8-cell grid for listing the effects (gains and losses) relating to each option: things I will gain; things I will lose; things others will gain; things others will lose; gains in approval of myself; losses in approval of myself; approval by others; disapproval by others (see Fig. 3.1). The balance sheet procedure has been found to be an effective technique for promoting adherence to decisions and preventing post-decisional regret. For example, Mann (1972) conducted a field experiment in which 30 seniors at Medford High, Massachusetts, filled in decision balance sheets relating to their options for college several months prior to making their choice. Students who were given the balance sheets were compared with a control group of students. The "balanced-sheet" students tended to consider a wider array of college options, to take into account more self-related considerations and expressed less regret and concern about their choice 6 weeks after notifying the colleges of their decision.

The Gofer course provides students with lots of practice in filling out balance sheets.

GOFER

Option 1 *stay at school*

	Gains	Losses
	THINGS I WILL GAIN	THINGS I WILL LOSE
	– More education.	– I will not earn money.
	– Be with best friends.	– I will have to do lots
	– Play volleyball every	of homework.
	Wednesday.	
	THINGS OTHERS WILL GAIN	THINGS OTHERS WILL LOSE
	– The family will do	– Parents will have to
	better in making decisions	support me for another
	(I'll be studying GOFER)	year.
	GAINS IN APPROVAL OF MYSELF	LOSSES IN APPROVAL OF MYSELF
	– I will feel more	– None.
	confident.	
	APPROVAL BY OTHERS	DISAPPROVAL BY OTHERS
	– Parents will approve.	– A friend who has
	– Best friends will	started work will
	approve.	think I'm crazy.

FIG. 3.1 GOFER: The balance sheet (an example) (simplified version, based on Janis & Mann, 1977).

make Gofer female, partly in recognition of the invitation extended to us in 1984 by the Curriculum Development Centre of Australia to develop a course in decision making that would assist girls "by developing awareness of their limited role in decision making and increasing their skills and knowledge to become effective decision makers and partly to redress the gender imbalance in cartoon heroes." Australian educational authorities in the mid-1980s were concerned that girls were making poor choices in opting not to finish high school and in opting not to choose science and math subjects, thereby limiting their future career choices. We ended up writing a course suitable for boys and girls, on the principle that decision making is a universal activity, and that adolescent males and females require instruction in the principles of decision making which, in our judgment, apply equally to both sexes.

The starting point in our journey was a theoretical map known as the conflict theory of decision making (Janis & Mann, 1977). Janis and Mann maintain that good decision-makers satisfy seven criteria when making an important choice:

1. Thoroughly canvass a wide range of alternatives.
2. Survey objectives to be fulfilled and values implicated by the choice.
3. Weigh the negative and positive consequences that could flow from each alternative.
4. Search for information relevant to the alternatives.
5. Assimilate new information without bias.
6. Carefully reevaluate consequences prior to choice.
7. Plan for implementation and post decisional contingencies.

Few adolescents, let alone adults, would be interested in memorizing a list of seven abstract terms and concepts. We took on the challenge of simplifying and translating the somewhat difficult language and concepts of conflict theory so that they would be acceptable to high schoolers, without compromising the integrity of the theory.

The word "GOFER" emerged out of our painstaking attempt to translate the seven criteria of vigilant decision making into simple language. Thus, surveying objectives and values became Goals; canvassing a wide range of alternatives became Options; searching for information became Facts; weighing the negative and positive consequences became Effects; and planning for implementation became Review. When put together, goals, options, facts, effects and review become "GOFER" and a simple, but handy, acronym was born. The association between the term GOFER and action (Go for it!) allowed us to add a sixth step of sound decision making—GO-FER IT, or carry out the decision by putting it into action. We soon hit upon the idea of a cartoon character who would eventually learn to accomplish all of these exemplary steps of vigilant decision making. Gofer, the thinking dog's alternative to Snoopy, was created by our illustrator, and appears throughout (and on the covers of) our two books, as a reminder of the acronym and as a somewhat endearing figure with whom all but the most dog-fearing student can identify (see Fig. 3.2).

GOFER AND GOOFER

We also assumed that a comprehensive course in decision making should go beyond a prescriptive analysis of decision making. We believed that it was also important to teach students to recognize and understand faulty decision-making in order to provide a basis for correcting their own decision habits and to respond with some insight into the decision strategies of oth-

FIG. 3.2

ers. Again, Janis and Mann's conflict theory was a highly useful map and guide.

The core of Janis and Mann's conflict theory is a description and analysis of five major patterns for coping with difficult decisions under stress. The "ideal" pattern is vigilance, which is exemplified by the seven criteria of sound decision making identified previously. The other four patterns are regarded as poor ways of dealing with decisional conflict: For example, complacency, in the form of unthinking adherence or change to simple courses of action; defensive avoidance, in the form of procrastination, shifting responsibility onto others, and wishful thinking or rationalization; and hypervigilance, in the form of impulsive or panicky choice. We reasoned that it is important for adolescents to identify both good and poor decision-making patterns and to understand the underlying causes of both if they are to accept the relevance of decision making as a coherent body of knowledge.

Conflict theory specifies the antecedent conditions of each coping pattern in terms of combinations of magnitude of conflict, presence or absence of deadline pressures, and extent of optimism or pessimism about finding a solution to the decision problem. Although the GOFER course does not include an analysis of the antecedent conditions of the five coping patterns, it does contain a detailed description of each pattern, how to identify them, and how to counteract tendencies to rely on any of the four faulty patterns when confronting a difficult decision.

Again, we simplified the terminology of the coping patterns so as to provide a more popular and accessible set of concepts. Vigilance, became, as stated, GOFER. It is hardly surprising that we then called the four faulty coping patterns "Goofers." Translated into adolescents' language, unconflicted (unthinking) adherence to an ongoing course of action became "drift on"; unconflicted (unthinking) change to a new course of action became "follow the leader"; defensive avoidance, the tendency to escape or avoid making choices, became "cop out," and its three manifestations—

procrastination, shifting responsibility, and wishful thinking or rationalization—became "put it off," "pass it on," and "kid yourself," respectively. Finally, hypervigilance became simply "panic." These new terms proved to have considerable appeal, and it is quite common to hear students who have studied GOFER use them freely in their out-of-school interactions and activities.

OVERVIEW OF THE GOFER COURSE

In the first book, *Basic Principles of Decision Making,* students examine the concept of decision making and how decision tasks change according to age. They learn about the GOFER strategy as a sequence of steps to follow for making sound decisions. They discover the consequences of missing a step on the quality of decisions. They then examine the concept of a "batting average" in decision making, poor patterns of decision making ("Goofers") such as "drift on," "follow the leader," "cop-out," and "panic," and what to do about tendencies to use "Goofers." Students also learn how to recognize and define decision problems; how to clarify the goals and values involved in major choices; how to generate options; how to check the reliability of information; how to assess risks; how to compare options; and how to "hatch" decisions, including announcement, selling the decision, implementation, fine tuning, and if necessary, undoing mistakes.

In the second book, *Decision Making in Practice,* decision principles are applied to five problem areas: decision making in groups; friendship decisions; subject choice in school; money decisions; and applications of decision principles in various professions such as medicine, management, life insurance, technology, environmental science, and psychology. Each chapter in Book 2 contains the following six elements which serve to reinforce decision making as an articulate, systematic, and knowledge-based activity.

1. *A statement of some key choices or dilemmas relating to the problem area.* For example, the section on friendships begins with examples of decision problems: to choose someone as a friend, to stop having someone as a friend, to introduce someone to your friend, to tell off a friend, to disappoint a friend or humiliate and upset a friend, to forgive a friend, to tell a friend's secret to someone else.

2. *A statement of basic facts and information to provide a context to the decision problem.* For example, the friendship section contains a brief overview of social psychological principles relating to first impressions, similarity and attraction, social comparison and social reality, stereotypes and ingratiation.

3. *A selection of GOFER steps which are given most attention.* For ex-

ample, in the friendship section, considerable attention is given to work on new options for solving friendship problems and how to terminate as gracefully as possible a friendship that is no longer satisfactory.

4. *A selection of other principles and concepts to be included.* For example, we expect that ending and giving up friendships is often tinged with regret, so we included material on the concept of regret, how to recognize it, and how to cope with it.

5. *Practice in decision aids and tools.* In the friendship section, as in many other parts of the course, students are given practice in filling out decision balance sheets. Students are set the exercise of filling out balance sheets for the options in the following dilemmas: leaving school at age 15 with all their friends or staying on until age 17; traveling home in a car with their friend who has been drinking or insisting on a taxi; selecting school subjects in accord with their friend's expectation or in accord with their own preferences (see footnote 1).

6. *Assessment of learning.* In the friendship section, most of the assessment relates to testing for understanding of goofers in friendship decisions—such as recognition of "follow the leader" ("Sophie wasn't certain if she still wanted to be friends with Fiona, so when the other girls turned their backs on Fiona in the canteen, Sophia did too").

To repeat, we include each of the six elements as a standard format in each of the applied decision chapters. This serves as a model for the preparation of additional materials to cover decision areas not included in the course—such as, for example, health-related decisions, career decisions, decisions about leaving home, and so forth—according to the teacher's interest and student's needs.

The most difficult chapter of the book introduces students to decision analysis and to strategies for choice, such as maximax, minimax, expected value, satisficing and multiple attribute utility.[2] This chapter also teaches students how to "structure" decisions with the aid of decision tables and decision trees. We called this part of the course "Building on GOFER" in recognition of the reality that GOFER "shows you how to be careful and thoughtful in the way you make decisions, but it doesn't tell you which option you should choose."

The Instructor's Manual for the course includes a supplementary sec-

---

[2]In non-technical language, maximax is the optimistic strategy of choosing the option which yields the best possible gain if all goes well. Minimax is the pessimistic strategy of choosing the option which incurs the least possible loss if things don't go well. Expected value is the strategy of considering both the probability and the value of outcomes when choosing between options. Satisficing is the strategy of choosing the first option that meets the minimum requirements, i.e., is "good enough" to choose. Multiple attribute utility is the strategy of considering the importance of attributes or features of options and the utilities or values of each option on those attributes when making a choice.

tion, "Decision making for teachers," which covers three areas of concern to teachers: decisions relating to classroom teaching and management, personal decisions about professional development as a teacher, and policy decisions in the school. We wrote this supplementary section because we wanted instructors to face their own decision problems as teachers and to observe how GOFER can be applied to these problems. We assume that a key to the success of the course is the teacher's own experience in applying the core concepts of GOFER and in recognizing their relevance to everyday problems.

Duration

We suspect that many decision courses produce little benefit because they attempt too much in too little time. It is unrealistic to expect an 8-10 hour program in decision making to have long-lasting effects. Good learning and retention depend upon exposure to information and practice in skills over an extended period of time during which it is likely that the student is making some personal choice about school subjects, friendships, what to do with money, et cetera. Accordingly, the GOFER course comprises a substantial program of readings and exercises taught ideally over 40-50 contact hours spaced over at least 1 year and preferably 2 years. This enables the teacher to consolidate the course materials and apply the course principles to personally relevant decisions as they occur. Ross (1981) noted that programs designed to teach decision skills to high schoolers produce changes only very slowly and a full year may be required for improvements to take place.

WHEN TO TEACH A COURSE IN DECISION MAKING?

A simple, but not trite, answer to the question is, "While the student is still in school and is able to benefit from a course in decision making." In Australia, schooling is compulsory until age 15 years, after which adolescents are free to leave in order to find work or whatever they see fit. Although a growing proportion of young Australians remain in high school through the senior year (year 12), the drop out rate after 15 years is very high. Thus, in 1986, 10% of Australian 15-year-olds, 33% of 16-year-olds and 60% of 17-year-olds did not participate in school. Several factors lead to the importance of teaching decision making before the age of 15, before large numbers of students drop out of school.

1. The decision to drop out of school is, in itself, often ill-informed and shortsighted. It is often made without careful consideration, and its conse-

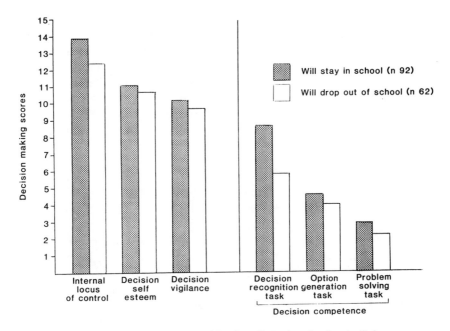

FIG. 3.3 Comparison of 15 year olds who will stay in school and will drop out of school.

quences may be highly negative. It is likely that a course in decision making, in which students learn *inter alia* the costs as well as the "benefits" of leaving school could serve to convince many that the wiser option is to remain in school. We hope, in future evaluation of GOFER, to investigate whether students who study GOFER are more likely to continue high school than other students.

2. It is apparent that students who drop out of school are those most in need of instruction in decision making to remedy deficits in their confidence and competence as decision makers. In 1985 we tested a sample of 154 15-year-old students in a South Australian high school, measuring them on Nowicki and Strickland's (1973) locus of control scale, Mann's (1982) measures of decision self-esteem and decision vigilance, and on three indicators of competent decision making—the ability to recognize in a scenario who has to make decisions and what these decisions are, the ability to generate many options for resolving a dilemma, and the ability to solve problems of a logical nature. We followed up the sample 2 years later to trace those who completed high school and those who dropped out before completion. We found that 92 of 154 (60%) remained in school, and 40% dropped out. As Fig. 3.3 shows, at age 15 the future "drop outs" were less internal, less confident, and less proficient than the future "continuers." The decision to drop out is itself corroborative evidence of a weakness in

decision making. Accordingly, those students most in need of instruction are no longer in school after 15 to receive such instruction. It is sound policy to program the course in decision making during the time of compulsory schooling, so as to (a) provide sufficient knowledge about sound decision making necessary to ensure that major decisions, like dropping out of school, are made carefully, and only after the option of continuing in school is given sufficient attention; and (b) to strengthen the decision-making competence and knowledge of a large group of students who will soon have to face difficult choices outside of school with fewer skills than their counterparts who remain in school.

3. There is substantial evidence that mid-adolescence, in particular the age 14–15 years, marks a period of rapid increase in the cognitive skills and maturity necessary for competent decision making (Mann, Harmoni, & Power, 1989). Mann and colleagues (1989) reviewed the research literature dealing with age-related changes in decision making performance. They identified nine indicators of competence, all of them coincidentally commencing with the letter C: choice, comprehension, creativity, compromise, consequentiality, correctness, credibility, consistency, and commitment. Older adolescents, those age 15 and above, demonstrate a greater knowledge of the steps involved in systematic decision making (e.g. Ormond, Mann, & Luszcz, 1987), and show greater competence in correctness of choices (e.g., Greenberg, 1983; Weithorn & Campbell, 1982) and in commitment to a course of action (e.g., Taylor, Adelman, & Kaser-Boyd, 1983, 1985) than younger adolescents. The evidence also suggested that younger adolescents were weaker in several aspects of decision making—in identifying a range of risks and benefits (Kaser-Boyd, Adelman, & Taylor, 1985), in foreseeing the consequences of novel alternatives (Lewis, 1981) and in gauging the credibility of information provided by so-called "experts" (Lewis, 1981). No research evidence was available to enable a comparison between younger and older adolescents on three components: willingness to make a choice, ability to compromise, and consistency of choice. We predict, however, that 14- and 15-year-olds would show better performance on those components than young adolescents. In sum, we argue that most 14–15-year-olds are prepared cognitively and emotionally to benefit from a comprehensive course in decision making that builds upon skills they have begun to show with some reliability. This leads to the conclusion that the 14th year is the appropriate age for studying decision making. Broadly speaking, this fits in with psychological knowledge about the 14-year-old's interests, abilities, and concern about decision making (cf. Mann, Harmoni, & Power, 1989). This is not to say that a course in decision making is of little use to 16- and 17-year-olds (although we suspect that by then the horse has bolted) or that an 11-year-old would not benefit from such a course. However, we have tailored our decision making course, concepts, and exercises to the period of mid-adolescence and we would expect that

many 16–17-year-olds would regard Gofer as rather juvenile and most 11-year-olds would find it too difficult.

The GOFER materials themselves are graded in level of difficulty so that, for example, the first chapters introduce simple concepts gradually, whereas the applied chapters, especially "Building on GOFER," contain quite difficult abstract concepts relating to decision analysis.

EVALUATION

It is important that decision courses are evaluated properly so as to provide educationists and teachers with a basis for determining whether or not to use the program. Many authors of decision courses fail to provide an adequate evaluation of the effectiveness of their programs. The degree of student acceptability of the course and the amount of learning skills taught in the program constitutes a basic form of evaluation. A more rigorous evaluation is the extent to which students subsequently and correctly apply the skills they have learned in their personal decision making.

The GOFER course was evaluated in two studies in which students who were trained in a trial version of the course were compared with control students to measure differences in knowledge of decision making and self-reported decision habits (Mann, Harmoni, Power, Beswick, & Ormond, 1988). After completing the writing of Book 1, the authors looked around for schools at which to conduct a formative evaluation. Teachers at two large metropolitan schools approached to trial the material agreed to cooperate by adhering to the course outline and including even those bits they thought were of low interest. The authors planned an elegant evaluation research design to test the effectiveness of the course materials, which would include a waiting control. Unfortunately, the reality of school administrative and curriculum arrangements took precedence over niceties of evaluation design. We had to settle for a much briefer coverage of GOFER than we wanted and we settled for a design that did not include a waiting control.

The first evaluation study was conducted on a sample of 40 12-year-olds in a State school. The students were taught a trial version of GOFER in a course of 20 class sessions (equal 13 contact hours). The control students were 51 age-peers at another school, matched for ability in Mathematics and English. Three months after completion of the GOFER course the two samples were compared on measures of self-esteem as a decision maker, self-reported decision habits, and knowledge of decision strategy. The treatment group scored significantly higher than the control group on each measure, testifying to the effectiveness of the course materials (see Table 3.1).

The second evaluation study was conducted on a sample of 122 15-year-

TABLE 3.1
Evaluating GOFER

First evaluation study: Decision habits in the treatment and control groups.
Year 8 students

Measure	Treatment group (n = 40) Post-test Mean	Control group (n = 51) Post-test Mean
Decision self-esteem	9.50	7.60
Vigilance	9.97	8.32
Maladaptive	12.78	19.21

Second evaluation study: Decision habits in the treatment and control groups.
Year 10 students

Measure	Treatment group (n = 122) Pre-test Mean	Post-test Mean	Control group (n = 219) Post-test Mean
Decision self-esteem	10.79	12.30	10.76
Vigilance	10.02	11.06	9.80
Maladaptive	15.35	12.69	15.31

olds in a private school. These students received 16 hours of instruction in a trial version of GOFER as part of a year-long course in vocational decision making. They were compared with age peers from three high schools in Adelaide, Australia. The treatment group was pretested on a battery of decision tests 3 months prior to taking the course and post-tested 1 year later, several weeks after completing the course. Once again, a significant difference was found between students who took the course and the control group on measures of self-esteem as a decision maker and self-reported decision habits (Table 3.1).

A comparison across the two evaluation studies is instructive. Mann and colleagues (1988) found that 12-year-olds trained in GOFER (Study 1) reported decision habits equal to, if not superior to, untrained 15-year-old controls (Study 2). This finding indicates that decision training for 12-year-olds is entirely appropriate. It also suggests that the effect of GOFER is to accelerate the 12-year-olds' knowledge and understanding by about 3 years to the level of untrained 15-year-olds.

We measured student's acceptance of the trial version of GOFER in our sample of 15-year-olds. Approximately 45% of students who participated in the trial were administered a post-course questionnaire that measured their opinions on aspects of the course. Twenty per cent found the course interesting (26% found it boring); 31% described the course as useful (6% described it as useless); and 75% reported they learned something (6% dismissed the course as a waste of time). In order to determine whether these responses represent high or low praise for GOFER we should obtain student opinion of their other subjects. Inasmuch as some students reject school and learning, the range of responses is not surprising, but they also show that the course may not be acceptable to all students and this should be recognized by the teacher.

The formative evaluations also enabled us to learn from the teacher's experience in using the trial version of GOFER. Teachers reported that many students had difficulty with the concept of goals clarification, the first step of GOFER. We revised the materials to provide more concrete examples of goals and we recommended that teachers deal with goals and values briefly in the first few lessons, and provide a more extensive coverage in the later applied lessons, dealing with subject choice, money decisions, and friendship.

We also learned that many students found some of the material repetitive, and this led us to identify exercises that could be dropped. We learned that students liked most those parts of the course that tackled real-life problems, so we revised the homework exercises to reinforce the practical aspects of decision making.

We also found a remote country town named Moonta, 200 kilometers from Adelaide, where the school counselor in the Area School undertook to trial GOFER as part of a course on social education for 15-year-olds. Fourteen students took the course. The instructor, a skilled and enthusiastic teacher, achieved considerable success. Paul is an example of a student who benefitted from GOFER. Paul had been "coasting" in the non-academic stream, but decided after completing GOFER to repeat Year 10 and enter the academic stream to prepare for admission to a Teachers' College. Karen is another example of success. Karen was pregnant at the beginning of the school year, but came back to school after the birth of her child to learn something about decision making and career options for young mothers. The Moonta Area School evaluation taught us much about the importance of the teacher for the success of a course in decision making. A key to the success of the GOFER course is the teacher who takes the role of "coach" rather than instructor, is prepared to disclose some of her/his own experiences in decision making, and is willing to accept the greater independence and questioning of authority that invariably accompanies the growth of students' decision-making skills and confidence.

We were also gratified by reports that parents of the Moonta students had noticed positive changes in their youngsters—greater independence, responsibility, and maturity—and had commented on this to the school principal. In the year after the introduction of GOFER at Moonta Area School, the teacher agreed, following repeated requests, to offer a modified version of the course to interested parents in the town.

So far we have evaluated GOFER in terms of a number of self-report measures of decision habits, opinions about the GOFER course, knowledge acquired about decision making, and testimonial evidence about the success of the course in promoting change. Most of these are "soft" indicators of the effectiveness of the course. Ross (1981) pointed out that the critical task of decision-making programs is to transfer skills and confidence learned in the classroom to real life settings. The difficulty of producing and administering a reliable measure of actual decision-making competence in the out-of-school context remains as a barrier to testing the effectiveness of GOFER and other decision courses, in assisting students to deal with personal dilemmas and problems. Examples of such measures include voluntary attendance at information-giving sessions, punctuality in meeting deadlines for decisions, reliability in maintaining commitments, and willingness to plan and execute long-term career and life goals rather than settle for immediate, short-term gratifications.

The decision to stay in school as opposed to dropping out constitutes a "hard" measure of decision making competence. Brennan, Beun, and Anderson (1988) designed course materials based on Janis and Mann's conflict theory of decision making to reduce the drop-out rate among at-risk high school students in Denver, Colorado. We propose to conduct long-term follow-up studies of students who received instruction in GOFER to determine whether they are less likely to drop out from high school than other students. The predicted difference, if found, could be due to direct influence of the course (learning how to choose wisely) or to indirect influences (participation in an interesting, rewarding subject rather than suffering another failure experience). In any case, a prime indicator of the effectiveness of courses in decision making is whether they counteract the tendency of many adolescents to choose the easy option and drop out of school.

ATTITUDES AND VALUES ABOUT DECISION MAKING

A prior condition for learning is the belief that the material to be studied is of some relevance. The teacher faces a more difficult task if the adolescent (and the parent) believes that the domain of decision making is solely the concern of adults, and is of no concern to adolescents. Research by the GOFER team (Mann, Harmoni, Power, & Beswick, 1987) showed that a substantial minority of young Australian adolescents, approximately one in five, hold beliefs and attitudes indicative of negative attitudes and stereotypes about decision making. Some of these attitudes are no doubt based on ignorance, others due to poor experience in the home.

In Book 1 there is an exercise, "Decision Poll", that serves to identify student attitudes, and gives the teacher the opportunity to correct the most glaring ones. The items include: "Young people . . . don't make any important decisions"; "There is little you can do to become a good decision maker"; and "Girls are poor decision makers compared with boys." Table

TABLE 3.2
Decision Making Poll: Percentage of Students Who Agree with the Item

Decision Attitudes	13 year olds		14 year olds		15 year olds	
	m n = 55	f n = 42	m n = 54	f n = 34	m n = 41	f n = 75
1. Decision making does not affect young people because they don't make any important decisions.	29%	2%	9%	15%	7%	3%
2. Bad decisions made by others are those with which you disagree.	42%	52%	47%	34%	25%	20%
3. People are either good decision makers or bad decision makers. There is little you can do to become a good decision maker.	17%	12%	22%	18%	13%	1%
4. People who take a long time when making decisions are not sure of what they want.	46%	50%	56%	44%	22%	37%
5. Girls are poor decision makers compared with boys.	19%	10%	16%	5%	10%	1%
6. Important decisions affecting young people should be made by adults.	26%	12%	10%	18%	13%	7%
7. Important decisions affecting young people should be made by the young person.	63%	76%	64%	54%	55%	61%

Source: Mann, Harmoni, Power, & Beswick (1987)

3.2 presents the percentage of students in agreement with these items and shows that some adolescents (and no doubt many adults) hold these attitudes. It also shows that fewer 15-year-olds than 14-year-olds and fewer 14-year-olds than 13-year-olds hold these attitudes. The age change reflects the adolescents' increased awareness of the importance of decision making. The implication for teaching a course in decision making is that prior attention must be given to dealing with and correcting these attitudes, and more time should be given to addressing these attitudes among younger students.

The teacher must also deal with another, more difficult attitudinal problem, namely parents' perception that the GOFER course, which seeks to develop greater independence, autonomy, and responsibility among adolescents, may constitute a potential challenge to their authority. This problem is much sharper in multicultural schools attended by students from traditional cultures in which family values of deference, respect, and loyalty to the kin group dominate over such western values as individualism, independence, autonomy, self-assertiveness. The values GOFER represents are unabashed individualism, even though the student is instructed to be responsible and consider the effects of her/his choices on others.

We have no brilliant advice to offer on this matter. In our teacher trainer workshops we suggest that teachers in multicultural schools discuss the issue with parents, and introduce additional materials, especially in regard to valid and acceptable cross-cultural differences in goals and values underlying personal and group decisions. We are in no doubt, however, that GOFER would be considered a rather exotic specimen in Japanese schools. Although Gofer is a mixed creation born out of a theory conceived by a North American (Irving Janis) and an Australian (Leon Mann), the values espoused by the course appear to have broad appeal in western countries. The course is under active consideration for adoption in Israel and Sweden, although the Israelis are appalled by the idea that such a nonserious creature as a dog should embody the principles of sound decision making. They have insisted that GOFER is transmuted into a Kibbutz type who wears shorts, sandals, and a bell shaped hat.

Gofer's persona is not really an important factor in determining the course's international prospects. More pertinent is the local relevance of figures, statistics and other information provided in each chapter as a context to such decision problems as subject choice, money matters, legal rights, and responsibilities. For example, information contained in GOFER about different ages pertaining to legal rights and responsibilities in Australia would have to be revised in accord with the facts for each country.

IMPLEMENTATION OF THE COURSE

It would be so much easier if the author's task ended at the point of publication of the course materials. We recognized even before publication day that the course materials would be destined to gather dust on library shelves unless we offered assistance to curriculum managers, educationists, counselors, and senior teachers in how to introduce and support the course. After all, responsibility for a 50-hour course in decision making is a formidable challenge to even the most committed teacher and very few teachers have studied decision-making theory and practice during their professional training.

The GOFER kit was published as a set of course materials supplemented by a comprehensive Instructor's Manual. But the Instructor's Manual does not ensure that the course will be taught effectively. We have now devised a program of in-service workshops designed to introduce the course to senior educationists and teacher trainers. Our intention is that the graduates of these workshops will become the first generation of "accredited" GOFER resource personnel. We have conducted a series of GOFER workshops on the invitation of State Education Departments in Australia. These workshops, typically 2 to 4 days in length, cover the theory and practice of decision making, the adolescent as a decision maker—his or her abilities, motives, confidence, willingness to learn, attitudes toward decision making, the development of competence in decision making during adolescence, and an examination of approaches to assist adolescents to become better decision makers, focusing on the GOFER program. The workshops are limited to about 25 participants as emphasis is placed upon syndicate work, encouraging participants to design additional materials and exercises based upon GOFER principles, and attending to the question of how to establish a close resource and support network among teachers offering the course. By the end of the workshop, participants have the knowledge to lead their own teacher-training workshop, to assist in dealing with problems teachers may have in interpreting and working with the course, to act as a resource person for ideas in teaching the course, especially in regard to the creative integration of GOFER into the wider curriculum, for example, in health education, vocational training, literature, and environmental studies.

It should be noted that the workshops have proven to be beneficial to the authors and (we hope) to the participants. Many creative ideas for introducing, teaching, and supporting the course emerge in the workshop discussions, as well as suggestions about case materials and examples of student problems with decision making in the school, home, and street. In sum, our own knowledge and understanding of adolescent decision making has been expanded by the experience of leading workshops for teacher–trainers. What we initially took on as a chore has turned out to be a source of interesting ideas and stimulation.

REFERENCES

Brehm, S. S., & Brehm, J. W. (1981). *Psychological reactance: A theory of freedom and control*. New York: Academic Press.

Brennan, T., Beun, B., & Anderson, F. (1988). *At-risk student decision making and dropping out: Utilizing Janis and Mann's Conflict theory to design interventions*. Unpublished manuscript. University of Colorado at Denver.

Corbin, R. M. (1980). Decisions that might not get made. In T. S. Wallsten (Ed.), *Cognitive processes in choice and decision behavior* (pp. 47–67). Hillsdale, NJ: Lawrence Erlbaum Associates.

Festinger, L. (1957). *A theory of cognitive dissonance*. Evanston, IL: Row, Peterson.

Greenberg, E. F. (1983). An empirical determination of the competence of children to participate in child custody decision-making (Doctoral dissertation, University of Illinois). *Dissertation Abstracts International, 45,* (0-1) 350-B.

Janis, I. L., & Mann, L. (1977). *Decision making: A psychological analysis of conflict, choice and commitment.* New York: Free Press.

Kaser-Boyd, N., Adelman, H., & Taylor, L. (1985). Minor's ability to identify risks and benefits of therapy. *Professional Psychology, 16,* 411-417.

Kiesler, C. A. (1971). *The psychology of commitment.* New York: Academic Press.

Lewis, C. C. (1981). How adolescents approach decisions: Changes over grades seven to twelve and policy implications. *Child Development, 52,* 538-544.

Mann, L. (1972). Use of a "balance-sheet" procedure to improve the quality of personal decision making: A field experiment with college applications. *Journal of Vocational Behaviour, 2,* 291-300.

Mann, L. (1982). *Decision Making Questionnaires I and II.* Unpublished scales. Flinders Decision Workshops, The Flinders University of South Australia.

Mann, L., Harmoni, R. V., & Power, C. N. (1988). *Gofer: Basic principles of decision making* and *Gofer: Decision making in practice.* Woden, ACT: Curriculum Development Centre.

Mann, L., Harmoni, R. V., & Power, C. N. (1989). Adolescent decision making: The development of competence. *Journal of Adolescence, 12,* 265-278.

Mann, L., Harmoni, R. V., Power, C. N., & Beswick, G. (1987). *Understanding and improving decision making in adolescents.* Unpublished manuscript, The Flinders University of South Australia.

Mann, L., Harmoni, R., Power, C., Beswick, G., & Ormond, C. (1988). Effectiveness of the Gofer course in decision making for high school students. *Journal of Behavioural Decision Making, 1,* 159-168.

Nowicki, S. V., & Strickland, B. R. (1973). A locus of control scale for children. *Journal of Consulting & Clinical Psychology, 40,* 148-154.

Ormond, C. L., Mann, L., & Luszcz, M. (1987). *A metacognitive analysis of decision making in adolescence.* Unpublished manuscript, The Flinders University of South Australia.

Ross, J. A. (1981). Improving adolescent decision-making skills. *Curriculum Inquiry, 11,* 279-295.

Taylor, L., Adelman, H. S., & Kaser-Boyd, N. (1983). Perspectives of children regarding their participation in psychoeducational decisions. *Professional Psychology: Research and Practice, 14,* 882-894.

Taylor, L., Adelman, H. S., & Kaser-Boyd, N. (1985). Minors' attitudes and competence toward participation in psychoeducational decisions. *Professional Psychology: Research and Practice, 16,* 226-235.

Weithorn, L. A., & Campbell, S. B. (1982). The competency of children and adolescents to make informed treatment decisions. *Child Development, 53,* 1589-1598.

Chapter 4

Thinking and Decision Making

Marilyn Jager Adams
Carl E. Feehrer
Bolt Beranek and Newman Inc.
Cambridge, Massachusetts

Making decisions. There is probably no mental activity on which we spend more time and energy. Indeed, there is probably no conscious activity on which we should spend more time and energy. Except as we actively make decisions, life just happens to us.

Clearly, everything we do influences life's course, but it is through the process of making decisions that we influence it willfully. Ideally, decision making is the process by which we influence life purposefully and with due consideration of what we need and what we don't need, what we want and what we don't want, what we know and what we don't know, what we can do and what we can't do, and how much it's worth to us. Yet, that's a lot of considerations. And so, we find that among mortals, the ideal and the actual do not often coincide.

In developing curricular materials on decision making, our goal was not to teach the students to behave like ideal decision makers. It was, instead, to develop in them a sense of the multilayered and multidimensional nature of the decision space. It was to allow exploration of the importance of the various dimensions of the space and discovery of the connections between them. And, it was to develop appreciation of the many and often-overlooked ways in which decision making is relevant.

Our materials on decision making were, moreover, developed as just one series of lessons within a larger curriculum package entitled *Odyssey: A Curriculum for Thinking* (Adams, 1986). As such, their more general purpose was to convey to students, in just one more way, that all manner of problems, even seemingly impenetrable problems, can be productively thought about.

THE *ODYSSEY* FRAMEWORK

The *Odyssey* curriculum is built on the premise that there are two keys to productive understanding: information and interpretation. If you already have all the information you need and you still can't understand, then what you need is more careful interpretation. If you have thoroughly interpreted everything you know already and you still can't understand, then what you need is more information.

As an instruction, this may sound uselessly simplistic. As a conviction, however, it is enormously powerful. In essence, the message is "Whatever it is, it can be understood." The overall goal of the *Odyssey* curriculum is to develop this conviction in its students.

The way that *Odyssey* pursues this goal is by teaching students that the way to interpret a complex problem productively is to make it simpler. To this end, the students are given a single, simple analytic framework and lead to apply it—to investigate its use and utility—over and over, across a diversity of problem types and "cover stories." As examples, the activities include solving logical and algebraic word problems; interpreting and composing texts of a variety of genre, including instructions, advertisements, allegories, jokes, mystery stories, business letters, and expository passages; working with graphs and tables; solving constrained resource allocation problems; generating and testing hypotheses; identifying fallacies of reason; understanding social conflicts and alternate points of view; playing with word meanings and aspects of formal grammatical and rhetorical structure; investigating the designs of objects and procedures, and inventing or "speccing out" new ones; constructing and interpreting factorial designs; and, of course, analytically working through decisions.

The *Odyssey* curriculum was thus designed upon a reciprocal goal structure. On one hand, we sought to show the students how, by applying the basic *Odyssey* framework, each such complicated challenge could be reduced to a manageable and understandable problem space. On the other, by exercising the *Odyssey* framework again and again across so varied a range of problem types and cover stories, we sought to develop the strength and flexibility of the *Odyssey* framework itself such that the students might readily recall and apply it in whatever challenges they might face beyond the confines of our course. (For a more detailed discussion of the theoretical rationale of the curriculum, see Adams, 1989.)

The *Odyssey* curriculum, in short, provided both the conceptual framework that was to support the decision-making lessons and that which the

TABLE 4.1
Which Radio is the Best Choice?

Radio A

Reception: 12 stations
Tape Capabilities: Plays cassettes. Does not record.
Power Requirements: Standard 110 outlet or 5 "D" Cell batteries
Price: $25

Radio B

Reception: 20 Stations
Tape Capabilities: Plays cassettes. Records on cassettes.
Power Requirements: Standard 110 outlet only
Price: $75

Radio C

Reception: 40 stations and shortwave reception
Tape Capabilities: None, but can be added at cost of $20
Power Requirements: Standard 110 outlet only
Price: $125

Note. From *Odyssey: A curriculum for thinking. Volume 5: Decision Making* (p. 142) by C. E. Feehrer and M. J. Adams, 1986, Watertown, MA: Charlesbridge Publishing. © BBN Laboratories Incorporated and The Republic of Venezuela.

decision-making lessons were to support. As this reciprocal structure may be best understood through illustration, let us examine some of the decision-making materials (see Feehrer & Adams, 1986).

Interpreting the Decision Space

The setting is a seventh-grade classroom in a barrio of Barquisimeto, Venezuela. The students range from 10 to 17 years of age. They come from the neighborhoods of poor and poorly educated people known as "marginales." Their school skills and book knowledge are disorientingly weak, but their countenances are inspiringly familiar: They are the faces of bright-eyed, busy adolescents.

The teacher has asked them to examine a list describing three radios and to decide which they would most like to buy (see Table 4.1). The discussion is lively. One student makes a firm pitch for Radio C. It's the best. Yes, offers another: It has shortwave reception; you could listen to radio programs from all over the world. But it costs too much, protests somebody else. You could save the money, suggest another. And just as a subconversation breaks out on earning money, the point is raised that Radio C won't run on batteries—it must be plugged in to be used. As the discussion turns to the many situations in which portability is important, the class begins to settle on Radio A. Then someone points out that Radio A is incapable of recording. The suggestions pour forth. You could make cassette recordings on

TABLE 4.2
Comparing the Radios Dimension by Dimension

Dimensions	Radio A	Radio B	Radio C
Reception	1	2	3
Tape Capabilities	1	3	2
Power Requirements	3	2	1
Price	3	2	1
Total Preference	8	9	7

Note. From *Odyssey: A curriculum for thinking. Volume 5: Decision Making* (p. 148) by C. E. Feehrer and M. J. Adams, 1986, Watertown, MA: Charlesbridge Publishing. © BBN Laboratories Incorporated and The Republic of Venezuela.

someone else's radio, suggests one student; but you could really make great cassettes if you had shortwave reception, comes another; you could get someone else to bring their portable radio and keep yours at home, offers a third; . . . .

So far, the role of the teacher has been one of observing the repartee or, if necessary, of fomenting it by pointing out divisive differences between the radios whenever convergence seems close. Now, however, she or he interrupts with the observation that the students favor certain aspects of each of the radios. The radios differ from each other in so many different ways. Isn't there some way that they could be compared more productively? Isn't there some way to organize their similarities and differences so as to support more methodical discussion? At this point in the *Odyssey* curriculum, this is not an unfamiliar query and the students—either on their own or with little prompting—suggest that the radios be compared dimension by dimension.

The teacher writes the labels for the three radios on the board and asks the students which dimension to consider first. Working with only this dimension, the teacher then ranks each radio based on the students' votes, giving a score of 3 to the most preferred and a score of 1 to the least preferred. Continuing in this way, the class develops a dimensionalized preference table, as shown in Table 4.2. Summing the ranks in each column, they agree that Radio B (or whichever radio actually wins out) is, on balance, the preferred choice of the class as a whole. Further, acknowledging that Radio B is not necessarily the first choice of any given student, the decision space is now explicitly organized in a way that supports clear discussion of the personal weightings and trade-offs that may underlie individual departures from this decision.

The students then work through and discuss several more such problems. Across problems, the guidance provided by the teacher or in their workbooks is methodically reduced. The goal is to develop the students' independent ability to analyze decision spaces in this manner.

By the beginning of the next lesson, they are sufficiently facile with the procedure that the dimensions of comparison no longer need be labeled and separated for them. Instead, they are asked to decide between two wristwatches whose dimensions of comparison are neither itemized nor labeled but jumbled together in a manner more similar to the order in which we may tend to notice and resonate to the attributes of choice alternatives in real life. "Imagine that you want to buy a new wristwatch and have found two that you like very much. Watch A costs only $25.00, but it has a cheap plastic band. Watch B has a handsome 14 kt. gold band, costs $125.00, but loses 20 minutes a day. Watch A, which comes in a plain cardboard box, loses 1 second every 3 months and does not have alarm, date, or stopwatch functions. Watch B, on the other hand, does have alarm, date and stopwatch functions, and it comes in a beautiful black leatherette gift box, lined with satin." (Feehrer & Adams, 1986, p. 155). Secure in the method and logic of their procedure, the students transform this prose to a comparison table with little help or hesitation. As they have done in other lessons on other topics, they focus on each distinguishing property, identify its overarching or dominant dimension, and search out its value on the comparison watch: price ($25.00 versus $125.00); band (plastic versus gold); accuracy (excellent versus poor); box (cardboard versus elegant); extra functions (none versus alarm, date, and stopwatch). In this way, through their now familiar and—up to now—reassuringly helpful procedure, the students analytically establish that Watch B is the preferred option overall.

But this time something is wrong. This time, there are not just a few, but many dissenters from the tabular decision. This time, virtually everyone agrees that the tabular winner is not simply suboptimal by their own personal standards but foolish.

The solution is put on the board for checking. Virtually everyone agrees on the rankings between the two watches on each individual dimension, and the arithmetic is correct. Still, with the table on the board, it is clear that Watch B is preferrable to Watch A along the majority of its dimensions of comparison. Although some students have analyzed the functions (alarm, stopwatch, date) one by one, that only seems to exaggerate the disturbing numerical advantage of Watch B.

The teacher is nonplussed: Here is the table; here are the numbers; it seems clear that we should buy Watch B. But the students still object. The teacher presses: Why? What's wrong with Watch B? It costs too much and barely keeps time, comes the response. Those are good points, concedes the teacher, but what about all these other ways in which Watch B is better than Watch A? The students' response is firm: The watches' boxes, straps, and special features are just not as important as their price and accuracy.

The students, in short, have discovered quite by themselves the importance of weighting the dimensions of a decision space. Thus understanding its logic, it is easy to give them a procedure for entering such weights into their tables. To this end, the method adopted in the *Odyssey* curriculum consists only of ranking the dimensions in terms of importance, and then multiplying the rank preference of each property on each dimension by its dimension's rank importance. For each of the subsequent problems that are presented to the students, this technique yields results that are wholly rational, and clearly superior to any unweighted solutions.

The drawback to this technique, of course, is that it is crude. Once the students had become facile with this technique, our intention (foiled by the classroom days available to us) was to entrap them with problems that involved some dimensions that were roughly comparable to each other in importance versus others that were wildly incomparable in terms of importance. In this way, we planned to lead them to discover the logic of fractional weightings—again, instead of trying to explain it to them. Plans notwithstanding, the technique with which we left the children captures the essential logic of the utility function: For any decision problem, there may be a number of dimensions to be compared; although each must be considered, some should influence our choice more than others.

Beyond that, two more general aspects of these lessons deserve emphasis. The first is that pivotal points are not told to the students. Instead, they are discovered by the students. Problems and worksheets are used not only for purposes of exercising methods and logic that the students are to learn, but equally for purposes of eliciting those methods and logic from the students. Indeed, the sort of constrained discovery learning illustrated above was the principal means through which major logical insights and their limitations and corollaries were established throughout the *Odyssey* curriculum (see Adams, 1989). In Piaget's words:

> Children should be able to do their own experimenting. . . . In order for a child to understand something, he must construct it himself, he must reinvent it. Every time we teach a child something, we keep him from inventing it himself. (Piaget, 1972, p. 27)

This is not to say that direct instruction is of no value. To the contrary, such instruction subserves the very valuable functions of directing students' attention to phenomena of interest, of refining or emphasizing selected relations among them, and of providing means of reinforcing such knowledge and recalling it across contexts. In recognition of this, verbal summary, rules, graphic support, and labeling are methodically exploited throughout the *Odyssey* curriculum. Even so, rules, definitions, labels, and explanations cannot substitute for perceptual, conceptual, and procedural experiences. At best, they can allude to such experiences. The process of constrained discovery is intended to create maximal support for direct instruction.

The second aspect to be emphasized is that the children mastered the logic and method of these multidimensional decision problems to the point of independent application (at least to classroom problems) in the span of just two 45-minute lessons. This was possible only because they were familiar already with so many of the relevant concepts and relations. They were familiar already with the processes of constructing and using tables. They were familiar already with the nature and interpretation of ordinal relations. They were familiar already with focusing on particular attributes or properties of interest in a situation. But most of all, they were familiar with the notion of partitioning conceptual spaces in terms of their dimensions of variation.

The ability to parse the world into alternate sets of constrastive dimensions is fundamental to physics, mathematics, formal logic, and virtually all formal disciplines. *Odyssey* was built on the premise that such explicit analysis is of fundamental utility for cogent thinking in any domain. In the earliest lessons in the curriculum, the attributes of interest and their overriding dimensions were concrete and perceptually salient. Little by little, working at first with such dimensions as color, form, number, and function, the students were led to discover the utility of such analyses and the logical comparisons they support—classification, hierarchical classification, ordering, and analogical comparison. Little by little, these same analytic processes were refined, extended, and combined to interpretations of word meaning, of the viewpoints of characters and authors, and of jokes, advertisements, and algebra-like word problems. Whatever the domain and always by means of constrained discovery, the students were repeatedly led to invoke and apply the same basic logical concepts and processes. The goal, again, was to make the analytic framework seem so readily familiar and so broadly useful to the students and that they would resort to it on their own, beyond the confines of the course.

Formal Versus Real-World Concepts of Decision Making

In their very use, formal approaches to preference and choice force the decision maker to make explicit the dimensions of consideration along with the favorability and likelihood of their outcomes. Beyond that, they provide a procedural frame for rationally computing and contrasting the overall merits of a set of choice alternatives. To this extent, such analyses are clearly very useful. Interestingly, research on decision making suggests that people who have been taught to appreciate the mertis of such an approach may credit themselves with its use more often than they use it.

Soelberg (1967) provided a classic study of such delusion. The decision makers whom he studied were MIT Sloan School (business school) students. Compared to most randomly chosen adults, in other words, all were exceptionally well-versed in the methods and merits of dimensional utility analysis. The decision-making situation that he studied was the process through which the students chose among their actual job offers as they finished school. It was, in other words, a "real-world" rather than an artificial problem. Compared to the random real-world problem, however, it was fairly similar to the well-structured and quantifiable "textbook" prototype; moreover, its situation of application was not very far removed from the classroom context in which such textbook applications had been developed. Through the use of a nonintrusive interview technique, Soelberg examined the dynamics of the students' job selection process. For each student, he began shortly after her or his set of job offers was first considered and continued the interviews over the months until a final selection had been made. As evidenced by his ability to predict the students' ultimate choices, Soelberg inferred that they generally became committed to a particular alternative very early in the process. After that point, most of their "decision" activity was directed not toward evaluating, but toward justifying their choice. And this was very much despite the students' training and assertions to the contrary.

Indeed, at the outset of the study, Soelberg's students independently assured him that their decision would proceed by weighting all relevant factors with respect to each alternative and that their choice would be made by "adding up the numbers." Yet, Soelberg observed, if the students did run through this procedure at all, it was only after they had implicitly decided among the alternatives.

During the job search process, no evidence of factor weighting was apparent. Instead, the alternatives tended to be screened along a number of noncompared goal dimensions. The alternatives tended not to be systematically compared with one another even on termination of the search process, and there was little evidence that the students had constructed a transitive rank ordering of their merits and demerits.

Typically, reported Soelberg, the students terminated their search process only after having identified a preferred choice. Just as typically, however, the students professed great uncertainty about their preferences at this point. Moreover, the students seemed genuinely unaware that any tacit choice had been made.

During the remainder of the selection process, the students directed their efforts toward resolving the residual uncertainties and problems connected with their choices. Engaging in "a great deal of perceptual and interpretational distortion," the students managed to promote their preferred alternatives and to demote all competitors. By the time each was done, each had developed a fine decision structure, complete with goal attribute weights, that showed "unequivocally" that her or his preferred choice was her or his best choice.

We have reviewed Soelberg's study not as a diversion but because it illustrates several aspects of the decision-making process that we perceived as key conceptual points for our students. The first is that in the real world it is often difficult to divide the decision-making process into the distinct conceptual phases that the textbook world presumes. In particular, the presumption of formal utility functions is that the alternatives of a decision or their relevant dimensions will have been enumerated before they are evaluated. Necessarily, however, unless the effective set of choice alternatives is to exhaust the potential space (but nobody really considers all possible jobs), the process of setting up the decision space involves evaluation of the candidate alternatives. Similarly, it is often only through the discovery and exploration of candidate alternatives that the dimensions of evaluation are established.

A second and, it seems to us, closely related point is that it is easy to cheat the evaluation process without any awareness or intention of so doing. In particular, people's biases and hypotheses about the outcome of a diagnosis or decision strongly influence their perception, memory, and interpretation of information on which it might otherwise be based (e.g., Chapman & Chapman, 1971; Grabitz & Jochen, 1972; Hoyt & Centers, 1972; Salancik & Kiesler, 1971). And the greater the time and effort that an individual has invested in developing such biases and hypotheses, the stronger and less mutable their influence (Nickerson & Feehrer, 1975). By showing students how the very generation of the decision space may itself be the product of hypothesis generation and evaluation, we hoped we might help them to guard against its distorting influence.

A third, equally related, but still more important issue to our minds centered on the basic notions of what decisions are and of the circumstances in which they are made. Within the formal literature on the topic, decision making is equivalent to choosing. As mentioned above, formal utility models generally assume prior and independent establishment of the space from which the choice will be made. Thus, to the extent that the generation of the decision space must itself be the product of decisions, the utility of utility functions is already limited. But formal decision-making models also take for granted the beliefs and values with which decision makers weight the components of their decision space. Even the language of the discipline is powerfully loaded toward the exclusion of such considerations: Applied to the alternatives in the decision space, formal decision-making models describe the rational choice, the optimal choice, the choice that maximizes the favorability of the outcome—but only given the beliefs and values by which those alternatives were weighted. Questions as to the appropriateness of the decision makers beliefs and values are, as Fischhoff (1988) put it, "not in the department of decision theorists."

In fact we have no interest in picking at the terminology of the decision-making literature; it is the way it is for understandable historical reasons. On the other hand, in designing the *Odyssey* curriculum, our goal was not one of giving students terminological access to that literature but of giving them reflective insight into the presence, process, and consequences of decisions in their own lives. Very often, as mentioned earlier, the generation of the decision space is itself the product of decisions, and we wanted the students to appreciate it. But beliefs and values are also largely a matter of decision and choice, and to the best of our abilities we wanted the students to understand that, too.

In the real world, after all, it is not as though the information one encounters comes labeled as true, partly true, or false. It is not as though it normally comes complete with lists of its sources, proofs, and conditions of pertinence. Very few of the rules and facts we "know" are unquestionably true; of those that are, still fewer are unconditionally true. The knowledge and values one accepts—or chooses to apply in any situation—are themselves a matter of personal decision.

Constructing the Decision Space

In brief, the process of weighting the alternatives of an established decision space is a decision problem that pivots on one's beliefs and values. The process of setting up the alternatives of a decision space is a decision problem that pivots on one's beliefs and values. Settling on the beliefs and values by which one does either, is a decision problem that pivots on the thoughtfulness with which one reviews, critiques, and ascertains one's beliefs and values. To this end, the sound decision maker's only recourse is to collect, compare, and carefully interpret information.

Where the decision space is not predefined (as it was, for example, in the radio selection problem described earlier), this generally means collecting more information than one actually needs. After all, one is not in the position to assess the relevance, credibility, or relative weight of the information until the space has been defined, and the space cannot be properly defined until the information it properly subsumes has been acquired. For the reader who is also a researcher, such informational overreaching is a familiar fact of life. We are accustomed to reading beyond the boundaries of what we will write; we are accustomed to collecting those extra data and conducting those retrospectively superfluous analyses: It's all part of ensuring that we have reached the boundaries of the information we really do need to solve the problem at hand.

To convey this sense to our young students, we confronted them with a similarly ill-defined research problem. By design, the problem, presented as a story, was broken across pages such that the text on each page set up questions that we wanted the students to try to answer and issues that we wanted them to discuss in the course of so doing. To involve the students in some of the messier aspects of information organization and interpretation, they were also given pages of data with which to work. The research problem was presented in the guise of a detective story.

As the story begins, someone has robbed the bank. Captain Alcott, Detective Segal, and Detective Hayes must solve the crime. As the officers find a number of people in the bank when they arrive, they are immediately faced with a decision: Should they clear the bank out or not? If they ask everyone to stay for questioning they might find a witness or they might waste valuable time; if they ask everyone to leave, they might lose a witness or they might save valuable time. The two possible outcomes of each alternative are clear and so, too, are their valences. On the other hand, the police do not yet have any basis for assessing their likelihoods. What should they do? They should quickly poll to see if anyone in the bank witnessed the robbery: To resolve the uncertainty as required to make their decision, they should gather information.

Detective Segal quickly returns. Not only has he found a witness, but the witness identified the robber as Bob Jackson. Segal argues that they should arrest Bob Jackson immediately: If they do, they'll get a commendation; if they don't, they might lose him and get fired. True, acknowledges the cautious Captain, but only if the witness was correct. And thus the students are led to appreciate not only that the outcomes under consideration are less than certain but also that the decision space is incomplete and cannot be properly evaluated without recognizing the costs and benefits of their complements. What should the officers do? They should gather more information.

Having asked everyone for information as to the appearance or identity of the robber, Detective Hayes then returns with her report. No one got a very good look. The robber had been wearing a mask and, besides, made them all hide their eyes. Nevertheless, several of the witnesses suggested that the robber looked or sounded like Bob Jackson, and the rest produced descriptions that were consistent with Jackson's appearance.

The question is posed again: Should the officers arrest Jackson or not? The decision space and its outcomes are still the same. The new information has changed their apparent likelihoods only. But that's enough. This time the decision is affirmative. The Captain sends Detective Hayes to arrest Jackson. Pointing out the remaining uncertainties, however, the Captain asks Detective Segal to stay with him at the bank—to gather more information.

Several false leads later, Detective Hayes discovers that Jackson was in the hospital at the time of the holdup. He could not have been the robber. The police have no leads, no suspects. What can they do? They must gather more information.

At the Captain's decision, the officers then collect all the information they can from every witness and the closed-circuit television, writing everything in their notebooks. When they regroup, the officers have reports not just of the robber and his behavior, but also of the customers, of their clothes, of who butted in line, of who was marrying whom, of the cars out front, and on and on. Put together, the three lists are overwhelmingly long and frustratingly diffuse. To interpret them, the students must first find a way to reduce them.

As the students observe that not all of the information appears equally useful, they are challenged to go through each notebook, marking each observation as relevant or irrelevant. The first purpose of this process is to make clear to the students—through their own debate—that relevance is in the eye of the perceiver, the apparent relevance of a fact depends on what one has in mind while assessing it. The second point is that relevance of a clue or diagnostic cannot be definitively determined until the diagnosis is known; although this point is central to the between-student debates, it becomes inescapable only much later in the lesson. The third point is that apparent relevance is itself multidimensional; in this case, some of the seemingly relevant information pertains to who the robber might be, some to who witnesses are, and some to how the robbery was executed.

Studying the newly collected information, Captain Alcott finds reason to hypothesize that Loretta Beasley, uniquely missing among the people who had been in the bank at the time of the robbery, may have been an accomplice. The students are asked to examine the information for any that would support or refute this hypothesis. Admittedly, we had stacked the deck with consistent information and, as the story continues to unfold, they are offered still more. As it turns out, Captain Alcott's hypothesis is wrong; Loretta Beasley is wholly innocent. However, by helping the students to mislead themselves we hoped to dramatize people's susceptibility to commitment and its influence on the perception and interpretation of information.

In the course of pursuing the Beasely hypothesis, the students are led to notice that there are discrepancies and disagreement in the information that the police have gathered. To help the police to assess these inconsistencies, the students are asked to collapse the data. The information is first organized by categories—the robber's physical characteristics, what the robber wore, what the robber carried, the robber's behavior, information about the witnesses present, and information about suspicious vehicles. From this information, the students are then asked to fill in a spreadsheet: the rows of the spreadsheet have already been labeled with "relevant" attributes of the robber or the robbery taken from the officers' notes; in the internal columns the students are to cite the information obtained; in the summary column, they are to indicate whether or not the various reports on each attribute are consistent with one another. There are some attributes in the table for which the police have collected but one single report. Working with these entries, the students are led to agree that the concept of consistency simply doesn't apply when only one datum is available. More than that, these single-entry items are used to elicit the point that wherever the possibility of erroneous observations exists, multiple observations are extremely important.

The attention of the police and the students is then turned to the inconsistent entries in their spreadsheets. Recognizing that at least one of each such set of entries is likely to be erroneous, they are challenged to assess their relative credibility. Working through this challenge, they discover that credibility is also a multidimensional construct. Most obviously, the credibility of an observation is seen to increase with the number and proportion of sources that reported it. Where the reports are divided, however, that is not enough. And so their attention is directed to the sources. In general, the information from the closed-circuit television is judged to be more credible than witness reports, and witness reports are judged to be more credible than local news broadcasts. Yet, having decided that, the students are quickly led to recognize that the credibility of any given witness depends on the position that she or he was in to observe the reported information.

Finally, the issue is raised that some variables are intrinsically more observable than others. For example, a person's exact age or weight is not easy to assess at a glance. In view of this, the students record the range of the reports on these dimension instead of discounting any for being discrepant. There is, after all, no advantage and obvious potential cost in pretending that you have accurate observations on information that could not have been accurately observed.

In contrast with age and weight, some attributes are easily observable. Thus, getting three reports from eye-witnesses that the robber wore a tan raincoat and one from the local news that he wore a black cape, it is relatively easy to suspect that the latter report was in error. On the other hand, the students also encounter disagreement among eyewitnesses who should have been equally credible about information that should have been unmistakably observable and difficult, in context, to confuse or forget. This discrepancy turns out to be a key clue—if not yet interpretable.

The results of the students' credibility analysis suggest several new leads—none of which pans out—and several previously overlooked but potentially useful sources of information to be examined. Frustrated by the apparent lack of progress, Detective Segal expresses a thought that has surely occurred to many of the students:

"It's just that the more we work, the more information we get rid of. At the rate we're going, we'll throw out all of our information before we arrest anybody," he laments. "Take it easy, Segal," says the Captain. "We haven't thrown away any information. We just put some aside. Tell me, why did we put it aside?" "We did it because it looked irrelevant, inconsistent, or incredible. We did it because it looked useless," replies Detective Segal. "That's it," agrees the Captain. "We put the information aside because it *looked* useless. If we had been sure it was useless, we could have really thrown it away. Now that would have been progress" (Feehrer & Adams,

1986, pp. 127–128). There follows, first among the officers and then among the children, a discussion of the process of elimination, the hazards of unwittingly confusing good information with bad, and the ultimate value of not committing oneself to a wrong answer in any case.

Working from the unexplained inconsistencies in the eyewitness reports, the search for a suspect becomes focused on the eyewitnesses themselves. By reorganizing information from the officers' notebooks, including some that had been previously put aside as irrelevant, a pattern of inconsistencies and possibilities is detected. More information is again needed, but this time the officers and the students know precisely what they are looking for. The crime is solved and, as it turns out, with plenty of corroborating evidence.

EVALUATION OF THE CURRICULUM

To evaluate the impact of the *Odyssey* curriculum, approximately half of its 100-odd lessons were taught by teachers from the Venezuelan school system to 450 seventh graders (12 classes) in barrio schools in Barquisimeto, Venezuela. The 12 experimental classes were selected in conjunction with 12 control classes, matched, insofar as possible, on school and classroom parameters as well as on students' ages, initial abilities, socioeconomic status, and so on. (For a more detailed discussion of the evaluation effort, see Herrnstein, Nickerson, deSanchez, & Swets, 1986.)

All 900 of the students completed a battery of tests at the beginning and end of the school year. One set of these tests was designed by us to assess the students' mastery of the course material per se. The remainder of the battery was put together with an eye toward assessing the general rather than the specific carryover of the course. These tests were selected not to match the specifics of the course but to provide a broad range of aptitude and achievement measures.

More specifically, the battery included three sets of standardized tests: the Cattell Culture Fair Test (Cattell & Cattell, 1961), the Otis–Lennon School Ability Test (Otis & Lennon, 1977), and a set of eight achievement and general ability tests—three of Guidance Testing Associates' Tests of General Ability (Manuel, 1962a), three of Guidance Testing Associates' Tests of Reading (Manuel, 1962b), one from the Puerto Rican Department of Education, and one developed by our own staff to assess arithmetic skills. In addition, we collected qualitative assessments of the course from teachers, students, and supervisors and administered some less formal tests of reasoning and writing; these measures corroborated the results of the standardized tests.

As must be expected, the test scores of all students, both experimental and control, increased across the school year. However, the gain of the experimental students was significantly greater than that of the control students on each of the tests. One way of indicating the magnitude of the effects is to express the gains realized by the experimental group as a percentage of the gains realized by the control group. In these terms, the gain of the experimental group was 21% greater than that of the control group on the Cattell test, 46% greater on the Otis-Lennon, 68% greater on the achievement and general ability tests. The gains of the experimental students were also significantly greater (117%) on our tests of what had been taught—but that is not a very telling index of what, in any transferrable way, they might have learned from those lessons.

A moving endorsement of the decision-making materials per se comes from work at the Ethan Allen School, Wisconsin's maximum security correctional facility for youth. As an experimental complement to a treatment program centered on cognitive–behavioral intervention and errors in criminal thinking, Dr. David Smith and colleagues administered the *Odyssey* program to seven young men. Smith reports substantial increase in the youths' grade point averages and their scores on several tests of creativity. In addition, however, the *Odyssey* students committed many fewer serious in-house infractions than their seven controls. Every one of the *Odyssey* students made himself eligible for release from the institution by the end of the year, as compared to only one of the seven controls. One year after their respective releases, none of the *Odyssey* students had been sent back to the school; in contrast, five of the controls had been sent back.

The numbers are small but the effects are dramatic, and Smith believes the difference derives from the *Odyssey* course and the decision-making strand in particular. The course, in his words "treated the students like they had a mind and could use it." The decision-making strand gave them the structure and challenge for considering the results of their behaviors.

SUMMARY

Our goal in writing the *Odyssey* curriculum was to develop an effective course, not particularly on decision making, but on thinking in general. The basic premise underlying the curriculum is that productive thinking in any domain rests squarely on two ingredients: information and interpretation. The topic of decision making was included within the curriculum because we saw it as a useful vehicle for purposes reinforcing this premise; we wanted the students to appreciate that decision making profits from the kind of thinking that they had been studying. Conversely, however, we hoped they would appreciate that productive thinking necessarily involves decision making at all levels. Decision making, in summary, is the pivotal and, at best, reflective and willful determinant not just of what we choose given any set of alternatives, but very often of the very membership of those alternatives and always of the knowledge, beliefs, and values from which we estimate their worth and likelihood.

REFERENCES

Adams, M. J. (1989). Thinking skills curricula: Their promise and progress. *Educational Psychologist, 24,* 25–77.

Adams M. J. (Ed.). (1986). *Odyssey: A curriculum for thinking* (Vols. 1–6). Watertown, MA: Charlesbridge Publishing.

Cattell, R. B., & Cattell, A. K. S. (1961). *Culture fair intelligence test (Scale 2, Forms A & B).* Champaign, IL: Institute for Personality and Ability Testing.

Chapman, L. J., & Chapman, J. (1971, November). Test results are what you think they are. *Psychology Today,* pp. 106–110.

Feehrer, C. E., & Adams, M. J. (1986). *Odyssey: A curriculum for thinking. Volume 5: Decision Making.* Watertown, MA: Charlesbridge Publishing.

Fischhoff, B. (1988). Judgment and decision making. In R. J. Sternberg & E. E. Smith (Eds.), *The psychology of human thought* (pp. 153–187). New York: Cambridge University Press.

Grabitz, H. J., & Jochen, H. (1972). An evaluation of confirming and disconfirming information in decision making. *Archiv für Psychologie, 124,* 133–144.

Herrnstein, R. J., Nickerson, R. S., deSanchez, M., & Swets, J. A. (1986). Teaching thinking skills. *American Psychologist, 41,* 1279–1289.

Hoyt, M. F., & Centers, R. (1972). Temporal situs of the effects of anticipated publicity upon commitment and resistance to counter-communication. *Journal of Personality and Social Psychology, 22,* 1–7.

Manuel, H. T. (1962a). *Tests of general ability: Inter-American series (Spanish, Level 4, Forms A & B).* San Antonio, TX: Guidance Testing Associates.

Manuel, H. T. (1962b). *Tests of reading: Inter-American series (Spanish, Levels 3 & 4, Forms A & B).* San Antonio, TX: Guidance Testing Associates.

Nickerson, R. S., & Feehrer, C. E. (1975). *Decision making and training: A review of theoretical and empirical studies of decision making and their implications for the training of decision makers.* (Technical Report: NAVTRAEQUIPCEN 73-C-0128-1). Orlando, FL: Naval Training Equipment Center.

Otis, A. S., & Lennon, R. T. (1977). *Otis–Lennon school ability test (Intermediate Level 1, From R).* New York: Harcourt Brace Jovanovich.

Piaget, J. (1972). Some aspects of operations. In M. Piers (Eds.), *Play and development.* New York: Norton.

Salancik, J. R., & Kiesler, C. A. (1971). Behavioral commitment and retention of consistent and inconsistent attitude word-pairs. In C. A. Kiesler (Ed.), *The psychology of commitment: Experiments linking behavior to belief.* New York: Academic Press.

Soelberg, P. O. (1967). Unprogrammed decision making. *Industrial Management Review, 8,* 19–29.

Chapter 5

Toward Improved Instruction in Decision Making to Adolescents: A Conceptual Framework and Pilot Program

Jonathan Baron
University of Pennsylvania

Rex V. Brown
Decision Science Consortium, Inc.
Reston, VA

INTRODUCTION

Educated people must know how to make up their mind intelligently. When they have a decision to make, like which career to pursue, or who to vote for, or what to do with their company's assets, they weigh the pros and cons in a balanced, reasonable way. If they have a question of fact to resolve, like whether the stock market will go up or down, or who stole the cookies, they weigh the evidence fairly. The better they can perform these tasks, the better off they, and society at large, are in a number of ways.

Despite the importance of this ability, very little educational effort goes into teaching people how to make decisions. Given the fact that many decisions seem to be poorly made (whether personal, professional, or civic), such instruction would not be superfluous. Moreover, we argue, there is every reason to think that such instruction can be effective if properly done. In this paper, we make the argument for instruction in decision making in the schools, particularly in early adolescence. We outline the foundations of such instruction in the field of decision analysis and in the psychology of decision making and learning. We then illustrate our ideas from a middle school program we are piloting in Reston, VA and Philadelphia, PA., and finally propose an approach to measuring the impact of such instruction on real-life decision-making.

Why Do People Need to Be Taught Decision Making?

Rational decision making may be defined as thinking that uses methods that are most likely to satisfy the goals that the thinker would have on reflection (Baron, 1985). This definition takes into account real differences in people's goals. On the other hand, by limiting itself to "goals that the thinker would have on reflection" it acknowledges that people do not always act to attain the goals that are best for them, from their own perspective. The part of the definition referring to likelihood acknowledges the fact that decisions should be evaluated from the perspective of what is known to the decision maker at the time, rather than what is known only in hindsight (see Baron & Hershey, 1988).

People exhibit systematic biases in thinking (Baron, 1985, in press a; Kahneman, Slovic & Tversky, 1982; Nisbett & Ross, 1980), which lead them to depart from this standard. People tend to be biased toward options they already favor, they tend to neglect consequences for other people or consequences that occur in the distant future, they attend to irrelevant factors (such as sunk costs that cannot be redeemed), and they ignore relevant factors (such as differences in probability ; see Baron, 1988). We discuss these biases further in the next section.

Adolescence as a Crucial Time

Instruction in decision making cannot wait until college or even high school. Many serious and apparently irrational decisions, with consequences inconsistent with the decision-maker's long-term goals, are made by adolescents. As evidence of this, we cite a number of phenomena peculiar to this age.

Teenage Pregnancy.   Teenage pregnancy is widespread in the U.S. and in many less developed countries. The determinants of teenage pregnancy are complex, but at least some of them may be related to more general problems in making decisions. Steinlauf (1979) showed that scores on a test of problem solving in daily life correlated with the number of unplanned pregnancies in female adolescents who had already been pregnant once. Interviews with teenagers suggest that unplanned pregnancies often result from a failure to think probabilistically ("It can't happen if we do it just once"), as well as a more simple failure to think at all about the consequences of sexual activity either at the time or beforehand, or about possible protective measures.

Behavior Disorders.   Adolescents are disproportionately represented among criminals, drug users, and victims of suicide. Many lifelong self-destructive habits, such as smoking, begin in adolescence. All of these behaviors may result in part from a failure to consider adequately the consequences of acts, especially distant consequences. Adolescents may fail to recognize the precedent-setting effects of single acts (e.g., why one cigarette is likely to lead to another, and another) and they may fail to consider the long-term consequences of such habits for themselves and others. Even suicide may be, in part, a result of poor thinking. Suicide has been treated successfully by cognitive therapy, which emphasizes: (a) search for counterevidence against sweeping negative generalizations, and (b) more reflective coping and decision making.

Aids.   The recent AIDS epidemic has made the preceding problems more urgent. Improved decision making will not by itself stop the spread of this disease. However, accurate information about consequences of sexual behaviors and drug abuse will not affect behavior unless people think about such (distant) consequences and take them into account. In addition, practices that lead to AIDS may result from neglect of small probabilities, neglect of precedent setting, and failure to consider alternatives.

Reports presented by the National Assessment of Education Progress (1981) and the National Commission on Excellence in Education (1983) argued that children in American public schools, although possessing vast factual knowledge, show deficiencies in their abilities to reason critically in a wide variety of inference and problem-solving related tasks. The reports concluded that many students approach such tasks superficially and without adequate consideration. These general deficiencies may manifest themselves in the problems just mentioned as well as in school work.

Need for Improved Adult Decision-Making

Problems in decision making do not end in adolescence. For many of the health related decisions the die has been largely cast in youth, but a whole range of new major decisions open up, such as those related to marriage, careers, and resource allocation. In addition, adults as citizens and leaders make decisions with societal impact.

It has been argued that the economic strength of nations is as much due to superior education as to more conventional considerations, such as the availability of capital (Rostow, 1971). It is surely not that citizens of advanced countries appreciate Shakespeare's sonnets better or know more of the history of classical Greece. The decline of the British Empire is said to date from the decline of classical training in the schools. Mastery of technical skills has a role to play, but is not the whole story: Only a fraction of the population becomes engineers or physicists. Economic strength surely lies in a more general intellectual competence. Although the typical American's reasoning power may be ahead of his counterparts in other lands, there remains great room for improvement. Concern is widespread that the gap is closing, and that our standard of living is jeopardized as a result.

The quality of decision making in a democratic society manifests itself in the quality of the government. It is said that people get the government they deserve. If the populace is proficient as decision makers, elected leaders will be forced to demonstrate competence in their public decisions. This is as true in industrial democracies as in fragile democracies elsewhere.

Scope for Improvement Through the Schools

We contend that there is much that can be done to improve reasoning and decision-making abilities through teaching programs in the schools. Whether reasoning can be taught in school was a topic of wide debate among educationists at the turn of the century, and the resulting general consensus was that it could not. However, recent evidence (Nisbett, Fong, Lehman, & Cheng, 1987) indicates that reasoning can be taught, if it is taught in the right way and if the substance of what is taught is appropriate to problems that students will face.

FLAWS TO BE CORRECTED: HEURISTICS AND BIASES

As suggested earlier, the preceding examples of poor decision making may be mediated by a number of heuristics and biases that have been studied or postulated by psychologists and economists. Although many such biases have been discovered (see Baron, 1988), only a few seem to us to be broadly relevant in the course of people's lives as well as in the professions.

Biases can be divided into those that involve search and those that involve inference. When we think about a decision, we search our memories and the outside world (including each other) for goals that we have or should have, options, and evidence about the extent to which the options achieve our goals. Evidence often consists of imagined outcomes and their probabilities. We then make tentative inferences (and final inferences after further search) concerning the options. Baron (1985, 1988) proposed that we generally search too little to justify the confidence that we hold in our inferences (see Koriat, Lichtenstein, & Fischhoff, 1980, and Hoch, 1985, for evidence on this point).

Biases of Search

Insufficient Search.   One common manifestation of insufficient search is impulsiveness (Baron, Badgio, & Gaskins, 1986; Messer, 1976). Children and adults differ in their willingness to sacrifice accuracy for speed in problems that require thinking. Those who tend to make many errors for the sake of speed have more difficulty in school (and even on IQ tests, which often reward speed); thus it would seem that thinking too little is a more common problem than thinking too much.

Single-mindedness. People tend to make holistic decisions in terms of a single dominant dimension. They are apparently unwilling to make trade-offs—or less willing than they ought to be (Baron, 1985; Gardiner & Edwards, 1975; Montgomery, 1984; Slovic, 1975; Tversky, Sattath, & Slovic, 1988). This may be seen as a form of insufficient search: insufficient search for goals. One manifestation of single-mindedness is the framing of decision problems in terms of "local" goals such as "profit maximization" or "national interest." Favoritism toward one's group may result from failure to understand the arbitrariness of group membership as a moral concern or as insufficient thought about the legitimacy of the other group's point of view.

Myside Bias. It has been argued by Francis Bacon and more recent authors (Baron, 1985; Janis & Mann, 1977; Kruglanski & Ajzen, 1983; Nisbett & Ross, 1980) that the irrational persistence of belief is one of the major sources of human folly. Irrational belief persistence may also be involved in educational difficulties. A good student, like a good scholar, must remain open to counterevidence and criticism. Belief persistence is also relevant to political attitudes and actions. Sharp disagreements—of the sort that lead to intolerance, lack of cooperation, and even war—are often characterized by belief persistence on one or both sides. Part of the problem here is that search is limited to evidence that supports an initial opinion. In addition to the studies of Koriat, Lichtenstein, and Fischhoff (1980) and Hoch (1985), Baron (1989, in press a), Frey (1986), and Perkins (in press; Perkins, Bushey, & Faraday, 1986) reported and reviewed direct evidence for this claim.

In matters of morality, there seems to be strong temptation to analyze situations in a way that is favorable to oneself. People tend to attend to reasons why their side has been treated unfairly and to neglect reasons why the other side has been. There is good reason for teaching the value of "giving the benefit of the doubt," for it is exactly what people tend not to do.

Two goals that are often neglected insidiously are the desires of the decision maker in the future (Thaler & Shefrin, 1981) and the desires of other people (Messick, 1985), both now and in the future. These are related in that the decision maker in the future is a somewhat different person (Parfit, 1984). In addition, both types of neglect may be caused by overattention to the satisfaction of immediate desires, and both are counteracted by the virtue of self-control.

Biases in Inference

Other Biases Concern Inference.   Many of these biases can be understood as overgeneralizations of rules of inference that are often useful (Baron, in press b). Myside bias, for one, operates in inference as well as search (Lord, Ross, & Lepper, 1979).

Sunk-cost Effect.   Sometimes people stick with plans even though they believe that the future will be better if they were to give them up (Arkes & Blumer, 1985, p. 124; Thaler & Shefrin, 1981). This sort of rationale occurs in public policy-making as well as in our personal lives. "To terminate a project in which $1.1 billion has been invested represents an unconscionable mishandling of taxpayers' dollars" (Senator Denton, 11/4/81; quoted by Arkes & Blumer, 1985).

Endowment Effect and Framing Effects.   A number of biases in decision making seem to stem from the adoption of a particular reference point. For example, in the endowment effect (Thaler, 1980), people overvalue what they have as opposed to what they might obtain. Kahneman and Tversky (1981) and Thaler (1983) have documented a number of effects of this sort.

Omission Bias.   Harmful commissions are considered worse than equally harmful omissions (Spranca, Minsk, & Baron, in press). For example, many people would prefer to do nothing and expose a child to a 10 in 10,000 chance of death from a disease than to vaccinate the child against the disease, if the vaccination has some risk of causing death itself, even if the risk is much lower (Ritov & Baron, in press).

Neglect of Uncertain Outcomes or Imperceptible Outcomes.   "Why give to charity when my money might be wasted?" "It's OK to rip off the insurance company because the resulting premium increase will be so little that nobody will notice."

   All of these fallacies may cause poor decisions, that is, decisions that do not best serve the goals that the decision maker would have on reflection, including moral goals. The prevention of these fallacies, and others like them, through education is surely a worthwhile goal. It is arguably a premier goal for education, given the very real consequences of poor decisions.

CONCEPTS TO BE ABSORBED

An Avenue for Enhancement: Personalized Decision Analysis (PDA)

There are many promising avenues for correcting decision-making biases. One avenue is warning people about them, another is to use heuristics. Nisbett and Ross (1980) suggested heuristic reminders to oneself, such as, "Don't throw good money after bad" (sunk-cost effect) or, "Believing is seeing" (belief persistence). A final avenue, and the one we focus on, is teaching certain formal rules of rational decision making. We will exploit the fact that every bias can be shown to flout the precepts of these rules and can be corrected using them (logically, if not necessarily psychologically).

Modern decision analysis began with Pascal's wager, and has undergone steady development since that time. Mathematical decision theory is taught in business schools, medical schools, and elsewhere. However, the basic ideas behind the theory are accessible to young adolescents. They involve thinking about decisions in terms one's options and the possible conse-quences of each opinion.

Personalized decision analysis (PDA), also known as applied statistical decision theory, produces prescriptions for personal decisions based on the quantification of a person's expectations and desires. It derives from a well-established body of logical/mathematical theory, statistical decision theory (Savage, 1954). In its most familiar form, possible options are specified, uncertainty about their possible outcomes is measured by probabilities, and the desirability of these outcomes is measured by utilities. The preferred op-tion is the one with the highest value for the probability weighted utility of its outcomes (Raiffa, 1968). The utility may reflect multiple attributes (Keeney & Raiffa, 1976).

PDA techniques and computer models are increasingly used in business and government on major decisions. Examples include deciding how to dis-pose of nuclear waste or when to launch a new product (Brown, 1987; Ul-vila & Brown, 1982). PDA is also taught at leading professional schools (Watson & Buede, 1987). No doubt many decisions have been improved by PDA, but applying PDA to a decision does not necessarily change the thinking patterns the decision maker brings to the next decision. Such change would require making the link between PDA and prevention of er-rors, and a great deal of practice in PDA.

The basic PDA message can be communicated simply and persuasively as an ideal of good decision making (see Appendix A). PDA concepts can provide a useful backdrop for informal decision making. Structurally sim-ple analyses, say, modeling a few clear cut options, their assessed impact on broad attributes of concern, and value tradeoffs between them, can give useful direct guidance. Often the use of PDA concepts involves no more than appreciation that a decision involves specifying options, predicting consequences, and evaluating them.

Formal analysis is not required in order for PDA to provide useful skills. Informal observations of trained decision analysts indicate that they spend very little time constructing quantitative models in making personal or, for that matter, professional business decisions. Nevertheless, the concepts of decision analysis figure importantly in their decision making. Appendix A describes an analysis with nothing more quantitative in it than the summing of pluses and minuses. One of the authors (Brown) used this analysis to help him decide whether to have his hip replaced.

PDA has been found particularly useful as a vehicle of communication between participants in a decision. For example, policy discussions between directors at Decision Science Consortium, Inc. (all of them decision analysts) are often couched in decision analytic terms (but without numbers or formal charts). This appears to enhance both the quality of each individual's contribution and the ability of his colleagues to understand and respond to it.

How Formal Training Can Help

The issue that now concerns us is whether the normative principles of PDA can help people in general to learn effective thinking before poor habits become ingrained. We believe that this can—and should—be explicitly taught in schools; but that it is not now being done, at least not routinely. The trouble is that there are almost no teaching materials as yet available that are adapted to young minds and deal with everyday (as opposed to professional) decisions. After there is some progress there, the institutional problems of getting the material into the curriculum and training the teachers can be addressed (see Campbell & Laskey, chap. 6 in this volume).

Essence of Course.   We have attempted such instruction in a course designed for young adolescents. A 6–8 unit core course is described by Laskey and Campbell (chap. 6 in this volume). It essentially teaches students to make decisions by "going through the GOOP." By this we mean they: determine what *G*oals are important to them; examine the *O*ptions available to them; predict the *O*utcomes of each option; and consider the *P*robabilities of any outcomes that are uncertain.

Students are shown that these considerations can be quantified and used in a plausible calculation to identify the "best choice." They are taught two alternative logical ways of analyzing a decision: in terms of "expected utility" and "multiattribute utility."

In the first they learn how to associate each outcome of each option with a utility and probability number, multiply the two and add to get the option's "expected" utility. In the second, they decompose the same expected utility into components contributed by different attributes of value, each contribution, in turn, decomposable as the product of score on the attribute and an importance weight.

Students are expected only to be able to understand and be persuaded by the principle involved. They are not expected, or at least not required, to be able to model any of their own choices explicitly in this way.

Role in Overcoming Biases. We listed previously several problems with decision making, and reasons why instruction in decision making may be helpful. These included insufficient search, myside bias, singlemindedness, neglect of others, temporal myopia, the sunk-cost effect, the endowment effect, omission bias, and the framing effect(s) involving status quo. Each of these deficiencies may be remedied by formal instruction.

Insufficient search is overcome by the very idea of formal analysis. For this purpose, it does not much matter what sort of formal analysis is done. Any such analysis slows down the process of decision making, allowing reasons to affect the decision that might not have done so if the decisions were made impulsively. Also, PDA may help focus attention where search is needed: different sorts of evidence are relevant in thinking about utilities of outcomes and probabilities of events, and a conflict of two goals can lead to search for a new option that satisfies both goals.

Similarly, myside bias is overcome by the idea that formal analysis is most useful if it avoids tinkering to force a pre-decided answer. If it is to be a real "second opinion," the first opinion must be put aside. Again, it does not matter much what sort of analysis is done, provided this stance is taken.

Singlemindedness ought to be reduced by increasing search and by fairness to opinions other than the first. Additional stress on the search for goals may also be required.

The sunk-cost effect is counteracted by a particular feature of PDA, the fact that it is future-oriented. It analyzes the effects of decisions on future outcomes and puts aside the past, because the past cannot be affected by our decisions. One of the main effects of formal training (as distinct from any training in decision making) should therefore be to reduce the sunk-cost effect. Similarly, the emphasis on future consequences will reduce blind obedience to precedent. "We've always done it that way," is no argument when the consequences are now unacceptable. Finally, attention to future consequences will obviate the distinction between omission and commission.

The endowment and framing effects may be avoided by the adoption of an impersonal perspective when assessing utility. That is, when one imagines various outcomes and how desirable they might be, one should not regard any particular outcome as the "given" one. Rather, one should treat them all as new, as if one were another person (with the same tastes as the decision maker but with unknown status quo) coping with these outcomes for the first time.

Temporal myopia and the neglect of others may be countered by making sure that the goals considered include the future interests of the decision maker and the interests of others affected by a decision. Students must be made aware that future effects of decisions may include those that arise from precedent setting. For example, a violation of the law may be harmless in a given case, but it may make future violations (by the violator and others) more likely, and these may not be so harmless. We cannot tell people how much they ought to weigh the future, the interests of others, and the effects of precedent. What we want to avoid is the assignment of zero weights out of failure to consider these goals at all.

PDA may also help people to clarify their goals. Often, our initial impulses are governed by goals that seem less important on reflection, such as avoidance of embarrassment or the desire to maintain the belief that one's past decisions were well made (Baron, 1988). Avoidance of negative emotions—such as those produced by saying "no" to a request—may also influence decisions in a way that would not stand up to the kind of reflective examination required in PDA.

Research on Normal Child Development Progression and Processes

So far, we have argued that poor decisions may result from inadequate skill in decision making, and we have argued that, in principle, the teaching of PDA might remedy some of the deficiencies. We now turn to the question of whether the relevant aspects of PDA may be understood by middle school children.

How difficult is decision analysis to understand? We might get some clue from the fact that decision analysis is formally analogous to number of other mathematical and physical systems. One that has been studied extensively (e.g., Siegler, 1976, 1981, 1985) is the balance beam task, in which a child must indicate whether a beam will balance or tilt to one side or the other. The weights and their distance from the fulcrum are varied. By systematically varying weight and distance, it is possible to determine what rule children use to predict balance.

The analogy with decision analysis is this: For multiattribute analysis, the two sides may be seen as options, each weight may be seen as the utility of an option on a dimension, and the distance may be seen as the importance of the dimension. (Alternatively, weight and distance may be reversed.) For expected-utility theory, importance may be replaced with probability. (The highest probability could correspond to the end of the beam.) In sum, it would seem that children of the target age can understand concepts formally analogous to those of decision analysis. This is especially true if the concepts are taught directly, rather than asking children to abstract them from experience. This finding is confirmed by experiments reported by Martin and Brown (chap. 10 in this volume).

PEDAGOGY

Pedagogy: General Principles

How might we best teach general principles of decision making? The answer is related to other research on the teaching of other strategies and heuristics for thinking.

Decision Analysis as a Design.   Perkins (1986) proposed a theory of knowledge as design. This theory also serves to explain what it means to understand something. He suggested that understanding involves knowing three things.

First, there is the structure of the thing to be understood, the piece of knowledge, or what Perkins calls (for other reasons) the design. The student must know a general description of the design. For decision analysis, the structure involves analysis into options, consequences, each with probabilities and utilities, possibly on each of several attributes, and a method for combining these quantities. Typically, this description will make reference to other concepts already known (or understood) for the relevant purpose. For example, the idea of weighing attributes against each other is analogous to a balance scale. Appropriate interpretation of the description is practically always facilitated by the use of at least one model or example in which the interpretation is given for a specific case (see Martin & Brown, chap. 10 in this volume).

Second, there is the purpose of the design, to make better decisions. Students may have to be convinced of the need to improve decision making. One way of doing this is to show that students disagree with each other, or that they disagree with themselves when the same decision is described in different ways (Kahneman & Tversky, 1984). Students may be given an open-ended decision problem as homework. Typically, we have found that most students think their solution will emerge as the best after discussion, but they are usually wrong. Another method is to look at examples of erroneous decisions from real life, both from history and personal experience.

The third part of understanding is the argument that the design in fact serves the purpose. One argument for PDA is that it maximizes long-run utility. The analogy with gambling may be helpful. Additional arguments for the need for PDA as a tool stem from the existence of biases. More generally, a teacher may demonstrate repeatedly how the use of PDA can lead people out of traps that they recognize clearly as traps once they are out of them. In addition, it may be argued that PDA grows out of, and formalizes, the methods of decision making that students use anyway.

Determinants of Transfer

We hope that training in PDA will transfer out of the context in which it is given. The literature suggests several ways to facilitate such transfer.

First, understanding itself is a powerful determinant of transfer (Katona, 1940; Wertheimer, 1945). When a tool is misunderstood it is likely to be misapplied, or its application will not be attempted at all.

Second, the general principles should be made explicit, and students should be told that the principles are generally useful (Belmont, Butterfield, & Feretti, 1982; Brown, Campione, & Barclay, 1979; Woodrow, 1927) and where they can be used (Brown & Palincsar, 1982). In an interesting demonstration of the importance of using general terms, Schleser, Meyers, and Cohen (1981) trained children to be more careful in the Matching Familiar Figures Test (MFFT). Children were instructed to talk to themselves while doing the task. In a "specific" condition, the talk concerned only the task itself, for example, "I have to pick one of these pictures which is just the same as the one here. I have to look very closely at each part of the picture. I have to go slowly. I have to compare each. . . ." In a "general" condition, the talk was of the sort that could apply to many different tasks, for example, "I'm going to answer a question. I have to stop and think about what the question is asking. . . ." Although both groups showed considerable improvement at the MFFT, only the group given the "general" training showed transfer to a second task involving perspective-taking.

Third, variety of experience is important. Gick and Holyoak (1983) found that transfer of a principle of problem solving was facilitated by the use of two examples plus instruction to attend to their similarities, as opposed to one example. It has also been suggested (by Baron, 1978, and others) that students may be trained to transfer by giving them new problems and suggesting that they apply methods they have learned. This would seem to be part of the use of multiple examples.

Fourth, studies of intrinsic motivation (e.g., Lepper & Greene, 1978) have suggested that simple maintenance of new learning is less likely when the goal emphasized during the learning (e.g., grades) is different from the goal in effect outside the classroom. Deci and Ryan (1985) found that grades may be used if they are presented as informative feedback rather than reward.

Finally, Baron (1985) suggested that transfer is more likely to occur if it involves a change in "style" that in turn is maintained by changed beliefs or motives. (Much of the literature just reviewed can be understood in this light.) For example, Baron, Badgio, and Gaskins (1986) carried out an 8-month training program designed to reduce insufficient search ("impulsiveness") and myside bias ("rigidity"). The overall effects were large enough to show up in (blind) teacher ratings of academic performance when children graduated from the school where the training was done and attended new schools

Debiasing. An additional body of relevant literature concerns efforts made to counteract various biases in probability judgment and decision making. Most of the early studies carried out by Kahneman and Tversky, and others, suggested that biases such as neglect of base rates and nonre- gressiveness in prediction tasks could be found even in people who ought to know better, such as groups of mathematical psychologists. These early studies indicated that the biases were not totally removed by such training, but they did not involve systematic comparison of trained and untrained groups.

More systematic studies (reviewed by Fischhoff, 1982) have shown that simply warning students of the existence of a bias does not usually help. Certain biases are, however, overcome through extensive practice with feed- back in a particular domain (e.g., calibration of weather forecasters). In other cases, biases are overcome through instruction to consider evidence against one's original hypothesis (Anderson, 1982; Koriat, Lichtenstein, & Fischhoff, 1980; Slovic & Fischhoff, 1977). Such consideration of reasons on the other side will be a natural part of training in decision analysis. In- deed, it has been argued (e.g., Gardiner & Edwards, 1975) that one of the main advantages of analysis is that it forces consideration of attributes that would ordinarily be ignored or discounted. Recent evidence also indicates that ordinary courses in which decision analytic or statistical questions are discussed can affect the magnitude and prevalence of biases (Fong, Krantz, & Nisbett, 1986, Experiment 4).

Nisbett, Fong, Lehman, and Cheng (1987) provided additional evidence for general effects of instruction in specific academic domains. For exam- ple, statistical and methodological reasoning (e.g., knowledge about the need for control groups) was facilitated by graduate study in psychology and medicine, but not by study of law or chemistry. Formal logical reason- ing was facilitated by study of law, medicine, and psychology, but not chemistry. They also reported additional evidence of transfer after specific training in appropriate heuristics.

Naive Theories? One decision that teachers must make concerns how much to build on what students already know about decision making. Al- ternatively, PDA could be presented as an entirely new method. A great deal of recent work (e.g., Gentner & Stevens, 1983) suggests that students of technical subjects such as physics come into the learning task with "na- ive theories," which are not always replaced by simple instruction. Putting aside the general validity of this claim, it would seem that the rudiments of decision–analytic thinking are already present in most people (Klayman, 1985). There is no real conflict between naive and expert theories, so much as conflict among different naive theories within the same individual. Thus, it seems reasonable to try to build on the thinking of students that already corresponds to decision analysis.

A RESEARCH AND PILOT TEACHING PROGRAM

We are currently embarked on a program to develop and test a PDA-oriented curriculum for teaching decision skills to adolescents, incorporating as best we can the insights developed earlier. In addition to progress reported in this chapter, several elements are dealt with in more detail elsewhere in this volume: the design and evaluation of an eight-session core course (Laskey & Campbell, chap. 6 in this volume); teaching experience with the core course (Graumlich & Baron, chap. 7 in this volume); a four unit follow-on module and experiment involving use of balance beams (Martin & Brown, chap. 10 in this volume); and issues of getting such courses adopted in the schools (Campbell & Laskey, chap. 13 in this volume).

Principles Underlying Curriculum Development

The principal thrust of our research project is to determine whether learning some version of formal decision analysis can help adolescents make sound decisions.

Although our main pedagogical objective is to instill sound analysis of decisions without necessarily using quantitative procedures, our pedagogical hypothesis is that this can be achieved effectively by teaching formal techniques of PDA. If students acquire some facility at analyzing decision problems formally, they will become adept at using informal counterparts of formal analysis in everyday decisions.

The teaching material consists of a combination of: qualitative exposition of principles of good thinking and the common biases that interfere with it; formal quantitative technique to cancel these biases (including worked examples); and discussion of real problems to illustrate quantitative and qualitative analysis and the relation between them. The problem discussions represent the major part of any course session and build loosely on the case method of instruction as practiced at the Harvard Business School (Brown, Kahr, & Peterson, 1974). A major difference is that, whereas all the material in a Harvard business case is supplied in a written case study, our students often draw on their own experiences and available sources of information.

Progress to Date

In all, we taught eight course segments under a variety of circumstances: urban versus suburban, with and without a host teacher, 6th grade to high school, gifted to regular. Details are listed in Appendix B. The material taught covered *Goals*, *Options*, *Outcomes* and *Probabilities*. Decision making was described as "going through the GOOP." The primary quantitative procedures taught were subjective expected utility (SEU) and multiattribute utility analysis (MUA). Pedagogic treatment varied somewhat, partly in response to differences in the circumstances, and partly in response to lessons learned.

A measure of teacher interest in, and comfort with, the program is that five of the six teachers involved in Reston are arranging to adapt and teach the concepts in their regular classes in the year 1989–90, with technical support from decision skills specialists.

General Conclusions About What Students Learned

Three levels of learning are worth distinguishing:

Level 1: Qualitative Concept.   All middle schoolers (possibly even the inner city students with better teaching) can absorb and, with practice, make practical use of the qualitative "GOOP" paradigm (consider Goals, Options, Outcomes, Probabilities), with about eight classes of teaching. These concepts can readily be integrated with any given applied area and can be readily taught by most certified teachers, with no more than a week of in-service training.

Level 2: Quantitative Procedure.   Gifted eighth graders can learn and understand quantitative procedures such as expected utility and multiattribute utility (for addressing decisions where uncertainty and conflicting objectives dominate, respectively), with about four additional classes each. Specifically, they can work through model analyses of preset problems and complete an analysis that has been prestructured by a decision analysis expert. This will serve to enhance basic grasp of issues in a decision. Two days of in-service training on each technique should be sufficient for certified teachers to teach this material. Regular seventh-grade students may develop demonstrable mastery only of qualitative techniques.

Level 3: Useful Application.   It is unrealistic to expect that students, even if led by a very skilled teacher, can use either of the two formal procedures on a new decision problem and have numerical output of real practical value without very substantial training for both students and teacher. The critical skill, which professional decision analysts take years to acquire, is creating the structure of an adequate model and making appropriate use of the model output. However, the qualitative parts of the program appear to have practical value, and the quantitative parts might reinforce the learning of the qualitative ones.

Practical Implications

The core course, as taught at Langston Hughes Middle School in Reston, is probably teachable, as is, as a stand-alone course. It corresponds roughly to Levels 1 and 2 as described and takes up between eight and sixteen classes. Three or four classes would be saved by working with one rather than two of the quantitative paradigms (SEU or MUA).

An equally viable strategy would be to integrate decision analysis concepts and procedures into an existing course, developing the concepts only as needed (as discussed by Swartz & Perkins, 1989). The demands on teacher training would probably not be excessive and would depend on which of the three knowledge levels were targeted. Science, civics, and history appear to be the most natural host courses.

Given institutional realities, intimate integration into an existing curriculum is probably easier to implement than the insertion of a separable module. This approach has the advantage of being acceptable to regular teachers, and of demonstrating to students relevance of the material in a number of subject areas. It has the potential disadvantage that the decision making content may be weakened by teachers whose primary interest is mastery of subject matter content.

MEASURING THE IMPACT OF DECISION TRAINING

The Measurement Problem

Lack of Appropriate Methodology. There is a fairly well-established methodology for evaluating student mastery of the content of decision skill courses, as there is of conventional academic courses. It has been applied, with some distinctive features, to variants of our own core course, with reasonably encouraging results (Laskey & Campbell, chap. 6 in this volume).

However, much less has been done to evaluate the impact of such courses (or indeed of any decision aiding intervention) on the quality of real-life decisions—our primary objective. Promising measures of decision impact have been attempted. Some, for example, are based on self-reported competence (Adams & Feehrer, chap. 4 in this volume); some on performance in contrived experiments with "school solutions" (von Winterfeldt & Edwards, 1986); and some on expert evaluation of hypothetical decisions (Shanteau et al., chap. 9 in this volume).

However, none of them appears to permit very firm inference about real practical impacts. Moreover, we are aware of no persuasive general methodology for gathering appropriate data and drawing appropriate inferences of this kind. Certainly we have not ourselves developed any convincing evidence on whether our students make better choices as a result of our courses. Much less do we have any empirical basis for testing a more important hypothesis: that *some* training along these lines, suitably improved and extended over time, will produce more competent decision making adults. (However, let it be added that conventional school courses have not had to pass comparable tests before being adopted!)

Approach to a Solution. The challenge is twofold: to measure the quality of an actual decision process (e.g., a school graduate applying for his first job); and to gauge the impact on that quality of alternative hypothetical "treatments" (e.g., the effect of a statewide decision-training program on the careers of its graduates).

We propose the following conceptual framework of a methodology for meeting those two challenges. It draws on ideas put forward by Brown, Campbell and Laskey (1990). We are developing plans to implement it in the evaluation of decision courses such as ours.

The essence of our approach is plural evaluation. For any given evaluation task (such as the present one), there may be a number of alternative potential evaluations, each of them flawed in different ways. Pursuing two or more with a view to reconciling any conflicts may yield a credible "plural evaluation" (Brown & Lindley, 1986). Our intent here is to develop an integrated battery of decision quality measurement techniques. The methods are largely fashioned after existing ideas. None stands alone as adequate, but are to be combined into a whole that stands stronger than its parts.

Measuring the Quality of an Observed Decision

By the quality of a decision process, we mean the extent to which it produces decisions that can reasonably be predicted (from available information) to satisfy the goals that the decision maker would have on reflection. In PDA terms this can be interpreted as the decider's expected (probability weighted) utility.

Note that the decider's and society's utility may not always coincide. A satisfying career might contribute to national economic stagnation. A visitor to Russia commented that Gorbachev must be making good decisions, because more people were smiling on the streets of Moscow! However, Gorbachev may be headed for a fall, although the people may thrive.

The decider's utility can be thought of as the product of a process with a causal chain: from the decider's skills, to a decision procedure, to the specific action taken, to the outcome of the action to the utility of the outcome. Any given quality measurement typically focuses on one level in this chain. It may characterize or predict the skills, the procedure, the actions, or the outcomes. In each case the consequences at that level in the chain are evaluated in terms of convenient surrogates for the utility they will lead to.

Brown, Campbell and Laskey (1990) discussed some of these surrogates in more detail, and suggested how they might themselves be empirically and theoretically validated. The following are examples at each level in the chain.

Characterizing the Decider's Skill.   This is the simplest and most common method typified by a written test or exercise.

Characterizing the Decision Procedure.   This is often a comparison with the researcher's conception (often controversial) of an ideal procedure (e.g., "going through the GOOP," in our case). Or, an acknowledged expert in the domain (e.g., career counselor) can judge whether the subject "seems to have gone about his choice the right way."

Characterizing the Action Taken.   Alternatively, we can sample resulting actions and evaluate those. It is usually easier to tell what action has been taken than the procedure that produced it. Note that the quality of an action is not an infallible guide to the quality of the process (an irrational person may make a smart move by dumb luck).

The same two basic approaches to evaluation are available. The researcher can try to determine what the "right" course of action is, for example, by performing his own PDA. (However, there is no assurance his choice is any better than the subject's.) Alternatively, a domain expert can be asked—this time what she/he would have done in the same circumstances (see Shanteau, Grier, Johnson, Berner, chap. 9 in this volume). In a real (rather than hypothetical) situation, a difficulty is in assuring that the subject and expert are using the same information.

Characterizing the Outcome.   It is probably easiest to evaluate an outcome (i.e., we can usually tell if things turned out successfully). However, it is most difficult to predict what outcomes a process will produce, or attribute them to a process after they have occurred unless there is a large sample. (Good decision processes can have bad outcomes, and vice versa.) Candidate outcome measures proposed by Brown, Campbell and Laskey (1990) as surrogates for utility include: subjective reports of regret, decision reversals, objective measures of success (like money), even subjective measures of happiness.

Assessing the Impact of Decision Training

Formulating the Research Task.   Our object is not just to evaluate the quality of actual decision making, though that is clearly important in establishing whether the system is "broke," before going on to figure out whether and how to "fix it." We need also to determine what difference a proposed course would make (or did make) to the quality of a subject's decision process. That process (with or without intervention) may not be available for direct observation. In our example of gauging the long-term effect of a statewide decision training program on the careers of school graduates, the only data we have to go on might be a comparison of the short-term career decisions of students at a certain school, some of whom have taken a pilot decision course.

Figure 5.1 shows, schematically, the measures one might want to take to evaluate the state course just before its introduction (Fig. 5.1a) and then a year afterwards (Fig. 5.1b). The area between the with- and without-intervention curves in each case corresponds to the cumulative net impact of intervention on performance in each case. (Interpretation of this figure and of its implications is given in Brown, Campbell & Laskey, 1990, from which it is reproduced.)

Designing the Research Strategy. The task to be addressed is: how to design research on which such measures can be based, bearing in mind that the research strategy needs to be both feasible (technically and economically) and sound (giving credible conclusions). The research options basically consist of defining each of four standard elements in the design of an experiment (or sample enquiry):

1. Subject—who is tested, and in what control/treatment grouping.
2. Task—what decisions are evaluated.
3. Treatment—what teaching intervention.
4. Response—what is measured.

The researcher's art is to pick a cost-effective combination of these. At each level there is a trade-off between *feasibility* (including cost) and *fidelity* (how faithfully the experiment corresponds to the target effect, i.e., phenomenon of real interest).

For example, one of the most feasible ways of getting subjects would be to find a cooperative (and perhaps atypical) school and look at one class that happens to have had a decision course, and another, for comparison, that has not, as similar as is practicable. For any high degree of fidelity, however, you might (if you could afford it) need to take a representative sample of schools, with control and treatment groups carefully matched. Table 5.1 shows some relatively feasible and some relatively faithful options for each element of research strategy.

The best design depends on available funds, the need for accuracy and how errors (lack of fidelity) in elements combine in a given design. A theo-

TABLE 5.1
Experimental Options for Measuring Target Effect
(career impact of proposed course requirement)

EXPERIMENTAL ELEMENTS TO BE DEFINED	FEASIBLE OPTION	FAITHFUL OPTION
Subjects: in the pool sampled	Convenient school	Representative sample of school system
grouping within pool	Two uncontrolled classes	Two matched and controlled samples
Decision task settings	First job choice	Sequence of career decisions
Teaching treatment	Group pilot course	Extensive proven program
Quality response	Knowledge of material	Lifelong career satisfaction

retical framework for evaluating alternative designs is proposed in Brown (1969). However, its practical implementation is not close, and for now we must almost certainly rely on the ad hoc skill of the researcher.

CONCLUSION

We have argued that there is a need for training in decision making. The consequences of poor decision making are so severe that teachers need not be hesitant to try to influence students for the better. Although some students may see instruction in decision making as an intrusion, the same may be said for instruction in history. In the long run, most students will be grateful for the training in decision making that they and others have received. (Bad decisions affect others as well as those who make them.)

We have argued further that the formal theory of decision analysis provides a good starting point for instruction. PDA may someday be seen as yet another case in which a scholarly field has made its way into the curriculum—just as various social sciences have made their way to form what we now call social studies, and just as the mathematics and natural sciences once accessible only to scholars are now considered routine. PDA is one of the unique contributions of the social sciences to human affairs, and it should be appreciated as such by our educational system.

We have discussed a body of literature indicating that PDA is within the intellectual grasp of those who need to learn it. We have developed and tried out specific courses; the results suggest not only that the task is feasi-

(Decision Skills Course)

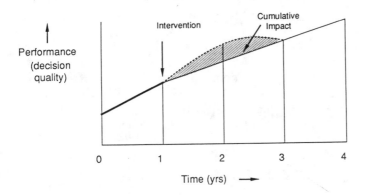

a. Assessed before intervention takes place

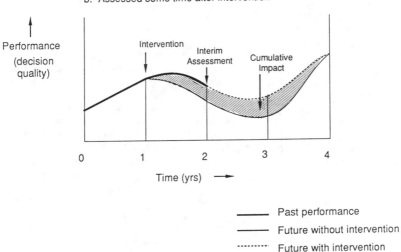

b. Assessed some time after intervention

——— Past performance

——— Future without intervention

·········· Future with intervention

FIG. 5.1 Evaluating the impact of an intervention. [Reproduced with permission from Brown, Campbell, & Laskey (1990)].

ble but also that materials developed are already usable and useful. And finally, we have explored ways in which the practical impact of courses such as these might be realistically evaluated.

Of course, much work remains to be done in the development of approaches that succeed in capturing the interest of children, especially those who are not already intellectually motivated, in helping them make and understand real decisions. The major challenge ahead, however, and one we are just beginning to grapple with, may be to overcome institutional hurdles to adding radically new curriculum, however valuable, in already overburdened school systems. (See Campbell & Laskey, chapter 13 in this volume.)

ACKNOWLEDGMENTS

This work was supported by the National Institute of Child Health and Human Development under grant #2-R44-HD23071-02 to Decision Science Consortium, Inc. The paper has benefited from many helpful suggestions from Dr. Kathryn B. Laskey and Dr. Vincent N. Campbell.

REFERENCES

Anderson, C. A. (1982). Inoculation and counterexplanation: Debiasing techniques in the perseverance of social theories. *Social Cognition, 1,* 126–139.

Arkes, H. R., & Blumer, C. (1985). The psychology of sunk cost. *Organizational Behavior and Human Decision Processes, 35,* 124–140.

Baron, J. (1978). Intelligence and general strategies. In G. Underwood (Ed.), *Strategies in information processing* (pp. 403–450). New York: Academic Press.

Baron, J. (1985). *Rationality and intelligence.* New York: Cambridge University Press.

Baron, J. (1988). *Thinking and deciding.* New York: Cambridge University Press.

Baron, J. (1989, August). *Actively open-minded thinking versus myside bias: Causes and effects.* Paper presented at the Fourth International Conference on Thinking, San Juan, Puerto Rico.

Baron, J. (in press a). Harmful heuristics and poor thinking. In D. Kuhn (Ed.), *Developmental perspectives on teaching and learning thinking skills.* Basel: Karger.

Baron, J. (in press b). Beliefs about thinking. In J. F. Voss, D. N. Perkins, and J. W. Segal (Eds.), *Informal reasoning and education.* Hillsdale, NJ: Lawrence Erlbaum Associates.

Baron, J., Badgio, P., & Gaskins, I. W. (1986). Cognitive style and its improvement: a normative approach. In R. J. Sternberg (Ed.), *Advances in the psychology of human intelligence, Vol. 3* pp. 173–220. Hillsdale, NJ: Lawrence Erlbaum Associates.

Baron, J., & Hershey, J. C. (1988). Outcome bias in decision evaluation. *Journal of Personality and Social Psychology, 54,* 569–579.

Belmont, J. M., Butterfield, E. C., & Feretti, R. P. (1982). To secure transfer of training instruct self-management skills. In D. K. Detterman & R. J. Sternberg (Eds.), *How and how much can intelligence be increased?* Norwood, NJ: Ablex.

Brown, A. L., Campione, J. C., & Barclay, C. R. (1979). Training self-checking routines for estimating test readiness: generalization from list learning to prose recall. *Child Development, 50,* 501–512.

Brown, A. L., & Palincsar, A. S. (1982). Inducing strategic learning from texts by means of informed, self-control training. *Topics in Learning and Learning Disabilities, 2,* 1–17.

Brown, R. V. (1969). *Research and the credibility of estimates.* Boston: Harvard University, Graduate School of Business Administration, Division of Research.

Brown, R. V. (1987). Decision analytic tools in government. In Karen B. Levitan (Ed.), *Government infostructures.* Westport, CT: Greenwood Press.

Brown, R. V., Campbell, V. N., & Laskey, K. B. (1990). *Measuring decision quality with application to career strategy and the impact of decision courses.* Unpublished working paper, Reston, VA: Decision Science Consortium, Inc.

Brown, R. V., Kahr, A. S., & Peterson, C. R. (1974). *Decision analysis for the manager.* New York: Holt, Rinehart & Winston.

Brown, R. V., & Lindley, D. V. (1986). Plural analysis: Multiple approaches to quantitative research. *Theory and Decision, 20,* 133–154.

Deci, E. L., & Ryan, R. M. (1985). *Intrinsic motivation and self-determination in human behavior.* New York: Plenum.

Fischhoff, B. (1982). Debiasing. In D. Kahneman, P. Slovic, & A. Tversky (Eds.), *Judgment under uncertainty: Heuristics and biases* (pp. 422–444). New York: Cambridge University Press.

Fong, G. T., Krantz, D. H., & Nisbett, R. E. (1986). The effects of statistical training on thinking about everyday problems. *Cognitive Psychology, 18,* 253–292.

Frey, D. (1986). Recent research on selective exposure to information. In L. Berkowitz (Ed.), *Advances in experimental social psychology* (Vol. 19, pp. 41–80). New York: Academic Press.

Gardiner, P. C., & Edwards, W. (1975). Public values: multiattribute utility measurement for social decision-making. In M. F. Kaplan & S. Schwartz (Eds.), *Human judgment and decision processes.* New York: Academic Press.

Gentner, D., & Stevens, A. L. (Eds.). (1983). *Mental models.* Hillsdale, NJ: Lawrence Erlbaum Associates.

Gick, M. L., & Holyoak, K. J. (1983). Schema induction and analogical transfer. *Cognitive Psychology, 15,* 1–38.

Hoch, S. J. (1985). Counterfactual reasoning and accuracy in predicting personal events. *Journal of Experimental Psychology: Learning, Memory, and Cognition, 11,* 719–731.

Janis, I. L., & Mann, L. (1977). *Decision making: A psychological analysis of conflict, choice, and commitment.* New York: Free Press.

Kahneman, D., Slovic, P., & Tversky, A. (Eds.). (1982). *Judgment under uncertainty: Heuristics and biases.* New York: Cambridge University Press.

Kahneman, D., & Tversky, A. (1981). The framing of decisions and the psychology of choice. *Science, 211,* 453–458.

Kahneman, D., & Tversky, A. (1984). Choices, values, and frames. *American Psychologist, 39,* 341–35.

Katona, G. (1940). *Organizing and memorizing: Studies in the psychology of learning and teaching.* New York: Columbia University Press.

Keeney, R. L., & Raiffa, H. (1976). *Decisions with multiple objectives.* New York: Wiley.

Klayman, J. (1985). Children's decision strategies and their adaptation to task characteristics. *Organizational Behavior and Human Decision Processes, 25,* 179–201.

Koriat, A., Lichtenstein, S., & Fischhoff, B. (1980). Reasons for confidence. *Journal of Experimental Psychology: Human Learning and Memory, 6,* 107–118.

Kruglanski, A. W., & Ajzen, I. (1983). Bias and error in human judgment. *European Journal of Social Psychology, 13,* 1–44.

Lepper, M. R., & Greene, D. (Eds.). (1978). *The hidden costs of reward.* Hillsdale, NJ: Lawrence Erlbaum Associates.

Lord, C. G., Ross, L., & Lepper, M. R. (1979). Biased assimilation and attitude polarization: The effects of prior theories on subsequently considered evidence. *Journal of Personality and Social Psychology, 37,* 2098–2109.

Messer, S. B. (1976). Reflection-impulsivity: A review. *Psychological Bulletin, 83,* 1026–1052.

Messick, D. M. (1985). Social interdependence and decision making. In G. Wright (Ed.), *Behavioral decision making.* New York: Plenum.

Montgomery, H. (1984). Decision rules and the search for dominance structure: Towards a process model of decision making. In P. C. Humphreys, O. Svenson, & A. Vari (Eds.), *Analyzing and aiding decision processes*. Amsterdam: North Holland.

National Assessment of Educational Progress (NAEP). (1981). *Reading, thinking, and writing: Results from the 1979-1980 national assessment of reading and literature*. Report No. 11-L-01 Denver, CO: Education Commission of the States.

National Commission on Excellence in Education. (1983). *A nation at risk: The imperative for educational reform*. Washington DC: U.S. Government Printing Office.

Nisbett, R. E., Fong, G. T., Lehman, D. R., & Cheng, P. W. (1987). Teaching reasoning. *Science, 238*, 625-631.

Nisbett, R. & Ross, L. (1980). *Human inference: strategies and shortcomings of social judgment*. Englewood Cliffs, NJ: Prentice-Hall.

Parfit, D. (1984). *Reasons and persons*. Oxford: Clarendon Press.

Perkins, D. N. (1986). *Knowledge as design: Critical and creative thinking or teachers and learners*. Hillsdale, NJ: Lawrence Erlbaum Associates.

Perkins, D. N. (in press). Reasoning as it is and could be: An empirical perspective. In D. Topping, D. Crowell, & V. Kobayashi (Eds.), *Thinking across cultures: The third international conference on thinking*. Hillsdale, NJ: Lawrence Erlbaum Associates.

Perkins, D. N., Bushey, B., & Faraday, M. (1986). *Learning to reason*. Unpublished manuscript, Harvard Graduate School of Education.

Raiffa, H. (1968). *Decision analysis*. Reading, MA: Addison-Wesley, 1968.

Ritov, I., & Baron, J. (in press). Reluctance to vaccinate: Commission bias and ambiguity. *Journal of Behavioral Decision Making*.

Rostow, W. W. (1971). *The stages of economic growth*. New York: Cambridge University Press.

Savage, L. J. (1954). *The foundations of statistics*. New York: Wiley.

Schleser, R., Meyers, A. W., & Cohen, R. (1981). Generalization of self instructions: effects of general versus specific content, active rehearsal, and cognitive level. *Child Development, 52*, 335-340.

Siegler, R. S. (1976). Three aspects of cognitive development. *Cognitive Psychology, 8*, 481-520.

Siegler, R. S. (1981). Developmental sequences within and between concepts. *Monographs of the Society for Research in Child Development, 46* (2, Serial No. 189).

Siegler, R. S. (1985). Encoding and the development of problem solving. In S. F. Chipman, J. W. Segal, & R. Glaser (Eds.), *Thinking and learning skills. Vol. 2: Research and open questions* (pp. 161-185). Hillsdale, NJ: Lawrence Erlbaum Associates.

Slovic, P. (1975). Choice between equally valued alternatives. *Journal of Experimental Psychology: Human Perception and Performance, 1*, 280-287.

Slovic, P., & Fischhoff, B. (1977). On the psychology of experimental surprises. *Journal of Experimental Psychology: Human Perception and Performance, 3*, 544-551.

Spranca, M., Minsk, E., & Baron, J. (in press). Omission and commission in judgment and choice. *Journal of Experimental Social Psychology*.

Steinlauf, B. (1979). Problem-solving skills, locus of control, and the contraceptive effectiveness of young women. *Child Development, 50*, 268-271.

Swartz, R. J., & Perkins, D. N. (1989). *Teaching thinking: Issues and approaches*. Pacific Grove, CA: Midwest Publications.

Thaler, R. (1980). Toward a positive theory of consumer choice. *Journal of Economic Behavior and Organization, 1*, 39-60.

Thaler, R. (1983). *Mental accounting and consumer choice*. Unpublished manuscript, Cornell University, Ithaca, NY.

Thaler, R. H., & Shefrin, H. M. (1981). An economic theory of self-control. *Journal of Political Economy, 89*, 392-406.

Tversky, A., Sattath, S., & Slovic, P. (1988). Contingent weighing in judgment and choice. *Psychological Review, 95,* 371–384.

Ulvila, J. W., & Brown, R. V. (1982, September–October). Decision analysis comes of age. *Harvard Business Review,* pp. 130–141.

von Winterfeldt, D., & Edwards, W. (1986). *Decision analysis and behavioral research.* New York: Cambridge University Press.

Watson, S. R., & Buede, D. M. (1987). *Decision synthesis: The principles and practice of decision analysis.* New York: Cambridge University Press.

Wertheimer, M. (1945). *Productive thinking.* New York: Harper & Row.

Woodrow, H. (1927). The effect of type of training upon transference. *Journal of Educational Psychology, 18,* 159–172.

APPENDIX A: ILLUSTRATIVE ANALYSIS
OF A PERSONAL DECISION

The following true example was used as a running case to illustrate the decision analysis techniques taught in one iteration of the decision skills core course (in fact the seventh grade version described in Laskey & Campbell, chap. 6 in this volume).

Author Brown, at the outset of the course in the Spring of 1989, was faced with the decision of what do about a somewhat painful arthritic hip. His doctor's initial opinion had been that he was too young at age 55, and the condition was not yet bad enough, to justify a hip replacement operation. "Give it another five years, and see if its gets worse." However, he was prepared to go along with whatever Brown wanted.

An appointment was set up for two months later to render a decision— in fact just after the end of the decision skills course. Throughout the course, the concepts and techniques developed were exercised in the context of this problem, and on the last day of class a majority of students recommended that he have the operation right away—and he did.

Central Multiattribute Analysis.   Table A-1 shows the main analysis that preceded the vote. It was synthesized by the author from input developed by the class in the course of interrogating him about his values and uncertainties. (He thus served in the dual capacity of case discussion leader and consulting client.)

First, options were narrowed down to two: to have the operation at the next available opportunity (in June), or to wait at least a few more years. (Other possible options, such as exploring alternative "resurfacing" treatments, were discarded on informal grounds.) Then pros and cons (attributes) were elicited from the "client," with the importance of each reflected in the number of pluses or minuses. Absence of either indicated that things got neither better nor worse than they were now. Netting out pluses/minuses indicated that under both options things were expected to get worse, but having the operation now was better than waiting (two rather than four minuses). This therefore appeared the preferable option.

TABLE A-1
Evaluation by Attributes of Hip Replacement Decision

	OPTION I		OPTION II	
ATTRIBUTES	REGULAR OPERATION NOW		WAIT UNTIL WORSE	
	Effect of option	Score	Effect of option	Score
Inconvenience now	Give Blood	–	Maybe later	
Risk of death	Slight	–	Maybe later	
Fear of operation	Bone sawed	– –	Maybe later	–
Cost of operation	$5,000	–	Maybe later	
Pain of operation	Some	–	Maybe later	
Inconvenience after operation	Month out of action	–	Maybe later	
Regular exercise	O.K.	+ + +	Less and less	– –
Comfort	O.K.	+ +	Not too bad, but get worse	–
NET EVALUATION		– – [a]		– – – –

[a]Preferred option

Supplementary Analysis of Uncertainties. The preceding analysis takes no explicit account of a number of important uncertainties, although implicitly they influence the pluses and minuses in Table A-1, (e.g., a high probability of dying on the operating table would increase the minuses for the attribute "risk of death" under Option I).

To help make sure that uncertainties were adequately considered, the key ones were identified and quantified, as shown in Table A-2, again based on questioning the "client." No attempt was made to incorporate these events and probabilities into any further formalization (such as the maximization of expected utility), but the students were encouraged to bear them in mind when making their final recommendation. They could do so, either by reconsidering the pluses and minuses they had assessed earlier in each row, or by adjusting the final tally for each option to reflect a holistic sense of the impact of new thinking about uncertainties.

The net effect of this final round of analysis was to make the "operate now" less attractive relative to "wait" (no doubt because of a greater attention to its attendant risks, even though these were seen as not particularly serious). Nevertheless, most students still considered it the preferred option—as did the client patient.

He notified the doctor, who accepted the rationale and went along with the decision. The operation was a complete success.

Technical Observation. Note that Table A-1 amounts essentially to a simple multiattribute utility analysis (MUA). However, unlike conventional PDA versions of PDA, the utility contributions from each attribute are not decomposed into importance weights and scores. (Some students were so-

TABLE A-2
Supplementary Probability Analysis of Hip Replacement Decision

OPTION I: REGULAR OPERATION NOW		
POSSIBLE OUTCOMES	PROBABILITY	
Operation has to be redone eventually	Unlikely	5%
Insurance won't pay (claim operation is "not necessary")	Fairly unlikely	10%
Operation doesn't work	Very unlikely	1%
Die on operating table	Extremely unlikely	.1%

OPTION II: WAIT TILL HIP GETS WORSE		
POSSIBLE OUTCOMES	PROBABILITY	
Less nasty treatment becomes available	Could happen	30%
Die before operation is necessary	Unlikely	5%

phisticated enough to realize pluses and minuses might not simply add, so that net minuses would need adjusting, for example, to allow for double counting in the attributes.)

In fact author Brown's own analysis of his decision corresponded very closely to this model. In particular, he also chose a simple model structure, which did not decompose utility contributions into importance and score. (Unlike conventional linear additive multiattribute utility models, which, he believes, impose an unnecessarily distracting burden for most personal decisions, even for professional decision analysts, as in this case). He also took account of uncertainty in substantially the same form as Table A-2, and in the same informal way. This reflects his general view that PDA should be more intuition-intensive and less model-intensive than is commonly the case. There were some distinguishing features of his private analysis. A few subtle additional attributes were added. Allowance was made for nonadditivity of some attributes. The evaluation of attribute contributions to utility was more finely graduated than a whole number of pluses or minuses, and involved a good deal more complex deliberation than was shared with the class. However, the prescription for action came out the same as from the class analysis.

APPENDIX B: COURSES TAUGHT AS PART OF DSC PROJECT

List of courses developed and taught by researchers involved in a DSC project entitled, "A Formal Approach to Teaching Children Decision Making," and sponsored by the National Institute of Child Health and Human Development, Grant #2-R44-HD23071.

Introductory Core Course

- Langston Hughes Intermediate School, Reston, VA: Fall 1988. 8th Grade G&T English/Social Studies Class. Taught by Kathryn Laskey with pre- and post-test administered by Vincent Campbell. Host Teachers: Ellen Rugel and Beth Myers. 8 units of 50 minutes.
- Langston Hughes Intermediate School, Reston, VA: Spring 1989. 7th Grade Science Class. Taught by Kathryn Laskey with pre- and post-tests administered by Vincent Campbell. Host Teacher: Katy Davis. 8 units of 50 Minutes.
- University of Pennsylvania Discovery Program, 1988. Saturday morning program for gifted 5th to 8th graders. Taught by Jonathan Baron. 4 sessions, 2 hours each.
- Parkway School (10th Grade, inner city), Philadelphia, PA: 1988–1989 School year. Taught by Jonathan Baron. No host teacher. 14 units of 45 minutes. Taught twice.
- Houston Elementary School (6th Grade, gifted enrichment class), Philadelphia, PA: Taught and hosted by Greer Graumlich. 1988–1989. School Year. 11 units of 60 minutes.

Science Add-on Module (Balance Beams)

- Langston Hughes Intermediate School, Reston, VA: Spring 1989. 8th Grade G&T Science. Taught by Rex Brown with analog device testing performed by Anne Martin and Nancy Poudrier. Host teacher: Mary Bailey. 4 units of 50 minutes.

Special Introductory Segment on Probability and Expected Value

- Langston Hughes Intermediate School, Reston, VA: Spring 1989. 7th grade math class. Taught by Anne Martin. Host teacher: Carol Isaacs. 4 units of 50 minutes.

Plans by host teachers for integration of decision making skills into regular course curriculum at Langston Hughes in the 1989/90 school year are as follows:

Katy Davis:	7th Grade Science
Mary Bailey:	8th Grade Science and in TA Working Group
Carol Isaacs:	8th Grade Math
Beth Myers and Ellen Rugel:	8th Grade Combined Social Studies/English (Career decisions).

Chapter 6

Evaluation of an Intermediate Level Decision Analysis Course

Kathryn Blackmond Laskey
Decision Science Consortium, Inc.
Reston, VA

Vincent N. Campbell
Decision Systems, Inc.
Reston, VA

INTRODUCTION

A democratic society depends on a citizenry with the ability to think critically about issues facing society and make intelligent decisions about how society should respond to these issues. Increasingly, the American economy depends on a workforce that can think and make decisions at a level of sophistication much higher than that required of previous generations. The research described in this chapter responds to a growing call for instruction in critical thinking and decision making.

Good decision making can be defined as thinking that leads to choices that are most likely to satisfy the goals that the thinker would have on reflection (Baron, 1985, 1988). The basic hypothesis addressed by our research is that decision-making skills can be improved by formal instruction in the principles and techniques of good decision making. To test this hypothesis, we have developed and evaluated a unit in decision making for intermediate school students. The intermediate level was chosen because this is the age at which children begin to be able to think more formally, and because they make decisions at this age that will affect the future course of their lives.

The course adapts techniques drawn from personalized decision analysis (PDA) to the intermediate level. PDA draws from decision theory, cognitive science, and recent work in critical thinking to create systematic decision-making methods that complement people's natural decision making strengths while compensating for natural weaknesses. The PDA course teaches students to think systematically about their goals for a decision, the options they face, and the likely outcomes of each option. They learn to organize this information in a standard format. This systematic approach encourages students to take account of all the relevant information as they make a decision. Students are taught to weigh uncertainty and their trade-offs between goals both qualitatively and quantitatively.

The remainder of this chapter is organized as follows. The next section describes the decision making unit as it was taught in a Fairfax County, Virginia, intermediate school. The following section presents our methodology for formally evaluating the effect of the course, and the results of the evaluation. We then describe informal evaluations performed as part of the teaching project. The final section summarizes our conclusions and discusses what we have learned from the experience of teaching the course.

A UNIT IN DECISION ANALYSIS

Course Content

The decision analysis unit described in this section (Baron, Laskey, & Brown, 1989) was designed for early adolescents. Versions of the unit have been taught to gifted eighth-grade students and to seventh-grade students at Langston Hughes Intermediate School in Fairfax County, Virginia. The unit was also taught to tenth-grade students in a Philadelphia inner city school and a variant of it to sixth graders in a Philadelphia gifted program. This chapter presents evaluation results for the Fairfax County students only.

The Fairfax County classes were taught by one of the authors (Laskey), with the regular classroom teacher observing and helping at times to direct the class discussion. The classroom teachers plan to adapt the material and teach it as part of their curriculum in the future.

The unit teaches personalized decision analysis (PDA) using decision problems designed to mirror the kinds of situations faced by the students in their lives. The unit consists of eight lessons, each taking one 50-minute class session. Because the unit was evolving as it was being taught, the specific content of the lessons varied for the classes in which the course was taught. The following unit description applies to the most recently taught set of lessons, the version taught to the Fairfax County seventh graders.

The most basic goal of the unit is to teach students a systematic procedure for reflecting on decision problems and determining the option that best satisfies their goals. The lessons stress that good decision making depends on *process* more than *product*. That is, the quality of the product of decision making depends on the quality of the process by which that product was generated.

In qualitative terms, PDA is a systematic way of reflecting on and incorporating into the decision process the answers to the following three questions:

1. What do I want?
2. What can I do?
3. What might happen?

Our decision-making unit teaches students an acronym to help them remember this process: Good decision makers go through the GOOP. That is, good decision makers:

1. Determine the *Goals* that are important to them.
2. Examine the *Options* available to them.
3. Predict the *Outcomes* of each option.
4. Consider the *Probabilities* of any outcomes that are uncertain.

Students learn that good decision makers systematically consider each of the GOOP elements before making a decision, and select the option for which the probable outcomes best satisfy the decision maker's goals. Each of the structured decision analytic techniques presented to the students (multiattribute utility analysis, expected utility analysis) is presented as a way to systematically take GOOP elements into account in making a decision.

The course was first taught in the fall of 1988 to a double class of 48 gifted eighth graders. It became clear that the scope was ambitious for eight lessons, even for gifted eighth graders. When the course was repeated for seventh graders in the spring of 1989, two lessons were dropped and the remaining six lessons were expanded into eight. A brief review follows of the expanded eight-lesson unit, as well as the two lessons taught only to the eighth graders.

Lesson 1: Decisions—Good or Bad?

In this lesson, the GOOP framework is presented in the context of a decision that the group analyzes. The decision problem should be of interest to the students. (We were fortunate that a member of the course development team was actually facing an important decision: whether to have an operation to replace an arthritic hip with an artificial joint). The decision problem is presented to the class. Students ask questions and offer suggestions. At appropriate points in the discussion, the teacher introduces the words *goals, options, outcomes,* and *probabilities.* Students, teacher, and

Analysis of: 1988 Presidential Election

Attributes:	Option: DUKAKIS		Option: BUSH	
STRONG ECONOMY	Economy stronger	✓	Economy weaker	
CLEAN ENVIRON-MENT	Probably won't be better		Stay the same or better	✓
DEATH PENALTY	NOT HAVE		Yes for serious crimes & drug dealers	✓
LOWER CRIME	Worse or stay same		Same or better	✓
STRONG DEFENSE	Defense will lower		Stable or stronger	✓
DRUG PROBLEM	Get people involved, reduce a little		lower a lot	✓
NUCLEAR WEAPONS	reduce		keep as is	✓
POVERTY	help	✓	some help	
SOCIAL SECURITY	help/improve	✓	not much	

Other options:

FIG. 6.1 Example Multiattribute Chart. The responses shown here are those of one of the eighth grade students.

class guest together write the decision maker's goals, options, outcomes, probabilities, and recommended decision on a GOOP worksheet. Time is reserved at the end of class for students to form small groups and begin filling out a GOOP worksheet for another example problem.

Lesson 2: Decisions Affecting Multiple Goals

In this lesson, students learn a qualitative version of multiattribute utility analysis. Again in the context of a decision problem, they learn to identify a set of *attributes,* or dimensions that measure how well each option satisfies the decision maker's goals. They are given a template *multiattribute chart,* which lists attributes down the left side and options across the top (a sample is shown as Fig. 6.1). Each entry in the table is a verbal description of the predicted outcome with respect to the corresponding attribute if the corresponding option is chosen. The class fills out a multiattribute chart together and discusses the recommended decision. Then students break into small groups and begin working on a multiattribute chart for a problem to be finished as homework. Students learn that the multiattribute chart helps to avoid *single-mindedness*, or making a decision on the basis of one goal that seems most important at the moment. Students learn that it is common for decision makers to neglect non-salient goals. Among the commonly neglected goals are the future consequences of our decisions and the effects of our decisions on other people.

Lesson 3: Weighing Goals

Students learn a numerical technique for scoring each option using a multiattribute chart. First, each cell in the table is assigned a number between 0 and 100, called the *simple utility* of that option on that attribute. The simple utility measures how desirable the outcome is with respect to that attribute, with 0 meaning "very bad" and 100 meaning "very good." Next, students assign a *weight* to each attribute. The weight measures the importance of that attribute to the decision maker. Weights are multiplied by simple utilities to form *weighted utilities*, and the weighted utilities for an option are summed to form its *total utility*. The numerical analysis recommends the option with the highest weighted utility, but students are encouraged to use the analysis only as a guide. The class as a group fills out a numerical multiattribute chart for one of the decision problems from the previous class. Then the class breaks into small groups to begin working on another problem.

Lesson 4: Using Multiattribute Analysis to Make Decisions

The purpose of this class is to review the techniques discussed so far (GOOP analysis, qualitative multiattribute analysis, and quantitative multiattribute analysis), to assess the kinds of decision problems for which each might be a useful aid, and to discuss how the analysis fits into the actual decision-making process. The question is discussed whether the option that scores highest on a numerical multiattribute analysis *has* to be the best choice. Sources of error in numerical analyses are discussed: incorrectly assessed numbers, missing attributes, double counting of attributes. (One student in the eighth grade gifted class spontaneously raised the issue that attributes may combine nonadditively; this point was not raised with the seventh graders.) Even after doing a multiattribute analysis, students' justifications of recommended decisions tend to sound single-minded, and students tend not to mention the bad features of their recommended decision. This tendency is pointed out and discussed: Multiattribute analysis helps us to remember to weigh *both* pluses and minuses of each option. Students are taught a simple technique for generating new options or modifying existing ones: Try to modify an option to improve its score on the attributes on which it scores poorly, or try to combine two options to get the best feature of both.

Lesson 5: Unknown Outcomes and Evidence

In this lesson, students explicitly consider the uncertainty associated with decisions. Students identify uncertainties in several sample decision problems, and identify the possible outcomes of the uncertain events. They discuss how important those uncertainties are to the decision. Students discuss, for several decision problems, ways of gathering information to reduce the uncertainty. For each problem, students evaluate different sources of information and discuss which are most and least credible. The concept of *probability* is introduced as a way of describing our degree of uncertainty about outcomes. Likelihood terminology (very likely; toss-up; unlikely; nearly impossible) is introduced.

Lesson 6: Probability as a Guide to Action

Often evidence gathering does not eliminate uncertainty. Students learn in this lesson how to use what they know about uncertain outcomes to decide which option to choose. The best option to choose depends both on *how good* and *how probable* is each of its outcomes. Students begin on a problem in which only one of these dimensions varies (e.g., whether to use a pinch hitter with a .230 or a .310 average). They then consider cases in which both dimensions vary. A probability chart is given as a template. Students list the possible outcomes for each option and give a verbal description of the probability of each outcome. A probability chart is filled out in class for a sample problem, and students begin working in small groups on a second problem.

Lesson 7: Probability Weighing of Unknown Outcomes

In this lesson, students learn to compute a *probability weighted utility*, or expected utility, for options involving uncertainty. On one of the problems analyzed in the previous class, students assign utilities and probabilities to the possible outcomes for each option. The utility of each option is multiplied by its probability, and the values are summed to get the *expected utility* for each option. In our class, we used a balance beam to illustrate probability weighted utility. Each arm of the beam represents an option. Weights corresponding to the probabilities are hung at distances from the fulcrum corresponding to utilities. The side that goes down when the beam is released is the side with the highest expected utility. Changes in probabilities and utilities are explored both numerically and via the beam to explore their effect on expected utility. At the end of the class, students begin working on an expected utility analysis of a new decision problem. (In chapter 10, Martin & Brown describe a set of experiments using the balance beam to represent probability weighted utility.)

Lesson 8: Review: Techniques for Good Decision Making

This lesson reviews the fundamentals of good decision making: It is actively open-minded, it considers goals, options, outcomes, and probabilities. Students consider one or more sample decisions, and review the techniques they learned in class. Students recall problems that can occur when decisions are made without sufficient thought. Common decision-making errors are discussed in terms of the GOOP framework: goals may be neglected; decisions may be made on the basis of a single salient attribute; not all options may be considered; decision makers may assume that the outcome they want will happen; decision makers may fail to think of a possible outcome; uncertainties may be neglected; and decision makers may fail to act according to their better judgment. Going through the GOOP before making a decision is a systematic way to avoid the thinking errors that can cause poor decision making.

Additional Lesson A: Present and Future

The first additional lesson examined decisions involving future consequences. It was pointed out that people commonly neglect to consider future consequences in making decisions, and that this neglect can contribute to poor decision making in areas such as drug use, study habits, and sexual behavior. Students discussed whether some degree of neglect of the future was justified. Ways of policing ourselves to avoid the temptation of the moment and act according to our better judgment were discussed.

Additional Lesson B: Self and Others

The second additional lesson examined social dilemmas, or decisions in which individual benefit conflicts with societal or group benefit. Examples included deciding whether to litter, to pay one's taxes, to recycle, to do one's share of the housework, and to take a shortcut across the grass. Students played a simple social dilemma game as a class exercise and structured the social dilemma as a multiattribute problem with attributes dealing with benefit to oneself and to society. Students discussed the ethics of social dilemma decisions and what societies could do to foster more cooperative behavior.

Another difference between grades was that information gathering and source credibility were covered in the seventh-grade lessons on uncertainty, but were omitted in the eighth grade due to time pressure.

Pedagogy

The basic pedagogical format was an instructor-led class discussion, followed by small-group work on an assignment to be completed at home. (There were instances, especially in the eighth-grade class, in which no time remained for small-group work at the end of the period.) Usually the instructor worked on an example decision-making chart on an overhead projector, while students followed on their own copies. The instructor elicited discussion about the decision problem, suggestions on what to write on the chart, and comments about the completed example. The example then served as a template for the small-group exercise.

When possible, additional tools and activities were incorporated. A guest was brought into the class to discuss a real decision problem he was facing. This aroused students' interest and provided a concrete example of the utility of the techniques they were learning. A balance beam was used to illustrate the concept of expected utility. In the eighth-grade class, the class played a social dilemma game that made concrete the effect of individual actions on the collective good, and the need for mechanisms to encourage cooperation. Also in the eighth-grade class several games were used to illustrate probability concepts.

FORMAL EVALUATION OF DECISION-MAKING COURSE

A set of short term and long term student skill objectives was formulated at the start of the project, and students' progress toward these objectives was carefully evaluated for each of the two Fairfax County courses. Although the course was evolving as it was being taught, instruction remained directed toward these core objectives.

For both the seventh- and eighth-grade courses, the primary evaluation instrument was a performance test given at the start of the course, and again at the end using a parallel form of the test. This appears to be the first time a decision skills performance test has been used to evaluate a curriculum, as nearly as we can tell from the available literature (cf., Beyth-Marom et al., chap. 2 in this volume).

In addition, a questionnaire asking students for their own appraisals of the course was given at the end. Observation of student reactions and difficulties during each class, and discussion with the regular class teachers (who observed the classes) provided an ongoing informal evaluation, and was the basis for many changes made during the course.

Performance Test

The test was constructed, tried out on a few students not in the course, and revised in preparation for its use in this evaluation. The test consisted mainly of a set of exercises or decision problems. It measured transfer of skills to new situations, in that the decision problems in the tests were not those used during instruction. The formats for analysis in the test also differed in minor ways from those used in class.

A sample problem (WENDY) is shown as Fig. 6.2 to illustrate the approach used.

Note that the open-ended answer to "How did you decide this?" was completed and handed in before the student saw the structured analysis that followed. The purpose was to assess what the student would do without a structure first, then to assess the student's understanding of the specific analysis framework presented. The sequence of exercises in the test as a whole also followed this principle. Exercises providing no structure at all were given first, then exercises such as WENDY which had both an unstructured and a structured part.

For the eighth-grade tests, the sequence of exercises is shown as Fig. 6.3. Forms S and D are parallel forms of the test.

Table 6.1 lists the course objectives addressed in the evaluation, and shows which exercises were used to measure progress toward those objectives. All exercises except PROBABILITY had an open-ended response asking how to decide an issue as the initial question. These open-ended questions were scored on several objectives.

The eighth-grade results showed clearly that students did not report applying formal decision analysis to their own life decisions, and it was thought even less likely that seventh graders would do so. The critical incident exercise (Exercise GOOD in Table 6.1) was therefore omitted for the 7th grade pre- and posttests. Minor wording changes in CITY, WILLIAM, and ACID were also made before use with the seventh graders. The only other grade level difference in the tests was that in the seventh grade ACID was moved in the sequential order from third to last.

Experimental Design

Eighth grade. In the eighth grade, a control class was given performance tests on the same pre- and posttest days as the taught class. The control class, also a double class, had the same teachers and comparable students to the taught class. Both were G & T classes to which the assignment criteria were not discernibly different, so the students in the two classes were treated as random samples from the same population.

All 48 students in the taught class were given Form S as a pretest and Form D as a posttest. This was intended to enable the teacher to use the pretest items for instructional purposes, if needed, while retaining Form D as new content (except ACID) for the posttest.

The 45 students in the control class were divided randomly into four subgroups, as follows:

It's late August and Wendy has just been given money to buy a winter coat. Last year's coat is too small now, so she has to get a new one. She shops around and finds two she likes, but each one has some advantages and disadvantages. Here are her thoughts:

The brown coat is more stylish, so I like its looks better. Style is the most important thing to me.

The blue coat matches my other clothes better, so I could wear it with more outfits. This advantage is almost as important as the style difference. The blue coat also costs less, and I can use whatever I save to buy something else I want. This cost saving is as important to me as the difference in matching other clothes, but less important than the style difference.

The brown coat is a little heavier, and will keep me warmer when it is very cold. However, I can always wear a sweater inside, so warmth is far less important to me than any of the other differences.

Which items in the list below are Wendy's choices (options)? Write "C" beside those items. Write "V" beside the items which are values or goals (attributes) that Wendy used to evaluate her options. Write "N" beside an item that is neither a value nor a choice.

_____ Buying the brown coat
_____ How well her coat matches her other clothes
_____ What she thinks of the style of a coat
_____ Whether she will get the money to buy a coat
_____ Buying the blue coat
_____ How much the coat costs

If all Wendy's thoughts are true, and nothing else about buying a coat matters to her, which coat should Wendy buy?

_____ Brown coat   _____ Blue coat

How did you decide this? (Please give as much detail as you can on the lines below.)

_____

_____

_____

_____

_____

One way of analyzing which coat Wendy should buy is shown below. The numbers under the options are scores. The weights show how important 100 points are for each attribute. Using these numbers, which option would she choose? _____

	OPTION		
ATTRIBUTES			WEIGHT
	Brown Coat	Blue Coat	
1. Style	100	40	10
(Last year's coat scores 0 on style)			
2. Match clothes	0	100	5
3. Coat savings	0	100	5
4. Warmth difference	100	0	1

How much would the weight for warmth have to be to make the brown coat and blue coat equally good choices for Wendy? (Guess if you are not sure.) _____

FIG. 6.2.   Sample exercise from performance test.

FORM S

CITY. Decision: which city a person should accept a job in. Unstructured response.

GOOD. Recall of a recent good decision made by the student; format follows the critical incident technique (Flanagan, 1954). Unstructured response.

ACID. Decision: what should be done about acid rain. Page of information; then a blank matrix with columns for "Options," rows for "Goals (attributes)," student enters options, goals, and (in cells) effects; then is asked to select best option and explain decision.

WENDY. Decision: which coat to buy (see Fig. 6.2).

PROBABILITY. Two multiple-choice questions. Student selects numerical probability which best fits a described event.

STRANGER. Decision: whether to walk or run when followed by a stranger, given two probabilities to combine to get answer. Unstructured response, followed by structured analysis with numbers given.

FORM D

WILLIAM. Decision: which career a person should choose. Format parallels CITY in Form S.

GOOD. (Same as in Form S)

ACID. (Same as in Form S)

NINA. Decision: where to go for a vacation. Format closely parallels WENDY.

PROBABILITY. Two questions closely paralleling Form S in format.

HOOKEY. Decision: whether Joe will play hookey, given two attributes of value and a probability of getting caught. Format parallels STRANGER.

FIG. 6.3.   Exercises used in performance test.

	Pretest	*Posttest*
Group C1:	Form S	Form D
Group C2:	Form S with numeric models omitted.	Form D
Group C3:	Form D	Form S
Group C4:	Form D with numeric models omitted.	Form S

Comparison of pre–post test-score gains among these subgroups served to measure the following extraneous effects of the test itself:

C1 minus C2, and C3 minus C4: Estimate gains due to learning from the numeric models presented in the pretest, apart from other pretest content. There were no significant gains of this type overall, so on items other than numeric models, results for C1 and C2 were pooled, as were results for C3 and C4.

Mean of C1 and C3 gains: Estimate gains due solely to having taken the pretest. Only 1 of 20 of these "retest effects" was significant ($p < .01$), so no adjustment was made to gains for retest effects.

Half of (C3 minus C1): Adjustment of taught group gains for differ-

TABLE 6.1
Learning Objectives and Exercises

Area	Objective	Exercises
QUALITATIVE ANALYSIS	Construct own analysis of a decision, trading off importance of outcomes on different goals, and avoiding errors.	All open-end
	Analyze decision using a GOOP chart (relating options, goals, and outcomes).	ACID
	Can think of arguments against own view.	ACID
	List outcomes (pros and cons) relevant to a decision.	All open-end
	Distinguish goals from options in a stated problem.	WENDY/NINA
NUMERIC ANALYSIS	Construct own numeric analysis, given no structure.	All open-end
	Calculate multiattribute utility (MAU) from numeric problem data.	WENDY/NINA
	Make decision consistent with data (MAU).	WENDY/NINA
	Calculate utility using numeric probability data (EU).	STRANGER/ HOOKEY
	Make decision consistent with data (EU).	STRANGER/ HOOKEY
	Convert statement to numeric probability.	PROBABILITY
RATIONAL STATEMENTS	Asked how to decide an issue, answer: Be rational, think it through, etc. Avoid biases and errors. List pros and cons, goals. Use GOOP, relate options to goals. Search, seek new options.	All open-end
APPLY PDA TO OWN LIFE	Voluntarily apply PDA outside school.	GOOD

ences in difficulty of the two test forms. There were significant differences in difficulty of the two forms, and these differences varied by exercise. Gains were therefore adjusted separately for each exercise, so that gain results would reflect only what was learned, and not arbitrary differences between forms.

Seventh Grade. We assumed that extraneous effects of the test would be similar in the two grades, so form difficulty was the only test effect controlled in the seventh grade. The seventh grade teachers also did not use test exercises during instruction. This allowed us to use a simpler design in the seventh grade, requiring no control group. The 24 students in the class were divided randomly into two groups of 12. One group was given Form S on the pretest and Form D on the posttest. The other group was given the forms in the reverse order, that is, Form D on the pretest and Form S on the posttest. Summing the performance gains for the two groups on each exercise thus controlled for differences in form difficulty.

Procedure

Administration of Tests.   The performance test was administered in parts, as described earlier, and each part was handed in before beginning the next. Only one student did not complete the test in the 50 minutes available, and was given a few minutes to complete it after class. The pretest was given to all groups a day or two before instruction began, and the posttest was given within a day or two after the course ended.

Scoring.   All tests were scored by one author (Campbell), using a standard scoring key that includes guidance for scoring responses to open-ended questions. As an informal reliability check, a college student was trained on scoring for 3 hours, then independently scored approximately half of the open-ended exercises in the eighth-grade posttest. Disagreements with the author occurred on 10% to 15% of the scores, and were resolved by discussion.

All exercises except PROBABILITY were complex and were scored on several different course objectives, as described in the results section. A desired response or response pattern was generally given one point credit on the objective. For the quantitative analysis objectives, answers were given one to three points depending on the complexity of the problem and the accuracy of the answer, as specified in the key. In this way we established a scoring scale of what we judged to be equivalent units of achievement, for the purpose of summing scores across exercises and across objectives.

Statistical Methods.   All structured responses were analyzed using one-tailed t-tests on gain scores, with zero gain being the expected gain if there was no learning. Open-ended answers were scored on several categories. Where the frequency of responses was moderate or high, a t-test was used. For categories in which there was a low frequency of responses, a chi-square test (with Yates correction) was used to compare pretest and posttest numbers of responses in the category. All gains reported without qualification in the results section would have occurred by chance less than 1 time in 1,000 ($p < .001$), unless a weaker significance level ($p < .01$ or $p < .05$) is stated.

Results

General Summary.   Students taught the course made substantial gains in some areas and little or none in other areas, and the pattern was fairly consistent, though there were wide individual differences in performance on each exercise.

The eighth graders as a group made significant gains in performing both qualitative and numeric analysis of hypothetical decision problems, whereas the seventh graders showed gains only in qualitative analysis. Analyses were nearly always made in response to a structure provided by the test, rather than one created by the student. In both groups, a formal PDA was rarely constructed in response to open-end questions (e.g. "How would you decide. . . ?") where no framework or model was provided. Most students in both grades usually answered such open-end questions by describing the arguments favoring (and sometimes opposing) the chosen option, on both the pretest and the posttest. Although their arguments were usually sensible, they seldom explicitly mentioned rational processes. When an explicit framework was provided in the text to structure the same decision, students often showed gains in ability to use the framework appropriately to analyze the decision.

As noted, the eighth graders showed no evidence of having voluntarily applied PDA to their own life decisions during the 2 months between pre- and posttesting. The seventh graders were not given this exercise (GOOD).

Table 6.2 summarizes the results for both grades by area and specific objective. In the results columns, the significance level is given; "NS" means no significant gain.

Qualitative Analysis.   Of the three broad areas tested in the seventh grade, all significant gains were within one area, qualitative analysis. As in the eighth grade, the gains were mainly on two exercises: ACID and WENDY/NINA. The acid rain analysis (ACID) corresponded most closely of all exercises to the type of analysis process the seventh graders did in class, though classwork was always on personal decisions whereas ACID analyzed societal decision. It was to be expected that this exercise would show the greatest gains. On the pretest only one seventh grader used the multiattribute chart effectively (named three options, and differentiated them sensibly on at least two goals), whereas 15 (62%) did so on the posttest. The corresponding gain for the eighth graders was from 42% to 85%. In thinking of arguments opposing one's own decision on the acid rain problem, neither grade level made significant progress.

The number of seventh graders who distinguished goals from options with no more than one error on the WENDY/NINA matching question increased from 50% on the pretest to 75% on the posttest; the comparable gain (adjusted) for the eighth graders was from 71% to 94%.

The most difficult objective, constructing an analysis with no structure given, was achieved to a significant degree in qualitative analysis by the eighth graders; only one had constructed such an analysis on the pretest, but on the posttest 50% did at least a partial analysis trading off importance of outcomes on different goals. The number who showed logical errors and biases in their answers declined slightly but not significantly from pre- to posttest. The seventh graders showed no gain at all in constructing analyses from scratch.

TABLE 6.2
Results by Grade and Objective

Area	Objective	Signifance Level of Gain	
		7th	8th
QUALITATIVE ANALYSIS	TOTAL QUALITATIVE	.001	.01
	Construct own analysis of a decision.	NS	.001
	Analyze decision using a GOOP chart.	.001	.001
	Can think of arguments against own view.	NS	NS
	List outcomes (pros and cons).	NS	NS
	Distinguish goals from options.	.05	.001
NUMERIC ANALYSIS	TOTAL NUMERIC	NS	.01
	Construct own numeric analysis.	NS	NS
	Calculate multiattribute utility (MAU).	NS	.001
	Make decision consistent with data (MAU).	NS	NS
	Calculate utility using numeric probability (EU).	NS	.001
	Make decision consistent with data (EU).	NS	NS
	Convert statement to numeric probability.	NS	NS
RATIONAL STATEMENTS	TOTAL RATIONAL STATEMENTS	NS	.05
APPLY PDA TO OWN LIFE	Voluntarily apply PDA outside school	NA	NS

NS = Not Significant
NA = Not Applicable

No gain in listing pros and cons was expected or observed in either grade. We knew after the first pretest that nearly all responses to open-end questions were of this type, as discussed above. Because answer space on each test page was limited, we half expected a decline in this score on the posttest due to substituting process answers for content answers. The decline was not significant.

Numeric Analysis. Only two eighth graders constructed a numeric utility model on the posttest in answer to an open-end question with no structure given (none did on the pretest). However the group showed substantial gains in calculating utility correctly given numeric data structured by options and goals. On the WENDY/NINA multiattribute utility analyses (MAU), the percent who calculated correct answers rose from 31% on the pretest to 54% on the posttest. On the STRANGER/HOOKEY analyses, involving probability, the percent correct rose from 33% to 71%.

In view of the above results we were rather surprised that neither grade (eighth or seventh) showed any gains in making the correct choice among options. This may have been due largely to the fact that the choice question came first, and then the utility calculation, even though the two questions were on the same page. Students do have a tendency not to go back and change previous answers, even after new contradictory evidence is derived. If we had asked for the calculation first, they might have paid more attention to their own calculations and as a result might have shown a gain on choosing the right option as well.

On the pretest, a high percentage (88%) of the eighth graders could correctly convert a verbal statement of a problem into a numeric estimate of probability. There was no significant gain beyond this initially high level. For the seventh graders, the change was from 60% to 65% (NS). Probability estimation was not a major focus of the lessons, but it was covered to some degree.

Rational Principles Stated. The total number of rational process statements volunteered by taught eighth graders increased slightly ($p < .05$) from pretest to posttest. Very few seventh graders stated verbal support for a rational process, even on the posttest, in response to open-end questions. The seventh graders tended to give shorter answers to all questions, and to complete the test faster than the eighth graders (the seventh graders' tendency toward brevity was observed in homework exercises as well). Apart from grade level, perhaps the G & T students (eighth grade) were a little more willing and able to respond to the challenge and compose longer answers.

INFORMAL EVALUATION OF DECISION-MAKING COURSE

In addition to the formal evaluation just described, the course was evaluated informally by students, classroom teachers, and researchers. Student reactions to the material were assessed both by the authors and by the regular classroom teachers who observed the decision-making lessons. These reactions included some time spent in class discussion of student perceptions of the material they were being taught. In addition, students filled out an evaluation questionnaire in which they evaluated the material for difficulty, relevance, and whether they thought they would use it in their lives.

Observation of Student Response

Students understood and easily applied the GOOP terminology to fill out GOOP worksheets for decision problems. They had little difficulty making qualitative multiattribute charts for decision problems. In the eighth-grade class, students performed a multiattribute analysis of the 1988 Presidential election using the chart shown in Fig. 6.1. This class was particularly effective, due to the high degree of student interest and involvement. The lesson also graphically demonstrated decision biases, especially single-mindedness.

The complexity of the issues involved demonstrated the usefulness of a structured tool like the multiattribute chart, and the students' interest helped them to master the concepts quickly.

Although students had little difficulty producing multiattribute charts, the effect of the systematic analysis was not so clear when students were asked to state why they recommended a particular decision. Their responses often appeared single-minded. For example, one exercise described a girl, Marian, faced with a choice between band and basketball as an after-school activity. In explaining a recommended decision, a student might say "Marian should join the band because it would prepare her for a career as a musician." But students rarely added comments reflecting trade-offs between goals, such as: "Her career is more important than being on the basketball team with her friends." This may be due to a tendency to *justify* a decision once it has been made by amassing arguments in its favor. But even when students were explicitly instructed to include both pros and cons in their discussions and to discuss trade-offs, the tendency toward single-minded responses remained. This observation is consistent with the formal evaluation results, which showed no gain in students' tendency to cite arguments opposing their own position. However, on homework exercises many students did discuss how the decision maker could modify an option to achieve some of the advantages of the option not chosen, e.g.: "Marian could do band after school, but join a Saturday basketball league."

Students at both the seventh and eighth grade levels had little difficulty with the numerical manipulations required for quantitative multiattribute analysis. However, we feel that insufficient time was devoted to justifying the need for using numbers to keep track of trade-offs among goals, or to developing methods for checking the validity of the numbers. In informal comments, students indicated that the qualitative multiattribute analysis would be useful for decisions they faced, but not the numbers. Based on reading homework assignments, we had the sense that the numbers were assigned without sufficient thought and may not have accurately reflected the students' values. We feel that insufficient class time was given to numerical utility for students to see its value or internalize the process.

When presented with a decision problem involving uncertainty, the seventh-grade class could come up with events whose outcomes were uncertain, suggest potential sources of more information, and judge the credibility of the sources. Both seventh- and eighth-grade students had difficulty thinking up examples of decisions they faced that involved uncertainty. We suspect this is in part because people do not tend to explicitly encode uncertainties for most everyday decisions.

Although students were familiar with the concept of probability and its measurement on a percentage scale, we were surprised that they apparently did not consider it natural to use probability as a guide to decision. When presented with a stark example (Bob's TV works 60% of the time and Bill's

50% of the time; whose TV should they use to watch the game?), most students chose according to probability. But this broke down when they were faced with any extraneous factors. Students were given an example of whether a baseball manager should replace the .130-average pitcher with a .290-average pinch hitter in the bottom of the ninth with two out, one run behind, and the bases loaded. Several argued vociferously that in either case the batter might or might not get a hit, and so the manager should leave the pitcher in. (When this example was modified in a different class, so that the manager had already decided to replace the pitcher but the choice was between a .290 and a .330 hitter, students readily agreed on the hitter with the higher average.)

It appears to us from these observations that students readily agree that a higher probability of a good thing or a lower probability of a bad thing is good, *all other things being equal*. But when asked to integrate probabilistic information, even qualitatively, with differences in value on other attributes, students have difficulty.

Students also had difficulty with the concept of identifying a set of mutually exclusive outcomes for a decision involving uncertainty. This difficulty was at least in part due to our lesson structure, which we intend to modify in the future. We attempted to simplify the probability problems by asking students to assess holistic utilities, rather than integrating the probabilistic with the multiattribute analysis. Throughout the course, students had learned to decompose outcomes into attributes, assessing separately the outcome for each attribute. Now they were being asked for a different kind of decomposition. For each option, students assessed a set of mutually exclusive and exhaustive possible outcomes, *aggregated* over all attributes. Probabilities and utilities were then assessed over these aggregated outcomes. In retrospect, it is understandable that this would prove difficult. As an example of confusion between the two frameworks, consider the problem of whether Linda should buy a vase for her mother now, or try to get it for $5 less at another store. The other store may be out of the vase and she cannot get back to the first store, so she risks having no vase for her mother. For this problem, one typical student listed the possible outcomes of going to the second store as: (1) pay $5 less; (2) don't get vase; (3) mother is happy. Note that (1) and (3) describe different attributes of the same outcome (get vase), whereas (2) describes a different outcome. This student and many others listed a mix of outcomes and attributes, confusing the two frameworks they had learned. There was not sufficient time in either class to teach them how to discriminate which framework was appropriate for a given problem.

The balance beam seemed to be a very effective tool for illustrating the concept of expected utility. Students were interested in guessing which side went down. Numerical calculations could be demonstrated on the balance beam. The balance beam was particularly effective in demonstrating the effect of changes in probabilities and utilities on which outcome is preferred (see Martin & Brown, chap. 10 in this volume).

Students perceived the material on probability and expected utility as more difficult than the material on multiattribute analysis. Their homework assignments reflected less mastery of the material taught in class.

The eighth-grade students who had the "Self and Others" lesson were involved and interested in the social dilemma game, and quickly saw its relevance to examples of real-life social dilemmas. Even with prompting, they had difficulty seeing the relationship to the multiattribute analysis they had just learned: The choice of whether to cooperate in a social dilemma involves trading off benefit to yourself against benefit for others. The relevance of multiattribute analysis seemed more intuitive in the lesson on trade-offs between present and future than in the lesson on social dilemmas.

In summary, the most effective parts of the decision making unit were the qualitative GOOP and multiattribute analyses. This observation was shared by both the research team and the classroom teachers. Students, in class discussion, indicated that they thought these aspects of the course were useful and they might apply them to future decisions (although some students, not surprisingly, expressed the opinion that none of what they had learned was useful). Numerical multiattribute and probability analyses, as taught in this course, appeared to be less effective and less motivating to students. It remains unclear whether this was due to insufficient time devoted to these topics, suboptimal pedagogy, or lack of readiness on the students' part. Qualitative treatment or uncertainty was, in our assessment, less successful than the qualitative multiattribute analysis, but more effective than the quantitative methods. These impressions are consistent with the formal evaluation results cited earlier.

Student Evaluation Questionnaire

After the eight-session course was over, students were asked to fill out a questionnaire evaluating their feelings about the course. Table 6.3 summarizes the results of the questionnaire, broken down by class (the two numbers preceding each response indicate the number of seventh and eighth graders, respectively, who gave that response). Comments were solicited for each question.

From Table 6.3, we see that the dominant response was that the material they had learned was a good way of approaching some (but not most) decisions; that they would apply it to important (but not ordinary) decisions; and that they would apply some (but not most) of what they had learned.

Comments indicated that decisions *not* suitable for decision analysis included trivial decisions and time-constrained decisions. Some of the eighth graders indicated that very important decisions or life-and-death decisions

TABLE 6.3
Results of Student Evaluation Questionnaire
(First number: 7th Graders N = 21. Second number: 8th graders N = 38.)

1. Do you think the way of analyzing decisions you learned in this course is a good way to approach making decisions?

4	10	Yes, for most decisions.
12	24	Yes, for some decisions.
5	4	No, not for most decisions.

2. Once you have learned the material in this course very well, do you think you would use it to analyze decisions you face in your life? (Check as many as apply.)

11	24	Yes, for important decisions.
4	3	Yes, for ordinary decisions.
6	10	No.

(2 students checked both important and ordinary; 1 checked both ordinary and no.)

3. Do you think you will apply the things you have learned to decisions you have to make?

5	6	Yes, I will apply most of what I have learned.
12	28	Yes, I will apply some parts of what I have learned.
4	4	No, I will not apply what I have learned.

4. Do you think the decision making class was:

3	0	Too hard.
N/A	3	Too hard for regular class, but OK for gifted and talented.
14	29	About right.
3	5	Too easy.

5. Do you think the class went:

1	4	Too fast.
N/A	2	Too fast for regular class, but OK for gifted and talented.
8	18	About right.
11	13	Too slowly.

6. Do you think you had enough practice to learn the material?

18	21	Yes.
3	16	No.

7. Some people say that units in decision making should be included in many courses. For example, the methods you learned could be used to analyze environmental decisions in science class, or decisions made by past and present world leaders in social studies class. Do you think this is a good idea?

16	20	Yes.
4	14	No.

were not suitable for decision analysis. Interestingly, a suicide example was used in the seventh grade class as an illustration of the importance of considering probabilities (would telling a counselor decrease the probability that a friend would commit suicide, and should this outweigh a promise to the friend not to tell?). The regular teacher followed up this class with a discussion of what to do when a friend threatens suicide; this discussion made heavy use of the decision analysis concepts they had learned. The teacher felt that the suicide lessons were among the most effective and worthwhile aspects of the class. None of the seventh graders mentioned life-and-death decisions as a category not suitable for decision analysis.

Students complained that the charts and numbers were too difficult and time-consuming. ("If you are buying a vase in a store as in Linda's problem by the time you have decided to go to the other store the vases will be gone. Perhaps you could develop some quicker processes.") There were class discussions on the level of analysis appropriate to different kinds of problems, and it was pointed out that just thinking about GOOP elements could improve decisions for which it was not worth doing a detailed analysis. Some students' comments reflected this, but others seemed to come away with the impression that they were being told to make charts for all their decisions. ("Ordinary decisions can usually be made without charts and graphs. I've done good so far.")

A number indicated that they would think more about their decisions in the future, or remember to be open-minded. But some shared the sentiment expressed by one student: "The decisions were thoroughly discussed by you but my emotions still take precedence over any numbers that are recited to me."

Despite our and the teachers' impression that too much material was compressed into too short a time, the students indicated that course difficulty was about right and that pace was about right or too slow. This may have been due to a reluctance to admit to having difficulty. In their comments, students confirmed our impression that probability was an area that needed further practice.

Students responded favorably to the suggestion that decision-making material be included in a number of courses. One expressed our basic hypothesis that formal instruction will improve informal decision processes: "I think that if they grow up with this class they might not write it down but a little will stick in their head." But one student said, "The whole class was boring. Everyone will hate school more if this is put in the curriculum."

A final open-ended question was included asking for suggestions on how to improve the course. In general, students asked for more variation in activities, more student involvement, more group activities and more practice on specific parts, especially the probability. Some said the course was too boring and they spent too much time staring at the overhead. They liked the balance beam and the games, and wanted more activities like those. One suggested group projects, and having each group present its project to the class. There were comments that the problems should be made more realistic and relevant to students' lives; others said the problems were good. Students suggested that there was too much time between classes (classes were a week apart); this sentiment was shared by the classroom teachers.

DISCUSSION AND LESSONS LEARNED

We have demonstrated that students can master some decision analytic concepts in an eight-session course. A majority of the students at both grade levels gained in ability to analyze a decision problem in some fashion. In the seventh grade the gains were in qualitative, but not numeric, analysis. In the eighth grade over half the taught group used numbers correctly, but showed little inclination to apply them to the decision at hand. The advantage of using numbers was not explicitly taught to either group. This may account partly for absence of numeric analysis gains in the seventh grade, and the disparity between the eighth graders' calculations and their decisions. We believe an important element in future instruction in decision making should be to show that numbers help to keep track of numerous comparisons and relate them logically. This was missing from the experimental course reported here.

Of course, some decision analysts would argue that qualitative analyses are sufficient for the lay person most of the time. Even if this is true, those few complex decisions in which numbers would help may be very important ones. Moreover, some argue that understanding how a numerical analysis works improves people's informal decision-making skills. Our students received too brief an exposure to numerical methods to test this hypothesis.

Another conclusion, drawn mainly from post-course discussion with students and teachers, is that students need a good deal more individual study to master the PDA principles presented, and considerably more practice in applying them to specific problems. In our course the ratio of discussion and lecture to individual and small group practice was perhaps 80% to 20%. We now think these proportions should probably be reversed.

Whether more practice on problems would lead students to apply the skills to their own lives remains open to question. Most school work seems to be reserved in a separate compartment of the brain from "real life." It may be that students would need repeated practice in applying PDA to their own personal decisions, and to perceive that the analysis helps them better reach their goals. For students to even begin this process may require individual counseling, or some dramatic event, to launch them through the "school–life barrier." Yet an eight-lesson exposure to a decision analysis course still rough around the edges prompted a substantial majority of students to say they would apply some of what they had learned to their lives. We remain optimistic about the potential of formal instruction in decision analysis, and we suspect that repeated exposure over a period of years would positively affect everyday decision making.

The teachers with whom we worked were uniformly enthusiastic about the usefulness and relevance of formal instruction in decision making at the intermediate level. Teachers felt that the best chance for adoption was not as a stand-alone unit, but as an integral part of the existing curriculum. They felt that decision analysis had great potential as a tool for enriching students' understanding of course material and its relevance to the real world. The civics and science teachers intend to apply what they have learned to develop enrichment lessons as part of their regular curriculum.

The English teacher was positive about its potential for other classes, but felt that she could apply only the material on decision biases to her own curriculum. The consensus among the teachers was that this material would make a relevant and useful addition to courses in science, civics, social studies, health and family life, and career counseling. Students also indicated that they felt it was a good idea to include instruction in decision making in a number of courses.

Our experience teaching this experimental course has taught us a number of lessons that we plan to apply in future attempts to teach decision analysis at the intermediate and secondary levels. The specific suggestions that follow owe a great deal to insightful comments by the classroom teachers with whom we worked.

The first area of potential improvement is in course content. Our experience shows the strong desirability of developing a more unified treatment of probability and multiattribute utility. Students were confused by a proliferation of different charts. We are now working on a single decision-making template that can be used for multiattribute problems both with and without uncertain outcomes. In a time-constrained introductory course, we recommend focusing on qualitative analyses. Attention should be diverted from the mechanics of numerical calculations, and devoted to how to apply a qualitative decision analysis template to help make a choice between options. We do believe, however, that numerical techniques are valuable components of a second course or a longer first course, and that understanding of the qualitative techniques will be increased when students see how to use numbers to keep track of complex trade-offs.

Our second set of suggestions relates to pedagogy. Much more attention needs to be paid to developing students' understanding of why learning decision analysis is a good idea. They need to see demonstrations of the problems to which thoughtless decision making can lead. They need to see that thoughtlessness has costs even on minor decisions. The course must avoid giving the impression that decision analysis means making charts and calculating numbers. More attention needs to be devoted to good informal decision-making processes, and how these informal processes avoid the problems associated with thoughtless decision making. Formal procedures need to be understood as a way of applying the principles behind the informal procedures when decisions get complex enough that the informal procedures bog down.

Especially at the intermediate level, students need to be active participants rather than passive listeners. Our course attempted to involve students as much as possible. We were limited in this by the amount of material we attempted to cover, by the large size of the eighth grade class, and by habits ingrained in us by our experience as college teachers. Both teachers and students made valuable suggestions for keeping students involved. A key is variety: Do not overuse any one instructional method. As noted earlier, more small group work would be desirable. This could include a project to be completed cooperatively by the group and presented by a group member to the class. Students needed more practice and reinforcement of the techniques, especially guided in-class practice. Games and visual aids improved students' motivation and interest in the material.

Both of these suggestions—more emphasis on the relevance of decision analysis and more active student involvement—serve the goal of getting students to "own" the tool of decision analysis. Only when students feel ownership are they likely to apply decision analysis outside the classroom.

ACKNOWLEDGMENTS

Without the assistance of our cooperating teachers, the development of these lessons would have been impossible. Thank you for providing us with class time, for enthusiastically supporting our efforts, for putting up with our relative inexperience with classroom teaching, for providing us with valuable feedback on how to make the class sessions run more smoothly, and for giving us suggestions on how to improve our material. Thank you Mary Bailey, Katy Davis, Carol Isaacs, Beth Myers, Ellen Rugel, and Greer Graumlich.

Our thanks also extend to Ed Thacker, principal of Langston Hughes Intermediate School, for giving us support, and especially for allowing us to test our materials in Fairfax County. Thanks are also extended to Fred Vincent, principal of Parkway School in Philadelphia, for allowing the team to test our materials there, for attending classes, and for giving suggestions on more effective teaching strategies. Thanks to Jon Baron, for sharing his experience teaching the same material to very different students.

And many thanks to our students, who had to put up with the inevitable rough edges of a pilot project, and who did not hesitate to tell us what they did and didn't like about what we were doing.

Finally, this work would not have been possible without the support from the National Institute of Child Health and Human Development, Grant Number 2-R44-HD23071-02.

REFERENCES

Baron, J. (1985). *Rationality and intelligence.* New York: Cambridge University Press.
Baron, J. (1988). *Thinking and deciding.* New York: Cambridge University Press.
Baron, J., Laskey, K. B., & Brown, R. V. (1989). Decision making lessons. Reston, VA: Decision Science Consortium, Inc.
Flanagan, J. C. (1954). The critical incident technique. *Psychological Bulletin, 51,* 327–358.

Chapter 7

Teaching Decision Making in the City: Two Experiences

Greer Graumlich
Henry H. Houston Elementary School

Jonathan Baron
University of Pennsylvania

This chapter reviews two attempts to teach decision making in Philadelphia Schools. The teachers were the two authors. Baron is a psychology professor with only a little previous experience teaching secondary-school students. Graumlich is an experienced teacher. Both efforts used the versions of the DSC course described by Laskey and Campbell (chapter 6). This course emphasized the analysis of decisions in goals, options, outcomes, and probabilities (GOOP), and it included discussion of actively open-minded thinking, goal trade-offs, simple multiattribute analysis, probability, self and others, and future consequences. Although little formal evaluation was done, we believe that we have learned something from these efforts that should be of use to others who try to teach decision making in urban schools.

GRAUMLICH'S CLASS

Graumlich taught the lessons over a 6-month period to a class of 18 mentally gifted sixth-grade students in a large urban public school. Each lesson was presented on the same designated day of the week and lasted approximately 1 hour. We provide here a discussion of each of the lessons, which were not quite the same as those used in other versions of the course.

147

Lesson 1: Pretest; Introduction of Concepts

The students submitted their responses of a pretest, called "Brainstorming Decisions Sheet," which asked: what a decision was; what decisions the student made recently; what the student's most important decision was and how it was made; what the standards are for evaluating decisions; what the common errors are; how to avoid them; what the techniques of decision analysis are; what the difference is between good decisions and good outcomes; and whether well made decisions lead to good outcomes on the average. Most students could define a decision, but few could list multiple factors to be considered when making a decision. None of the students was familiar with the techniques of decision analysis. Few students could explain the difference between good decisions and good outcomes. Few students responded that they were aware of the fact that the decisions they made influenced others.

The students were told to keep the unanswered pretest questions in mind throughout the lessons. This technique served to heighten the students interest in learning more about decision making. The questions asking about past decisions made the students aware that they do, in fact, make many decisions. The pretest also anticipated the idea of formal decision analysis.

After completing the pretest the students proceeded with Lesson 1, roughly as described by Laskey and Campbell (chapter 6). We discussed going through the GOOP (goals, options, outcomes, and probabilities) and made a GOOP chart as a visual aid. Each student began a decision-making notebook. Definitions of vocabulary words and concept explanations and examples were put into the decision-making notebooks by the students. The notebooks served as a helpful tool throughout the decision-making lessons. The students frequently referred to their notebooks for information they had forgotten and that they knew would help them to better understand the concepts on which they were currently working.

Lesson 1 continued with definitions of value trade-offs, myside bias, and what it meant to be actively open-minded. The students participated with enthusiasm when they were allowed to give their own examples.

The principal of the school happened to choose this particular time to observe Graumlich's teaching. In her report, she wrote, "It is obvious that the teacher has put a great deal of thought into arranging and sequencing the steps of this lesson. The focusing activity (Brainstorming Decisions sheet) was excellent. I like the way the students are taught to really listen to each other . . . I am particularly impressed with the infusion of vocabulary development into the lesson. Nuances and shades of meaning are treated thoroughly and carefully. *This lesson is one most adults I work with should have.*"

Lesson 1A: Picking a Decision Problem and Writing Down the GOOP

The students were presented with two dilemmas in Lesson 1A: One concerned an aspiring basketball player who had to choose between an academically excellent magnet school without a basketball team and an academically inferior neighborhood school with an excellent team; the other concerned an aspiring flute player's choice between band and basketball. For homework each student was to choose one of the dilemmas and write the goals, options, outcomes, and "predictions" (a term used in this early version of the course), the GOOP, of the dilemma of their choice. Surprisingly, each student wrote about both dilemmas! They went through the GOOP in an appropriate and detailed fashion, perhaps because the dilemmas were related to the kinds of situations these students were experiencing in real life: Many were in the midst of deciding whether or not to go to a magnet school; and many were trying to decide between extracurricular activities. Many students hesitated in giving advice as to what the students in the fabricated examples should do.

Lesson 1B: Creating "Personalized" Scenarios for Value Trade-offs and Myside Biases

At this point each student began a decision-making notebook to keep notes, handouts, and homework assignments. Frequently during subsequent lessons, the students asked if they could review their notes. Frequent use of the notebook served to keep the students familiar with vocabulary, to focus their attention on central issues, and to remind them of the details of the steps of formal decision-making techniques. After the notebooks were created, the concepts of myside bias and value trade-offs were reviewed, using students' own experiences.

Lesson 2A: Doing a Multiattribute Table From a Republican or Democratic Viewpoint

Lesson 2A involved learning to make a multiattribute table. A political topic—voting Democrat or Republican—was suggested. As was the case with Baron's students, this topic fell flat. Although the students learned the steps of doing a multiattribute table and successfully completed a table on the Democrat/Republican topic, the lesson was less enthusiastically received than others. Every class member said they would vote as a Democrat and many of their oral responses seemed to be "parroting" comments they had heard their parents make. The students seemed to be unable to identify wholeheartedly with the political issues. These sixth graders seemed to be more interested in working with topics relevant to decisions they would make themselves in the near future.

Lesson 2B: Making a Multiattribute Table

To "recover" from the political dilemma of the previous lesson the students were presented with doing a multiattribute table for a dilemma about Sara's choice between a part time job baby-sitting and a job with her friend at Burger King. (Although the baby-sitting pay was lower, Sara had many ties to the family and the child, and she was interested in child development as a career.) Because the students were familiar with the topic, they could focus on the concept of what a multiattribute table achieved as well as learning the mechanical tasks involved.

As a homework assignment, to reinforce what had been presented in class, the students were given a list of topics involving decisions to be made: selling arms to Iran for hostages, using steroids, doing homework, and serving food in the school cafeteria. The students had to describe how one of these decisions might be made in a single-minded way. Then they were to pick one of the topics and make a multiattribute table. Again the students showed a keen interest in most of the topics and did detailed work for homework.

The assignments that were given subsequent to the pretest had a "grade" put on them. Usually the students earned a grade of 4 or 5 on a grading scale of 1 to 5 with 5 being the highest grade a student could achieve. Also, these assignments had many positive comments placed on them before they were returned to the students. Good grades and positive comments may have been helpful in sustaining the interest and enthusiasm of the students throughout the lessons.

Lesson 3: Anticipating Future Consequences

The concept of thinking about future consequences was the main topic of Lesson 3. The topics of doing homework, practicing an instrument, developing healthy habits seemed relevant to the students. In class, they discussed in detail the future positive as well as negative consequences involved with each of the topics. Throughout this lesson, almost every hand was up—the students wanted to share their own stories and give insights they had learned. The students were given lots of verbal praise for participation. The negative consequences of acting impulsively or being short-sighted were enumerated. The students seemed to leave this lesson keenly aware that taking the time to consider the future consequences of their decisions was well worth it.

Most of the previous lessons had ended within an hour. Lesson 3 was allowed to go on for 1½ hours. This was too long a time period for the students. They began to lose a bit of interest. Subsequent lessons were limited to 1 hour even though many of the students "groaned" because they wanted to continue discussing the topics.

A handout was distributed to each student for the future consequences lesson. This handout, as well as all of the other handouts, were valuable aids to the students in understanding the vocabulary and concepts of the lessons. The students kept the handouts in their decision-making notebooks and referred to them often.

As homework for Lesson 3 several of the students did well in listing decisions that require self-control. However, some missed the point with regard to writing about the methods of self-control they had used. A special review of this topic was presented and the students, with the help of the handout, then successfully redid their homework.

Lesson 4A: Thinking About Others as Well as Yourself

Thinking about others brought a multitude of responses from the students. They gave numerous examples of school related situations where "chipping in" or "doing one's share" was an issue. The verbal participation of the students was so overwhelming that at this point it was decided that a student would be selected to write the class responses on the board instead of the teacher. This technique helped to develop the students' sense of ownership of the lessons.

In one part of the lesson, students played an imaginary social dilemma game in which each student privately wrote C or D on a piece of paper. Students were to imagine that those who wrote D would get $1, regardless of what others did, but that writing C would give *everyone else* $1 and nothing for the person who wrote it. In discussing this game, the students concluded that they should cooperate (C) because, they reasoned, if they defected (D), they would feel bad.

Lesson 4B: Getting People to Cooperate More

When the students were given the assignment to think of a social dilemma in which too few people cooperate and were asked to write how people could be made to cooperate more, the social dilemmas they chose included: limiting the use of automobiles and aerosol cans as a means of controlling pollution, working to stop the selling and usage of illegal drugs, caring for the homeless, putting an end to drunk driving, curtailing shoplifting, cooperating with the police force, keeping endangered species alive, and working on adolescent apathy toward school.

The lesson had mentioned electing a leader, making group rules, and changing goals as three methods of getting people to cooperate. In addition to these methods the students suggested: enlightening the public more about the issue, sending booklets, stopping the production of harmful substances, encouraging people to cooperate, hiring guards, having meetings, and paying people to cooperate. This brainstorming encouraged the students to think about the task of getting people to cooperate. Many of their suggestions seemed appropriate.

Lesson 5: Weighing Goals

When assigned to make an original multiattribute table, many of the students could readily proceed when they were allowed to use a previous sample as a guide. The "each one teach one" teaching technique was employed for those students who were still having difficulty making a multiattribute table. Students who understood what to do were paired with students who did not. The results were positive: Each student created an interesting table.

The most important concept that the students obtained from this lesson was stated by one of the students as follows: "We use a multiattribute table to show what is most important to us."

Only one student was upset with the "outcome" of her multiattribute table. Her outcome indicated that she should purchase a breed of dog different from the breed that she originally said she had wanted to purchase. This student's multiattribute table was put on the board and analyzed by the class. This analysis clarified the importance of assigning the correct weights. It also indicated to this student, as well as to the other students, that perhaps what they originally think they should do may not, in fact, be appropriate when many variables are taken into account and weights are attached to each variable. This was a particularly good lesson because the student was upset and the other students wanted to help her see what doing a multiattribute table was all about.

Lesson 6: Understanding the Meaning of Probability

The guessing game of predicting which color the teacher would say was played during this lesson and, as predicted, most of the students attempted to discover patterns and begged the teacher to slow down as she was calling out the letters of the game so they could memorize her verbalizations. Eventually, the students grasped the point that when things are unpredictable its best to go with the probabilities.

The most interesting point of this lesson was that the students learned to think about relative sizes of sets. When the chances of a student becoming a pro basketball player were determined, the students were amazed at the probability! The impact was profound on several students who had begun to seriously consider basketball as a career. The basketball example captured the students' interests and, because the outcome had been so dramatic, the students wanted to go on to calculate the probabilities of becoming pros in additional careers in which they had interest. The students enjoyed determining relative sizes of sets and seemed to realize the importance of taking the variable of probability into account when making a decision.

The discussion of subjective probabilities further piqued student interest. When the students learned the real as opposed to the biased probabilities regarding the tornado vs. lightning, drowning vs. leukemia, and other examples, the impact was again profound. As a result, the students wanted to acquire data firsthand from reliable sources to help them make decisions in the future.

The lesson culminated with a discussion of setting a precedent and the realization that probabilities add up. The students volunteered the following examples of how a pattern or habit was created through precedent setting and repetition: eating a sugar/fat rich snack; taking steroids; spending your allowance as soon as you get it; and taking a drug. These examples were discussed enthusiastically.

Lesson 7: Considering Probability and Expected Utility

Lesson 7 began with the students responding (enthusiastically) to the statement on the board "Risks can sometimes be worth taking and sometimes not." The students said they would determine whether or not to take a risk by how big a loss was at stake. At the time of this lesson Philadelphia was having its $121 million lottery. Most students thought everyone should buy a reasonable amount of tickets but not spend the rent money on tickets. Most of the students brought forth mature insights as well as the ability to take future consequences seriously into consideration (possibly as a result of the earlier lesson).

Lesson 8: Discussion, Revision, and Completion of the Posttest and Comparing the Responses of the Pretests with Those of the Posttests

Before the posttest was administered, as a review, the students were presented with a blank copy of the pretest (see Lesson 1) and asked if they needed clarification on any of the answers to the questions. The students said they easily could answer questions about the nature of a decision and recent decisions, but they requested that the question about "the most important decision you ever made in your entire life" be changed to "what do you think the most important decision you will ever make in your entire life might be?" They felt that the decisions they had made to date were minor. This rationale was accepted and the question was changed.

The students could not easily answer the question about the standards by which a decision can be evaluated as having been well made or poorly made. The only other question from the pretest for which the students requested further explanation was one about the techniques of formal decision analysis. Discussion revealed that the students were familiar with the techniques but did not realize that the techniques they knew were the stuff of "formal" decision analysis. Students were able to list common errors in decision making, ways to avoid these errors, and the difference between good decisions and good outcomes. Several noted that well-made decisions generally lead to better outcomes.

When asked (later) to choose the one unit from the entire year's curriculum that had the most impact on him, one student responded, "Decision making of course, since I'll be doing it the rest of my life and how I do it will affect me forever." When asked, the majority of the students "decided" that taking the time to use decision making techniques that they had learned would benefit them greatly in future decision making. This attitude also showed itself in the thoroughness with which students did their homework and in the number of examples they used from their own lives throughout the unit.

Teaching decision making seemed to help these students consider goals, options, outcomes, and probabilities before they made a choice. Many of the students who participated in the lessons initially made very single/closed-minded comments and argued their biases quite forcefully. At the culmination of the decision-making lessons these same students were found taking the time to list multiple considerations, putting weights on options, and considering future consequences to themselves and others. For example, from the posttest, one student listed the consequences of dropping out of school to become a "rapper singer," another weighed the attributes of videos when deciding which to rent, and a third mentioned considering others when deciding whether to use drugs or alcohol. Adoption of these decision-making behaviors by the students perhaps gave them an antidote to the high dosage of impulsive, single-minded behaviors which they are administered daily via soap operas, their peers, and sometimes their family members themselves.

BARON'S CLASS

Baron taught the lessons in two successive terms (1988–89) at Parkway School, an alternative public high school in West Philadelphia (the origins of which are described by Silberman, 1970). Few students from Parkway go on to college. Classes met at the University of Pennsylvania. They were offered as an elective, which met for 45 minutes once a week. (Nominally the period was 55 minutes, but there was a Burger King near the path from the school building and the University.)

In the first term, the class consisted of 12 boys and girls. In the second term, the class consisted of 8 boys. The principal of the school, Dr. Fred Vincent, made occasional visits, and for the second term, an undergraduate student, Mark Patrick, attended most of the classes and took notes. The instructor (Jonathan Baron) wrote his own notes after each class. From these notes, a few repeated observations stand out, some psychological, others pedagogical. No other evaluations were made.

Students' Difficulties with Probability

One psychological finding was that students really do make apparent errors in thinking about decisions. When one class was asked for examples of decisions, in the first meeting, one young man who was approximately 5'8" tall and weighed 135 pounds said (with a straight face) that he had decided to be a professional football player. Although one of the other students was quick to criticize this decision, most of the students went along with it when a similar example was discussed in class the following week.

Students have difficulty with probabilistic arguments. When students were asked the probability of getting three heads in a row, the modal answer was "three." Most students did not know that weather forecasts were often stated in probabilistic terms.

The problems were not just matters of knowledge. During a discussion of teenage pregnancy, the instructor would make arguments like "teenagers are more likely than adults to have underweight babies." One student said, "Yes, but some teenagers have healthy babies." This student made similar arguments whenever such arguments were made. It seemed that this student was unwilling to think in terms of probabilities as relevant. In a discussion of why people neglect the future, several students said "because the world might end," again not considering probability.

To try to make the point that probabilities matter, the instructor discussed a medical operation that might help a baseball player with a bad shoulder but might also make his condition worse (so that he couldn't play at all). The dialogue went something like this:

Instructor: If you were the player, what would you want to know before you decide?

Student: I'd ask the doctor what he would do.

Instructor: What if he said it was up to you?

Student: I'd ask him to decide.

Instructor: OK, what if you were the doctor, how would you decide?

Student: I'd ask the patient to decide.

Instructor: Is there anything we've been talking about that might help here? (We had been talking about probability.)

Student: No answer. (Asked again. Still no answer.)

Instructor: What if the doctor said that it failed the last five times he tried it?

Student: Then I'd have the operation, because the time is coming up to succeed.

Instructor: What if it succeeded the last 20 times?

Student: Then I wouldn't have it because it's time for it to fail.

In a discussion of whether one should wear seat belts, students were at a loss when they were told that seat belts could sometimes make accidents worse, as when a car fell in a lake. Such problems were found in the Reston students as well as in these inner-city students.

One example did succeed in inducing the students to attend to probability: "You are a baseball manager. It's the bottom of the 9th and it's the pitcher's turn to bat. If you win, you get to the play-offs. You are one run behind. The bases are loaded and there are two outs. There are two batters you can put in for the pitcher. They are pretty much the same, except that one has a batting average of .300 and the other has a batting average of .225. Which would you put in? Why? If this happened again, would you do the same thing?" This example served as a reminder of the principle through a discussion of several other examples.

One exercise (based somewhat on the ideas that Swets describes in chapter 13) that did not work, as a means of teaching about the use of probability, was to ask the students to guess which of two events (the teacher writing B or G on the board) would occur, when one event was three times as likely as the other. Students were supposed to learn to guess the more probable event all the time, but, in the two classes in which this was done, one student did better by guessing than this strategy would have done. (Subsequent calculations indicated that this will happen reasonably often in a class of reasonable size.) The exercise therefore did not help convince others that going with the more probable event all the time was the best strategy, and this lesson had to be explained in other ways (e.g., the baseball manager).

The Concept of Bias

Another finding was that the students did not habitually use concepts of "bias" or "inconsistency" to which we could refer in arguing for certain methods of decision making. For example, an in-class demonstration was based on the experiment of van Avermaet (Messick, 1985). Students were told that each of them had just done a psychology experiment in which the ones on the right side of the room worked for 90 minutes and did 3 questionnaires each and the ones on the left side worked for 45 minutes and did 6 questionnaires (of the same sort) each. They were then asked how each of them would divide $7 fairly between himself or herself and a person on the other side. Everyone gave themselves more and justified this by saying that their dimension (number or time) was more important. Students seemed not to understand why this experiment was interesting or why it indicated any sort of bias. Students' understanding of the concept of consistency seems to be a ripe area for future research.

Motivation and Interest

Pedagogically, these students seem to have some special needs. When the talk turned to abstractions, the students tended to doze off, start twittering, looking at the clock, and so forth. Examples that strike academics as elegant are not appreciated. For example, to discuss temporal myopia, we used an example of a preference switch: A child prefers one piece of candy now to two pieces in a day, but prefers two pieces in two days to one piece in one day—the same decision made a day sooner. This example shows how myopia can produce inconsistency. Most students were not particularly bothered by the idea of inconsistency, so they did not see this as part of an argument against myopic decisions.

Students also do not like to have their ignorance of certain topics exposed. Discussion of the 1988 presidential election went poorly, apparently because most students were unaware of the issues. In the next term, the idea of multiattribute analysis was introduced with a different example, how to spend a $50 present, and the discussion was much livelier.

On the positive side, the students really enjoyed learning about the probabilities of various events out of "The odds on virtually everything" (Editors of Heron House, 1980). Other examples that seem to work well (at least with boys) are those from sports.

Students also liked exercises on the computer. A simple decision-analysis program—which did multiattribute analysis and expected-utility analysis—was written for the course. Students enjoyed playing with it, although they required a great deal of close supervision. The major pedagogical advantage of the program is that it avoided arithmetic mistakes, which were extremely frequent in any pencil-and-paper analysis the students attempted. It did not avoid (frequent) mistakes in setting up a decision analysis, such as confusing outcomes and options, or outcomes and attributes, or assigning incorrect utilities (e.g., higher utilities for higher values of "price" on the grounds that price was an index of quality, even though quality was coded separately).

The most useful examples, however, were those that involved decisions close to the students' lives and interests, such as those involving consumer decisions (e.g., tennis shoes), sports (especially for the boys), or how to counsel a friend considering suicide.

Pedagogical Technique

In general, what worked well as a teaching technique was introducing a concept and asking the students to apply it to examples, such as shortsightedness. Physical analogies seemed to help (Martin & Brown, chapter 10).

An analogy for temporal myopia is this: Find two points, one slightly above eye level and the other quite a bit above it—such as the tops of two blackboards. The lower point should be closer to you, with you and the points forming a line. Then walk toward the points. From a distance, the lower point appears lower. As you get very close to the lower point, it will appear to be above the upper point in the visual field. This is what happens to rewards (such as getting drunk in the evening vs. not being hung over the next morning) as you approach the time at which the lower but sooner reward is available (e.g., getting drunk).

CONCLUSION

In both classes (Baron's and Graumlich's), examples of decision problems close to the students' interests seemed to capture students' interests the most. Both classes found probabilities interesting when the probabilities concerned real events (e.g., probabilities of making it to the pros in various sports). This result suggests one way to integrate the teaching of probability concepts with other subjects, for example, by discussing the probability that a spaceship shot into space will hit a star, or the probability that two unrelated people will have the same genes.

The differences between the two classes was the result of several factors: Graumlich's greater variety of techniques (the notebook, for example), the students' academic interests, and the amount of homework that the students did. She also fostered from the outset a sense of "ownership," and the students' initial enthusiasm seemed to carry them through some lessons that might not, in themselves, have aroused it.

Children are required to make decisions from the time they enter school until they leave. Adults assume that children will automatically acquire decision-making skills as they mature and grow. Teaching decision-making lessons helped us understand that decision making should be looked upon as a learned "skill." Decision making, like any other skill in the curriculum, needs to be taught through planned lessons, not just in one unit but across several different courses. By teaching children how to organize their thinking to make decisions we will not be leaving to chance the experiences necessary to give children the necessary tools for them to be successful in life and to contribute to society. Most school systems have mandated their teachers to provide students (K through high school) with lessons on staying away from strangers and saying "no" to drugs. Children need to know how to make decisions to appropriately address these as well as the myriad of other challenges they are expected to meet daily.

ACKNOWLEDGMENT

This work was supported by the National Institute of Child Health and Human Development under grant #2-R44-HD23071-02 to Decision Science Consortium, Inc.

REFERENCES

Editors of Heron House. (1980). *The odds on virtually anything*. New York: G. P. Putnam's Sons.

Messick, D. M. (1985). Social interdependence and decision making. In G. Wright (Ed.), *Behavioral decision making* (pp. 87–109). New York: Plenum.

Silberman, C. E. (1970). *Crisis in the classroom: The remaking of American education*. New York: Random House.

Chapter 8

Teaching the Foundations of Social Decision Making and Problem Solving in the Elementary School

Maurice J. Elias
Leslie R. Branden-Muller
Michael A. Sayette
Rutgers University

Researchers and clinicians have shown that diverse problems experienced by some adolescents, such as substance abuse, teenage pregnancy, delinquency, suicide and depression, and school failure and drop out, are associated with deficits in social decision making and problem solving (Asarnow, Carlson, & Guthrie, 1987; Benard, Fafoglia, & Perone, 1987; Flaherty, Marecek, Olsen, & Wilcove, 1983; Freedman, Donahoe, Rosenthal, Schlundt, & Mc-Fall, 1978; Kalafat & Underwood, 1989). With this realization has come an increased emphasis on improving clients' problem solving as a goal of clinical treatment (e.g., D'Zurilla, 1988; Haley, 1976; Kazdin, Esveldt-Dawson, French, & Unis, 1987; Rotter, 1978). There is also a broader trend toward developing individuals' so-called "critical thinking skills," reflected in the dramatic growth of curriculum-based and other approaches to "teaching thinking" in the schools and in the return of notions like "practical (or social) intelligence," that is, the importance of one's ability to solve problems and make decisions in everyday life contexts (Marzano, Brandt, Hughes, Jones, Presseisen, Rankin, & Suhor, 1988; Sternberg & Wagner, 1986).

From our perspective, these relatively recent developments are both timely and long overdue. We view social decision making and problem solving as a distinctly human characteristic. Its cultivation in children is a *developmental right,* which means to us that it is necessary to incorporate the goal of improving social decision making into the mainstream of educational practice (and therefore into the training of teachers and educational administrators—cf. a fuller discussion in a special issue of the *Journal of*

School Health, 1990, on Comprehensive School Health Education). Because these skills are so basic and their influence is so pervasive, it is unfair to continue the prevailing (implicit) practice of "reserving" skill development efforts for children and adolescents who have experienced interpersonal difficulties related to their skill deficits.

For over a decade, members of the Improving Social Awareness–Social Problem Solving (ISA–SPS) Project have been engaged in an action-research enterprise in schools, developing curriculum-based approaches for teaching social decision-making to children. The Project views social decision making as the "fourth R" in basic elementary education (Elias & Clabby, 1989). The work of the ISA–SPS team has been informed by two important perspectives:

1. *A developmental perspective:* Our curriculum design and research encompasses grades Kindergarten through 12. This has allowed us to understand the pattern of development of social decision making and problem solving, its relationship to more general trends in cognitive and socioemotional functioning, and the factors that seem to encourage and limit its growth. We have become convinced of the benefits of providing a solid foundation of social decision-making skills in the elementary grades. As with reading and language skills, it is possible to learn social decision making at virtually any point in one's school career. However, the receptivity of children of elementary school age and the way in which they are able to integrate social decision making into diverse aspects of their functioning suggest the likelihood of strong preventive and promotive gains from early teaching (Spivack & Shure, 1985).

The developmental reasons for the benefits of early initial teaching can be derived from two comprehensive reports on the health status of early adolescents and the adequacy of our current system of middle grades education (Carnegie Council on Adolescent Development, 1989; Wheelock & Dorman, 1988). The multitude of psychosocial, physical, cognitive, and relational changes that accompany the onset of puberty have significant implications for instruction in social decision-making. First of all, there is greater developmental diversity in early adolescence than in other major periods for school-aged children. That diversity results in part from the wide variability in the onset, progression, and comprehensiveness of pubertal and related physical and cognitive changes. This creates considerable difficulties in the design of curriculum and instruction. Although the problems are by no means insurmountable, educators agree that helping children consolidate, access, and apply their information and skills in the social, affective, and health domains is at least as realistic and feasible a set of goals as embarking on significant content or process initiatives.

A second point is that adolescents of high-school age are more likely to possess and use abilities that Piaget labelled "formal operations." Their abilities to see various sides of a problem, view the world from perspectives other than their own, focus on long- and short-term consequences to self and others, and cognitively create and retain decision-making schema that include plans with multiple contingent elements allow for considerable receptivity to engaging, well designed instructional procedures. But perhaps most critically, these adolescents are likely to possess the perspective needed to have the *motivation* to learn, retain, and apply social decision-making strategies. These incentives may vary; they may be focused around jobs, careers, college, dating, driving, relationships with parents or teachers, experimentation with and use of chemical substances, or one's social position. However, developmental theory and data suggest that significant instructional initiatives in social decision making in high school are likely to have more enduring benefits than those in the middle grades (especially in the absence of reinforcement of these initiatives in high school).

A final point, however, raises a caveat and suggests why we have chosen to place an emphasis on instruction in the elementary grades. This period is one in which children are developing attitudes, habits, and orientations toward thinking and learning that set patterns for the future. The incentive systems for children in the elementary grades also tend to be relatively uniform; pleasing teachers and parents, getting along with peers, being successful in at least some school and leisure activities, and having fun are common priorities. Social decision-making skills are easily linked to these priorities, and thus children can be helped to see the relevance of social decision-making instruction. When competently implemented, social decision-making instruction in the elementary grades enhances children's orientation toward being decision makers and problem solvers in social situations, increases self-efficacy, and primes children's receptivity to future instruction, whether in middle school or high school (Elias & Clabby, in press).

2. *A contextual perspective:* We have been impressed with research findings reporting (a) the difficulties of generalizing gains in behavioral treatment across settings and (b) the domain specificity of human problem-solving abilities (Bransford, Sherwood, Vye, & Rieser, 1986; Kendall & Hollon, 1980). It appears that generic training in critical thinking skills (or in thinking skills linked "across the curriculum" to various academic areas) is unlikely to transfer to the interpersonal domain without explicit instruction (Sternberg & Martin, 1988). These findings can be addressed in our educational system by planning context-focused training in the domain of socially-based decision making and problem solving. And within the social domain, instruction must be carefully designed to foster application in salient contexts for children, such as peer relationships, teacher-student relationships, and the management of interpersonal relationships with classmates and parents while trying to do one's school work.

We must also be careful to consider that social decision-making occurs in an *emotional context*. The problems that children encounter and the decisions they must make all have implications for their psychosocial functioning and their developing sense of identity. Raven (1987) astutely pointed out that children's displays of so-called "cognitive" or "academic" excellence are invariably associated with some form of affective intensification—positive or negative—experienced in themselves and in others with whom they are interacting. He suggested that the educational field will benefit from acknowledging that for most practical and instructional purposes, cognition and emotion should be considered as co-occurring and functioning in an integrated (although not clearly specified) manner. At the very least, Raven's work shows that significant oversights can result from a purely cognitive orientation to learning and instruction.

For the present paper, we wish to take up Raven's point and examine the ways in which current approaches to improving children's social decision making and problem solving address the role of emotions. To do so, we have selected three approaches, each of which acknowledges the role of emotion and can be considered an example of a widely held, widely cited point of view. We will compare the approaches' theoretical positions and the way in which those positions get translated into instructional/curricular procedures. The approaches and their positions are outlined next, followed by a more detailed discussion of each:

Social Information Processing.   This approach to improving social decision-making is closely linked to the analogy of computers. Information from the environment is "input," subjected to various encoding and associational operations ("throughput"), and then followed by a behavioral response ("output"). Emotions are viewed primarily as "noise" in the system and as interfering with maximally effective processing.

A Problem Solving Approach.   From this point of view, emotions are seen as either facilitating or inhibiting decision making, depending on whether the arousal accompanying the problem or decision is positive or negative or of high or low intensity. Negative emotions (defeat, dread) "disrupt" problem solving and decision making, whereas positive emotions (hope, happiness) are seen as motivating and reinforcing.

The Improving Social Awareness–Social Problem Solving Perspective.   In the ISA-SPS approach, an attempt is made to operationalize the perspective that there can be no genuine differentiation of emotion and cognition (Piaget, 1981). Recent research is supportive of the ISA–SPS position, indicating that attentional and memory processes are organized and guided along networks that contain affective, or sensory, features as their defining elements (Cowan, 1988). Thus, a "memory" is best understood as containing emotional as well as cognitive "information." Even memories of "facts" are likely to contain contextual information related to the time, place, circumstances, feelings, and so forth, accompanying the learning, reinforcement, or elaboration of those facts.

A COMPARISON OF APPROACHES

Social Information Processing

Proponents of social information processing models have been intrigued by the question of how children learn competent interpersonal behavior, and the associated questions of how incompetent interpersonal behaviors—particularly with peers—are sustained and how they can be changed. Preeminent among current work in this area is that of Dodge (1986). Dodge borrowed from cognitive, social, and developmental psychology in formulating his social information processing model of social competence. For example, Flavell's (1974) notion of social inferences has been integrated into Dodge's model. According to this position, children must first be aware that other people have thoughts. Next, they must realize that they must make inferences about these other people. Third, they must *make* the inferences about others' thoughts and finally use these inferences to determine their own behavior.

Dodge extended Flavell's primarily cognitive model to behavior by using concepts from Goldfried and D'Zurilla (1969). They discussed behavior as following a sequence that includes understanding the context, searching for possible responses, deciding which of the possible responses is best after anticipating the consequences of the different options, and executing the selected response. Dodge (1986) believed that a series of cognitive processes is necessary in order to display competent social performance. These processes are viewed as occurring in a sequential, temporal order and, like the model espoused by Goldfried and D'Zurilla, include encoding and interpreting environmental cues, generating a behavioral response, selecting a response, and behaviorally enacting the response selected (Dodge, 1986).

From these assumptions, Dodge derived a five-step model of social information processing, with each step representing a separate skill. Step 1 involves the encoding of environmental cues. Step 2 calls for the interpretation of these encoded cues. Step 3 refers to the response search process when the child generates a variety of possible solutions to the problem. Step 4 is the stage where potential responses are evaluated in terms of the anticipated consequences leading to the selection of an optimal response. Step 5 involves the enactment of self-evaluation of the response selected in the preceding stage.

Dodge's model stresses the importance of domain specificity. As children's behaviors are a function of a variety of cognitive processes, it is important to conduct assessments and, when necessary, intervene at each of the five steps. In addition, it is unwise to assume that a program training a child to respond nonaggressively to provocation by another child will lead to a change in behavior that would generalize to a group entry situation. In training programs, the skills need to be addressed explicitly within a variety of contexts.

In addition to establishing more precision in assessing both the different skills and the contexts in which they are used, Dodge (1986) addressed the relationship between cognitive processes and the subsequent behavior. Recognizing that knowing what to do does not always predict behavior, Dodge suggested that the real time demands of processing social information may lead to processing overloads that cause a breakdown in behavior. This could be manifested in a failure to undertake a particular processing step, the display of a skill deficit, or the display of some form of bias in processing (Dodge, 1986).

One processing bias, deviant bias, refers to processing based not on skill deficits but on assumptions about a particular cue, interpretation, or response possibility ". . . simply because it is highly available" (p. 38 m.s.). An example of a deviant bias is a child responding to a stranger's smile by averting his or her gaze, whereas another child returns the smile; one interprets the cue as a threat, whereas the other sees a friendly gesture. Dodge maintained that such deviant biases "highlight the role of affect and emotion in information processing" (p. 38). He contended that biases are especially important when responding to ambiguous social cues and has shown empirically that biases reflecting a child's generalized expectancy that actions of others are hostile or threatening may lead ambiguous social cues to be followed by aggressive behaviors.

Although Dodge (1989) identified affect as an important target for future research, as well as a factor that can hinder the problem-solving process, it is not an integral component of his model. Dodge's approach to affect is in contrast to decision-making models that view affective factors as primary. Etzioni (1988) outlined a model whereby emotions and values *"shape to a significant extent decision-making, to the extent it takes place, the information gathered, the ways it is processed, the inferences that are drawn, the options that are being considered, and those that are finally chosen"* (italics original: p. 127). He posited that in the majority of decisions, affective and value-related factors dictate the course of action. For example, in some cultures, it is not the practice for adolescent males having difficulty with social relationships to discuss such problems with their mothers. On logical grounds, there may be occasions when this option is not only advisable, but optimal (such as the case of how to deal with a girlfriend). However, because of what Etzioni referred to as affective and value-related factors, such an option and related options (talk to a grandmother, female cousin, female guidance counselor) may never be perceived as possibilities to be considered. Thus, the logical consideration of finding the best sources of information to assist in decision making is constrained by nonlogical factors defining the universe of possible sources.

Another, more common set of cases includes career and college choices where "whole categories of positions are not considered at all. . . ." (Etzioni, 1988; p. 131). Rates of dropouts, firings, quittings, and similar indicators combined with reports of school and job counselors suggest that the processes used by adolescents and young adults to arrive at their choices contain lacunae that Etzioni would attribute to the operation of affect and value (or at least to errors in the use of rational decision-making procedures). Another example is that of a child or adolescent imbued with the value of being "tough." When embroiled in an argument with a friend, such a child is likely, in Etzioni's terms, to exclude from deliberation "major subsets of facts, interpretations, and approaches" (p. 131) that would be expected from a "rational" or "cognitive" decision-making framework. One would have to understand the child's fear of parental reaction to his or her *not* being tough to predict the child's decision-making process, ultimate choice, and subsequent behavior. Etzioni also emphasized that emotion is not necessarily disruptive; it can also play a positive role, such as in the "selection of ethical means over others" (p. 138).

The elevation of affect to a position that is no longer peripheral to information-processing capacities in social decision making is a perspective that is not well elaborated or incorporated into current computer analogy. Although a central role for affect does not necessarily challenge the integrity of Dodge's model, it does call into question its applicability to the multitude of decisions facing children and adolescents. The type of model proposed by Dodge may be utilized in only a small proportion of problem situations. If Etzioni's (1988) contention is accurate, then it is necessary to examine models that elaborate a more balanced relationship between affective factors and the way in which information about social cues and situations is organized and processed.

A Problem Solving Approach

Resolving interpersonal problems and making social decisions are processes in which we engage every day of our lives, and whose main principles exist in two forms. The first is a prescriptive, or normative, model that delineates how people should solve problems in order to be maximally effective. This model has five components which include various skills and abilities. The second is a clinical problem-solving training or treatment model. It is built on the prescriptive model's theoretical framework, and it involves a series of steps intended to increase problem-solving ability (D'Zurilla & Goldfried, 1971), to increase social competence, and to reduce stress

(D'Zurilla, 1986). We examine both of these models to see to what extent the theoretical model incorporates affect and cognition, and whether the intervention model attempts to treat the client in both the affective and cognitive domains. We take our prototypical models from D'Zurilla (1986), a comprehensive version of the seminal D'Zurilla and Goldfried (1971) article.

Theoretical/Prescriptive Model of Problem Solving

D'Zurilla's prescriptive model is cognitively based. A brief summary of this model serves to highlight the cognitive nature of the problem-solving model. The five stages of D'Zurilla's (1986) problem-solving model are: Problem Orientation, Problem Definition and Formulation, Generation of Alternative Solutions, Decision Making, and Solution Implementation and Verification. The stages are ordered in a logical fashion, and although they are most useful when applied in the order presented, they can be followed with some flexibility; one might shift back and forth from one stage to another as insights gained in one stage influence previous and subsequent considerations.

Stage 1: Problem Orientation

This phase is designed generally to facilitate problem-solving performance throughout the problem-solving process. Problem orientation has four functions: (a) to increase awareness of problems and to introduce the idea of problem solving; (b) to encourage positive expectations for problem solving and to divert attention from negative and preoccupying thoughts; (c) to encourage persistence against emotional stress and difficult situations; and (d) to facilitate a positive emotional state and discourage disruptive emotional distress.

The major cognitive variables that are associated with a general problem-solving style (i.e., how one approaches a problematic situation) are problem perception, problem attribution, problem appraisal, personal control, and time/effort commitment. A brief description of these variables follows.

Problem Perception.   Problem perception involves recognizing and labeling problems. In order to recognize and label problems properly, one must learn to conceive of a problem as a situation, "and learn to use [one's] maladaptive responses (e.g., anxiety, ineffective behavior) as cues to monitor [one's] transitions with the environment and identify the problematic situation that is causing these responses" (D'Zurilla, 1986, p. 23). For example, an anxious, young, hard-working sales representative striving to do well may label his problem in terms of pleasing his boss without being aware that the "real" problem is the conflict between his demanding work schedule and his family responsibilities. With the problem perceived only in terms of his boss, it is unlikely that the sales representative will be successful at reducing his anxiety; indeed, his subsequent problem-solving efforts may exacerbate his anxiety.

Problem Attribution.   This deals with one's attribution of problems in living to environmental factors, to harmless, passing, or changeable personal factors, or to stable personal defects. Those who believe that problems are a normal part of life and not due to stable personal defects are more likely to initiate problem solving confidently.

Problem Appraisal.   Problem appraisal is the person's judgment of a problem as it relates to his/her social and personal well-being. Problems can be viewed as challenging or as harmful or threatening. Positive appraisers—those who view problems as challenges—are more likely to engage enthusiastically in problem solving than negative appraisers. Problem attribution influences problem appraisal.

Personal Control.   This variable deals with the personal-control cognitions of "outcome expectancy" and "self-efficacy expectancy" (Bandura, 1977). Those who perceive they have control over a situation and that they are capable of solving a problem have less anxiety, better adaptive coping behavior, and are more likely to initiate problem-solving behavior and persist in the face of obstacles.

Time/Effort Commitment.   This involves the chances that a person will accurately estimate the time needed to solve a particular problem successfully and the likelihood that the person will devote enough time and energy to problem solving. Adolescents encountering difficulty in school often underestimate the time and energy needed to resolve their problems. Perhaps their greatest omission is a consideration of the interpersonal sequelae of their difficulties (i.e., reactions and perceptions of teachers and parents and the ways in which these influence their reactions to the adolescent's subsequent problem-solving efforts).

Stage 2: Problem Definition and Formulation

This stage of the problem-solving process is very important, as "a well-defined problem is half-solved" (D'Zurilla, 1986, p. 26). One defines the problem by gathering as much relevant information about the problem as possible, clarifying the nature of the problem, setting a realistic problem-solving goal, and reexamining the importance of the problem for personal well-being.

Consider, for example, the following situation. An adolescent whose parents are divorced has not heard from his father for a while. He may think his father is ignoring or rejecting him. But, if he gathers more information, he may find that in reality his father has been very busy. The adolescent must then redefine the original nature of the problem (that his father was rejecting him) to take into account the external demands of the situation on both himself and his father, as well as his needs for contact and company with his father. So, if the adolescent's goal is to see his father more often in the next few weeks to make up for lost time, he may fail in his attempts if his father (due to external demands) is not readily available. The adolescent would also need to assess whether not seeing his father is the real problem and think about whether there are any antecedent problems (such as anger at his mother, jealousy at siblings who have better relationships with his parents, guilt over his perceived role in the divorce, etc.). Finally, when the problem is understood and the goals are stated, the adolescent needs to reassess the significance of the problem and consider the extent to which it can be defined in a manner in which he has more control over its possible resolution than it would seem at present (i.e., with him *waiting* for contacts from father and *assuming* rejection).

Stage 3: Generation of Alternative Solutions

In this stage, the person is encouraged to be creative in coming up with an many novel ways of dealing with the situation as possible. Using "brainstorming," a technique that gets the problem solver to generate as many ideas as possible while deferring judgment of suggestions, the problem solver maximizes the possibility that the best solution will be among the suggestions.

Stage 4: Decision Making

The task of decision making is to evaluate the available solution alternatives by comparing and judging them, and then to select the "best" one for implementation. Decision making is based on the expected utility model, according to which one considers the value and likelihood of the anticipated consequences, decides whether the alternatives are feasible and acceptable, and looks at the cost and benefit of alternatives. Specifically, utility judgments are based on (a) the "likelihood of achieving the problem-solving goal", (b) "the quality of the expected emotional outcome", (c) the "amount of time and effort expected to be required", and (d) one's "overall personal–social well-being" (D'Zurilla, 1986, p. 35). D'Zurilla suggested improving decision making by helping the decision maker realize that there are alternative decision frames (that is, conceptualizations and formulations) for any problem and that she has certain beliefs, values, and emotions that color the desirability of any particular solution. In effect, the decision maker should try to reframe the problem and consider different ways to express the same proposed solution, because seeing the solution in various lights can change the attractiveness of the solution.

Stage 5: Solution Implementation and Verification

In this stage, the problem solver implements the solution in real life and assesses the solution outcome and the solution effectiveness. The problem solver's assessment is based on his/her cognitive/behavioral conception of self-control, which may be divided into four components:

Performance.   The problem solver examines whether obstacles prevented him/her from performing effectively. For example, adolescents often misattribute social failures to "catastrophic" deficits in physical appearance. But a "zit" may be less the cause of performance failure than poor planning, awkward interpersonal skills, or distracting thoughts due to family problems or impending academic demands.

Self-Monitoring.   The problem solver records or measures solution behavior and his/her success at producing the appropriate behavior. For example, adolescents who must lower the amounts of their phone bills would self-monitor by keeping a record of the calls they make.

Self-Evaluation.   The problem solver "compares the observed solution outcome with the predicted or expected outcome for that solution" (D'Zurilla, 1986, p. 40).

Self-Reinforcement.   If self-evaluation revealed that the problem solver met his/her goals, he/she rewards him/herself. This is a critical step because self-reinforcement rewards effective problem-solving performance and "strengthens perceived control and self-efficacy expectations" (D'Zurilla, 1986, p. 40). According to D'Zurilla, the reward can be tangible, such as buying something the person has desired, or a self-statement such as, "I did a good job. I'm proud of myself." It is likely that children and most adolescents respond best to tangible forms of self-reinforcement.

The Role of Emotion

A careful reading of this clearly cognitive model discloses that D'Zurilla's prescriptive model is not devoid of an affective component. Affect plays an implicit role in the prescriptive model: to clear up the problem solver's thinking so that he/she can problem solve more efficiently. For example, in the Problem Orientation stage, D'Zurilla encourages the problem solver to learn to use what might be called maladaptive affective responses (e.g., anxiety) to help identify what it is in the environment that is contributing to those responses. In addition, he suggests that being challenged by the problem rather than threatened makes it more likely that the problem solver will be enthusiastic and thereby raise his/her chances of solving the problem adequately. Furthermore, the prescriptive model says that the problem solver can expect to have less anxiety when he/she has greater self-efficacy and control. Again, this increases the likelihood of the problem solver making a sound decision.

D'Zurilla devoted an entire chapter of his 1986 book to "The Role of Emotions in Social Problem Solving." Specifically, D'Zurilla recognized three sources of emotional arousal during problem solving:

The Objective Problematic Situation.   D'Zurilla (1986) proposed that most problematic situations involve emotions that cause stress (e.g., feelings of loss, frustration, uncertainty, conflict, unpredictability, complexity, novelty, and ambiguity).

Problem-Orientation Cognitions.   This refers to one's beliefs, evaluations, and expectations of the problem and of one's ability to solve the problem successfully. People can approach a problem situation and deal with problem solving as a challenge or a threat. When viewing the problem situation as a challenge, the person experiences exhilaration and positive excitement; when viewing the problem situation as a threat, the person experiences fear or anxiety.

Specific Problem-Solving Tasks.   Different emotions can be aroused at each step of the prescriptive problem-solving model. Those emotions in turn influence the way one approaches subsequent stages of the model. Emotional arousal before or during problem solving can interfere with or facilitate problem-solving performance. Negative affect can inhibit performance, as can high levels of arousal. Positive affect facilitates performance, as do low and moderate levels of emotional arousal, which increase motivation and alertness.

D'Zurilla stated that emotions from all three sources can facilitate or inhibit problem-solving performance, depending on whether the person experiences the emotions as pleasurable or as painful and the degree to which he/she is emotionally aroused (i.e., the degree to which he/she experiences autonomic nervous system arousal).

Training Model of Social Problem Solving

D'Zurilla's (1986) training model explicitly reflects the view that emotions can influence one's ability to solve problems. To the prescriptive steps, he added "Use and Control of Emotions in Problem Solving," a section that described how people can be instructed to use their emotions to facilitate problem-solving effectiveness. D'Zurilla (1986) suggested that one way emotions may be used is "as a cue for problem recognition" (p. 110). For example, a negative emotional response signals that one has just encountered a problematic situation and that one may engage in problem solving. Emotions can also be used "to facilitate motivation for problem solving" (p. 110); one can adopt a positive approach toward problem solving. In addition, emotions can be a problem-solving goal. That is, one's goal can be to increase positive affect and/or reduce negative affect. For example, during decision making, emotions can serve as a possible consequence to consider when thinking about solution outcomes. Emotions can also serve as a criterion for evaluating the solutions one has tried in the implementation phase. Finally, emotions can reinforce effective problem-solving behavior. Carefully applying effective problem-solving rules and principles can result in successful problem solving, leading to positive emotional reactions.

Analysis of D'Zurilla's Problem-Solving Approach

Although D'Zurilla's explanation of the role of emotions is more explicit in his intervention model, affect is no better *integrated* here than in the prescriptive model. The preceding description is just one unit in the training model which is otherwise comprised of the same general steps as the prescriptive model, joined by one last unit, 'Motivation and Generalization." "Use and Control of Emotions in Problem Solving" stands as a separate section, sandwiched between Problem Orientation and Definition and Formulation.

Furthermore, emotion-oriented techniques in therapy, as described by D'Zurilla (1986), serve mainly to ensure optimal cognitive conditions. These techniques focus directly on minimizing disruptive emotional arousal which can interfere with problem solving at each stage. Such techniques largely focus on relaxation and desensitization methods. At times, D'Zurilla maintains, specific emotion-focused techniques are not necessary. The adult client may only need training in how to "recognize potentially disruptive emotions and cognitions"; "identify the various resources they already have available for coping" with the negative effects of stress (such resources may be music, hobbies, pleasant imagery, distraction, social support, exercise, etc.); or "use these resources when needed to minimize, control and prevent these effects so that problem-solving performance will not be disrupted" (D'Zurilla, 1986, p. 112).

We believe that such a treatment of affect will not suffice. Intervention models should intertwine affect and cognition even if they do not specify the precise nature of the interrelationship between the two. Proponents of an independent systems model and proponents of an integrative model believe, although for different reasons, that the therapy we employ should include both affective and cognitive components. For example, Rachman (1981) believed that we should access both affect and cognition in therapy because it may be hard to influence affective experiences through attacking cognitions if affect and cognition are partially independent or if affective reactions precede cognitions. Greenberg and Safran (1984) advocated incorporating affect into therapeutic techniques because clinical problems may involve a "breakdown of the emotional synthesis process" (p. 7). They believed "an important focus of therapy should be the integration of the different levels of processing involved in the construction of emotional experience" (p. 7). These considerations are equally relevant to a preventive and/or education-oriented intervention approach.

The Improving Social Awareness–Social Problem Solving Project

One program that integrates affect and cognition in many stages is the Improving Social Awareness–Social Problem Solving (ISA-SPS) Project (Elias & Clabby, 1989; Elias & Clabby, in press), a preventive/educational intervention approach. This program is centered around a curriculum comprised of eight steps which are introduced sequentially, and which together help build skills needed for healthy social and emotional growth. These steps are presented in the language in which they are taught:

1. Look for signs of different feelings.
2. Tell yourself what the problem is.
3. Decide on your goal.
4. Stop and think of as many solutions to the problem as you can.
5. For each solution, think of all the things that might happen next.
6. Choose your best solution.
7. Plan it and make a final check.
8. Try it and rethink it.

The ISA-SPS program recognizes that in order for children to engage in the social decision-making and problem-solving steps in the most effective manner possible, the children must be given the proper tools. Therefore, the eight steps are preceded by a "Readiness" phase that prepares the children for working on decision-making and problem-solving skills. This phase of the curriculum is meant to give children the means to be in control of impulses to be distracted or angry, to be aware of the presence of different emotions, to recognize different emotions, and to acquire ways of dealing with different emotions. A considerable amount of emphasis—as well as curricular priority—is spent acquainting children with their emotional selves. Also, much emphasis is placed on understanding the emotional expression and experience of others. Special techniques and diverse activities and games provide the structure for these affect-enhancing lessons.

The one technique in the ISA-SPS curriculum that emphasizes using emotions solely to facilitate cognitive activity is "Keep Calm" (Elias & Clabby, 1989), a technique that helps children recognize when they are upset and might lose control and provides them with a way to keep in control. The children are told to engage in self-talk to "stop" and to "keep calm." Children are trained to take deep breaths, with specific instructions about inhaling, exhaling, counting, and other forms of distraction. They are taught that they should continue to use this technique until they are calmer. Teachers and children use "Keep Calm" in a variety of settings.

Most other Readiness lessons focus explicitly on affect and recognize the importance of both affect and cognition. One technique, the "Sharing Circle," encourages children to deal with each other on an emotional level. Sitting in a circle with their classmates, children are encouraged to state their name and something about themselves, such as "how they are feeling at that time." This technique provides an opportunity for children to get more comfortable with one another and with expressing something about themselves. It is used as a starting point in nearly all Readiness lessons.

Another unit introduces several techniques that focus on an awareness of feelings: "Feelings Flashbacks," mirroring exercises, and role playing (Elias & Clabby, 1989). In Feelings Flashbacks, each child in the class selects a card with a specific feeling written on it and shares with the class a specific time or situation when he or she felt that way. Other children are encouraged to ask questions. Mirroring exercises require one child to mirror another's expressions, movements, and position. For example, if one child looks sad, then happy, then scared, then tired, the child mirroring must reflect these same emotions. Children switch roles frequently and may share their experiences.

The curriculum provides for both inanimate and animate role plays. In the inanimate role plays, children "identify with and become an object" (Elias & Clabby, 1989, Unit 8, Topic 13). They are asked to identify how they would feel if various things were done to them as this object, for example, if they were a table, how they would feel if cold fruit juice spilled on them. The other children are asked to observe the role-player and identify the feelings he/she displays. In a similar fashion, interpersonal role plays aid the children in recognizing feelings in others and expressing feelings themselves.

Once the class has worked through the part of the curriculum that prepares the children to work together as a problem-solving team, the children learn to use feelings as a cue that they have a social problem, that is, a conflict or disagreement with a person or group of people. The children learn that they can notice that they have a personal or interpersonal problem because they get a "not so good" feeling (i.e., unhappy, sad, pressured; Elias & Clabby, 1989, Unit 9, Topics 1–6). This "not so good" feeling is also introduced as a "Feelings Fingerprint"—a characteristic way of experiencing how one feels when upset or stressed (Clabby & Elias, 1987).

The Feelings Fingerprint is a key part of the first of the social decision-making and problem-solving steps, "Look for Signs of Different Feelings." During this step, children learn to become more sensitive to their own and others' feelings by learning to recognize and verbalize those feelings (Unit 9, Topics 5 and 6). Typically, they hear a story or watch a videotape or film depicting how children feel as they encounter a variety of everyday problems. The children may also engage in activities that demonstrate that different children may show various feelings differently, or that provide children with the opportunity to nonverbally act out certain feelings while the other children in the class guess what feeling that is. This latter game is known as "Feelings Charades." Once the children have a good grasp on their own and others' feelings they proceed to the next step of the social decision making and problem solving model.[1]

The ISA-SPS approach, like that used by D'Zurilla for training, treats affect explicitly. The ISA-SPS approach, however, goes one step beyond D'Zurilla's model by integrating affect into the model: "Look for Signs of Different Feelings" is the first social decision-making and problem-solving step in the ISA-SPS model. Each time children face a social problem, they are taught to proceed through each problem-solving step, beginning with a continual review of feelings in self and others and how to use them.

Children are taught both facets of looking for signs of different feelings. The first emphasizes signs of feelings in *themselves;* the second emphasizes signs of feelings in *others.* Deficient "feelings vocabularies" and inaccurate labeling of feelings are associated with children who are viewed as having behavioral or emotional disturbances. In our view, these children do not adequately label their feelings and are likely to engage in avoidant, distracting, or sedating activities as a coping strategy. Similarly, inaccurate labeling in social situations is also likely to lead to coping responses that will be judged as maladaptive. Therefore, through the use of pictures, television programs, movies, and other visual stimuli, children are encouraged to look

---

[1]Although the curricular examples of "Readiness" activities are focused on children in the elementary school grades, the skills being discussed are equally relevant to successful social decision making in adolescence. Clinical case records and practice confirm repeatedly, for example, that adolescents experiencing psychosocial dysfunction often have impoverished feelings vocabularies, and view their "Feelings Fingerprints" as generalized aversive stimuli to be avoided, terminated, deadened, and so forth, as quickly as possible. These points are made by the work of Selman (1980), who studied the interpersonal negotiation strategies—and errors— of adolescents in treatment facilities. From our perspective, early skill building can help avert a history of interpersonal difficulties which then tends to make the process of unlearning and remediating skill deficits in adolescents especially challenging.

carefully at the sources of information about feelings that exist all around them. They are taught to identify how they may mistakenly neglect to consider the feelings of others in situations and/or project their *own* feelings and expectations upon others rather than accurately observe and interpret cues in themselves and in their environment that are there to be seen.

The ISA-SPS model also succeeds at integrating affect and cognition because it works feelings into many parts of the curriculum; other problem-solving steps include some mention of affect. For example, when learning the step "Tell yourself what the problem is," children are told that a problem is defined as "something that happens to someone or between two people that usually leads to 'not so good,' upset, or uncomfortable feelings." In the step that encourages children to generate alternative solutions to a problem, children are shown that one's own feelings or those of others (e.g., "Bob might feel good because he is trying something"; "Inez felt that her ideas were useful because they might help her family feel better") can be appropriate measures of the potential viability or success of one of the alternatives proposed (although by no means the only such measures). In step five, "For each solution, think of all the things that might happen next," children learn that consequences are "a feeling or an action that follows, or happens after, something else; ask yourself 'what might happen next' or 'how would you feel after . . .'" and that a best solution is "a way to solve a problem that comes closest to meeting your goal without harming yourself or others." The project thus incorporates affective and cognitive elements to forge a curriculum that explicitly underscores the importance of emotion in problem solving.

Context of Application

Earlier, we noted concerns about situation specificity and the necessity of training for desired applications. In the ISA-SPS approach, these concerns are addressed in three primary ways:

1. For each Readiness and Instructional Phase topic, instructional activities begin with a discussion of the practical, everyday rationale for a particular skill. The goal is to elicit from children situations in their lives in which the skill could be applied; these situations are then available to be used as examples during the lessons.

2. The ISA-SPS curriculum contains a specific set of scripted lessons organized into what we call the Application Phase (Elias & Clabby, 1989). Here, the eight social decision-making and problem-solving steps are used as a framework for analyzing academic and interpersonal tasks, including creative writing, social studies, understanding the media, correcting personal weak points, overcoming stereotypes and prejudice, and making transitions to new classes and schools.

3. Much credence is given to the value of creating a climate and culture of social decision making and problem solving in the school, and also extending this to the home. Material and procedures exist to train parents, administrators, counselors, school-based support staff, and lunchroom aides in the same approaches being introduced in the classroom (Clabby & Elias, 1987; Elias & Clabby, 1989).

In summary, the ISA-SPS approach fosters affective and cognitive integration in a variety of specific, salient contexts to maximize the likelihood of having a tangible, lasting impact on children.

Toward A Multiple Decision Frame Approach

The ISA-SPS project is attempting to move toward a multiple decision frame (MDF) approach to social decision making and problem solving. Our MDF approach emphasizes the role of emotion in both the theory of decision-making processes and in the practice of teaching, enhancing, or correcting those processes in children as a preventive or remediative mental health strategy.

From the information processing perspective, we have come to understand the importance of being grounded in behavioral reality. This especially refers to characteristics, patterns, and limits of humans as processors of information. Further, it requires us to be cognizant of the interaction of such characteristics with properties of the external stimuli and the context of their presentation. Dodge's (1986) work is especially helpful because it points out tendencies for human decision making to be subject to "bias" or "error." Because human decision making is subject to developmental factors and to a variety of situationally based complexities, the sources and operation of "error" are widespread and subtle.

D'Zurilla's (1986) work, forged in clinical contexts, makes it clear that a theory of the operation of social decision making must be differentiated from a theory of instruction. In our view, emotion is not something "external" to the social decision-making process (i.e., something that facilitates or inhibits problem-solving performance), nor is it a by product of cognitive processes. With Piaget (1981), we view emotion as an "indivisible" aspect of social decision making. Piaget expressed well that there is no separate system for encoding cognition and affect. Therefore, emotions are a constant feature of human judgment and functioning.

One of the implications of such a perspective relates to our view that there are certain elements of social decision making and problem solving that can be identified as having heuristic value, although the precise nature of their operation and interrelationship is not well known. Next is a brief review of some of those elements which we have found necessary to "accommodate" in our instructional procedures.

Interpersonal realities introduce constraints into social decision-making processes. The vast majority of social decision-making circumstances are not optimal (Simon, 1983). People often face decisions when they are tired, under time limits, feeling pressured by competing demands for energy and attention, missing relevant information, not aware of all possible sources of help, unsure how details will play out, and influenced by irrational beliefs about personal or group or organizational goals (Elias, 1989a; Weick, 1971).

Emotional factors transform the meaning of social decision-making situations and the way in which possible solutions are sought. Emotional factors are intertwined with what can be thought of as cognitive and situational elements. Therefore, however one wishes to describe the way in which experiences with prior decisions are organized—whether as schema or in various forms of short- and long-term memory storage—one must include an affective aspect as part of the description. This is significant because it implies that knowledge of behavioral or social learning histories must go beyond "factual" occurrences and antecedent–behavior–consequence analyses and attend to the emotions surrounding and accompanying events, if one is to infer how previous circumstances will influence current social decision-making processes. The affect surrounding certain decisions, options, and situations may lead entire domains of knowledge—or potentially accessible knowledge—to be cognitively "off limits" because the goal of a logical problem-solving process may be incompatible with the goal of avoidance of the emotional sequelae of a situation. Some examples of situations in which certain classes of alternatives and consequences might be avoided, or omitted from consideration, include teenagers avoiding dating or group situations (i.e., because they fear ridicule or rejection, they will not consider alternatives—like calling their peers—which are likely to put them closer to the situations they wish to avoid) or children not asking for help they need in academics or in hobby activities (e.g., because they are concerned that even after receiving help, they might not be successful and would then have to confront the reality of their limitations and how this might affect their relationships with parents or teachers).

Social decision making occurs in the context of application of multiple decision frames. In the ISA–SPS approach, our use of eight social decision making "steps" is actually better conceptualized as our recommending that a social decision be made through the filter of multiple decision frames. We begin by invoking a feelings-oriented frame, followed by a goal-oriented frame, and then a possibilities and outcomes-oriented frame. Next, our emphasis on planning invokes a constraints/reality frame, followed by an obstacles-based reframing of the situation, in which the feelings and outcome frames are shifted to negative. Once action occurs, it is incorporated in a variety of "categories" for future use in subsequent decisions through a review and rethink frame. The social decision-making frames are linked to the skills taught in the Readiness phase and the content and linkages of the frames are expanded and intertwined through the application phase. Thoughtful decision making has been identified in recent reviews as flexible, nonlinear, and recursive (Marzano et al., 1988). The MDF framework readily includes these types of thinking. The MDF concept is consistent with the writings of Perkins (1986) and of Sigel and Kelley (in press), all of whom discuss the benefits of using metaphors, analogies, and alternative visual representations as strategies to enrich and modify decision frames. Finally, the multiple decision frame approach explicitly recognizes an individual as constructor of his or her own knowledge network. It therefore allows an incorporation of developmental factors and unique social and affective learning experiences into the frames to serve as a basis of reaction, analysis, and action.

Instructional Implications

The operation of thinking skills programs is usually described in an orderly, logical manner. We would like to depart slightly from this tradition and close with some carefully considered but far from completed propositions about how we think our program *really* works. We have already said that we believe children really learn and use our eight "steps" as *frames*. We are fairly confident that they retain a general sense of sequence in the use of the frames. However, we also believe that children derive sequences that are somewhat idiosyncratic, that they favor the use of "favorite" frames, and that their social decision making is characterized by interconnections and pathways among frames. Here are some other considerations highlighted by the ISA-SPS approach:

1. Our combination of readiness skills, social decision-making frames, and extensive student- and teacher-generated salient examples places numerous elements into what Kaplan and Kaplan (1982) described as a vast knowledge network. The extensive practice opportunities given to children increase automaticity and routinization of interframe connections as well as content-related affective–cognitive–behavioral sequences, all of which serve to reduce the number of "truly novel" situations one experiences (Bloom, 1986). This, in turn, reduces the likelihood of information overload or paralysis or premature action in stressful decision-making contexts.

2. Social decision making and problem solving are rooted in developmental realities. For elementary school-aged children, concrete situations involving school situations and relationships with peers, teachers, and parents are most salient; these become the primary application contexts for our program. Further, children and teachers are receptive to a curricular form of instruction. Our work maximizes this positive "set" by giving children experiences that are empowering, reinforcing, and familiar; at the

same time, these experiences begin to forge children's generalized expectancies for thinking through repetitive social decisions and interpersonal problems. However, we also recognize that middle school- and high school-aged students will require other instructional forms, forms that take into account their developing cognitive and affective capacities and their psychosocial realities, especially their search for a stable, satisfying personal and interpersonal identity. After working for nearly a decade to establish a viable and effective framework for curriculum and instruction in elementary schools, we view the secondary school level with much humility. Our action–research efforts are now directed toward this challenging area, with a particular focus on adolescents' decision-making around substance use, other health-related concerns, academic effort and performance, sexual behavior, and their sense of social responsibility and citizenship.

In our initial work, we have become convinced that the context surrounding social decision-making instruction exercises a strong influence on the form of that instruction in middle school and high school. Specifically, there are so many competing influences on the attention and interest of adolescents that the cumulative curriculum-based approach so successful in the elementary grades often lacks salience and impact at the secondary level (with the general exception of self-contained special education classes). Even the most "appropriately" designed and implemented curriculum and instructional approaches may simply lose to competition in the crowded marketplace of ideas, hobbies, feelings, and interests that adolescents encounter. Accordingly, for the middle and high school, we have begun to experiment with alternative formats, including more intensive focus on a smaller number of self-control and social awareness skills and introducing all eight decision making steps at the beginning of the Instructional Phase and continuing their use throughout the remainder of the program (Elias & Tobias, 1990). We view this shift in tactics as analogous to deciding to serve as a lighthouse in the fog rather than attempting to raise the cloud cover and improve overall visibility. (The latter efforts are more properly the focus of comprehensive school reform efforts.) We are also convinced that the remediative value of curricular approaches to teaching social decision-making to adolescents should not be assumed to be positive; other service formats (individual or group guidance or counseling, for example) may be more beneficial to overcome the effects of social learning histories marked by poor social decision-making and problem solving and negative personal and interpersonal sequelae (Elias, 1990).

3. Educational settings are diverse and pluralistic. This requires an approach that is relatively simple and uniform, that is, consistent from grade to grade and building to building and as applicable to special education as it is to regular education and students labeled as gifted and talented. The ISA-SPS approach has identified two sets of readiness skills—self-control and social awareness—and eight social decision-making frames. Our belief

is that if students master these skills and frames, they will be well equipped to handle many of life's challenges; indeed, the scope of many therapy, rehabilitation, and remediative programs is little different than to provide much of what we have identified as important skills. Thus, we have embarked on a course of deceptive simplicity, which derives its success from continuity across children's salient social contexts, continuity over time, and our explicitly assigning responsibility to children's social environments to elicit, shape, and reinforce elements of thoughtful social decision making.

4. The ISA-SPS approach emphasizes affective and situation-based encoding and representations of experiences. We encourage children to create their own specific frames and interconnections by emphasizing application, realistic planning, anticipation of obstacles, and rethinking (i.e., accommodating current frames to reflect past experiences and likely future circumstances). We never lose sight of children as emotional and social beings and therefore we strive not merely to generate logical problem solving, but rather to encourage thoughtfulness, affective awareness, social sensitivity, and the restoration of a humane balance of these considerations as the normative mode of functioning in social decision-making situations.

By blending information processing and logical problem-solving perspectives with our belief in the inextricable role of affect in social decision-making and the unrelenting presence of reality constraints that will keep problem solving from conforming to optimal models, we feel we have moved in a direction that is useful both heuristically and pragmatically. Although our conceptualizations are far from complete, we have seen positive results—in the form of skill gains, improved everyday decision making, more positive peer relationships, enhanced self-efficacy, and improved coping with stressors in middle school, relative to controls—emerge from the application of our multiple decision frame perspective, particularly in the elementary schools (Elias, 1989b; Elias & Clabby, 1989). By allowing our theory and practice of instruction to be complementary to and synergistic for our ideas about the social decision-making process (rather than isomorphic with these ideas), we feel we have enabled our approach to be more easily assimilated by children and then accommodated and developmentally constructed by them to be maximally applicable to their realities.

REFERENCES

Asarnow, J., Carlson, G., & Guthrie, D. (1987). Coping strategies, self-perceptions, hopelessness, and perceived family environments in depressed and suicidal children. *Journal of Consulting & Clinical Psychology, 55,* 361–366.
Bandura, A. (1977). Self-efficacy: Toward a unifying theory of behavioral change. *Psychological Review, 84,* 191–215.
Benard, B., Fafoglia, G., & Perone, J. (1987, February). Knowing what to do—and not to

do—reinvigorates drug education. *Association for Supervision & Curriculum Development Curriculum Update,* pp. 1–12.

Bloom, B. (1986). Automaticity: The hands and feet of genius. *Educational Leadership, 43*(5), 70–77.

Bransford, J., Sherwood, R., Vye, N., & Rieser, J. (1986). Teaching thinking and problem solving: Research foundations. *American Psychologist, 14,* 1078–1089.

Carnegie Council on Adolescent Development (1989). *Turning points: Preparing American youth for the 21st century.* New York: Carnegie Corporation of New York.

Clabby, J. F., & Elias, M. J. (1987). *Teach your child decision making:* New York: Doubleday.

Cowan, N. (1988). Evolving conceptions of memory storage, selective attention, and their mutual constraints within the human information-processing system. *Psychological Bulletin, 104,* 163–191.

DeFriese, G., Crossland, C., Pearson, C., & Sullivan, C. (1990). Comprehensive school health programs: Current status and future prospects. *Journal of School Health, 60*(4, whole).

Dodge, K. A. (1986). A social information processing model of social competence in children. In M. Perlmutter (Ed.), *Minnesota symposium on child psychology* (Vol. 18, pp. 77–125). Hillsdale, NJ: Lawrence Erlbaum Associates.

D'Zurilla, T. J. (1986). *Problem solving therapy.* New York: Springer.

D'Zurilla, T. J. (1988). Problem solving therapy. In K. Dobson (Ed.), *Handbook of cognitive-behavioral therapies* (pp. 85–135). New York: Guilford.

D'Zurilla, T. J., & Goldfried, M. R. (1971). Problem solving and behavior modification. *Journal of Abnormal Psychology, 78,* 107–126.

Elias, M. J. (1989a). Effective family decision making: Living the good life under the decision tree. *Creative Living, 18*(2), 8–12.

Elias, M. J. (1989b, August). Longitudinal impact of a social decision making and problem solving program on substance abuse and psychopathology. In R. Weissberg (Chair), *Follow-up studies of social competence promotion: Findings and future directions.* Presentation at the biannual conference of the Society for Research in Child Development, Kansas City, MO.

Elias, M. J. (1990). The role of affect and social relationships in health behavior and school health curriculum and instruction. *Journal of School Health, 60,* 157–163.

Elias, M. J., & Clabby, J. F. (1989). *Social decision making skills: A curriculum guide for the elementary grades.* Rockville, MD: Aspen.

Elias, M. J., & Clabby, J. F. (in press). *Problem solving and decision making in children.* San Francisco: Jossey-Bass.

Elias, M. J., & Tobias, S. (1990). *Problem-solving decision-making for social and academic success: A school-based approach.* Washington, DC: NEA.

Etzioni, A. (1988). Normative–Affective factors: Toward a new decision-making model. *Journal of Economic Psychology, 9,* 125–150.

Flaherty, E., Marecek, J., Olsen, K., & Wilcove, G. (1983). Preventing adolescent pregnancy: An interpersonal problem solving approach. *Prevention in Human Services, 2,* 49–64.

Flavell, J. H. (1974). The development of inferences about others. In T. Mischel (Ed.), *Understanding other persons.* Totowa, NJ: Rowman & Littlefield.

Freedman, B., Donahoe, C., Rosenthal, L., Schlundt, D., & McFall, R. (1978). A social-behavioral analysis of skill deficits in delinquent and nondelinquent boys. *Journal of Consulting & Clinical Psychology, 46,* 1448–1462.

Goldfried, M. R., & D'Zurilla, T. J. (1969). A behavioral-analytic model for assessing competence. In C. D. Spielberger (Ed.), *Current topics in clinical and community psychology* (Vol. 1, pp. 151–196). New York: Academic Press.

Greenberg, L. S., & Safran, J. D. (1984). Integrating affect and cognition: A perspective on the process of therapeutic change. *Cognitive Therapy and Research, 8,* 559–578.

Haley, J. (1976). *Problem solving therapy.* San Francisco: Jossey-Bass.

Kalafat, J., & Underwood, M. (1989). *Lifelines: A school-based adolescent suicide response program*. Dubuque, IA: Kendall/Hunt.

Kaplan, S., & Kaplan, R. (1982). *Cognition and environment: Functioning in an uncertain world*. New York: Praeger.

Kazdin, A., Esveldt-Dawson, K., French, N., & Unis, A. (1987). Problem-solving skills training and relationship therapy in the treatment of antisocial child behavior. *Journal of Consulting & Clinical Psychology, 55,* 76-85.

Kendall, P., & Hollon, S. (Eds.). (1980). *Assessment strategies for cognitive–behavioral interventions*. New York: Academic Press.

Lazarus, R. (1982). Thoughts on the relations between emotion and cognition. *American Psychologist, 37,* 1019-1024.

Marzano, R., Brandt, R., Hughes, C., Jones, B., Presseisen, B., Rankin, S., & Suhor, C. (1988). *Dimensions of thinking: A framework for curriculum and instruction*. Alexandria, VA: Association for Supervision & Curriculum Development.

Perkins, D. N. (1986). Thinking frames. *Educational Leadership, 43,* 4-11.

Piaget, J. (1981). *Intelligence and affectivity: Their relationship during child development*. Palo Alto, CA: Annual Reviews.

Rachman, S. (1981). The primacy of affect: Some theoretical implications. *Behaviour Research and Therapy, 9,* 279-290.

Raven, J. (1987). Values, diversity, and cognitive development. *Teachers College Record, 89,* 21-38.

Rotter, J. B. (1978). Generalized expectancies for problem solving and psychotherapy. *Cognitive Research & Therapy, 2,* 1-10.

Selman, R. (1980). *The growth of interpersonal understanding*. New York: Academic Press.

Sigel, I., & Kelley, T. (in press). A cognitive–developmental approach to questioning. In J. Dillon (Ed.), *Classroom questioning and discussion: A multidisciplinary study*. Norwood, NJ: Ablex.

Simon, H. A. (1983). Alternative visions of rationality. In H. A. Simon (Ed.), *Reasoning in human affairs* (pp. 7-35). Stanford, CA: Stanford University Press.

Spivack, G., & Shure, M. (1985). ICPS and beyond: Centripetal and centrifugal forces. *American Journal of Community Psychology, 13,* 226-243.

Sternberg, R. J., & Martin, M. (1988). When teaching thinking does not work: What goes wrong? *Teachers College Record, 89,* 555-578.

Sternberg, R., & Wagner, R. (Eds.). (1986). *Practical intelligence: Nature and origins of competence in the everyday world*. Cambridge: Cambridge University Press.

Tversky, A., & Kahneman, D. (1981). The framing of decisions and the psychology of choice. *Science, 211,* 453-458.

Weick, K. (1971). Group processes, family processes, and problem solving. In J. Aldous, T. Condon, R. Hill, M. Straus, & I. Tallman (Eds.), *Family problem solving* (pp. 3-32). Hillsdale, IL: Dryden.

Wheelock, A., & Dorman, G. (1988). *Before it's too late: Dropout prevention in the middle grades*. Boston: Massachusetts Advocacy Center.

Chapter 9

Teaching Decision-Making Skills to Student Nurses

James Shanteau
National Science Foundation

Margaret Grier
Joyce Johnson
Eta Berner
University of Illinois Medical Center

"Today's graduates lack problem-solving and decision-making skills" (Ruggiero, 1988)

"There are file cabinets full of failed efforts to train decision making" (quote from a professional colleague)

The purpose of this chapter is to present research that addresses the questions raised in these two quotes. Is there a need for specific courses to teach decision making? And, can the decision-making abilities of students be increased through such a course?

There have been numerous efforts to teach decision-making skills through training. Unfortunately, most of these efforts have had little measurable impact (e.g., Lichtenstein & Fischhoff, 1980). There are several possible reasons for this, including (a) use of unskilled subjects, (b) lack of motivation to learn, (c) absence of relevant training materials, and (d) inadequate evaluation instruments.

The research described in this chapter was designed to investigate alternatives to traditional training approaches. In particular, the results of a course are described that involved (a) preprofessional students, (b) a strong motivation to learn, (c) content-relevant training materials, and (d) specially designed evaluation measures.

Although the students in this study were college undergraduates, the findings have considerable relevance for teaching adolescents and young adults. Not only were the students in their teens and early twenties, the material in the course was quite basic. Thus, the approach used here could be directly applied to younger students.

Nurses' Decision Making

The purpose of this project was to investigate the effectiveness of teaching decision-making skills to student nurses. A special course was designed for nursing faculty to teach nursing students how to make better decisions and to solve problems more effectively.

Previous research showed that nurses' decision skills leave something to be desired. Three specific deficiencies have been identified.

First, nurses do not make effective or efficient use of available information. Nurses have been found, for instance, to extract exceedingly large amounts of information when making judgments. Consider the following numbers reported by Hammond, Kelly, Schneider, and Vancini (1966) in nurses' response to pain for a specific case:

- 165 cues used in making a decision
- 58 doctors' orders concerning pain
- 17 nursing actions that could be implemented

Not only are such numbers well beyond the capabilities of the human information processing system (Simon, 1957), but this situation may interfere with patient care (Sisson, Schoomaker, & Ross, 1976).

Second, deficiencies in nursing decisions have been reported in analyses of risk and uncertainty. Grier and Grier (1978) found that nurses were undermedicating patients in pain, in part because they overestimated the chances of drug addiction. Similarly, Bailey, McDonald, and Claus (1973) observed that despite the accepted goal of nurses to maximize patient care, they were more concerned about minimizing perceived risks. Such tendencies to overestimate risks may be becoming more exaggerated as the emphasis on malpractice and medical liability increases.

Third, shortcomings have been reported for nurses' abilities to evaluate alternatives and to choose appropriate actions. Gordon (1973), for instance, reported that nurses use habitual strategies regardless of the situational demands (also see Grier, 1976). The inflexible application of heuristic judgment strategies also has been found to lead to suboptimal decisions in a variety of nonnursing studies (Kahneman, Slovic, & Tversky, 1982).

Relevant Decision Research

In this section, some relevant literature from judgment and decision making is reviewed.

Information Utilization.   A critical component of expert judgment is the ability to appropriately define and use information that varies in relevance. Ideally, decision makers should select and use only that information which is most relevant. There is considerable evidence, however, that irrelevant or partly relevant information can adversely influence many types of judgments.

Shanteau and Gaeth (1983; Gaeth & Shanteau, 1984) found over 250 published papers that investigated the effects of irrelevant factors on behavior. The fields of study ranged from problem solving and perception to social psychology and learning. Effects of irrelevance have been observed for children, adults, and the elderly. Moreover, evidence has been obtained from both laboratory and applied settings.

To find out if the effects could be reduced by training, Gaeth and Shanteau (1984) compared two procedures for helping experienced soil judges. The training was designed to help judges ignore specific factors known to be irrelevant, but which nonetheless influence soil classifications, for example, excessive moisture. One training procedure involved a lecture format (similar to typical classroom approaches). The other involved interactive experience with hands-on practice (similar to a laboratory experience). The lecture approach produced some reduction in the influence of irrelevant information. However, a greater impact came from the interactive training, with measurable improvement 1 year later. Moreover, training to ignore one specific factor (e.g., excessive moisture) generalized to other irrelevant factors (e.g., small pebbles and rocks). In addition, the training improved the accuracy of the judgments.

Risk Assessment.   The difficulties that people have in dealing with probabilities and uncertainty have been documented for over 30 years. In the 1960s, there were numerous studies by Edwards and his colleagues on Bayesian probability-revision tasks. This research (summarized in Edwards, 1968) revealed that people generally gave estimates that were conservative or less extreme than predicted by Bayes theorem.

In the 1970s, Kahneman and Tversky (1972, 1973; Tversky & Kahneman, 1973, 1974) initiated a series of studies on heuristics (mental rules of thumb) and biases in probability judgment. Heuristics such as availability and representativeness led to biases or errors of judgment in naive subjects. Although these authors argued that heuristics also apply to experienced decision makers (e.g., Tversky & Kahneman, 1971), there is evidence that experts do better than nonexperts in some settings (Ashton, 1983; Schwartz & Griffin, 1986; Shanteau, 1989).

Recent research has focused on the assessments of risk and uncertainty. One common finding is that people's probability judgments are poorly calibrated—the responses are not consistent with outcome frequencies (Lichtenstein, Fischhoff, & Phillips, 1982). Other studies showed that basic probability concepts, such as conjunction, are judged inappropriately (Tversky & Kahneman, 1983).

Such fundamental misunderstandings of probability have led to the development of college courses on how to deal with risk and uncertainty. Some of the texts available for such courses include Baron (1988), Dawes (1988), Halpern (1989), and Huber (1980). There also are high school books on thinking under uncertainty (Beyth-Marom, Dekel, Gombo, & Shaked, 1985).

Alternative Evaluation.   Many of the earliest studies of decision making concerned choices between risky options. In his pioneering research, Edwards (1954) looked at the effects of subjective probability on gambling preferences. Similarly, early research by Coombs and Pruitt (1960) examined the influence of outcome distributions on choices between bets. The results of these studies consistently revealed that subjects did not maximize expected utility in making their decisions.

Other deviations from rational choice theory have been observed. Probably the most widely studied has been the preference reversal phenomenon in which subjects' choices are inconsistent with their ratings. First described by Lindman (1971) and Lichtenstein and Slovic (1971), preference reversals have been of considerable interest to economists. Despite numerous efforts to eliminate the effect by training or financial inducements, the phenomenon has proven to be quite persistent (e.g., Grether & Plott, 1979).

Although utility maximization is a fundamental and easily understood concept, there is little literature on how to convey this concept to subjects. One approach has been to point out the consequences of making intransitive or inconsistent choices. Adherence to preference reversals, for instance, can lead subjects to be a "money pump"—by choosing illogically, they lose money on every transaction. Such training, however, produces marginal improvements which generally fail to generalize (Einhorn, 1980). It is an open question, therefore, whether efforts to improve alternative selection can be successfully taught.

Teaching Program

In the course on nursing problem solving, emphasis was placed on the three decision making deficiencies described earlier: inappropriate information utilization, biased risk assessment, and suboptimal alternative evaluation.[1] In this section, the strategies used to teach each of these are outlined. It is worth noting that many of the techniques in the course were adapted from

---

[1]The special course included various topics on thinking, problem solving, and decision making. However, only the three decision-making issues of information utilization, risk assessment, and alternative evaluation are discussed here.

procedures originally observed in the training of expert agricultural judges (Shanteau & Phelps, 1977).

The course began with background information about judgment and decision making, for example, problem definition and alternative selection. General concepts were explained, such as "do not select dominated (inferior) alternatives" and "determine what information is relevant for making choices." Then, specific decision strategies were provided and students practiced use of the strategies in making nursing decisions. In evaluating available information, for instance, students were told to determine the relevance of each piece of information for the decision problem and to use only the most diagnostic. In addition, the dangers of seeking too much information were explained by showing that information overload can result from exceeding cognitive capabilities.

The course then shifted to other topics such as how to make decisions under uncertainty. Initially, general concepts and definitions from probability and statistics were taught. Then, various techniques for using probabilistic information were described. Specific rules such as Bayes theorem were explained as well as other concepts from formal decision analysis, (e.g., how to interpret and use conditional probabilities). These rules were taught both at the formal mathematical level and at a conceptual/intuitive level using relevant nursing examples.

Both general principles and specific rules-of-thumb were provided to make choices. In learning how to choose between alternative courses of action, for example, goal setting and the concept of utility maximization were explained in depth. Then, several specific strategies for making choices were offered, for example, the students learned about the basic principles of multiattribute utility analysis. In addition, the nurses were told how to work through an alternative-by-outcome table (see the example in Appendix 1).

Three other general aspects of the course are worth emphasizing. First, the basic concepts were offered initially in standard classroom settings by regular nursing faculty. This was supplemented by real-world clinical practice under the guidance of practicum instructors in hospital settings. This two-sided approach parallels the lecture/laboratory technique for teaching science and language courses.

Second, the concepts were described and demonstrated using specific nursing illustrations. Also, the students were encouraged to contribute examples from their own nursing experiences. By using familiar contexts, it was hoped that problems in understanding and generalizing decision-making concepts to new situations could be minimized.

Finally, having a positive attitude toward decision making and problem solving was emphasized. An effort was made to give students positive experiences and to increase their self-confidence in making decisions and solving problems. Shanteau (1987) argued that confidence plays an important role in expert decision making.

METHOD

Subjects

One hundred and fifteen third-year nursing students and seven nursing faculty participated in a year-long research project in the College of Nursing at the University of Illinois Medical Center. The instruments developed were administered to both students and faculty.

The second and third authors were responsible for developing evaluation materials and teaching the course to nursing students. Other nursing faculty, who supervised the practicum experience for third-year students, reinforced the course concepts in actual clinical situations. These faculty also served as the "expert" group.

Design

As shown in Table 9.1, there were three phases in the project; the sample sizes for each condition appear in the table. The first phase was a pretraining assessment of nursing decision-making skills before the course. The second phase involved taking the newly developed class on decision making and problem solving. The final phase was administration of a posttraining assessment after the course.

The course was taught to two groups of students: Group One completed just the posttraining assessment, whereas Group Two completed both the pretraining and the posttraining assessments. Comparison of these groups allows examination of effects from prior instrument administration. In addition, there were two groups of control subjects who did not take the course: Control One subjects completed just the pretraining assessment.[2] Control Two subjects completed both the pretraining and the posttraining assessments. No substantial differences emerged between the two control groups.

For the nursing faculty (the expert group), several workshops on decision making were offered. These workshops followed the testing of control groups (to avoid contamination), but preceded the teaching of decision-making skills to the students. The material presented in the workshops was based on the first

---

[2]The pretraining assessment for the Control One group was conducted at the beginning of the school year. Therefore, that group provides an uncontaminated measure of the initial performance level. In contrast, the other groups were evaluated at later times in the year when there could have been spin-off effects (on pretraining assessment) from other students taking the course.

TABLE 9.1
Research Design

Group	N =	Pre Training	Training	Post Training
Control One	11	Yes	No	No
Control Two	37, 25	Yes	No	Yes
Group One	41	No	Yes	Yes
Group Two	24, 26	Yes	Yes	Yes

author's experience in teaching a course on Problem Solving and Decision Making to undergraduate students. This material was supplemented with nursing examples provided by the second and third authors.

Assessment Materials

A special instrument was constructed to assess the decision-making and problem-solving abilities of nursing students. Parallel versions of the instrument were developed for the pretraining and posttraining conditions; there were no apparent differences in the difficulty of the two versions. Only the three sections of the instrument relevant for the present chapter will be described here.

To evaluate the amount of information used by nurses when making a decision, several scenarios were constructed. One of the scenarios appears in Table 9.2. Each piece of information is followed by a number. After reading the scenario, nurses were asked to determine whether the content for each numbered item was *essential, contributory,* or *noncontributory* for making a decision. The answers of the students were compared to those of the nursing faculty.

To determine the nurses' ability to evaluate probabilities, a hypothetical diagnostic problem, along with the associated conditional probabilities, was presented. One of the question sets appears in Tables 9.3a and 9.3b. After examining the probability values, nurses were asked to give a probability distribution for various patient conditions. The answers were compared to values computed from Bayes theorem and probability theory.

To evaluate the ability of nurses to select between alternative courses of action, a two-part procedure was developed; one of the forms is shown in Appendix 1. In the first part, students read a description of a nursing problem and made an initial (preassessment) choice of action. The nurses then completed an alternative-by-outcome trade-off table and made a final (postassessment) choice of action.[3]

---

[3]It has been suggested by a reviewer that the pretraining groups may have been hindered in their decision-making ability by having to work through an unfamiliar table. It was for that reason that subjects were asked to choose nursing actions before and after working through the alternative-by-outcome trade-off table.

TABLE 9.2
Sample Scenario

You are a nurse working in the first aid station of a large amusement park(1). It is about two o'clock(2) on a hot sunny afternoon(3) when a moderately obese(4) middle aged(5) woman(6) enters. She asks, "Can I sit in here for awhile(7)? I have such indigestion(8) and that sun is so hot I feel like passing out"(9). You learn that her name is Mrs. Kastor(10), and you note that her face is flushed(11) and shiny with perspiration(12). You suggest she lie down on the cot. After a few minutes, she suddenly sits up stating, "I can't stand the pressure on my chest when I'm flat(13). Let me sit in the chair instead"(14). Upon questioning further, you obtain the following information. She has had several previous episodes of indigestion after eating highly spiced foods in the past(15); the indigestion was relieved with antacid tablets(16). She tells you that she had two antacid tablets about an hour after lunch(17) which consisted of hamburger, french fries, and a soft drink(18). She then says, "Usually the antacid tablets work almost immediately(19). I can't understand why they aren't helping(20); perhaps I got too much sun"(21).

Upon questioning Mrs. Kastor about the discomfort she is having, she describes it as a feeling of fullness or pressure(22), placing her hand over the substernal area(23). She also describes an aching feeling(24) in her left shoulder and over the shoulder blade area(25). She states that no matter what position she assumes, the discomfort always seems to remain(26). She now recalls that she had a similar episode(27) about a month earlier(28) while cleaning her house(29), but states that "it passed over" after she sat down for about half an hour(30).

Physical examination reveals: temperature 98.8F(31); pulse 110 and regular(32); respiration 24(33); no evidence of dyspnea(34); pain not altered by change in position(35); blood pressure 174/96(36); heart sounds are normal(37), no irregularities of beat are noted(38). She is currently not taking any medication except for an occasional antacid tablet(39). Her last medical check-up was three months ago(40) and she relates that she was given "a clean bill of health" by her family physician(41).

End of Scenario

Each datum should be classified in only one of three ways in coming to a decision about this woman's health condition:
   (A) for essential information
   (B) for contributory, but not essential information
   (C) for noncontributory information

For each problem, the correct answer was determined by an independent group of senior nursing faculty. Students' answers were coded as correct or incorrect, based on the outcome. The process by which the answers were generated was not considered, so that it is possible that some students may have simply guessed correctly. However, there is no reason to expect that guessing rates would vary before and after training.

The expert group of nurses completed the same instrument as the student nurses. These nursing faculty were not involved in either the development or the validation of the assessment materials. Thus, they were blind to the content of the test instrument until the time of its administration.[4]

---

[4]Keeping the "expert" nursing group uninformed about the instruments avoided the possibility that they may have "taught the test" to students.

TABLE 9.3a
Likelihood Table

Symptom	Probability of Symptom		
	Condition I	Condition II	Condition III
A. Systolic blood pressure below 90	.80	.80	.80
B. Rapid, weak pulse	.75	.75	.40
C. Rapid, shallow respirations	.70	.50	.70
D. Cold, clammy skin	.60	.80	.20
E. Decrease in blood volume	.80	.30	.20
F. Skin color cyanotic	.40	.75	.30
G. History of rapid onset	.30	.60	.75

Note. The likelihood table contains the probabilities of given symptoms (A–G) in three hypothetical conditions (I, II, and III). For example, if a patient had "Condition I", one would expect to see cold, clammy skin 60% of the time, decreased blood volume 80% of the time, and so forth. The three conditions have an equal chance of being present. Using the information in the table (Table 9.3a), answer the questions on the next two pages. Use the space provided beneath each condition for all probability calculations.

TABLE 9.3b

Judgment #1

Mrs. Rogers was admitted to the hospital following several days of progressive weakness and fatigue. Upon admission laboratory reports showed a decrease in blood volume. Her skin color was extremely pale; blood pressure 84/58 and pulse 116.

Based on the above information and data in the Likelihood Table what is the probability that Mrs. Rogers has each of the three conditions? Designate your probability (0%-100%) on the blank line to the right of each condition listed below.

Probability

Condition I   _____
Condition II   _____
Condition III _____

Judgment #2

Mr. Lampere was admitted to the hospital. Your initial assessment showed blood pressure 70/40; pulse 110 and weak; respirations 32 and shallow; skin warm, dry, and pale. Laboratory reports were not available.

Based on the above information and the data in the Likelihood Table what is the probability that Mr. Lampere has each of the three conditions? Designate your probability (0%-100%) on the blank line to the right of each condition listed below.

Probability

Condition I   _____
Condition II   _____
Condition III _____

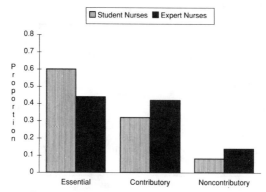

FIG. 9.1   Classification of items in scenarios by Control One student nurses (pretraining) and faculty nurses.

RESULTS

The results are separated into three sections: information utilization, risk assessment, and alternative evaluation. In each section, the pretraining and the posttraining results are described and compared. The results are averaged over parallel assessment forms.

Information Utilization

The nurses were asked to look at two cases (similar to Table 9.2) and evaluate the relevance of each piece of information. The results appear in Fig. 9.1. Without the course, the Control One student nurses rated 60% of the items as *essential* and less than 10% of items as *noncontributory*. In contrast, the faculty nurses (the experts) rated 44% of the items as *essential* and 56% of the items as either *contributory* or *noncontributory.* Using 95% confidence intervals, the patterns for students and faculty are significantly different.[5] Thus, naive nursing students rated more information as essential than expert nurses and less information as nonessential.

The effect of the course on information use can be seen in Fig. 9.2. Before training, the results for Group Two revealed that student nurses view a majority of information (67%) as *essential* and very little information as *noncontributory* (17%); the pattern of results is similar to the Control One results in Fig. 9.1. Following training, the results for Group Two show a reduction in the *essential* items to 50% and an increase of noncontributory items to 20%. The similarity of the posttraining results to the experts in Fig. 9.1 is noteworthy. Therefore, the students following training appear to

---

[5]Statistical tests were performed by comparing confidence intervals around means. Differences in 95% confidence intervals are equivalent to significant t-tests at the .05 level.

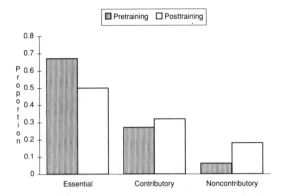

FIG. 9.2   Classification of items in scenarios by Group One and Group Two student nurses (pretraining and posttraining).

have become more discriminating in evaluating information and thus behaved more like the expert nurses.[6]

Risk Assessment

After examining a conditional probability table (see Table 9.3a), nurses were asked to give a probability distribution for various medical conditions. Relative to Bayes theorem, the student pretraining results (for Group Two) revealed a tendency to underestimate the most likely condition (number 1 in Fig. 9.3) and to overestimate the two less likely conditions (numbers 2 and 3). The results for the expert nurses were similar, with the same tendency to

---

[6]Interestingly, the posttraining only Group One results showed an even greater reduction in "essential" items (50%) following the course. Their results became even closer to the experts than Group Two. It is not clear why the course had more of an impact for this group.

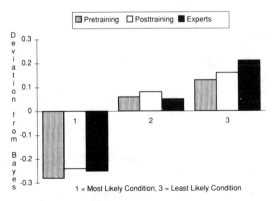

FIG. 9.3   Deviations of probability estimates from Bayesian values for Group Two student nurses and faculty nurses.

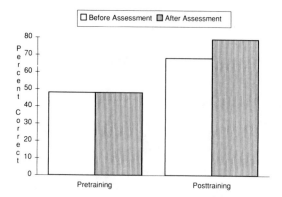

FIG. 9.4   Percent correct choices before and after training for Group Two
student nurses, before and after making tradeoff assessments.

underestimate the more likely condition and to overestimate the less likely
conditions.

Following the course, the probability distribution estimates were unchanged. The posttraining data values in Fig. 9.3 show a pattern similar to
both the pretraining results and to the expert results. It would appear, therefore, that teaching the nurses about risk and probability combination rules
had no impact on the nurses' ability to estimate probabilities.

As a follow-up to these analyses, the probability values given to complementary cases were examined, that is, the chance of an event occurring plus
the chance that it won't occur. It was found that the response values vio-
lated the basic definition of probability. Instead of summing to 1.0, the estimates for complementary cases summed to as much as 1.4. Comparable
results were found for the experts. Thus, there appear to be fundamental
difficulties in understanding probabilities that were not influenced by the
course.

Alternative Evaluation

Nurses examined a "Choice of Action" scenario (similar to Appendix 1)
and then made two sets of responses, before and after filling out an alternative-by-outcome trade-off table. The pretraining results in Fig. 9.4 show
that the student nurses chose the correct alternative less than half the time
(48%). The results were unchanged after filling out the trade-off table
(48%).

The results after training reveal a significant improvement in the students' performance compared to pretraining. Specifically, the pre-tradeoff
assessment results are 20% higher than before training (68%), and the post-
tradeoff assessment results are over 30% higher (79%); both are significantly greater as revealed by 95% confidence intervals. The difference

(11%) before and after filling out the trade-off table was not significant. The course, therefore, was effective in helping nurses select better courses of actions, with most of the improvement coming prior to completing a trade-off table.

DISCUSSION

There are four major observations that can be made about this research. The first reflects the pretraining results and the need for improvement in decision-making skills. The second concerns the effectiveness of the course in improving the nurses' judgments. The third involves the decision skills that can and cannot be taught effectively. Finally, the initial questions about the need for and the effectiveness of courses in decision making are addressed.

Decision Making Deficiencies

The need to improve the decision-making skills of student nurses is clear. The present pretraining results show that nurses identified too much information as essential, did not use probabilities appropriately, and selected the best course of action less than half the time.

Although such deficiencies have been noted in previous studies, it is notable that they were observed here in a nursing context. Prior research on decision biases has been criticized for using general knowledge questions instead of items familiar to subjects (Shanteau, 1978; Wallsten, 1983). In the present analyses, all materials pertained to nursing problems relevant to the students.

Similar evidence of biased decision making has been reported in other areas of medicine. In a series of studies of physicians, Elstein, Shulman, and Sprafka (1978) found that doctors interpreted incoming information as supporting present hypotheses, even though the information was in fact noncontributory. In a summary of the medical decision-making literature, Schwartz and Griffin (1986) reported that the same sorts of common biases observed in naive subjects can often be observed for physicians.

Not all studies of medical decision making, however, have obtained evidence of inappropriate decision making (e.g., see Christensen-Szalanski, Beck, Christensen-Szalanski, & Koepsell, 1983). It appears that there may be some medical settings in which more accurate decisions are made and other settings that lead to less accurate outcomes. Identifying the characteristics of each type of situation is an issue that deserves greater research (Shanteau, 1987).

Teaching Effectiveness

A comparison of the pre- and posttraining results reveals that at least some types of nursing decisions can be improved by a course on decision making.

Although the improvement was not equal across the three topic areas, the overall trend was for nurses to make better decisions after training than before. This improvement is quite encouraging.

It should be pointed out that the course did not teach nursing topics per se. Instead, the course focused on how to apply already existing nursing knowledge more effectively. Thus, the course dealt with the *process* of nursing decisions as opposed to the *content*. This is an important distinction because it suggests that efforts to teach the decision process can succeed—once there is a knowledge base in place.

Another aspect of the present course deserves comment. The teaching did not stop in the class. The concepts were reinforced by practicum experience that the nursing students had in hospital settings. It is not possible to say which aspect of teaching—classroom or practicum—had the greater impact. However, research of Gaeth (1984; Shanteau & Gaeth, 1983) comparing the two methods suggests that lecture-based training is necessary, but not sufficient, to alter decision behavior. Apparently, it takes the hands-on experience of a practicum (or laboratory) to cement the learning process. If so, that may explain why the lecture format used in most previous training studies has failed.

Skill Specificity

The improvements in nurses' decision skills after taking the course was not consistent across the three areas examined. Although the acquisition of information and the choice of actions improved following training, the use of probabilistic information did not. This suggests that nursing students have difficulty in understanding and applying formal concepts from decision theory (e.g., Bayes theorem). In contrast, the less formal concepts (i.e., "use only relevant information" and "maximize utility") may be more easily grasped. The implications of this observation will be considered for each area of training.

Information Utilization. Following the principle of "GI–GO" (garbage in–garbage out), a decision cannot be any better than the information on which it is based. Although there may be situations in which health-care professionals gather too little or the wrong types of information (Elstein, Shulman, & Sprafka, 1978), the concern here is with gathering too much information. The presence of excessive information, if it is nondiagnostic, can only diminish decision quality (Shanteau, 1975; Troutman & Shanteau, 1977).

The evidence from a variety of sources is clear—health-care students attempt to use excessive amounts of information (Hammond et al., 1966). So much is viewed as *essential* that information overload is an inevitable consequence. In contrast to students, professionals appear to be more discriminating in their use of information. Both here and in Hammond, Frederick, Robillard, and Victor (1989), health-care experts saw less information as essential.

Of course, training students to use less information won't necessarily improve decision making. The key is to differentiate between what is essential and what is nonessential. That requires knowledge and experience. Nonetheless, teaching about the importance of ignoring irrelevant information can improve the quality of even experienced decision makers (Gaeth & Shanteau, 1984).

Probability Assessment.   There is an extensive literature on the inaccuracies of probability judgment. In over three decades of research on probability assessment, the results have consistently pointed to suboptimal behavior. The present findings, for instance, mirror the reports of conservatism in probability revision tasks (Edwards, 1968); likelihood estimates are less extreme than that predicted from Bayes theorem.

Beyond conservatism, the present results show that there are more fundamental problems in nurses' use of probabilities. The finding that complementary probabilities sum to more than 1.0 suggests a deep-seated misunderstanding of basic concepts. It is notable that these misunderstandings were shared by faculty nurses. Given that the students' teachers did not understand probabilities, it should not be surprising that the students failed to improve after the course (also see Fischhoff, 1982).

However, the failure of students to learn should not be blamed entirely on the nursing faculty. The first author has had over 10 years of experience in teaching decision-making courses to undergraduates. Consistently, the most difficult area for students to grasp has been probability (Shanteau, 1984). Indeed, the course is now structured so that probability concepts are delayed as long as possible. Only after teaching other more easily grasped concepts, such as utility maximization, are principles of risky decision making introduced. This contrasts with the approach taken by writers of most undergraduate texts (e.g., Dawes, 1988; Yates, 1990). The relative success of these two approaches deserves further analysis.

Despite the present difficulties, there are domains in which probabilities are estimated accurately. Not only do weather forecasters make well-calibrated probability estimates (Murphy & Winkler, 1977), their accuracy appears to have been improving over the years (Lichtenstein, Fischhoff, & Phillips, 1982). Although this suggests that probability concepts can be learned, it is not clear how to translate from the specifics of weather forecasting to more general situations.

Alternative Evaluation.   The selection of the best option is fundamental to decision analysis. Before the course, students selected the best alternative less than half the time. In contrast, there was a substantial improvement following the course. However, most of the improvement came before filling out an alternative-by-outcome trade-off table. This suggests that the concept of utility maximization, as opposed to a formal trade-off assessment, is central to helping students make better choices.

A variety of decision aids and decision support systems have been developed to help decision makers. Many of these incorporate some variation of a multiattribute utility analysis (e.g., Gardiner & Edwards, 1975). Although there has been some debate about which system is superior, the present results imply that much of the improvement comes before the use of any particular quantitative aid. Apparently it is the overall approach that is important, not the specific technique. Determining whether this result generalizes beyond nursing will require additional research.

It is clear that nursing students can learn to make better choices. At their best, the student nurses were choosing correctly about 80% of the time. As good as that is, there is still room for improvement.

Concluding Comments

To sum up, we return to the two questions asked at the beginning of the chapter: Is there a need for teaching of decision making skills? And, can decision making be taught effectively? From the present research, the answer to both questions is definitely "yes."

The need for courses on decision making has been demonstrated both by scientific studies and by concerns raised by business leaders and politicians. Although classroom education can be effective in providing substantive knowledge, the ability of students to apply that knowledge has been questioned (e.g., Swoboda, 1989). It is noteworthy that the President's 1989 Education Summit concluded with calls for an increased emphasis on thinking ability (Hoffman & Broder, 1989).

The present research shows that a course on decision making and problem solving can be effective. The decision making skills of nursing students were significantly better following the course. The improvements in information utilization and alternative evaluation are notable. At the same time, the failure to improve risk assessments is troubling. This failure presents an important challenge for future research.

For teaching adolescents, the fact that the course was designed for nursing students is significant in three ways. First, the students were motivated to learn. Second, course concepts were taught using relevant examples. Third, evaluation materials reflected actual (nursing) problems. These are all components that can be incorporated into courses at any level.

Although some have suggested that teaching thinking skills may be "the fad of the 80's" (Ewen, 1988), the present success argues for an opposing view. As shown here, such courses can improve some decision-making skills (also see Nisbett, Krantz, Jepson, & Fong, 1982). There is still much work to be done, however, before we know how to teach all the skills necessary for making better decisions.

ACKNOWLEDGMENTS

This research project was supported, in part, by Public Health Service training grant NU 25084 from the Division of Nursing, HRSA. The senior author was supported, in part, by Army Research Institute contract MDA903-80-C-0029 during the period of this project.

James Shanteau is Director of the Decision, Risk, and Management Science Program at the National Science Foundation; he is on leave from Kansas State University. Margaret Grier is now Associate Dean, College of Nursing, at the University of Kentucky. Joyce Johnson is an Associate Professor of Nursing at the University of Illinois College of Nursing. Eta Berner is now a statistical consultant at the University of Connecticut.

REFERENCES

Ashton, R. H. (1983). *Research in audit decision making: Rationale, evidence and implications.* Vancouver: Canadian Certified General Accountants' Monograph No. 6.

Bailey, J. T., McDonald, F. J., & Claus, K. E. (1973). An experimental curriculum. In F. G. Abdellah (Ed.), *New directions in patient centered nursing.* New York: Macmillan.

Baron, J. (1988). *Thinking and deciding.* Cambridge, UK: Cambridge University Press.

Beyth-Marom, R., Dekel, S., Gombo, R., & Shaked, M. (1985). *An elementary approach to thinking under uncertainty.* (S. Lichtenstein, B. Marom, & R. Beyth-Marom, Trans.). Hillsdale, NJ: Lawrence Erlbaum Associates.

Christensen-Szalanski, J. J. J., Beck, D. E., Christensen-Szalanski, C. M., & Koepsell, T. D. (1983). Effects of expertise and experience on risk judgments. *Journal of Applied Psychology, 68,* 278–284.

Coombs, C. H., & Pruitt, D. G. (1960). Components of risk in decision making: Probability and variance preferences. *Journal of Experimental Psychology, 60,* 265–277.

Dawes, R. M. (1988). *Rational choice in an uncertain world.* San Diego: Harcourt Brace Jovanovich.

Edwards, W. (1954). The theory of decision making. *Psychological Bulletin, 51,* 380–417.

Edwards, W. (1968). Conservatism in human information processing. In B. Kleinmuntz (Ed.), *Formal representation of human judgment.* New York: Wiley.

Einhorn, H. J. (1980). Learning from experience and suboptimal rules in decision making. In T. S. Wallsten (Ed.), *Cognitive processes in choice and decision behavior.* Hillsdale, NJ: Lawrence Erlbaum Associates.

Elstein, A. S., Shulman, L. S., & Sprafka, S. A. (1978). *Medical problem solving: An analysis of clinical reasoning.* Cambridge, MA: Harvard University Press.

Ewen, I. (1988, July 1). Quoted in "The teaching of thinking skills." *The Manhattan Mercury,* p. C6. (Reprinted from the *New York Times*).

Fischhoff, B. (1982). Debiasing. In D. Kahneman, P. Slovic, & A. Tversky (Eds.), *Judgment under uncertainty: Heuristics and biases.* Cambridge, UK: Cambridge University Press.

Gaeth, G. J. (1984). *The influence of irrelevant information in judgment processes: Assess-

ment, reduction, and a model. Unpublished doctoral dissertation, Kansas State University.

Gaeth, G. J., & Shanteau, J. (1984). Reducing the influence of irrelevant information on experienced decision makers. *Organizational Behavior and Human Performance, 33,* 263–282.

Gardiner, P. C., & Edwards, W. (1975). Public values: Multiattribute utility measurement for social decision making. In M. F. Kaplan & S. Schwartz (Eds.), *Human judgment and decision processes.* New York: Academic Press.

Gordon, M. (1973). *Information processing in nursing diagnosis.* Paper presented at American Nursing Association Nursing Research Conference, San Antonio, TX.

Grether, D. M., & Plott, C. R. (1979). Economic theory of choice and the preference reversal phenomenon. *American Economic Review, 69,* 623–638.

Grier, M. R. (1976). Decision making about patient care. *Nursing Research, 25,* 105–110.

Grier, M. R., & Grier, J. B. (1978). The system for delivering pain medication: The patient's pain, the physician's order, and the nurse's choice. In *Proceedings of the Fourth Illinois Conference on Medical Information Systems.*

Halpern, D. F. (1989). *Thought and knowledge: An introduction to critical thinking* (2nd ed.). Hillsdale, NJ: Lawrence Earlbaum Associates.

Hammond, K. R., Frederick, E., Robillard, N., & Victor, D. (1989). Application of cognitive theory to the student–teacher dialogue. In D. A. Evans & V. L. Patel (Eds.), *Cognitive science in medicine: Biomedical modeling.* Cambridge, MA: MIT Press.

Hammond, K. R., Kelly, K. J., Schneider, R. J., & Vancini, M. (1966). Clinical inference in nursing: Information units used. *Nursing Research, 15,* 236–243.

Hoffman, D., & Broder, D. S. (1989, September 29). Summit sets 7 main goals for education. *The Washington Post,* p. A3.

Huber, G. P. (1980). *Managerial decision making.* Glenview, IL: Scott, Foresman.

Kahneman, D., Slovic, P., & Tversky, A. (1982). *Judgment under uncertainty: Heuristics and biases.* Cambridge, UK: Cambridge University Press.

Kahneman, D., & Tversky, A. (1972). Subjective probability: A judgment of representativeness. *Cognitive Psychology, 3,* 430–454.

Kahneman, D., & Tversky, A. (1973). On the psychology of prediction. *Psychological Review, 80,* 237–251.

Lichtenstein, S., & Fischhoff, B. (1980). Training for calibration. *Organizational Behavior and Human Performance, 26,* 149–171.

Lichtenstein, S., Fischhoff, B., & Phillips, L. D. (1982). Calibration of probabilities: The state of the art to 1980. In D. Kahneman, P. Slovic, & A. Tversky (Eds.), *Judgment under uncertainty: Heuristics and biases.* Cambridge, UK: Cambridge University Press.

Lichtenstein, S., & Slovic, P. (1971). Reversals of preference between bids and choices in gambling decisions. *Journal of Experimental Psychology, 89,* 46–55.

Lindman, H. R. (1971). Inconsistent preferences among gambles. *Journal of Experimental Psychology, 89,* 390–397.

Murphy, A. H., & Winkler, R. L. (1977). Can weather forecasters formulate reliable probability forecasts of precipitation and temperature? *National Weather Digest, 2,* 2–9.

Nisbett, R. E., Krantz, D. H., Jepson, C., & Fong, G. T. (1982). Improving inductive inference. In D. Kahneman, P. Slovic, & A. Tversky (Eds.), *Judgment under uncertainty: Heuristics and biases.* Cambridge, UK: Cambridge University Press.

Ruggiero, V. R. (1988, December 8). Schools must make thinking skills the core of each course. *The Kansas City Times,* p. D-5.

Schwartz, S., & Griffin, T. (1986). *Medical thinking: The psychology of medical judgment and decision making.* New York: Springer-Verlag.

Shanteau, J. (1975). Averaging versus multiplying combination rules of inference judgment. *Acta Psychologica, 39,* 83–89.

Shanteau, J. (1978). When does a response error become a judgmental bias? *Journal of Experimental Psychology: Human Learning and Memory, 4,* 579–581.

Shanteau, J. (1984, November). *Teaching judgment and decision making.* Paper presented at Judgment/Decision Making Meeting, San Antonio, TX.

Shanteau, J. (1987). Psychological characteristics of expert decision makers. In J. L. Mumpower, O. Renn, L. D. Phillips, & V. R. R. Uppuluri (Eds.), *Expert judgment and expert systems.* Berlin: Springer-Verlag.

Shanteau, J. (1989). Cognitive heuristics and biases in behavioral auditing: Review, comments and observations. *Accounting, Organizations and Society, 14,* 165–177.

Shanteau, J., & Gaeth, G. J. (1983). *Training expert decision makers to ignore irrelevant information.* Alexandria, VA: Army Research Institute.

Shanteau, J., & Phelps, R. H. (1977). Judgment and swine: Approaches and issues in applied judgment analysis. In M. F. Kaplan & S. Schwartz (Eds.), *Human judgment and decision processes in applied settings.* New York: Academic Press.

Simon, H. A. (1957). *Models of man: Social and rational.* New York: Wiley.

Sisson, J. C., Shoomaker, E. B., & Ross, J. C. (1976). Clinical decision analysis: The hazard of using additional data. *Journal of the American Medical Association, 13,* 1259–1263.

Swoboda, F. (1989, September 29). A first step toward national school reform. *The Washington Post,* p. A3.

Troutman, C. M., & Shanteau, J. (1977). Inferences based on nondiagnostic information. *Organizational Behavior and Human Performance, 19,* 43–55.

Tversky, A., & Kahneman, D. (1971). The belief in the "law of small numbers." *Psychological Bulletin, 76,* 105–110.

Tversky, A., & Kahneman, D. (1973). Availability: A heuristic for judging frequency and probability. *Cognitive Psychology, 5,* 207–232.

Tversky, A., & Kahneman, D. (1974). Judgment under uncertainty: Heuristics and biases. *Science, 1985,* 1124–1131.

Tversky, A., & Kahneman, D. (1983). Extensional versus intuitive reasoning: The conjunction fallacy in probability judgment. *Psychological Review, 90,* 293–315.

Wallsten, T. S. (1983). The theoretical status of judgmental heuristics. In R. W. Scholz (Ed.), *Decision making under uncertainty.* Amsterdam: North-Holland.

Yates, J. F. (1990). *Judgment and decision making.* Englewood Cliffs, NJ: Prentice-Hall.

APPENDIX

Choice of Action

You are a registered, professional nurse working 3 to 11 P.M. on a general medical unit. Additional staff on your unit includes another RN, two LPNs, and one nursing assistant. The nurse in the coronary care unit calls to tell you that they are transferring Mrs. Kastor, 45 years old, to your unit, and requests a room assignment. The nurse informs you that Mrs. Kastor had a myocardial infarction one week ago but has been medically stable without chest pain for 3 days. She also tells you that both Mrs. Kastor and her husband are anxious over the proposed transfer. Mr. Kastor wants "only the best" for his wife and is concerned that she will not receive adequate observation and care when transferred from the coronary care unit.

APPENDIX TABLE 1
Floor Plan

2	4	6	8	10	12	14
1	3	5	Nurses' Station	9	11	13

The nursing diagnosis is: Moderate anxiety secondary to discharge from the coronary care unit.

The goal is: Mrs. Kastor will not show evidence of increased anxiety as a result of transfer from the coronary care unit.

The floor plan (Appendix Table 1) shows the location of each room on the floor. What follows are several considerations to be taken into account in selecting a room for Mrs. Kastor.

Considerations in Making Decision

1. Proximity to nurses' station. Requires frequent nursing observation due to anxiety voiced by both Mrs. Kastor and her husband and her recent history of myocardial infarction.
2. Amount of noise. Requires quiet environment to provide maximal rest after recent myocardial infarction.
3. Appropriateness of roommate. Requires roommate compatible in age and interests to provide meaningful stimulation to counteract possible boredom and depression due to disease condition and hospitalization.
4. Potential risks. Room environment should minimize risk of increasing Mrs. Kastor's anxiety and possibility of other medical complications.

Based on the above information, which of the following rooms would be best for Mrs. Kastor? Circle the letter of your selection in the test booklet.

A. Room 5—Mrs. B, 55 y/o, newly diagnosed malignancy, 5th hospital day

APPENDIX TABLE 2
Trade-off Table

Alternative	Outcome			
	Nursing Observation	Maximal Rest	Meaningful Stimulation	Avoidance of Complications
A. Room 5—Mrs. B. 55 y/o, newly diagnosed malignancy, 5th hospital day				
B. Room 6—Mrs. R. 25 y/o, viral hepatitis, 2nd hospital day				
C. Room 8—Mrs. P. 67 y/o, CVA, comatose, 3rd hospital day				
D. Room 10—Mrs. D. 80 y/o, thombo- phlebitis, 4th hospital day				
E. Room 13—Mrs. J. 40 y/o, duodenal ulcer, 2nd hospital day				

B. Room 6—Mrs. R, 25 y/o, viral hepatitis, 2nd hospital day

C. Room 8—Mrs. P, 67 y/o, CVA, comatose, 3rd hospital day

D. Room 10—Mrs. D, 80 y/o, thrombophlebitis, 4th hospital day

E. Room 13—Mrs. J, 40 y/o, duodenal ulcer, 2nd hospital day

In the table above (Appendix Table 2) estimate the probability, (0% to 100%) of each outcome (listed across the top of the table) occurring for Mrs. Kastor in each of the five rooms listed to the left of the table. For example: If Room 4 had a roommate who would provide meaningful stimulation, with a disease process that posed a low risk of complications, and would not interfere with rest, your probabilities might appear as in the sample below.

Alternatives	Nursing Observation	Maximal Rest	Meaningful Stimulation	Avoidance of Complications
Room 4—Mrs Ex, 46 y/o, hysterectomy, 6th hospital day	10%	45%	75%	85%

In the test booklet, rank the four outcomes according to which is most important for Mrs. Kastor's welfare: 1 for the most important and 4 for the least important.

Rank	Outcome
_____	A. Nursing observation
_____	B. Maximal rest
_____	C. Meaningful stimulation
_____	D. Avoidance of complications

Based on your responses in the Trade-off Table and your ranking of the outcomes, rank in the test booklet the rooms, according to which would be best for Mrs. Kastor. Use 1 for best and 5 for worst:

Rank	Room
_____	A. Room 5
_____	B. Room 6
_____	C. Room 8
_____	D. Room 10
_____	E. Room 13

Chapter 10

Analog Devices for Teaching Decision Skills to Adolescents

Anne W. Martin
Rex V. Brown
Decision Science Consortium, Inc.
Reston, VA

INTRODUCTION

Motivation

Personalized decision analysis (PDA)[1] is a well-articulated quantitative logic for inferring the action and inference implications of an appropriately defined set of assessments and evaluations, typically expressed as numerical probabilities and utilities (Raiffa, 1968; Watson & Buede, 1987). This type of analysis is increasingly used to help professional deciders, such as government officials and business men and women, to help make and defend their decisions (Brown, 1987; Ulvila & Brown, 1982). Much less effort has been devoted to applying the mathematical formulation to help untrained individuals make personal decisions.

This is unfortunate, given that the decision-making performance of much of the US Citizenry *exhibits serious deficiencies* (Baron & Brown, chap. 5 in this volume). A number of efforts are under way to improve personal decision-making abilities through a variety of qualitative and quantitative approaches (Baron & Brown, chap. 5 in this volume), including PDA.

---

[1]Sometimes also referred to simply as "decision analysis," though this does not distinguish the paradigm from the many alternative approaches to analyzing decisions.

skills of adolescents (and the adults they will become) by having them learn and internalize certain quantitative operations at the heart of formal PDA. These include such decision rules as maximizing subjective expected utility or multiattribute utility, and inference aids such as conditioned probability assessment and pooling inconsistent judgments.

The objective of our teaching effort is not so much teaching detailed arithmetic manipulation of formal decision-making structures as it is enhancing students' informal abilities to replicate the essence of those structures and implement the coherent decision strategies that the structures imply.

There is little reason to believe that our objective, which amounts to having students internalize a few important decision-analytic principles, would best be achieved by conventional numeric decision analysis training. In our experience of teaching decision analysis to a wide variety of students, from children to senior managers (e.g., see Brown, Kahr, & Peterson, 1974), we have discovered that many, if not most, of them exhibit discomfort with and resistance to working explicitly with the numbers and numerical calculations. Indeed, they often experience enough discomfort that they reject entirely any course where numbers are centrally involved.

A possible solution to this problem is to teach using graphic and/or physical devices as models; the spatial and physical characteristics of such devices (distances, weights, areas, volumes) render them much more concretely manipulable than numbers, while serving the same functions that numbers serve. This approach has been used successfully in user interfaces for professional decision-analytic computer aids (Barclay, 1986).

This chapter reports on an experimental effort to use one device, the balance beam, in an ongoing decision-skills teaching program at Langston Hughes Intermediate School in Reston, Virginia, during the 1988–1989 academic year (Laskey & Campbell, chap. 6 in this volume). Potential use of other devices involving the conservation of areas and volumes is discussed in Appendix A.

Balance Beam as Analog for Weighted Sum Comparison

The "weighted sum" is the core algorithm for four major PDA paradigms:

1. Additive multiattribute utility: The scores of options on different attributes are weighted by their relative importance.
2. Expected single-attribute utility: The utilities of possible consequences are weighted by their probabilities.
3. Conditioned assessment: An unconditional probability is calculated as the average conditional probability given possible contingencies, weighted by their unconditional probabilities.

4. Pooling conflicting estimates: Weights correspond to relative "confidence," measured by statistical precision.

Although weighted sums are "easy" to compute, they may still represent a block to understanding the underlying logic, especially to the nonnumerate adolescent. In any case, the computation becomes burdensome, especially in a sensitivity mode, where the subject experiments with different possible values for weights and/or scores being weighted. Our intent is to develop in students a cognitive capacity to exploit PDA logic when making judgments without having to absorb assessed or manipulated numbers. It is clearly an advantage if magnitudes do not need to be digitized.

The balance beam provides an exact analogy to the comparison of weighted sums. The physical principle is that a "weightless" beam balances at the point where the sum of the products of signed distances from it, multiplied by weights attached at these distances, is zero; if a fulcrum is at a fixed point on the beam, the beam tilts down on the side for which the sum of the products of distances and weights is greater.

The corresponding PDA operation chosen for initial study is expected single-attribute utility analysis for comparing two options (analogous to comparing the two sides of the balance beam with fixed fulcrum); sensitivity of expected utility model conclusions corresponds to sensitivity of the balance beam's direction of tilt to shifts in distance or magnitude of the weights attached. Figure 10.1 is a diagram of the balance beam device constructed for our teaching and experiments. It was designed to be large enough to be clearly visible from the back of a classroom[2].

When using the balance beam as a device for comparing the expected utility of two options with uncertain outcomes, we assign one side of the device to either option. The utility under each outcome of choosing an option is represented by distance from the center (the tenth dowel out represents a utility of 100; the fifth a utility of 50); the probability of that outcome is represented by the number of weights placed at the distance corresponding to its utility (each weight represents .05, so three weights at some point represent a probability of .15 of the corresponding outcome). Of course, no weights can be placed at the center point, which corresponds to zero utility for both options.

---

[2]Along the cross beam at 2-inch intervals (starting at the center and proceeding outward in both directions) are attached 20 wire hooks (10 per side) on which are hung wooden dowels. The dowels are a half-inch in diameter and each has an eyelet attached to its top (for hanging on the hook) and a 1-inch metal disk attached to its bottom (for holding weights). The weights are doughnut-shaped (each made of five metal washers glued together) and measure 1⅜" across and ¼" tall; 20 are red and 20 are blue. The remainder of the set consists of a pair of removable supports for holding the cross beam level.

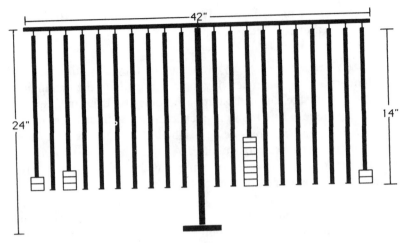

FIG. 10.1   Diagram of the balance beam.

Experimental Uses

During the 1988–1989 year, we experimented with the balance beam as a training device for two decision skills objectives:

1. To serve a pedagogical function in teaching students about decision analysis, applied explicitly both to personal and public decisions.
2. To serve as a device for enhancing students' abilities to make decisions better without explicit, numeric decision-analytic computation, that is, to improve their intuitive decision-making skills.

The first objective was addressed by having a DSC researcher (Brown), experienced at teaching decision analysis, use the beam experimentally in a series of classes designed to teach decision analysis to eighth-graders; this researcher's experience and conclusions are described in the next section.

The second objective was addressed using a more formal experimental approach; the experiments and their results are described in the following section, titled "Experiments on Developing Mathematical Intuition."

Why did we hypothesize that the balance beam would be an effective decision training device? Its promise seemed to lie in its concreteness and intellectual accessibility as compared to the theoretical and numerical character of decision-analytic formulas. The balance beam's concreteness (as opposed to the abstractness of expected utility formulas) may serve the same function as familiarity in the work of Reed and Evans (1987); these investigators found that for students' solutions to mixture problems, training in a familiar domain (temperature mixture) resulted in more improvement in the unfamiliar target domain (mixture of acid concentrations) than did training in the target domain. The balance beam also provides a visual image, recognized as mnemonic at least since the time of Simonides; a coherent image, basically a mental model, is likely to be much better remembered than a set of formulas. Finally, use of the beam is highly consistent with good pedagogic principles of providing concrete models early in the process of teaching complex knowledge structures (as recommended, e.g., by Perkins, 1986).

A reason that the balance beam might not have been a successful device for training decision skills is that there is some "conventional wisdom" based on limited interpretation of experimental work done for other purposes (e.g., that of Siegler, 1981; Siegler & Klahr, 1982) that people are not very good at predicting the behavior of balance beams. If the analog device proved not to be understandable (providing what Perkins called a "mental muddle"), it would not simplify or improve the process of teaching the analogous decision task. Thus, part of our experimental task was to test whether or not members of the middle school population in which we are interested could, in fact, understand balance beam behavior sufficiently to warrant its further testing as a decision training device.

CASE TESTING THE BEAM AS A PROBLEM-SOLVING AID

Stage Setting

Four consecutive class periods in an eighth-grade science class for "gifted and talented" students were devoted to the use of the balance beam in decision making. They came immediately following part of the regular science course curriculum dealing with the physical torque properties of a balance beam.

The class had previously taken another of our decision segments: an eight-session introduction to formal decision analysis, covering both qualitative and quantitative concepts at a broad level. One class had been devoted to expected utility and it had been exercised briefly using the balance beam.

The four-session science segment involved both controlled experiments with the balance beam and guided but uncontrolled problem solving in class using the beam[3]. The experimental aspects are discussed later.

The sequence of four classes on successive days was as follows. The regular teacher started with half an hour of teaching relevant physics of torque, and the rest of this class was given over to a pretest of the beam training experiment, discussed later. The second period exercised students' ability to

---

[3]Detailed teaching notes on the four-class module are on file at DSC. Interested readers should contact author Brown.

predict the behavior of a balance beam (in the form of both static comparison and sensitivity exercises). The next one-and-a-half periods were devoted to the analysis of two decisions, one personal and one public, that is, governmental. The final half hour was the experimental posttest.

Most of the sequence was first piloted on two students who had also taken the introductory decision course (and were not to be in the science segment).

Objective of Problem-Solving Exercise

Our intent was to address the following questions:

1. Does the beam help individuals or groups of students, previously exposed to PDA concepts, to solve the post-structure part of a problem, that is, after two options and up to a half dozen critical uncertain outcomes have been specified from oral case analysis?
2. Specifically, can it help to: elicit probability and value inputs; understand their implications, including preferred choice; override mismatches between model and perception; understand sensitivity on inputs?
3. Can it be done in keeping with requirements of an eighth-grade science course; that is, by exercising a physics concept (torque), and thinking through a decision with high scientific content (technological risk)?

Account of Problem-Solving Experience

The problem-solving activity, which occupied most of the second half of the four-class sequence, was introduced with a brief recapitulation of a relevant part of the core course (discussed by Campbell & Laskey, chap. 13 in this volume). Students showed rather weak retention of the material they had learned the previous term. For example, many seemed to confuse multiattribute utility and subjectively expected utility (and the balance beam does nothing to clear up the confusion).

In order to fit as closely as possible with the objectives of a science class, in our pilot we had tried to go straight to a realistic issue involving science policy. The cognitive burden of trying to assimilate both an unfamiliar analytic technique (i.e., using the beam) and a scientific issue on which they had almost no grounds for forming relevant judgments proved too great for very productive exercise.

Therefore, for the main class we "warmed them up" first on a personal decision where the judgments needed were very accessible to them. (The purposes of the science course would have been better served had we been able to come up with a science-oriented issue that was equally accessible, and thereby dispensed with warm-up entirely.)

For both decisions, students were given a homework assignment (see Fig. 10.2) that had them think through the problem. They were asked to go through the first steps of structuring their reflections qualitatively and writing them up on a standard form they had used before (see Laskey & Campbell, chap. 6 in this volume). It essentially involved following a basic drill we had urged on them in the previous course: consider Goals, Options, Outcomes, and Probabilities (what we called "going through the GOOP").

The use of a balance beam was only one element in the total pedagogic exercise of analyzing each case problem. For the purposes of this chapter, we are concerned specifically with the contribution of the balance beam to the total process. Many other important issues generic to PDA surfaced, but we do not address them here.

Personal Decision.   The first choice presented was a simple one to which they could all relate: which of two part-time jobs a student should pursue. If they try for McDonald's they either get a serving job or they don't. If they apply at an industrial corporation, and are accepted, they will either mop floors or be selected for a "plum job." The implied model structure was unambiguous in this case, and was readily elicited from the class (see Fig. 10.3).

One student, Eric, volunteered to be the subject whose hypothetical decision was to be aided. When asked for his initial inclination, he opted tentatively for the McDonald's job. His probabilities and utilities (to the nearest 5% and 10% respectively) were then elicited in a standard form, with which students were already familiar (from the earlier decision-skills course).

(Two other students were charged with setting up the beam correspondingly and operating it. An event that ended up being assigned zero utility would be located at the fulcrum, with no place to hang the event rod. This problem was handled by stacking its probability washers in front of the support post.)

The familiar PDA problem of getting the initial probability numbers to add up to one went away as soon as the numbers were replaced by their washer analog. It was visually clear that a fixed pile of washers were to be assigned to one event or another, for a given option.

The comparable, and equally familiar, problem of getting initial utility numbers for each option–event combination to lie plausibly on an interpretable 1–100 scale, on the other hand, was *not* helped a great deal by the analog of distance from the fulcrum. Within an option (i.e., one side of the beam) the analog helped clarity; but *between*-options comparability (i.e., on opposite sides of the beam) was probably impaired. For instance, utility

---

HOMEWORK ASSIGNMENT FOR CLASS 3 OF DECISION SKILLS
COMPONENT OF 8TH GRADE SCIENCE COURSE

1. Personal Job Choice

You have a choice of which of two jobs to apply for, for the summer vacation. You have only enough time available to do one interview. Prepare a GOOP chart to help you decide which of the two places to apply to.

One is with McDonald's, serving at the counter, for $4.50 an hour. More than half the 8th graders who apply get accepted. The other is with an industrial corporation. They always need people to mop the floors at $3.50 an hour, though they sometimes turn applicants down if they don't seem responsible enough to be given the run of executive offices. The company president also wants a companion for his child (same sex and age as you) when his family spends the summer touring Europe. All expenses would be paid, but you would not get any other pay. About 20 8th graders from Langston Hughes School (same sex as you) are expected to apply for this.

2. Public Policy Solar Satellite Choice

The US Department of Energy has been researching a new technology which, if successful, would solve any potential energy shortage for the next hundred years. It involves putting a massive satellite into orbit (perhaps 200 miles across). It would collect the sun's rays and transmit the energy through a narrow, immensely powerful beam to a collecting dish on the ground. This would be turned into electricity, which would power the entire United States. It would replace almost all existing sources of energy (oil, nuclear, coal, etc.) except for an emergency reserve. It would cost a trillion dollars over 20 years to set up. This is as much as the whole US federal budget for a year. However, it would recoup that cost in energy savings inside 5 years after that.

A government research group has been working on the problem for 10 years and has tested everything it could, short of actually building the satellite. Congress is about to vote on whether to approve going ahead. It is now or never. You are a Congressman. How would you vote, and why?

Use the format of the GOOP form (see section 2 of chapter 6).

3. Optional: Self-Generated Exercises

Can you think of any choice problem that has a science relevance, where uncertainty about a couple of possible outcomes is really critical? The choice should be narrowed down to just two options, and there should be one, two, or three possible outcomes for each option. For each option the outcomes should be stated so they are exhaustive and exclusive, i.e., just one of them must happen. List the outcomes in two columns under the option concerned.

FIG. 10.2.   Homework assignment sheet distributed before class 3.

PERSONAL JOB CHOICE

MC DONALD'S OPTION			CORPORATION OPTION		
Outcome	Util.	Prob.	Outcome	Util.	Prob.
Hired as server Not hired	50 0	.8 .2	Plum job Cleaning Not hired	100 30	.05 .95 .0
[Expected Utility]	[40*]			[33]	

PUBLIC POLICY SOLAR SATELLITE CHOICE

"PROCEED NOW" OPTION			"NEVER PROCEED" OPTION		
Outcome	Util.	Prob.	Outcome	Util.	Prob.
Works great, solves energy problem Just adequate Disaster Doesn't work	100 60 0 20	.50 .30 .05 .15	Energy crisis Better solution becomes available Same as now	10 100 50	.5 .2 .4
[Expected Utility]	[71*]			[45]	

FIG. 10.3. Decision cases: Initial probabilities and utilities with implied preferred choice*.

improvement goes from right to left on the right-hand beam and left to right on the left-hand beam.

The class voted on which side would tip down, and ¾ got it right. The helpers demonstrated it by releasing the beam. The implied preferred choice—McDonald's—conformed to Eric's first guess. (The corresponding expected utility numbers, shown in brackets in Fig. 10.3, were noted, to remind students of the logic, but not used again in the case.)

Then began the important part of the exercise, which was to see how well the beam worked as a vehicle for exploring alternative perspectives on value and uncertainty, as measured by utilities and probabilities.

First Eric was encouraged to test the acceptability of his numbers by seeing what choice they implied. He readily adjusted some of them directly on the beam (i.e., without going back to the numbers) and tested their implications on the beam until he felt comfortable, both with the inputs and the choice they implied. The rest of the class were actively involved as "consultants" to the subject, urging that a washer be moved from here to there, or that position on the beam be moved up or down (probability and utility respectively).

There were technically tricky utility assessment issues to address, for example, having to do with time horizon and the role of future uncertainties. Although these have nothing directly to do with the use of a beam, it is clear that they must be satisfactorily addressed before the beam has any useful role to play. It cannot be taken for granted that a teacher inexperienced in practical decision analysis can do it without careful briefing on a particular prestructured problem, such as this.

The argument then shifted to considering how the decision for other students might differ, for example, because different things were important to them. A number of iterations of the beam set-up were tried, corresponding to different views, including sensitivity. ("How much more would you need to value getting the corporate plum job than Eric did, before that's what you would try for?" translated into, "How far would you need to move the 'plum job' rod to the right, before the beam tipped the other way?")

The total case exercise took about 40 minutes of lively discussion, with much apparent interest and class participation.

Social Policy Decision.   The balance of the preceding class and half the next one were devoted to a realistic issue in public technical policy: whether the U. S. should put a vast solar satellite into space, to become the major source of this country's energy for the next hundred years. This time the ground rules were slightly different: Students were to take the perspective of a member of Congress voting on whether the Executive Branch should go ahead or not. (Previously, the researcher had actually worked for some years on this issue for Congress.)

The researcher's immediate objective was to quickly elicit from the class (with prompting as necessary) a reasonable structure that fitted the expected utility paradigm and the beam's capability; that is, a few exhaustive outcomes, whose uncertainty drives the choice. This was to set up the use of the beam for *post-structure analysis,* which is its distinctive role.

It was clear from review of the homework assignments and the limited class discussion devoted to structure that these students could not have proposed a suitable structure on their own, at least not one that could claim any realistic correspondence with their perception of the real problem.

The format of the case analysis and discussion was basically the same as for the personal job exercise, and the result was comparable. There was a lively, productive, and focused discussion of the issues, with the class ending up voting down the venture.

However, the technical challenge of the project made it difficult for students to make the probability and utility judgments that were reflected in the manipulation of distances and washers. On the other hand, one of the students had received input from his father who was familiar with the background of the issue (it was at one time a real Congressional choice). The beam enabled us to see the impact of the father's views on the choice, via his values and uncertainties.

A potential defect of this particular beam surfaced here: It was constructed to handle probabilities only to the nearest 5%, and utilities to the nearest 10% (on a scale of 0-100). This is serious when dealing with rare events with serious consequences like a disastrous accident—a common case with issues of technological risk management. This consideration weakened the pedagogic purpose of satisfying the students that they were working with a realistic representation of the problem. (However, this problem could readily be solved by using some smaller washers.)

Student-Generated Exercises.   About half the class of 20 exercised the option of producing and handing in a case analysis of their own choosing. (There was no time to discuss the submissions in class.)

They were asked to structure their analysis in a form that fit the requirements of the balance beam analysis; that is, a few discrete outcomes to each of two options. Almost all of them had great difficulty in reducing the problem to this form, and having it represent a reasonably accurate model of their perceptions of the problem.

Discussion

By and large, both case analyses seemed, to researcher and the regular teacher who observed the class, to be quite satisfactory. Students canvassed by questionnaire on their reaction to different aspects of the four-session course put the beam-aided case analysis as the most worthwhile part. The discussion was certainly lively and well focused, and the beam appeared to provide an appealing organizing principle to the students, especially for group analysis that could accommodate various points of view without confusion.

The researcher's firm, but of course subjective, view is that the beam was of significant value in exploring the students' collective and individual views on the two case choices. In particular, the analysis appeared more effective than it would have been, either with a purely qualitative discussion or with a PDA that had the same structure but was implemented with numerical calculations (even if computerized).

A weak control group, that is, one broadly comparable but without the beam components, was provided by a different but broadly comparable case analysis experience. Another middle school class with similar training played the role of decision analysis consultant to the researcher who had the (real) choice of whether to have an arthritic hip replaced. The discussion and exploration of views in a PDA format was definitely slowed down and rendered opaque by having to be mediated through numbers and calculations.

However, it should be noted that these two cases were set up to fit the rather restrictive mold of problems that can be conveniently analyzed with the help of a balance beam: binary choice with a few critical outcomes. This is fine for teaching a logical PDA concept—expected utility—which these classes seemed to do very well, but it severely limits the range of useful explicit applications of the beam for solving real choice problems.

EXPERIMENTS ON DEVELOPING
MATHEMATICAL INTUITION

Students appeared to respond well to early uses of the balance beam as an explanatory device for expected utility analysis; a reasonable next question is whether training using the balance beam can actually improve students' decision-making performance. This question was especially interesting, given balance beam-related results found by Siegler (e.g., Siegler, 1981; Siegler, 1985; Siegler & Klahr, 1982), whose work suggests that 12- and 13-year-old children often do not perform well on balance beam tasks.

Siegler measured performance by the sophistication of the rule that subjects appear to be applying to balance beam prediction. Subjects using Rule I predict which side (if either) would go down based simply on weight (predicting that the side with the most weight will go down). A subject using Rule II also focuses on weight, but predicts using distance when weight is equal on the two sides (so that a Rule II subject would predict correctly that the side with its weight further from the fulcrum would go down). Rule III subjects attend to both weight and distance, but "muddle through" when weight and distance are in conflict, resulting in chance responding when the side with greater weight is not also the side on which the weight is furthest from the fulcrum. Finally, Rule IV subjects balance weight and distance appropriately, and make predictions consistent with the sums-of-products rule.

Over the course of a number of experiments, Siegler found little spontaneous use of Rule IV by 12- and 13-year-olds; about half of the subjects at these ages (40% to 60%) appeared to use Rule III. When these students were given feedback on conflict problems (i.e., problems of types that Rule III students do badly and Rule IV students do well), either self-directed or experimenter-directed, about 20% appeared to infer Rule IV. However, when 13-year-olds were given assistance in the form of quantified encoding (so that they were told how many weights were at which positions, not just left to observe this) and memory aids (in the form of a record of previously-done problems), about 80% appeared to apply Rule IV.

For our purposes, the key message to be gotten from Siegler's work seems to be that, although children of the age group in which we are interested do not do well spontaneously on balance beam tasks, at least there exist some conditions under which they can do such tasks rather well. This, combined with Piaget's finding (Inhelder & Piaget, 1958; Piaget & Inhelder, 1969) that children are capable of performing balance beam problems at about age 12, allows us to maintain our optimism about utility of the beam as a pedagogical device for children ages 12 and above.

Optimism is not certainty, however. Given Siegler's results and the fact that our balance beam is a more complicated version, with ten rather than four positions on each side of the fulcrum, it was deemed desirable first to establish that children from our population of interest could learn to do balance beam prediction problems without external aids; this was the topic of Experiment 1. Experiment 2 addressed the question of whether balance beam and/or calculator training on expected utility decision problems can improve students' performance on such problems.

Experiment 1—Learning to Predict Balance Beam Behavior

This experiment was conducted as part of the eight-grade mini-course on decision making described earlier. The study was designed to test the hypothesis that children can learn to predict which (if either) side of a balance beam will go down for a variety of kinds of problems.

Method

Subjects.   Subjects were 22 eighth-grade science students (ranging in age from 12 years, 11 months to 14 years, 3 months) who had been classified by their school system as "Gifted and Talented" (GT) and had chosen to accept the classification and take a GT Science class.

Experimental Procedure.   The procedure that was followed consisted of five steps:

1. Students were given a short lesson, including hands-on experience, in levers/balance beams. This lesson, which lasted approximately 30 minutes, was conducted by the regular teacher and drawn from standard curriculum materials; it included an explanation of the correct rule for predicting which side will go down and hands-on experience with small levers.

2. The experimenter conducted a discussion of the similarity in principle of the balance beam used by the experimental team and the levers on which the students had just been trained.

3. A 20-minute pretest was administered, consisting of 12 problems; eight were strictly prediction problems ("Will the balance tilt towards red or blue, or will it balance?"), and four were sensitivity problems ("Where would I have to put y more points—at this point or this point—just to tip the balance in the other direction?" or "If I put y more weight here, would

the balance tip in the other direction?") The balance beam was masked from the class while the problems were being set up; once each problem was set up, the class was allowed to observe the balance beam for 7 seconds. Students recorded their responses on multiple-choice answer sheets.

4. The students were given two kinds of balance beam instructions. One exercise consisted of a beam-guessing game that pitted one half of the class against the other; the game, which is described in Appendix B, occupied one 50-minute class period. The other exercise was the beam manipulation component of the class discussion of two decision cases discussed earlier. Beam manipulation occupied about 30 of the 80 minutes devoted to decision analysis training.

5. A 20-minute posttest was administered, consisting of 12 problems equivalent to the pretest problems and using the same format used for the pretest.

Stimuli.   The 12 balance beam problems used in the pre- and posttests are shown in Fig. 10.4. Training problems were similar. Most of the problems require use of Siegler's Rule IV for correct solution, though some, for example, Problems 1 through 3 in Fig. 10.4, can clearly be solved using Rules I or II. It should be noted, however, that these problems were designed for different purposes than Siegler's. The objective in this case was not precise diagnosis of level of cognitive development, but pragmatic empirical testing of performance on problems at the level of complexity of typical expected utility problems.

Experiment 1 Results

Results support the hypothesis that children's performance on predicting balance beam behavior can be improved. The subjects' mean score on the pretest was 7.4 (*SD* 1.44) out of 12 problems. The mean score on the posttest was 9.1 (*SD* 1.36) correct out of 12. A t-test performed on the distribution of difference scores (mean 1.728, *SD* 1.632, with 21 degrees of freedom) yielded a value of 4.966 (p < .001, two-tailed).

Table 10.1 shows frequencies of right and wrong answers on the 12 pre- and posttest problems. The most substantial improvement was seen on problems 4 (going from 8 to 15 out of 22 subjects predicting correctly), 5 (going from 17 to 21 correct), 7 (going from 13 to 18 correct predictions), 10, and especially 9 (going from 4 to 18). On Problems 1, 2, 3, and 11, there was little room for improvement, because almost all subjects got these problems right on the pretest. On Problems 8 and 12, the frequencies are not at all inconsistent with chance responding, though there could be a slight bias in favor of wrong answers. Finally, we speculate that Problem 6 is deceptive to many subjects; there was actually a decrease in the number

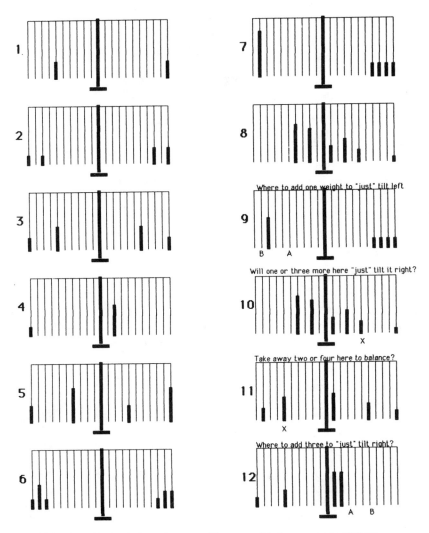

FIG. 10.4 Twelve balance beam problems used in the pre- and posttests.

of subjects getting this problem correct, and almost half of the subjects held firm on the wrong answer.

Experiment 2—Training Intuitive Expected Utility

Experiment 2 was designed to test the hypothesis that children can learn to apply intuitively ("in their heads") a normative approach to decision making, and in particular, that training involving the balance beam would fos-

TABLE 10.1
Numbers of Subjects Giving Right and Wrong Answers for Pretest and
Equivalent Posttest Problems—Experiment 1
(22 subjects)

Problem	Right pre/ Right post	Right pre/ Wrong post	Wrong pre/ Right post	Wrong pre/ Wrong post
1	20	0	1	1
2	22	0	0	0
3	21	0	1	0
4	7	1	8	6
5	17	0	4	1
6	7	4	1	10
7	10	3	8	1
8	4	4	6	8
9	3	1	15	3
10	7	3	8	4
11	20	0	2	0
12	4	5	5	8

ter such learning. This experiment took place in two seventh-grade math classes whose teacher classified them as performing on the same level.

The decision problem context used for this experiment was summer job choice, where the options were constructed to be amenable to expected utility analysis. The general problem type was explained as follows:

> Your school is having a job fair to help match up students who want summer jobs and local employers who want summer workers. Most students in your class do want summer jobs, and will participate in the job fair. The job fair is organized into a number of sessions, held at the same time in different places, and each session will give students the opportunity to apply for a different kind of job. Each student applying for a kind of job will be offered either one job of this type, or no job (if all the jobs for which that student was qualified are already offered to some other student). Because the sessions are separate but take place all at the same time, each student must decide beforehand what kind of summer jobs he or she is interested in and so which session to attend.

Subjects were instructed to imagine that they were advising a friend about making a job fair decision, and a procedure was described for how a student might help the hypothetical friend narrow down the options and assess probabilities and utilities (which were called scores) on outcomes. The information generated by this procedure (the application of which was described in a handout reinforced by discussion) was organized as shown in Table 10.2.

Method

Subjects.   Subjects were 49 seventh-graders (23 in the "balance beam" class and 26 in the "calculator" class) in standard seventh-grade mathemat-

TABLE 10.2
Organization of Job Fair Decision Information

FAST FOOD CHOICE (red)			PARK DEPARTMENT CHOICE (blue)		
Outcome	Score	Prob.	Outcome	Score	Prob.
McDonald's customer service	80	20%	Teaching crafts	100	15%
McDonald's cooking	30	40%	Maintaining nature trail	70	40%
Taco Amigo cleaning tables	10	35%	No job offer	0	45%
No job offer	0	5%			

ics classes; they ranged in age from 12 years, 0 months to 13 years, 8 months. Both classes had the same teacher and lesson plan, and met in the same classroom. Both met for 50 minutes in the afternoon; the calculator class met directly after the balance beam class. Neither class had prior exposure to decision analysis.

Experimental Procedure.

1. Both classes (on the same day) were given a short lesson in probability theory (a simple description of probability as a way of conveying how likely some event is, concrete descriptions of the basic rules of probability, class discussion of examples of the use of probability, and an exercise with dice).

2. Following the probability lecture, both classes received a hard-copy explanation of the job decision task, with discussion to make sure that the task was understood.

3. Next, both classes took a pretest, consisting of ten job-decision problems of the sort described above. Problems were presented using an overhead projector; each problem was presented for 20 seconds. The pretest task was to choose the better option for the hypothetical student.

4. On the following day, both classes received training on the job decision task:

The balance beam class's training used the balance beam as an expected utility computer. The experimenter performed an example demonstration of how the device could be made to represent the decision problem (distance from the fulcrum as the score of an outcome, amount of weight as probability of some outcome). Subsequent applications were performed by pairs of students, each setting up one choice or side of the balance beam. The remaining students watched and advised and, once a problem representation was set up, guessed which side of the balance would go down. Eight job problems were solved in this manner.

The calculator class's training was performed using small, hand-held calculators. Using an example decision problem, the experimenter demonstrated the steps involved in computing expected utilities (multiplying score by probability, then summing the products). After this demonstration, pairs of students with calculators computed expected utilities (posting intermediate and final results on the blackboard) for the options in the same eight problems that the other class had solved with the balance beam. Remaining students watched, made recommendations, and guessed which options would receive the higher score.

5. Six days later, both classes took a posttest consisting of ten problems equivalent to the pretest problems; in both classes, no decision aids (i.e., neither balance beam nor calculator) were provided.

6. Following the posttest, the classes were cross-trained—the balance beam class received an explanation of the computation of expected utility, and the calculator class was given a demonstration of the balance beam as an expected utility calculator.

Stimuli.   The categories of jobs among which hypothetical students had to choose, along with the names of the hypothetical students, were selected with the assistance of two eighth-grade consultants who were asked to check jobs and names for plausibility. Figure 10.5 shows the distributions of probabilities and scores for the ten pre- and posttest job problems; the eight training problems were similar to these ten. It should be noted that, though we present the problems in balance-beam format here, no balance beam was used for either group in the pretest or posttest; all job choices were presented in tables that listed job areas, outcomes, scores, and probabilities organized as in the Fast Food versus Park Department example in Table 10.2.

Experiment 2 Results

The balance beam training group improved significantly from pretest to posttest; average pretest score for this group was 5.3, with SD 1.66, and average posttest score was 6.2, with SD 1.57. The mean improvement from pretest to posttest for this group was .91 problems, with a standard deviation of 2.09 ($t = 2.088$; $p < .05$, two-tailed). Improvement in the calculator training group was marginally significant. The calculator group had a mean pretest score of 5.3, with SD 2.2 and a mean posttest score of 6.0, with SD 2.7; the t-test on differences (mean .69; SD 1.98) yielded a value of 1.777 ($p < .1$, two-tailed). Results of a test for differences in improvement between the two groups were not significant. A t-test on pre–post differences for the combined group of 49 subjects (collapsed across the two types of training, with an overall mean difference of .8 problems, SD 2.01) yields a value of 2.786 ($p < .01$, two-tailed).

Tables 10.3 and 10.4 show frequencies of right and wrong pre- and post-

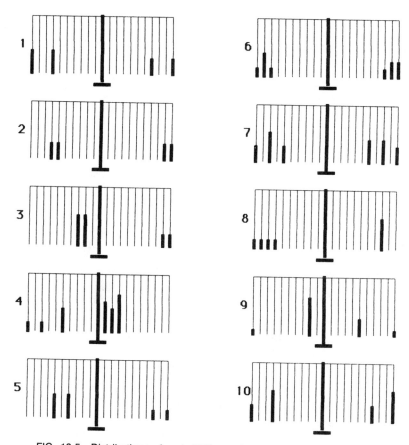

FIG. 10.5   Distributions of probabilities and scores for the ten pre- and posttest job choice problems (presented to subjects in tabular format).

test answers for the two groups. Generally the balance beam and calculator-trained groups tend to have about the same patterns on all problems. Both groups had high frequencies of right–right (right on both the pretest and the posttest) answers for Problems 1 and 2, which are very easy; balance beam problems equivalent to these can be gotten right using Siegler's Rule I or II as well as more sophisticated rules; right–right frequency was only slightly lower on Problem 5, which, in balance beam form, is always solved correctly by users of Rules I, II, and IV, but only sometimes by users of Rule III.

The problem on which both pre- and posttest performance was worst was Problem 9, for which the correct solution was "equal." This would be a very difficult balance beam problem; Rule III subjects might guess it correctly, but only Rule IV subjects with perfect encoding (i.e., subjects with precise information about the numbers and locations of all weights) could

TABLE 10.3
Numbers of Subjects Giving Right and Wrong Answers for Pretest and
Equivalent Posttest Problems—Experiment 2, Balance Beam Group
(23 subjects)

Problem	Right pre/ Right post	Right pre/ Wrong post	Wrong pre/ Right post	Wrong pre/ Wrong post
1	17	2	4	0
2	17	1	5	0
3	7	5	6	5
4	10	3	4	10
5	15	6	2	0
6	3	6	8	6
7	10	3	5	5
8	8	4	6	7
9	0	0	1	22
10	10	1	9	3

be expected to get it right. However, as a computational problem, it is quite
feasible; the fact that there was little improvement in the calculator group
suggests that the calculator subjects were not calculating on the posttest.
The most substantial improvement is seen in Problem 10 for both groups;
this is promising because, although the problem is relatively straightforward, its correct solution requires attending to both probability and utility
aspects of the choices. In Problem 3, there are noticeable differences in the
right–wrong frequencies of the two groups; however, this seems to be
mostly attributable to the calculator group's doing badly on this problem in
the pretest, and to have little to do with the differences in training. Overall,
the improvement seems to come from consistent, small increases in performance over most problems.

TABLE 10.4
Numbers of Subjects Giving Right and Wrong Answers for Pretest and
Equivalent Posttest Problems—Experiment 2, Calculator Group
(26 subjects)

Problem	Right pre/ Right post	Right pre/ Wrong post	Wrong pre/ Right post	Wrong pre/ Wrong post
1	22	1	3	0
2	22	2	2	0
3	2	5	6	13
4	3	6	5	12
5	19	2	3	2
6	4	4	10	8
7	12	6	5	3
8	7	4	6	9
9	2	1	3	20
10	11	2	8	5

Discussion

The results of Experiments 1 and 2 taken together leave us optimistic about the possibility of training middle school students' intuition using principles from decision analysis. Experiment 1 showed that training can improve their unaided performance at predicting the behavior of a balance beam, which is a promising analog device for teaching decision making. Experiment 2 demonstrates that (a) training an expected utility approach improves students' intuitive (unaided) decision performance, at least for problems in the same class as the training problems, and (b) the balance beam is effective for training intuition about expected utility problems.

Because our objectives, our problems, our experimental approach, and our performance criteria and methods of analysis (as well as our subjects) are different from those of Siegler, we cannot compare our results with his directly. We note, however, that our 12- and 13-year-old students, especially the eighth-graders, were capable of understanding balance beam behavior and improving at prediction of balance beam behavior.

No significant differences were found in later unaided performance of students given expected utility training using the balance beam and those trained using calculators (although the mean improvement for this sample was slightly higher for the balance beam group).

However, in both groups, a substantial majority (20 of 25 responses from the balance beam group, and 19 of 25 from the calculator group) of students responding to an anonymous post-experimental questionnaire opined that the balance beam was a better approach for helping students learn about PDA. (Numbers of responses are different from numbers of subjects because not all students were present on all days, and the anonymity of the questionnaires diminished the experimenter's ability to extract exactly one questionnaire from each subject.) Comments in favor of the balance beam included: ". . . easier and more fun"; ". . . it was easier to understand what was happening than with the calculator"; "it was interesting and people listened more"; ". . . the balance beam was the best analogy"; ". . . it is visual"; and ". . . it helped me weigh in my head." There were fewer comments in favor of the calculator. Most had to do with the availability of calculators for future use (one student suggested that the balance beam would be more useful if students were issued balance beams to use for decision making).

CONCLUSIONS

Findings

The empirical work described in this paper, comprising both controlled and uncontrolled teaching experiments, casts light on several issues, which can be taken as hypotheses for further testing. They pertain to the appropriate role of balance beams, and analog devices more generally, in helping adolescents, and the adults they will become, to be effective deciders.

Beam as Explanatory Device.   The problem-solving and experimental exercises suggest strongly that the balance beam can be a powerful aid for teaching basic decision-analytic concepts, such as expected utility, either through direct exposition or in the course of analyzing specific decision cases. It has strong intuitive appeal because of the directness and simplicity of the analogy, without the need for intervening numbers and arithmetic, which students may otherwise balk at.

Beam as Direct Aid in Analyzing Decisions.   With very little training, the beam can provide a convenient vehicle for individual and group evaluation of certain types of choice, notably for comparing paired options, in cases where the choice is dominated by a few uncertain outcomes. After the problem has been structured, the beam can serve to focus attention on critical probabilities and values, and rapidly and transparently compute action implications.

However, the problem-solving cases indicated very clearly that students with only a few hours of PDA training cannot be expected, on their own, to translate many decision problems into balance beam versions. This conclusion is supported by class discussion in the initial structuring phase of the satellite case, and by the earlier pilot classes. It is also consistent with our experience of using formal models to aid adult, including professional, decision making.

This suggests that the beam has only limited decision-aiding value, on its own, as an explicit *modeling* device (whether it is then manipulated physically or only in imagination). On the other hand, as the satellite case showed, the beam can be used very effectively by an experienced decision analyst to organize and focus decision deliberations. This is also consistent with our professional decision-aiding experience (notably in the context of computer-aided "decision conferences").

Beam as Device for Training Mathematical Intuition.   The beam, however, has a significant role to play when the expected utility operation *is* called for. Results of our experiments suggest that middle school students (a) can perform rather well on tasks requiring intuition about balance beam performance, and can get better with training; and (b) get better at option selection in a two-choice expected utility paradigm when they have balance beam training (and at least no worse when they have calculator training).

Unaided performance improvement following training was significant but small; there is clearly a need to refine methods of employment for the balance beam to increase the effectiveness of training. Recommended enhancements include training over a longer period of time (e.g., revisiting over the course of several weeks) and providing more opportunity for each student to interact with the device (perhaps by providing small individual balance beams).

That students' unaided performance on well-structured choice tasks improves after training with an analog device is promising, but of course not sufficient to allow us to conclude that use of the device will improve students' decision making. At minimum, more testing and probably expanded training will be required to ensure that students are capable of applying the lessons learned from working with decision problems that are already structured and quantified to the clearly messier decisions that they face in their own lives. In particular, training students in problem structuring using the balance beam has been carried through experimental teaching.

In decision skills courses that include the construction of expected utility models, balance beam training does seem to be an effective approach to grasp rapidly and precisely their meaning and action implications. However, no formal experiments have been done to test the efficacy of the balance beam as a device for training students to make decisions where the choice problem is not already well-structured. Its decision aiding value, therefore, is limited to those cases where a well-structured model is called for.

Directions for Further Research

Beam to Train Intuitive Choice. Neither the experiments nor the case analyses cast direct light on a critical hypothesis: that experience of working with a beam will help a subject *implicitly* to analyze binary decision dominated by "mushier" uncertain outcomes. Typical decisions are characterized by complex probabilistic profiles that may not justify thinking through explicitly as enumerable events with associated uncertainties.

Moreover, it may not even be appropriate for the subject to characterize his decision as a binary choice. On the one hand he may have a rich array of options to scan, for which binary comparisons, of the type two-sided beams fit, may not have a useful role to play. On the other hand, the subject may not be helped by *any kind* of concurrent evaluation of options. Klein (1989) and others have argued that "recognition-primed" deciding is a more promising paradigm, and indeed characterizes most experts. Balance beam training might even interfere with the development of that skill.

Extension to Other Analogs. The expected utility paradigm is in any case only designed to address one type of decision task, and the balance beam is only one analog that fits it. Research comparable to that presented here would be needed to test other combinations, as promising aids to decision aiding and training. For example:

- Decision-analytic weighted sum operations other than expected utility, such as linear additive multiattribute utility analysis (for decision tasks dominated by conflicting objectives).
- Analog devices other than balance beam for the same logical operation(s), such conservation of areas, using liquids (discussed in Appendix A).
- Use of analogs in the structuring phase of analyzing a decision, including problem recognition and identifying relevant outcomes.

APPENDIX A: ALTERNATIVE ANALOG POSSIBILITIES

Siegler and others have found (though we have not confirmed; see discussion of experiments, page 227) that adolescents often have cognitive difficulties with balance beams. We have considered—but not yet tested—other analog devices with the similar logical properties.

Conservation of Liquids and Areas as Weighted Sum Analog

Three important PDA operations are weighted sums: expected utility, conditioned probability assessment, and multiattribute utility (linear additive case). A weighted sum can be represented as the combined area of several rectangles. These can be physically formed in a number of ways, such as by liquids in rectangular troughs of uniform depth (so that volumes reduce to areas). Figure 10.6 shows the three cases schematically.

Areas have a major potential advantage over beams, in that they are not limited to paired comparisons (i.e., for only two options). Moreover, there is a palpable physical analog to the magnitude of the weighted sum (total area), rather than just a comparison, in the case of the beam (which side tips).

An added convenience, for the multiattribute utility analysis (MUA) case, is that the width of a trough can be set to correspond to an attribute weight, for all options, and the score is given by the height of the column, for any given option. A single trough structure can therefore be used for all options.

A promising (but untested) variant of the conservation of area analog, illustrated in Fig. 10.6, would be to use a single main trough, subdivided by movable partitions which would then form subtroughs, and even sub-subtroughs, corresponding to a hierarchy of weighted sums (as in hierarchical MUA case shown as Case c).

Physically, the equipment might be formed of clear plastic and opaque liquid. The main container would consist essentially of two parallel sheets

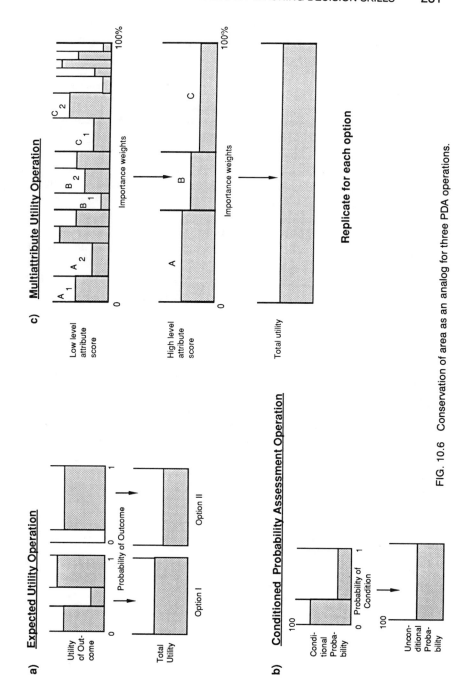

FIG. 10.6   Conservation of area as an analog for three PDA operations.

of clear plastic, blocked at the sides and bottom by strips creating three sides of a rectangle. The wide column thus formed could be partitioned by dividers slid into watertight grooves. Each partition would mark off a rectangular column.

In the MUA case (c) this would correspond to a given low level attribute. A rectangle would be formed by pouring an opaque liquid into the space. The width of the space would correspond to importance weight and the height to an option's score on the attribute. The subject could quantify each attribute by pouring liquid into each compartment. He would have the option of either controlling the total amount of liquid corresponding to the utility contribution of each attribute, by pouring from a graduated jug; or by controlling the height of the column.

The low level attribute columns could be grouped according to higher level attributes. By removing the partitions inside a grouping we could replace it by the higher order attribute and the liquid would settle in a way that gives the score on the attribute. (The weight would be automatically given by the wider column because high order weights are arrived at by summing lower order weights.) When all the internal partitions are removed, the height (and derivatively the area) gives total utility.

This procedure does not lend itself to successive partitioning of higher level attributes, but only the accumulation of lower level attributes. However, the weights can be assigned top down by successively finer insertion of partitions. The partition's visible edges could be color-coded in order to distinguish groups. Alternatively, the height of the partition could correspond to the level in the MUA hierarchy. (Clearly there is a nontrivial chore of developing appropriate equipment, which may stand in the way of the idea being used routinely, unless it took hold enough to give economies of scale.)

With the rectangular columns idea, using liquids, the eye can fairly readily determine an average that corresponds to the height of the liquid at the more aggregated level.

In the conditioned assessment case (b) only one piece of equipment is needed, whereas with MUA you either need two pieces of equipment or must empty one out between options.

In each of the three cases you could get finer decomposition; for example, two level conditioning of probabilities and different variants of each main outcome for expected utility.

Computer vs. Physical Analogs

A key question is whether the physical analog is better than a computerized version of it. The physical analog may be easier to understand, but a computerized version permits greater flexibility. The physical activity of pouring liquid in columns could be either a plus or a minus depending on whether you gain more from the concreteness and immediacy of the physical analog or from the speed and flexibility of the computer. It might make sense to train with the physical analog and then work with the computer as an actual decision aid.

They physical analog is, of course, much more cumbersome to construct and replicate. The computer can reverse the order, permitting successive refinement of a multiattribute hierarchy, that is, you break total utility down into a limited number of high level attributes and then reconsider the score (possibly the weight) of each, by subdividing it into lower level attributes. The computer would also make it easier to handle two options on a single display by having a zero horizontal line (corresponding to no difference between the options) and the columns can extend downwards as well as upwards (which you could not readily replicate with liquids).

We are coming more and more to think that the physical analog, at least as far as the column device is concerned, would only be used initially to get the idea across. However, the physical analog has the potential advantage of permitting the pouring out of measured amounts of utility.

Any given analytic operation could be represented by more than one physical analog in a kind of plural approach. A similar advantage to having a single analog for all weighted operations is economy of learning.

APPENDIX B: INTUITION TRAINING EXERCISES

Between the pretests and the posttests of the experiments described on pages 219-227, the subjects were given training of several kinds in intuiting the results of balance beam operations.

Beam Guessing Game

A sequence of 8 beam settings, of broadly increasing complexity, was shown to the class for 7 seconds. Then the students indicated simultaneously, by show of hands, which of the following they agreed with: (a) left side will tip down, (b) right side will tip down, or (c) they will balance. The correct answer was demonstrated on the beam.

The students were divided into two competitive teams. The winning side for this round was the one with more correct hands showing (i.e., failure to vote was treated as wrong). The dead time during set-up was taken up by researchers commenting on the process. Then the same beam setting was shown for a further 7 seconds and the class was asked to answer a binary sensitivity question of the form: "Will it take 2 or 4 washers shifted from A to B to just tip the beam the other way?" or "Should a washer be moved from A to B or to C to just tip the other way?" A running score was displayed of how many rounds each side had won (or tied).

A great deal of interest was generated by the closely contested match (even to the point of heated accusations of cheating!), and one jubilant side narrowly won. No doubt there *was* cheating, by people looking to see how others were voting before they cast their vote. This may have impaired the training somewhat for the "cheaters," and also inflated the apparent skill of the class.

Problem Solving

The second training exercise consisted of the beam components of the two case decision analyses referred to in the section describing case testing the beam, page 211. About 30 minutes in total involved working with the beam, with about 10 different beam settings corresponding to differing views on probabilities or utilities in the given case.

Every student had hands-on experience with manipulating the beam during set-up and demonstration, which was intended to enhance his training and to promote class involvement.

ACKNOWLEDGMENTS

This work was supported by the National Institute of Child Health and Human Development under Grant No. 2-R44-HD23071-02.

The authors wish to thank Mary Bailey and Carol Isaacs, teachers at Langston Hughes Intermediate School in Reston, Virginia, for experimental and lesson design assistance and access to their classes; Nancy Poudrier, assistant to Dr. Brown for help in developing stimulus materials and conducting experiments; Jeff Mandel for data analysis assistance; and David Schum for constructing the balance beam analog device.

REFERENCES

Barclay, S. (1986). *A brief description of HIVIEW and EQUITY.* Working Paper. Decision Analysis Unit. The London School of Economics and Political Science (University of London).

Brown, R. V. (1987). Decision analytic tools in government. In Karen B. Levitan (Ed.), *Government Infostructures.* Westport, CT: Greenwood Press.

Brown, R. V. (1989). *Notes for a decision analysis science add-on course.* Working paper (pp. 69–86). Reston, VA: Decision Science Consortium, Inc.

Brown, R. V., Kahr, A. S., & Peterson, C. R. (1974). *Decision analysis for the manager.* New York: Holt, Rinehart, and Winston.

Inhelder, B., & Piaget, J. (1958). *The growth of logical thinking from childhood to adolescence.* New York: Basic Books.

Klein, G. A. (1989). Recognition-primed decisions. *Advances in man–machine systems research, 5,* pp. 47–92. JAI Press.

Perkins, D. N. (1986). *Knowledge as design.* Hillsdale, NJ: Lawrence Erlbaum Associates.

Piaget, J., & Inhelder, B. (1969). *The psychology of the child.* New York: Basic Books.

Raiffa, H. (1968). *Decision analysis.* Reading, MA: Addison-Wesley.

Reed, S. K. & Evans, A. C. (1987). Learning functional relations: A theoretical and instructional analysis. *Journal of Experimental Psychology: General, 116* (2), 106–118.

Siegler, R. S. (1981). Developmental sequences within and between concepts. *Monographs of the Society for Research in Child Development, 46,* (2, Serial No. 189).

Siegler, R. S. (1985). Encoding and the development of problem solving. In S. F. Chipman, J. W. Segal, & R. Glaser (Eds.), *Thinking and learning skills, Volume 2: Research and open questions.* Hillsdale, NJ: Lawrence Erlbaum Associates.

Siegler, R. S., & Klahr, D. (1982). When do children learn? The relationship between existing knowledge and the acquisition of new knowledge. In R. Glaser (Ed.), *Advances in Instructional Psychology, 2,* (pp. 121–211). Hillsdale, NJ: Lawrence Erlbaum Associates.

Ulvila, M. W., & Brown, R. V. (1982, September–October). Decision analysis comes of age. *Harvard Business Review,* pp. 130–141.

Watson, S., & Buede, D. (1987). *Decision synthesis.* New York: Cambridge University Press.

Chapter **11**

Learning-Disabled Adolescents' Difficulties in Solving Personal/Social Problems

Joanna P. Williams
Teachers College, Columbia University

Our society is not providing its young people with the skills they need to face their problems. Over the past two decades, the suicide rate has climbed steadily in the United States, with the greatest increase in rate occurring among children and young adults (Statistical Abstracts of the U.S.A., 1987, p. 79). The overall crime rate among young people has been of serious concern over the same period and shows no sign of declining (Short & Simeonsson, 1986, p. 159). The incidence of violent crimes in schools has increased enormously, and the number of juveniles held in custody in public or private facilities has also grown steadily (Statistical Abstracts of the US, 1987, p. 170). A recent report of the Carnegie Corporation (Hornbeck, 1989) noted the turbulence and heightened vulnerabilities during the adolescent years and urged large-scale modification of the organization and curriculum of the schools, in a major attempt to curb some of these disturbing trends.

What is responsible for this increase in aggressiveness and destructiveness? Why are our young people so troubled? According to the National Assessment of Educational Progress (1985, p. 2), many adolescents show "little evidence of well-developed problem-solving strategies or critical thinking." Ennis (1987) defined critical thinking as "reasonable reflective thinking that is focused on deciding what to believe or do," and Baron (1985) pointed out that adolescents (as well as others!) often do not act in their own best interests specifically because they do not do such reflective thinking.

To try to understand the reasons for the great difficulties that so many people seem to have in managing their own lives, investigators have turned to the study of social problem-solving skills and their development in adolescents. "Social problem solving" refers to the cognitive behavioral process by which the individual discovers or identifies the most effective means for coping with problematic situations that are encountered in daily living (D'Zurilla & Nezu, 1981). Many studies have shown a relationship between problem solving ability and social competence (e.g., Ford, 1982; McKim, Weissberg, Cowan, Gesten, & Rapkin, 1982). Several studies have also demonstrated that problem solving ability and psychopathology area negatively correlated (Gotlib & Asnarow, 1979; Heppner & Anderson, 1985; Platt, Scura, & Hannon, 1973). In fact, effective problem solving has been shown to moderate depressive symptoms in people experiencing high levels of stressful life events (Nezu & Ronan, 1988).

Not all adolescents have such difficulties, of course. Those with learning disabilities seem to have particular problems in these areas. Although individuals are typically designated as learning-disabled on the basis of cognitive criteria (normal intellectual ability and a discrepancy between ability and academic achievement; Wong, 1986), and although most students who are labeled learning-disabled are so identified because of failure in learning to read (Stanovich, 1986), learning-disabled adolescents are at greater risk than their nondisabled peers not only in academic learning but also in all aspects of social competence, including peer acceptance, social skills, self-perception, and behavioral adjustment (Vaughn & Hogan, 1990). Most of these factors are associated with later difficulties such as social and vocational maladjustment and criminality (Pearl, Donahue, & Bryan, 1985).

One interpretation of these data is that LD students have general cognitive difficulties that interfere with social as well as academic learning (Vaughn & Hogan, 1990). For example, language deficiencies may lead to misunderstanding subtle social messages and hinder adequate verbal expression (Bryan, Donahue, Pearl, & Sturm, 1981), and metacognitive deficiencies may lead to poor monitoring and interpretation of social situations (Torgesen, 1980). Studies that focus specifically on interpersonal problem solving have also shown more difficulties for LD than for ND students (Bryan, Donahue, & Pearl, 1981; Oliva & LaGreca, 1988). These findings have prompted a recommendation by the Interagency Committee on Learning Disabilities that social skills deficit be considered a separate and primary type of learning disability (Gresham & Elliott, 1989).

TRAINING IN PROBLEM SOLVING

In response to the findings that many children, both learning disabled and normally achieving, exhibit difficulties in a wide variety of social skills, there has been a proliferation of instructional programs designed to improve these skills. Most of these programs have focused on young children between preschool age and fourth or fifth grades; there are relatively few training programs focused on adolescents. Blackbourn (1989), for example, taught specific social skills to elementary-school learning-disabled children (e.g., compliance, nonargumentative responding) by prompting and systematically attending to positive behaviors, and he found an increase in these behaviors as well as generalizations of them to other situations.

The effects of these programs have often been described as resulting from improvement in general problem-solving ability. However, their focus has usually been on behavioral change, and their effectiveness has been assessed in terms of behavioral outcomes. Because most of these studies do not involve multiple measures of behavioral change, their success may often be attributable to training in one specific behavior, for example, reducing aggression, rather than improvement in strategic problem solving (Urbain & Kendall, 1980); and if this is so, the likelihood of broad transfer is lessened. These programs have not typically been implemented on a large scale and accepted as a part of the regular school curriculum.

Over the past decade, there has been an upsurge of interest in problem solving as a general ability (Polson & Jeffries, 1985), which has led to the development of many instructional programs (Nickerson, 1989; Nickerson, Perkins, & Smith, 1985). Most of these have focused on cognitive aspects of problem solving, with assessment of ultimate training effects in terms of a traditional school orientation: performance on pencil and paper or computer-based tests of problem-solving ability. The expectation is that, because cognitive aspects of problem solving underlie any behavioral effects, these will transfer to real-world problem solving. These programs, like those previously described, have not been incorporated into the regular school curriculum.

A significant aspect of these training programs is their emphasis on abstract and formal content, for example, Instrumental Enrichment (Feuerstein, Rand, Hoffman, & Miller, 1980) and CoRT (de Bono, 1985). There is considerable controversy as to whether or not, in fact, this type of training transfers to problems other than those practiced in training. Bransford, Arbitman-Smith, Stein, and Vye (1985) reviewed several such programs. They suggested that these programs do help students to think and solve problems more efficiently, but they conclude that ". . . there is no strong evidence" of improvement in tasks different from the ones used in training (p. 202). Adams (1989), in a review of curricula in thinking skills, also concluded that transfer is limited. She did point out, however, that some programs are more successful at producing transfer than others, and she summarized the features that will maximize transfer: "A course on thinking skills should result in a single, well-integrated schema. The schema must be centered on the principles and processes the course was intended to develop, and it must be richly and diversely elaborated with concrete and real world instances of application" (Adams, 1989, p. 38).

There is another type of instructional program that retains the cognitive framework of those described above but that focuses on teaching specific skills and knowledge. These programs typically take the problem schema approach that Adams described. They teach a generic model of a *problem,* a general strategy for solving problems, and ways to utilize this general schema in solving specific problems.

This approach has led to a wide variety of clinical and educational applications. For example, Janis (1982) used a problem schema approach in individual counseling to help clients make effective life decisions. According to Janis, uncertainty about an important decision can cause stress that leads to poor decision-making; people can be taught to cope with their stress and improve their decisions by learning a general schema for decision-making. This schema involves five steps: (a) appraise the challenge, (b) survey alternatives, (c) weigh alternatives, (d) deliberate about commitment, (e) plan ways to encourage adherence despite initial negative feedback.

D'Zurilla and Goldfried (1971) identified five sets of cognitive operations that play a part in successful social problem-solving: (a) general orientation, (b) problem definition, (c) generation of alternatives, (d) decision making, (e) verification. Subsequent studies (D'Zurilla & Nezu, 1980, 1981) demonstrated that college students who were given training that was focused specifically on one or another of these cognitive operations, or aspects of a problem schema, improved in their problem solving. Spivak and Shure (1974, 1985) have used a similar schema as a basis for training interpersonal problem solving in kindergarteners and elementary school children.

This approach has also been utilized by investigators working in the field of learning disabilities. Larson and Gerber (1987) developed a social metacognitive training program for use with delinquent youth. One important component of this curriculum consisted of a series of lessons that presented a seven-step general problem-solving strategy, to use when attempting to make good decisions about social risk situations that might occur in the course of daily living. After 22 training sessions, both learning-disabled and nondisabled adolescent boys received fewer negative behavior reports and higher ratings on potential for rehabilitation; the learning-disabled delinquents' improvement was greater than that of the other boys.

Vaughn and her colleagues have developed interventions for teaching interpersonal problem solving to elementary and secondary students with learning disabilities (Vaughn, 1987; Vaughn & McIntosh, 1989). In these training programs, the schema for successful problem resolution includes problem formulation, generation of alternatives, solution selection, and solution implementation. Vaughn's training, which involves a problem schema incorporated into a complex set of classroom manipulations, has led to improvement in interpersonal skills shown in role-play situations and to increased acceptance by normally-achieving peers.

An extensive research and demonstration project at the University of Kansas has focused on helping learning-disabled students improve their thinking and problem-solving skills (Ellis, Deshler, & Schumaker, 1989; Schumaker, Deshler, & Ellis, 1986). This instruction includes curriculum packets, which also incorporate the use of a problem schema within the learning strategies that are taught. Results have demonstrated genuine gains in the ability to generate problem-solving strategies for learning-disabled adolescents who received this instruction.

Robin, Kent, O'Leary, Foster, and Prinz (1977) provided an example of the use of a similar problem schema in small-group counseling. Adolescents and their mothers were taught to: (a) define the problem, (b) list alternative solutions, (c) evaluate the solutions, and (d) plan implementations. This treatment led to improved problem solving in structured discussions of both hypothetical and real (to that particular parent–adolescent dyad) problems.

COMPREHENSION

The Use of Literature

Does reading about problems help people learn how to solve their own problems? The use of problem examples and discussion of them that is characteristic of many training programs (e.g., Shure & Spivack, 1978; Vaughn & McIntosh, 1989) suggests that it would. And indeed, over the years, people have attempted to improve social problem-solving by exposing children to literature.

A general assumption about the value of studying literature is that, by providing examples, literature enhances one's ability to cope with one's own experiences and the problems that arise from them. In fact, the field of bibliotherapy, which was very popular a few years ago, was based on this notion. In the late 1930s, Alice Bryan stated the objectives of bibliotherapy this way: (a) show readers that they are not the first to have such problems, (b) permit readers to see that more than one solution to a problem is possible, (c) help readers to see basic motivations of people involved in a particular situation, (d) help readers see the values involved in an experience in human terms, (e) provide facts needed for the solution of a problem, (f) encourage the reader to face his situation realistically (cited in Rubin, 1978, p. 29).

Many studies have investigated the effect of bibliotherapy on social and personal attitudes as well as on behavior. However, results are conflicting and confusing. As Klingman pointed out (1988), one difficulty in investigating the merits of bibliotherapy is that the technique has usually been accompanied by other procedures and has rarely been the primary intervention. Klingman himself used bibliotherapy as the primary intervention in a study involving Israeli kindergarteners. A series of weekly story-telling and discussion sessions proved successful in reducing these children's fear of the dark, as measured by self-report, parent report, and number of coping statements elicited before and after intervention.

This type of intervention can easily be fit into the daily school program—indeed, it is already part of it in the sense that the study of literature is a part of the regular curriculum. The research on problem schema and comprehension suggests that the use of bibliotherapy might well be enhanced by the addition of a schema approach. And the deep interest and involvement that can result from reading quality literature suggests that bibliotherapy has something valuable to contribute to the recent work in social problem-solving.

Schema Theory

Contemporary reading theory emphasizes the role of the structure of the text in guiding comprehension. This orientation mirrors the use of problem schemas in the literature discussed above, and has come to be called schema theory. That is, the reader who has a model or schema of a particular text genre—knows the components of a story, for example—will have expectations about what information can be gained from the story and will thereby show better comprehension. Patterns of recall, comprehension, and production are related to text structure (Kintsch & van Dijk, 1978).

Although there is a large literature on the effects of text structure, relatively little attention has been given to the *problem* as a specific genre. Meyer (1979, 1985) addressed the problem as a type of expository text, and Rumelhart (1977) and Black and Bower (1980) described the narrative mode as having problems embedded within it.

Applications of schema theory to reading instruction focus on ways in which knowledge of text structure can be used to improve comprehension. Essentially, general schemas and how to use them are emphasized. Williams (1986) used an analysis of the structure of expository text to improve learning-disabled students' ability to identify and generate main ideas. Bos and Anders (1987) developed an interactive teaching strategy that focuses on schema to enhance the comprehension of content-area texts in classrooms for learning-disabled students.

Singer and Donlan (1982) demonstrated that a problem schema can be used to teach students to comprehend narratives. These investigators taught 11th-grade students a general schema containing the components of short stories: plan, goal, action, obstacles, and outcomes that represent success or failure. The students were then taught how to derive from this general schema content-specific questions relevant to a particular story. This strategy was effective in improving comprehension. Manning (1984), working with reading-disabled third graders, gave instruction in cognitive monitoring (becoming aware of and regulating one's own thinking) and creative problem solving, which included an emphasis on a problem schema. The oral comprehension of these students was improved significantly as a result of this training. These studies demonstrate that knowledge of a problem schema is useful not only in instruction specifically focused on actual problem-solving but also for understanding texts that present problems.

OUR RESEARCH PROGRAM

This chapter describes some initial studies in a program of research designed to investigate ways in which learning-disabled adolescents deal with personal/social problems—problems that they must cope with in their everyday life and that will continue to be important throughout their lives. The ultimate goal of this work is to develop materials and strategies for use in instruction, so that when these students leave the school environment for the less supportive world outside, they will be better able to cope.

Ironically, the current trend toward increasing the emphasis on thinking and problem solving in the schools may have an unfortunate impact on handicapped students unless efforts are made to provide the special assistance in these areas that these groups need. Higher curriculum standards, competency examinations, and graduation requirements are putting pressure on students to perform. Learning-disabled children, many of whom have been mainstreamed, are encountering the realities and challenges of the regular curriculum. The fact that learning-disabled students' performance in both comprehension and problem-solving lags behind that of non-handicapped students is not surprising given the fact that much reading instruction for learning-disabled students, even at the junior-high and high-school level, focuses heavily on basic skills, sometimes to the virtual exclusion of comprehension instruction (Au, 1979).

We know that instruction focused on comprehension and problem-solving strategies can be highly productive. We also know that it is important to undertake such instruction within the context of the specific domain of interest. Yet one cannot simply decide to introduce new content into the curriculum; there are limits to the school day. There is a way, however, for essential content that is not now part of the standard curriculum to be incorporated into it: Use it as subject matter within formal instruction in reading comprehension. This approach will foster a desirable integration of important instructional goals and is feasible within existing institutional structures. The work reported here represents some beginning steps toward this goal.

Study 1

Our first study examined the ability of good and poor readers, both learning-disabled and nondisabled, to comprehend and solve personal/social problems presented in text. The objectives of this study were:

1. To develop a set of problems appropriate for use in the series of studies.
2. To investigate the effects of two variations in the way problems are presented on readers' comprehension and problem-solving performance.

By definition, the basic structural components of a problem schema remain the same across problems. The simplest formulation consists of (a) a *goal,* and (b) an *obstacle* to attaining the goal. However, the ways in which a problem is presented in a text can vary. There are other components of a problem schema, which may or may not be stated explicitly, for example, *choices* of alternative actions that might be taken. Also, other information besides schema components may be introduced; the text may present details of the setting, for example, or an initiating event.

In this study we addressed the distinction between two variations of presentation of a simple problem as it is presented in text. In each of the short narrative texts used, a character and his/her problem is presented. In the first variation, which we called a *No Priority* problem, the character's *goal* is presented, as well as the *obstacles* that make it difficult to achieve the goal, and two *choices* or alternative courses of action. With no further information provided, the reader cannot determine from the text what the character will do. The second variation, called a *Priority* problem, also presents the goal, obstacles, and choices for action. In addition, there is a statement of the character's *priority,* from which can be inferred which of the two choices of action he/she will make. In some sense, this Priority problem is not a problem (for the reader) at all, in that the priority determines the (probable) solution.

One important requirement for successful comprehension of text-presented problems is the ability to identify the source of information responsible for one's understanding. Working from a taxonomy developed by Pearson and Johnson (1978), Raphael (1984) found that readers who were able to differentiate between text-based information and background knowledge were better able to answer comprehension questions about texts.

The implication of the Raphael work, as of most other studies, is that background knowledge makes a valuable, positive contribution to comprehension. This is a valid implication if that knowledge is in fact relevant and accurate. However, background knowledge may sometimes be inaccurate or incomplete, and in such cases it may interfere with comprehension (Alvermann, Smith, & Readance, 1985; Spiro, 1979). Thus a reader must learn not only how to integrate information from diverse sources effectively, but also how to inhibit some of the background knowledge that is triggered automatically during reading. This involves the metacognitive ability to evaluate and modify one's inferences and conclusions.

Although the concept of background knowledge is considered to be all-inclusive, the relevant research usually deals with factual or descriptive knowledge and not with those aspects of one's knowledge that involve preferences, values, and so forth. The *problem* genre has a relatively strong tendency to involve a reader's values and other similar aspects of knowledge because of the natural thrust of this schema toward arriving at a solution.

Research relevant to the above considerations has, for the most part, been carried out within the context of problem solving, not within the context of reading comprehension. For example, it has been found that one of the characteristics of poor problem solvers is a tendency to confound the premises of the problem as stated with subjective opinions and feelings. In terms of a text comprehension model, this implies that the student brings in background knowledge and context that interfere with the solution of the problem. Such inappropriate strategies have been noted in a variety of studies. For example, Scribner (1977) found in several cross-cultural studies of verbal problem solving that one difference between African villagers who had gone to school and those who had not were that the latter failed to identify and use the explicitly stated premises of problems. It was not that these people were not using logical reasoning; rather, they were reasoning and drawing conclusions based on real-world knowledge and context that they themselves brought to the problem and justifying their judgments by appeals to fact, belief, or opinion rather than by reference to the information stated in the problem.[1]

These issues are relevant in the consideration of our two variations of problem presentation. With respect to the No Priority problem, a reader must learn to inhibit any unspecified solution or outcome and to leave the

---

[1]These ideas have been discussed at length and in a much wider context by Street (1984). On the one hand is the notion of an "autonomous" model of literacy as espoused by Hildyard and Olson (1978), which asserts that "written forms enable the user to differentiate the logical from the interpersonal functions of language in a way that is less possible in oral discourse" (Street, 1984, p. 3). This idea is rooted in Greenfield's (1972) conclusions on the basis of her work in Senegal that unschooled Wolof children "lacked the concept of a personal point of view and the cognitive flexibility to shift perspective in relation to concept-formation problems" (Street, 1984, p. 3). On the other hand is the notion of an "ideological" model of literacy (Street, 1984), which argues that literacy practices are embedded in ideology and social structure and that the autonomous model misleads and covers up rationalizations for political thrusts. These matters are quite beyond the scope of the work presented in this report and, arguably, are irrelevant to it.

matter unresolved. That is, there should be no premature closure on the outcome, or solution, to the problem. With respect to the Priority problem, which does imply a solution, the reader must learn to withhold his/her own values or preferences and to use only the character's priority as stated in determining the (probable) outcome. In either case, the reader must not, automatically and without evaluation, bring in extraneous information, whether factual or preferential.

In this study we compared adolescents who were good and poor readers, both learning-disabled and nondisabled, on their ability to comprehend these variations in problem presentation, in terms of both overall performance level and characteristic strategies.

Several different measures were used: (a) recall, as a means of general comprehension, (b) recall of the basic problem schema components, as an index of identification of main idea comprehension, (c) prediction of the character's probable solution, as a measure of problem-solving ability, and (d) identification of the information source that the reader used to predict the outcome, as an assessment of metacognitive awareness.

Text Problems vs. Real-Life Problems.   There is an important distinction to be made here. The preceding discussion deals with solving a problem on the basis solely of the text. It is outside the bounds of acceptable problem solution to change the terms of the problem in ways that violate the information given. In this way, these problems are similar to the typical school arithmetic problem. In real life, of course, one important aspect of problem-solving ability is the ability to change the terms of the problem in light of information perhaps not considered when the problem was first posed. There may be a way to remove an obstacle, for example, so that the goal can be achieved without being modified at all. Or an option can be formulated that is based on possibilities that the text does not refer to. This issue of how beyond-the-text context is considered is a critical one.

It is this difference, too, that Scribner (1977) pointed out. Adults who had not been to school did not—were unable to or refused to—solve problems solely on the basis of the information provided in the text if that information did not conform to their own perception of reality. It appears to be one of the general lessons of formal schooling that sometimes one must *restrict* context, or the amount of relevant information, in matters of both comprehension and problem solving. The most flexible reader/problem solver—the one who can judge whether, and when, and how to restrict *or* expand context—is usually the most advanced one.

In school, the most advanced problem solver is often the one who suitably restricts context. In "life," the most advanced—productive, successful—person is often one who expands context, by adding/changing options, obstacles, and so forth. In other words, he/she has modified the problem representation. This person, however, has probably also, after generating additional options, done some editing. By selecting among the options he/she has restricted the larger context that was generated. This ability to edit is often just as important to successful solution as the earlier step of expanding context, as research on brainstorming has demonstrated (Glass, Holyoak, & Santa, 1979).

Schooling may help by providing examples, which become prototypes, of "good" problems, those that have been restricted to appropriate dimensions. And decision making and problem solving instruction may help by providing a framework (schema) that not only suggests the appropriate slots to fill (issues to consider) but also what slots/issues are not appropriate to consider.

Subjects were drawn from three schools in New York City: a public junior high school, a private secondary school for learning-disabled students, and a private secondary school with a high academic ranking. The socioeconomic level of the students in both of the private schools was upper middle-class, and most of the students were Caucasian. In contrast, the population of the public school was equally split between Blacks and Hispanics, with a total of 5% Caucasian students. Sixty percent of the students qualified for free lunch or partial free lunch.

Twelve public school students, 9 males and 3 females, classified as learning-disabled by school placement, were drawn randomly from their ungraded classrooms. The other three groups were selected to match this group in gender distribution and age. There were no significant differences in the mean age among the four groups. The groups did, however, differ substantially in reading ability. See Table 11.1.

Based on interviews with 12 learning-disabilities specialists (teachers and clinicians), a variety of issues were identified as being of special importance to learning-disabled adolescents. These issues fell into several categories:

1. Issues that had to do with school, such as how to allocate sufficient time for studying, whether to get a high-school diploma.
2. Work-related issues, such as asking for a promotion, choosing a career.
3. Money issues, for example, planning a budget, keeping records of expenses, and how to shop knowledgeably.
4. Relationships with others: (a) authority figures—parents, teachers, bosses, and (b) peers—meeting people, making friends, dating, and working with people.
5. Other issues, such as how to spend leisure time, manage alcohol, stay away from drugs.

On the basis of these issues, short narratives were written and were read and critiqued by two LD specialists. A few texts were eliminated because they

TABLE 11.1
Characteristics of the Students

	Mean Age in Years (and SD)	Mean Grade-Equivalent Reading Score (and SD)	
Group		Vocabulary	Comprehension
1 LD-Public	14.7 (.8)	4.3 (1.6)[a]	4.4 (1.3)[a]
2 ND-Public	14.5 (.9)	6.3 (2.3)[b]	6.4 (1.9)[b]
3 LD-Private	14.8 (1.1)	8.2 (2.1)	7.3 (1.5)
4 ND-Private	14.3 (.6)	12.6[c]	12.6[c]

[a]Based on 8 scores
[b]Based on 9 scores
[c]In Group 4, 8 subjects scored at or beyond the ceiling score on Vocabulary, and 10 did so on Comprehension.

were judged too complex or not sufficiently interesting. Nine of the 34 remaining problems, selected because they represented a range of issues, were used in this study.

Following are examples of the problems:

1. Ann works at Macy's. She gets a discount on the clothes she buys there. She wants to buy a sweater, but she can't find one at Macy's that's the right color. She did see one at Gimbel's that's the right color. If she buys the sweater at Gimbel's, though, she won't get a discount and it will cost more than the sweater she could buy at Macy's. *Priority ending:* She cares more about getting the sweater in the right color than she does about how much it costs. *No Priority ending:* She isn't sure what to do.

2. Daniel is 16 years old and his mother has asked him to start thinking about his future. She'd like him to look for work this summer in an area that he's interested in, so that he can decide if he'd like to do that kind of work after he graduates from high school. He thinks that he'd like to be a car mechanic so he asked his sister's friend to teach him how to repair cars. He agreed to teach Daniel, but he can't afford to pay him a salary. Learning how to repair cars would prepare Daniel for a good job in the future, though. He has also been offered a job working at McDonald's and he'll earn money if he does that. He cares less about earning money this summer than he does about earning a good salary in the future.

3. Josh is 19 years old. He is putting himself through a 2-year program at a community college by earning money as a night watchman at a local factory. He is often able to study while he works. He wants to continue his education after he graduates and, in order to do so, he needs to save more money than he can with his current salary. He knows that there are going to be some construction jobs available in his neighborhood soon because a new building has been planned. Working on a construction job will be far

TABLE 11.2
Measures of Problem Representation

	Group[a]			
	1 LD-Pub	2 ND-Pub	3 LD-Priv	4 ND-Priv
Mean Proportion of Idea Units Recalled Correctly	.26	.36	.38	.59
Mean Proportion of Problem-Schema Components Reported Accurately	.27	.40	.31	.61
Errors per Idea Unit Recalled	.07	.03	.03	.03
Major Errors per Error	.53	.60	.47	.34

[a]Reading ability increases from Group 1 to Group 4.

more tiring than working as a night watchman and will leave him with little time for studying. He isn't certain what he wants to do.

Each subject read problems of only one type, either No Priority or Priority. All students read the "Ann" problem first; this was followed by two additional problems, assigned in all possible pair combinations such that across experimental conditions each particular problem occurred the same number of times.

Subjects were asked to read three problems, one at a time. After reading each problem, they were asked to retell it. Then they read the problem a second time and retold it again. Following the two retellings, subjects were asked a series of questions that focused on how they thought the character would solve the problem and on clarifying the source of their information. The retellings were scored using an idea unit analysis, developed on the basis of Johnson's (1970) pausal unit procedure, to determine how much of the text had been recalled.

Comprehension. To evaluate comprehension (how well the problem was represented), several different measures were used. These are presented in Table 11.2. The first measure was the proportion of idea units (Johnson, 1970) that were recalled correctly in the retellings.[2] As expected, performance on this measure improved as reading level increased, $F(3,40) = 28.56$, $p < .001$. However, even though the four group means were ordered appropriately, there was no significant difference between Groups ND-Pub and LD-Priv, $F(1,40) = .25$. There were no differences in recall or on any other comprehension measure between the No Priority and the Priority problems.

As an index of main idea comprehension, the data were analyzed to de-

---

[2]A complete description of the data analyses can be found in Williams (1988).

TABLE 11.3
Number of Each Type of Error as a Function of Group

	Group			
	1 LD-Pub	2 ND-Pub	3 LD-Priv	4 ND-Priv
Major Errors	16	9	8	11
Minor Errors	14	6	9	21

termine how well the students reported the components of the problem schema. Each subject was given a score on overall effectiveness in recalling the problem schema. One point was given for each component reported correctly: goal, obstacles, choices, and (depending on problem type) priority or a statement of uncertainty. Thus the score for each individual problem ranged from 0 to 4. We used a very stringent criterion in this scoring. On this measure, scores were ordered as would be expected: They increased as a function of reading level, $F(3,40) = 23.14$, $p < .001$, $ms_e = .75$. Although there was a reversal in the order of Groups LD-Pub and ND-Priv, the difference between the two groups was not large enough to be statistically significant.

We also looked at errors. An error was defined as an instance in which an idea unit was recalled inaccurately, or where the retelling contradicted the text. Errors were further categorized into two types: (a) major errors, which indicated substantial modifications of important idea units, and (b) minor errors, which included substitutions of proper names or paraphrases of detail information that were incorrect. An example of a major error was,

"Her classmate wasn't doing her work and was just a sit-there lazy." This was from the Katy problem; the correct version was that her classmate accused Katy of being lazy.

An example of a minor error was,

"And he asks his girlfriend's friend." This was from the Daniel problem; the correct version was that he asked his sister's friend.

Because the opportunity to make an error was a function of the total number of idea units recalled, the proportion of the total number of idea units recalled that were judged to be errors was used as the measure of overall error rate for each subject. See Table 11.3. The proportion, small for all groups, was significantly greater in Group LD-Pub, the lowest reading level, than in the other three groups, $F(1,40) = 9.37$, $p < .01$, which did not differ. With respect to the major versus minor classification, there was a tendency for the proportion of the total number of errors that was categorized

TABLE 11.4
Number of Problems Containing Importations

	Group			
	1 LD-Pub	2 ND-Pub	3 LD-Priv	4 ND-Priv
Plausible Importations	22	15	19	0
Implausible Importations	9	1	9	0

as major to be smaller for Group 4 (11/32) than for the other three groups (33/62), χ^2 (1) = 3.01, $p < .10$.

Next, we looked at the number of problems on which the subjects, during the retellings and interview, reported extraneous information that was not part of the text. Because of the distribution of scores and their lack of variation, a nonparametric test was performed. The proportion of problems containing such importations was greater for the two LD groups than for the two ND groups (59 vs. 16), $\chi^2_1 = 24.65$, $p < .001$ (see Table 11.4). The proportion of problems containing importations was also greater as a function of reading level, $\chi^2_3 = 31.72$, $p < .001$.

The importations were further categorized in terms of plausibility. Importations were considered plausible when they were judged to be reasonable elaborations of the problem text as stated; they were considered implausible when they would not have reasonably been able to be incorporated into the problem text as it was stated. An example of a plausible importation was, "Ann has to go to a party." In the text, no reason is given for why Ann wants to buy a new sweater.

The following transcription from one of the interviews provides an example of an implausible importation. In the text that the subject has just read (see page 248), Daniel is considering whether to spend his summer learning how to repair cars.

"What is Daniel's problem?"
"He wants a car . . . he just wants a car."

"And do you know what he'll do?"
"Anything."

"Anything? How do you know that?"
"Because it told me in the story, that he would do anything to get this car."

Table 11.4 presents, for each group, the number of problems on which there were plausible and implausible importations. Because of the low frequency of implausible errors, χ^2 was used, and groups were collapsed. The proportion of problems with implausible importations was greater for LD students than for ND students (18 vs. 1), χ^2 (1) = 15.21, $p < .005$. However, when the data were examined with respect to differences in reading level, there was no significant difference in the proportion of implausible importations (10 in Groups 1 and 2 vs. 9 in Groups 3 and 4).

The way that a problem is solved depends to a large extent on how it has been represented. What do the data tell us about these readers' representations? Idea units correctly recalled indicate how much of the problem has been represented, and problem schema components indicate the extent to which the main idea of the text has been represented. Errors and importations provide an indication of how the problem representation is different from the way in which the problem was presented in the text.

Of course, recall data do not reflect everything about the text that is in a reader's representation; they also reflect the selection/production constraints under which the reader is acting. Without careful probing—and perhaps even *with* careful probing—it would be impossible to determine precisely the nature of an individual's representation. However, the output of a recall can give a picture of differences in representations of different groups of subjects. From this perspective it appears that the poor readers, and the learning-disabled readers, had less accurate representations.

However, the relationship between reading level as measured by a standardized reading test and accuracy of representation was not a simple one. The expectation would be that Group LD-Priv would outperform Group ND-Pub, because of the difference in reading level on the standardized reading test in favor of Group ND-Priv. However, there was no difference between the groups on either proportion of idea units recalled or number of problem schema components recalled. In fact, Group ND-Pub's score was higher in the latter case than Group LD-Priv's score, although the difference between the two was not significant. These data suggest that the learning-disabled students were not using their reading ability on the experimental tasks as effectively as were the nondisabled students, and, moreover, that they did relatively more poorly as the task became more challenging and required higher-level thinking.

The importation measure speaks to the issue of problem boundaries. Our hypothesis was that learning-disabled subjects would not be as competent as nondisabled subjects in their ability to stick to the boundaries of the problem as presented in the text. The prediction was confirmed: The LD students imported information from sources other than the text into their representations of the problems more frequently than did the ND subjects, as described previously.

The way in which importations of extraneous information might change the problem representation is reflected in instances of LD subjects' use of extraneous information in elaborating their predictions. For example, one student, making the wrong prediction as to what Ann would do, said: "She'll buy the sweater at Macy's. Because she works there and she doesn't

TABLE 11.5
Number of Problems Answered Correctly

	Group			
	1 LD-Pub	2 ND-Pub	3 LD-Priv	4 ND-Priv
Question: Problem-solving				
Priority Paragraphs (max = 18)	10	16	12	17
Metacognitive Awareness				
Priority Paragraphs (max = 18)	11	10	11	17
No Priority Paragraphs (max = 18)	12	13	15	14

want to make . . . you know, like, supposedly work here and you're against another company. And you go and you buy something over there. So it makes where you work feel bad."

Group ND-Priv, the proficient readers, made a rather large number of errors overall. However, the fact that the proportion of major errors tended to be smaller in this group than in the other groups and also the fact that there were no importations in this group suggest that these proficient readers were in fact demonstrating more adherence to the problem boundaries than were the other groups, as would be expected. These minor errors suggest that the student had identified an idea unit—a category of information—that existed in the text and had coded it as a relevant category of information; and then, in recall, had constructed a specific idea unit that filled the slot appropriately if not correctly. For example, the student might remember that Ann could not decide between two sweaters but say that it was a matter of size instead of color. From this perspective, an importation could indicate a greater lack of comprehension than a minor error.

Problem Solving. Subjects were asked a two-part question: "Do you know what (Ann) will do?" and, next, "What will (Ann) do?" The answers were scored as a unit. In the Priority mode, an answer to this question that reflected the stated priority of the character was considered correct. Table 11.5 presents the number of correct responses to this question for each type of student. Twenty-two of the 36 problems administered to the LDs were answered correctly; this outcome was not different from what would have been expected by chance, $\chi^2 (1) = 1.78$. Thirty-three of the 36 problems administered to the NDs were answered correctly; this outcome was different from what would have been expected by chance, $\chi^2 (1) = 25.00$, $p < .001$. (There were no differences between the two LD groups or between the two ND groups.) Thus the LDs more often failed to recognize that there were clearly stated priorities or that those priorities could be used as the basis for an inference about what the character would do.

This question was asked in the No Priority mode as well, but the responses were not analyzed because the appropriate answer, "I don't know," is essentially uninterpretable. That is, such an answer might indicate either that the text did not indicate what the character would do (a response that a good reader would give, presumably) or that the subject did not know whether or not the text had indicated what the character would do (a poor reader's response, presumably).

It is important to note that performance on this problem-solving question was related to LD/ND status and not to reading level. This is exactly the pattern seen in the results of the implausible importation analysis. These data suggest that the degree to which the LD students brought in extraneous information, and appeared not to evaluate and edit for plausibility, was indeed a factor, as predicted, in their lack of ability to use the priority information effectively in making the appropriate prediction.

Metacognitive Awareness.   The next two-part question was, "How do you know what (Ann) will do?" and "Do you know that from what you read, or is that something you figured out yourself?" Again, these were considered together. For a subject in the Priority mode, a correct answer here was, "It says so in the text." For the No Priority mode, subjects were correct if they said, "I don't know" or "I figured it out" (or any variant of this, such as "I'm guessing"). Table 11.5 also presents the number of correct responses to this question as a function of group and type of problem. In the Priority condition, Group ND-Priv's performance was significantly different from that of the other three groups taken together, χ^2 (2) = 7.69, $p < .01$. In Group ND-Priv, the proportion of Priority problems for which this question was answered correctly was .94, significantly better than chance, χ^2 (1) = 14..22, $p < .001$, whereas the proportion answered correctly by the other three groups was .59, not significantly different from chance, χ^2 (1) = 1.85.

In the No Priority condition, the proportion of problems in which this question was answered correctly was .75, significantly different from what would be expected by chance, χ^2 (1) = 9.39, $p < .002$. There was no difference among Groups, χ^2 (1) = 1.48.

Only Group ND-Priv, the proficient readers, showed awareness of the source of the information on the basis of which their predictions were made. These results corroborate those of other investigators, who have noted that metacognitive abilities tend to develop late and are related to ability as well as age (Baker & Brown, 1984). Learning-disabled students typically perform poorly on tasks requiring metacognitive abilities (Ryan, Weed, & Short, 1986). In this study, however, the LD-Priv students, though depressed on other measures compared to the lower reading-ability ND-Pub students, were not poorer in terms of metacognition. This may simply

TABLE 11.6
Results of Multiple Regression Analyses

	Overall R^2	df	F
Retelling			
Reading Level	.663	1,46	90.48***
LD Status	.672	1,45	1.16
Problem-Schema Components			
Reading Level	.479	1,46	42.23***
LD Status	.556	1,45	7.80**
Errors			
Reading Level	.065	1,46	3.18
LD Status	.082	1,45	<1
Interaction	.187	1,44	5.67*
Importations			
Reading Level	.491	1,46	44.43***
LD Status	.642	1,45	18.86***
Prediction			
LD Status	.241	1,22	6.97*
Reading Level	.254	1,21	<1
Metacognition			
Reading Level	.073	1,46	3.62
LD Status	.076	1,45	<1

Note. Variables are listed in the order in which they were entered into the regression equation. Fs refer to the change in R^2 from one variable to the next.
   *$p < .05$
  **$p < .01$
 ***$p < .001$

be because our question lacked the sensitivity required to pick up meta-cognitive differences that possibly did exist.

Our interpretation is based on the findings of only one question. Given this caveat, it appears that these findings provide little evidence of strong metacognitive skill except in the group with the highest reading scores. A substantial proportion of the rest of the students could not identify the source of the information that they provided in their answer; they could not locate the information as either having been or not having been in the text that they had read. Such awareness is fundamental to critical reading in general and to any critical formulation of information in a problem schema in order to solve it within its appropriate context.

Further Analysis.   Multiple regression analysis was performed on each of the dependent measures with reading level and LD/ND status as independent variables. Group mean reading score (vocabulary and comprehension averaged) was used as the measure of reading level. In each case, reading level was entered into the regression equation first. See Table 11.6.

With respect to retelling scores, the linear regression on reading level scores accounted for a significant proportion of the explained variance; the addition of LD status did not contribute significantly to the explained variance independent of the contribution of reading level. With respect to the number of problem schema components reported (main idea comprehension), reading level was a significant variable, and so was LD status, which accounted for an additional 8% of the variance. The same pattern held for importations, with LD status contributing an additional 15% of the variance in importation scores. (If LD status were entered into the regression equation first, it would have accounted for 51% of the variance in importation scores, F (1, 46) = 48.07, $p < .001$).

Together, reading level and LD status did not account for a significant proportion of the variance in the error scores, although when the interaction between these two variables was added to the regression equation, there was a significant contribution to the explained variance in the error scores (19%). (This was the only case in which the addition of the interaction to the regression equation increased the amount of explained variance significantly.)

The prediction measure was the only one on which entering reading level first did not account for a significant proportion of the variance ($\chi^2 = .139$, F (1,22) = .07); however, when LD status was entered first, that variable did account for a significant proportion of the variance. The findings on the metacognitive measure were similar to those on the retelling measure: Reading level accounted for a significant proportion of the explained variance, and the addition of LD status to the regression equation did not increase it significantly.

Conclusion.   Reading level is clearly a powerful predictor of performance on these text-based tasks. Learning disability is also important: These data indicate that learning-disabled students do not use their abilities as effectively as do nondisabled students. They perform relatively more poorly on tasks that require higher-level thinking such as getting the gist of the problem and making the inferences necessary to predict outcomes. It is likely that this is at least partly because they construct less accurate representations of the text in the first place.

Study 2

In another study, which is reported in its entirety elsewhere (Williams, 1988), 24 learning-disabled male students from the same public school as was used in the first study, approximately the same age, were given three similar problems. The experimental procedure was the same as in the previous study, except that each text was read aloud by the experimenter as the student read his own copy silently.

Half the subjects were given versions of the texts that would have been appropriate had these particular texts been used in Experiment 1 (called the

Bare bones version). The other half received a version that contained three additional sentences, all of which gave reasons that would argue for the priority that in the last sentence was imputed to the character. This was called the Constrained version. The same two endings, Priority and No Priority, followed the additional three sentences in this version.

One of the three problems (Steve) follows:

Bare bones version:

Steve is 15 years old. He is good at sports but reads slowly. He has a hard time doing his homework in every subject but math. Steve has a younger brother named Jerry. Jerry is just 12 years old, but he is already a better reader than Steve. When Steve is having trouble with his homework and thinks about asking Jerry for help, he gets embarrassed. When Jerry asks for help in sports, however, Steve always shows Jerry what to do. Steve has a very important science test coming up soon, and he really needs help to understand what is in the science book.

Sentences added in the Constrained version:

A lot of the questions on the test will be about atoms and molecules. This is something Jerry knows a lot about. Besides, Steve realizes that his brother has never made him feel bad about being a bad reader. The test is coming up soon, and there is just no one else Steve can get help from.

No Priority ending:

Steve can't decide if he should ask Jerry for help or not.

Priority ending:

Steve would rather ask his brother for help than do badly on the test.

The added information did not help the problem-solving performance of these learning-disabled students: Across all subjects in the Priority condition, though their retellings had suggested that they had understood the problems, subjects performed at a chance level in terms of predicting what the character would do (19 out of 36 correct). In the Bare bones version of the Priority condition, 11 problems (out of 18; all 3 problems are included here) were answered in terms of the stated priority, and in the Constrained version, 8.

However, the presence of the additional three sentences did affect the subjects' metacognition. Contrary to what would be expected, students were *more* certain that they had figured the solution out for themselves (as opposed to reading it in the text) when there was added information in the text than when there wasn't. That is, subjects who were asked "How did you know that?" in the Priority condition gave the answer "I read it in the text" to 8 problems (out of 18) and "I figured it out" to 9 problems (the response to one problem was unclassifiable) in the Bare bones version. In the Constrained version, in contrast, only 3 problems were answered "I read it," and 15, "I figured it out." This difference, $\chi^2(1) = 3.75$, $p = .052$, suggests that these students judged (wrongly) that they had figured out the answer for themselves when there was extra, corroborating information that would support such a conclusion (though that conclusion has not really been drawn in the text) than when there was no such extra information. Perhaps the additional positive arguments for the solution made the students feel more sure of, and more comfortable about, the answer, and this feeling made them believe that the answer was "their own."

These findings suggest that, as in Study 1, LDs were not able to identify the source of the information that they provided in their answers. However, they did show some sensitivity to differences in the amount of information presented in the text, in that they were swayed by the presence of the additional information provided in the constrained problems.

A comparison of the other two problems permits a specific focus on how prior knowledge and beliefs influenced performance. In the problem about Joe, the character's priority was to accept a promotion at work that involved weekend hours rather than keep his dating routine. This would be perceived as a socially acceptable decision by these students (within the school setting, at least). In the problem about Gail, the character's priority, to concentrate her time on softball instead of her studies, would be perceived as not socially acceptable. Thus, in the Joe problem, there is no conflict between the priority actually stated in the problem and the priority that is likely to be generated by outside influences; but there is such a conflict in the Gail problem.

In the Priority mode, there was a difference between the two problems in the number of times that subjects chose the stated priority: on 9 of 10 (there were 2 unclassifiable responses) occasions, the correct (and socially acceptable) response to the Joe problem was given; and on only 4 of 9 occasions (3 unclassifiable responses), the correct (and not socially acceptable) response to the Gail problems was given. These subjects thus showed a significant shift in their predictions toward the incorrect response when the text posed a conflict between a response based on the stated priority of the character and a response deemed more socially acceptable (Fisher's exact $p = .05$, one-sided). Thus, they were very likely to bring in outside views— in this case, their judgment of social acceptability—to color (and to diminish the accuracy of) their interpretation of the text.

In this study we also looked at another measure, the ability to generalize.

In order to determine whether the students could generalize the problem schema, we asked them three questions about each story: "Have you ever been in a similar situation?", "Do you know of anyone who has ever been in a similar situation?", and "Can you think of a situation that would be similar? It does not have to have actually happened in real life."

If the answer to any of these questions was "yes," we asked the student to tell us about it. The maximum number of generalizations that could have been contributed was 216; 73 were offered. There were significantly more generalizations in response to the third question than to the other two. It may be that the students needed to warm up before being able to respond effectively, but there are other possible explanations. It may be easier, or less self-revealing, to make up a story than remember and tell one about yourself or a friend. There also may be a tendency to see one's own experiences as unique and thus not related to the target story.

Each generalization was evaluated in terms of completeness. We looked at whether or not it contained all the problem schema components represented in the target problem: the conflict, two choices, and an obstacle that rendered the choices mutually exclusive. If a generalization lacked a choice or an obstacle, it was categorized as fragmentary.

Twenty-eight of the 73 generalizations (13% of the total number of opportunities to generalize) were complete. One such example, taken from a subject who had been presented with the No Priority/Bare bones version of the Gail problem, was:

"Well, my friend won tickets to a concert and it was going to be on a school night and I had a test the next day and the concert was late and I wanted to go to the concert. I didn't know what to do. I ended up going."

Among the fragmentary generalizations, a few ($N = 7$) were almost complete. They lacked an explicit statement of an obstacle, but it appeared that an obstacle was implicit. One such generalization was about a boy who went to baseball practice. He was supposed to study afterwards but was too tired, and so he fell asleep. Here, the obstacle of fatigue is implicit. Other fragmentary generalizations ($N = 14$) definitely lacked an obstacle. For example, one student told a story about a girl who wanted to draw but needed help. The student ended by saying that the girl simply asked for the help; there was nothing in the story that made it difficult for her to ask.

The largest number of fragmentary generalizations ($N = 25$) were the least acceptable. In these generalizations, the student focused on a single aspect of the target problem and described it at length. For example, asked to make up a similar story after hearing the Steve problem (see page 257), subjects often described their own learning disability and failed to mention any other aspect of the original problem. One subject, who had heard the Priority/Bare bones version, said:

"Maybe when somebody's reading the newspaper from another country that knows English but does not know how to understand, doesn't know the words too much, he could have trouble reading the newspaper."

Conclusion. These data indicate that learning-disabled students are not able to identify the source of the information that they rely on when solving text-based problems. Their interpretations are strongly influenced by their prior knowledge and beliefs. This finding lends further support to the notion that learning-disabled students do not attend closely to the boundaries of such texts. In addition, these students demonstrate limited ability to generalize on the basis of a problem schema.

INSTRUCTION

Drawing on the variety of traditions that were discussed earlier in this chapter, Nancy Ellsworth and I designed an instructional program specifically organized around teaching learning-disabled adolescents to (a) identify a general problem-solving schema, and (b) to apply the schema to problems presented in short narratives to reach appropriate decisions (Williams & Ellsworth, 1990). The two studies reported in this chapter were the basis for many of the design characteristics of the program, including some of our decisions to put off incorporating certain features into our instruction. For example, although our ultimate goal is to use this instruction to further fundamental academic goals in reading comprehension and written expression, as well as to develop competence in problem-solving and critical thinking, we realized that we should focus on one thing at a time. We therefore put the reading/writing goals aside for our first study, and we concentrated on training decision-making.

We also simplified our initial instructional goals by laying aside—temporarily—certain of the more interesting of our findings. For example, our studies suggest that one of the distinctive difficulties exhibited by learning-disabled students lies in respecting the problem boundaries, which leads to poor problem representation and thence to poor problem solving. Our instructional focus must certainly address this issue. However, for the present initial foray into intervention, we did not address it. We focused primarily on the development of a schema and its application to problem narratives.

The content of the instruction—the problems and the schema—were based in large measure on the work reported in this chapter, modified as appropriate in response to two important considerations. First, we were planning instruction, and secondly, the population we were working with was somewhat older (high-school students).

The problems were somewhat longer than those used in our earlier studies. In general, the same issues were presented—getting along with family and friends, finding and holding a job, and so forth. Many of the problems that were used later in the instruction were suggested by the students themselves, as will be described below. All the problems were presented in the No Priority mode, and they were not as rigorously structured as those used in the research studies.

Here is one of the problems used in the study:

> Edward is a good athlete. He's on a winning football team, and he is sometimes the only lineman who can stop the other team. He gets along with all the other athletes, and he was voted most valuable player last year. He loves basketball also.
>
> Edward is not good with numbers, and he has a hard time remembering the plays. He often has to ask another player what the quarterback's call means. The other players don't seem to mind; in fact, they kind of make a joke of it. His coach gets really upset and yells at him, which makes Edward mad. The coach has threatened to kick him off the team if he doesn't learn all the plays within two weeks. Edward is so embarrassed that he feels like quitting the team.
>
> Edward isn't sure what to do.

The schema that we adopted for instruction was also somewhat different. It was more extensive; it involved generating, evaluating, and implementing alternative solutions. It consisted of a sequence of questions that would be applicable to problems in general—certainly to all the problems used in our instruction. Janis's work (1982) in individual therapy was an important source for the design of the schema.

The general schema included eight questions:[3]

1. What is the main problem?
2. What alternative solutions are there?
3. What additional information is needed to order to make the best decision? How could it be obtained?
4. What are the advantages and disadvantages of each alternative?
5. What is the best decision? Why? Is it appropriate?
6. What would be a good back-up decision?
7. What could the person do in implementing this decision to improve his chances of success?

---

[3]It should be noted that students derived these questions inductively during the early instructional sessions. The actual wording of the schema as it was generated by each instructed group was somewhat different, although the main point of each question in the schema was the same. For instance, for Question 2, one group's wording was "What are all the possible decisions?" rather than "What alternative solutions are there?"

8. What could he do to improve his chances of adhering to this decision despite some initial negative feedback? What problems might he encounter?

The instructional model used was based on both an inductive teaching approach and Vygotsky (1962). The instructor led the students, through discussion, to generate the problem schema. Each problem was presented for discussion as well, during which students generated alternative solutions and critiqued them. Along with this emphasis on inductive teaching went considerable support and guidance. For example, after the students had generated the components of the schema, the instructor explained how the problem schema was of value in helping to develop effective problem-solving strategies. (This was reiterated frequently.) The instructor also modeled the critical thinking processes that she herself used in making decisions concerning the specific problem narratives.

As the instructional sessions proceeded, the teacher's support became gradually less needed, and so she gradually withdrew it, leaving the students to rely on their own critical thinking processes and to gain confidence by doing so. This approach has been described as "modeling plus explanation and instruction marked by a gradual press for student independence in the context of supportive coaching" (Corno, 1987, p. 256) and is similar to that used in a wide variety of applications, such as the work on mediated learning by Feuerstein, Rand, Hoffman, and Miller (1980) and the reciprocal teaching model of Palincsar and Brown (1984).

The instructional activities for each session included:

1. Motivation. During the first session, the instructor gave examples of people who faced an important decision. The examples were supported by newspaper clippings. During the second session, the instructor told the students about a recent crisis that she herself had had with her teenage daughter, and she asked their suggestions for ways in which she could have better solved the problem. Thereafter, many of the students volunteered their own or their friends' problems on which a decision was needed, which provided excellent motivation.

2. Prereading Preparation. The instructor reviewed the general purpose of the program, and introduced the day's lesson.

3. Reading the Narrative. The instructor read the day's narrative aloud as students read silently from their own copies of the text.

4. Inductive Generation of the Schema. The instructor asked, "What questions should you ask yourself when you need to make a tough decision?" She recorded an abbreviated version of the students' schema on the chalkboard as they contributed. This procedure was followed during each session.

5. Application of the Schema. The instructor guided the group through

the application of the schema to the problem presented in the story. She began by saying, "What's the real problem here?" (Question 1 of the schema). Again, the chalkboard was used. The discussion continued until a decision had been reached and implementation and contingency planning had been accomplished. (The instructor's own contribution in terms of modeling, explanation, and support decreased gradually over the course of the instructional sessions.)

6. Conclusion. Each instructional session closed with an activity that recognized the progress made that day in learning to reach better decisions on personal problems. For example, the instructor might ask the students what they had accomplished during the session. Following their responses, she would suggest that they try to apply this decision-making strategy in their own lives.

Evaluation of the Program

The students who participated in the study were 70 learning-disabled students in two large (over 2,000 pupils each) New York City public high schools. The total enrollment of these schools included 19% Hispanic, 79% black, and 2% students of other ethnic origins; 61% received free or partial free lunch. The dropout rate was 52%.

All participants in the study had received individual psychological and educational evaluations and had been classified as learning disabled by the New York City Board of Education. They were provided one period of resource room instruction daily in a class with a maximum of five students, and they were mainstreamed for the remainder of their classes. All four grades from 9 to 12 were represented in the sample. The mean age of the 70 subjects was 16.5 years ($SD = .9$), and the mean grade-equivalent reading level, based on the Wide Range Achievement Test (WRAT), was 7.6 ($SD = 1.1$).

Some of these adolescents had children of their own, and some had criminal records or histories of drug and alcohol abuse. The amount of family supervision ranged from none, in the case of a boy who lived alone in the room that his father had abandoned several months before, to a great deal, in the case of an 18-year-old Puerto Rican immigrant girl whose mother accompanied her to and from school each day.

The 70 participants were selected in the following manner. Ninety-two students were given a pretest consisting of an audiotaped individual interview. In this interview, students were asked to recall two problem narratives, to describe the steps to be taken in solving a problem (to identify a general problem-solving schema), and to answer the eight questions in the problem schema with respect to each of the two problem narratives (to apply the general schema). The interviews ranged from 15–35 minutes in length.

We selected for instruction 10 intact special education LD resource room classes; all together, these groups included 35 students. The size of the classes ranged from two to four students. Ten comparison groups (total $N = 35$) were constructed from the remaining 57 students who had received a pretest. That is, a pseudo-group was formed to match each instructed group on number of subjects, grade level, number of group members with Spanish surnames, and reading level on the Wide Range Achievement Test (WRAT).

At the end of instruction, a posttest was administered to all 70 students. The posttest was the same as the pretest except that different stories (written in a similar format) were used.

There were seven 40-minute instructional sessions, given on a twice-a-week basis. The program was conducted as part of the regular resource room activities and took place in students' own classrooms. The comparison students received the usual program taught by their resource room teachers. The language arts program at the secondary level in these schools deals not only with basic reading and writing but also with comprehension and critical thinking through the study of literature and through general discussion. Our program was in keeping with this tradition; however, it provided a strong focus on one particular topic and a specific methodology, the schema approach.

One important criterion in developing the narratives for instructional use was that they be easily understood; we did not want the decision-making training to be affected by a lack of comprehension. We checked the comprehension of the two pretest narratives by evaluating recall. The two stories contained a total of 12 idea units identified as essential to comprehension. Recall of the narratives was excellent in terms of these important idea units: Both the instructed and comparison subjects recalled over 97% of them. On the two posttest narratives, the results were similar.

Five measures were used to evaluate students' ability to identify and apply the problem schema, scored on the basis of questions about each narrative. Separate analyses of covariance were conducted on the posttest scores on each of the measures, using pretest score as the covariate. On all five measures, there was a significant difference in favor of the instructed groups at the .01 level or better.

Table 11.7 presents the main findings. The first measure, Identifying the Schema, was a count of the number of parts of the problem schema that the subject could report (0–8). The other four measures focused on schema application. The score for Solution Generation was the number of acceptable solutions that each subject generated. For Fact Finding, the score was the number of additional pieces of information that the subject identified as being needed in order to reach the best decision. Implementation Planning was a measure of whether or not a subject devised a satisfactory plan to increase the probability of successfully implementing his/her decision, and Contingency Planning was a measure of whether or not a subject

TABLE 11.7
Instructional Study: Means and Standard Deviations
on all Posttest Measures

	Instructed Groups		Comparison Groups	
	Mean	SD	Mean	SD
Schema Identification[a]				
Mean No. of Components Reported	6.25	1.44	.35	.39
Solution Generation[a]				
Mean No. of Solutions Generated	5.15	.80	2.95	.39
Fact Finding[a]				
Mean No. of Additional Facts Identified	2.77	.70	.77	.32
Implementation Planning				
Proportion of Students with Satisfactory Plan	.73	.32	.36	.20
Contingency Planning				
Proportion of Students with Satisfactory Plan	.63	.27	.31	.15

[a]Adjusted scores.

stated a plan that could improve the likelihood of adhering to a given decision. In both cases, each subject's response was judged either acceptable or not acceptable, and the score for each group was the proportion of students in that group who succeeded.

Questions 4, 5, and 6 of the schema were not scored. The diversity of the students who participated in the study was great, and it was not reasonable to evaluate the personal appropriateness of the decisions that they offered.

In summary, our instructional program was effective in improving students' ability to identify a problem schema and to apply it to novel problem narratives similar to those used in training. These findings support the view that application of a general schema to problems presented in narratives can be an effective instructional method to improve decision making and critical thinking. Teenage students' needs in this domain are widely acknowledged, and those of learning-disabled adolescents are even greater; we suggest that the education of these students will be enhanced by the addition of instruction in critical thinking based on the use of a schema. Of course, this is just an initial step in developing such instruction. Transfer of the training to solving problems and making decisions in one's own life has not yet been demonstrated, and further research is needed to explore potentially effective ways of developing the transfer capability of this type of cognitive instruction.

Conclusion

We initially conceived of this program as an addition to remedial instruction in reading comprehension and writing skills. This goal is more modest than the goal of helping adolescents actually to improve their real-life decision-making skills and demonstrating that they have been so helped. It certainly appears form the students' enthusiasm generated in the present study that the discussion of urgent personal problems provides compelling motivation for attentive participation. Remedial instruction is often seen as boring, and to capture students' interest with a set of compelling materials is not always easy.

Instructionally, writing is a logical extension of the critical thinking process (Bereiter & Scardamalia, 1985). Writing narratives that describe problems can be introduced as a group writing experience and can progress to individual writing. Students can also record alternative solutions and additional facts needed before coming together for discussion, and they can compose their own decisions and the rationale underlying them. Providing sufficient stimulation is often the heart of getting students such as these to write, and the immediacy of the issues under consideration is likely to be successful in providing that incentive. Ellsworth and I are currently working on such ways to incorporate reading and writing instruction into the program.

We feel that this decision-making program is especially usable because of its simplicity and economy. It can be effectively implemented by classroom teachers without purchased materials or teacher aides. Although it was designed and evaluated on the basis of small group instruction, it would also lend itself to use with a larger group broken into smaller cooperative learning groups.

SUMMARY

These studies have shown that except for the highly proficient readers, the students did not demonstrate a high level of competence in comprehending and resolving these text-based problems. This was true even though the texts were written at a level that presumably did not exceed the competence of the poorest readers—and even though in the second study the texts were read to the subjects. The findings suggest that it would be useful to develop instructional materials in the area of text-based problem-solving, with a view not only toward improving reading comprehension and written expression but also "real-life" problem solving.

Learning-disabled students display particular difficulties in both the comprehension and resolution of these text-based problems, notably in the areas of developing accurate representations of the problem and keeping unconfounded information that is presented in the text and information derived from prior knowledge and beliefs. Such difficulties are manifested especially on tasks that require higher-level thinking.

The instructional program described here, which teaches adolescents to identify a general problem-solving schema and to apply it to text-based problems, is an attempt to improve the decision-making abilities of learning-disabled adolescents.

ACKNOWLEDGMENTS

This work was supported by a grant from the U.S. Department of Education (Office of Spcial Education Programs).

REFERENCES

Adams, M. J. (1989). Thinking skills curricula: Their promise and progress. *Educational Psychologist, 24,* 25–77.

Alvermann, D. E., Smith, L. C., & Readance, J. E. (1985). Prior knowledge activation and the comprehension of compatible and incompatible text. *Reading Research Quarterly, 20,* 420–436.

Au, K. H. (1979). Using the experience–text–relationship method with minority children. *The Reading Teacher, 32,* 677–679.

Baker, L., & Brown, A. L. (1984). Metacognitive skills and reading. In P. D. Pearson (Ed.), *Handbook of reading research* (pp. 353–394). New York: Longman.

Baron, J. (1985). *Rationality and intelligence.* New York: Cambridge University Press.

Bereiter, C., & Scardamalia, M. (1985). Cognitive coping strategies and the problem of "inert knowledge." In S. F. Chipman, J. W. Segal, & R. Glaser (Eds.), *Thinking and learning skills (vol. 2)* (pp. 65–80). Hillsdale, NJ: Lawrence Erlbaum Associates.

Black, J. B., & Bower, G. H. (1980). Story understanding as problem solving. *Poetics, 9,* 223–250.

Blackbourn, J. M. (1989). Acquisition and generalization of social skills in elementary-aged children with learning disabilities. *Journal of Learning Disabilities, 22,* 28–34.

Bos, C. S., & Anders, P. L. (1987). Semantic feature analysis: An interactive teaching strategy for facilitating learning from text. *Learning Disabilities Focus, 3,* 55–59.

Bransford, J. D., Arbitman-Smith, R., Stein, B. S., & Vye, N.J. (1985). Improving thinking and learning skills. An analysis of three approaches. In S. F. Chipman, J. W. Segal, & R. Glaser (Eds.), *Thinking and learning skills* (Vol. 1, pp. 133–208). Hillsdale, NJ: Lawrence Erlbaum Associates.

Bryan, T., Donahue, M., & Pearl, R. (1981). Learning-disabled children's peer interactions during a small-group problem solving task. *Learning Disabilities Quarterly, 4,* 13–22.

Bryan, T., Donahue, M., Pearl, R., & Sturm, C. (1981). Learning disabled children's conversational skills: The "TV Talk Show." *Learning Disabilities Quarterly, 4,* 260–270.

Corno, L. (1987). Teaching and self-regulated learning. In D. Berliner & B. Rosenshine (Eds.), *Talks to teachers.* New York: Random House.

D'Zurilla, T. J., & Goldfried, M. R. (1971). Problem solving and behavior modification. *Journal of Abnormal Psychology, 78,* 107–126.

D'Zurilla, T. J., & Nezu, A. (1980). A study of the generation-of-alternative process in social problem solving. *Cognitive Therapy and Research, 4,* 67–72.

D'Zurilla, T. J., & Nezu, A. (1981). Effects of problem definition and formulation on decision making in the social problem solving process. *Behavior Therapy, 12,* 100–106.

de Bono, E. (1985). The CoRT thinking program. In S. F. Chipman, J. W. Segal, & R. Glaser (Eds.), *Thinking and learning skills* (Vol. 1, pp. 363–388). Hillsdale, NJ: Lawrence Erlbaum Associates.

Ellis, E. S., Deshler, D. D., & Schumaker, J. B. (1989). Teaching adolescents with learning disabilities to generate and use task-specific strategies. *Journal of Learning Disabilities, 22,* 108-119.

Ennis, R. H. (1987). A taxonomy of critical thinking dispositions and abilities. In J. Baron & R. Sternberg (Eds.), *Teaching for Thinking* (pp. 9-26). New York: Freeman.

Feuerstein, R., Rand, Y., Hoffman, M. B., & Miller, R. (1980). *Instrumental enrichment.* Baltimore, MD: University Park Press.

Ford, M. E. (1982). Social cognition and social competence in adolescence. *Developmental Psychology, 18,* 323-340.

Glass, A. L., Holyoak, K. J., & Santa, J. L. (1979). *Cognition.* Reading, MA: Addison-Wesley.

Gotlib, L. H., & Asnarow, R. F. (1979). Interpersonal and intrapersonal problem solving skills in mildly and clinically depressed university students. *Journal of Consulting and Clinical Psychology, 47,* 86-95.

Greenfield, P. (1972). Oral or written language: The consequences for cognitive development in Africa, U. S., and England. *Language and Speech, 15,* 13-21.

Gresham, F. M., & Elliott, S. N. (1989). Social skills deficits as a primary learning disability. *Journal of Learning Disabilities, 22,* 120-124.

Heppner, P. P., & Anderson, W. P. (1985). The relationship between problem solving self-appraisal and psychological adjustment. *Cognitive Therapy and Research, 9,* 415-427.

Hildyard, A., & Olson, D. (1978). *Literacy and the specialization of language.* Unpublished manuscript, Ontario Institute for Studies in Education.

Hornbeck, D. W. (1989). *Turning points: Preparing American youth for the 21st century.* Report of the Task Force on Education of Young Adolescents, Carnegie Corporation of New York.

Janis, I. (1982). *Counseling on personal decisions.* New Haven: Yale University Press.

Johnson, R. E. (1970). Recall of prose as a function of the structural importance of the linguistic units. *Journal of Verbal Learning and Verbal Behavior, 9,* 12-20.

Kintsch, W., & van Dijk, T. (1978). Toward a model of text comprehension and production. *Psychological Review, 85,* 364-394.

Klingman, A. (1988). Biblioguidance with kindergarteners: Evaluation of a primary prevention program to reduce fear of the dark. *Journal of Clinical Child Psychology, 3,* 237-241.

Larson, K. A., & Gerber, M. M. (1987). Effects of social metacognitive training for enhancing overt behavior in learning disabled and low achieving delinquents. *Exceptional Children, 54,* (3), 201-211.

Manning, B. H. (1984). Problem-solving instruction as an oral comprehension aid for reading disabled third graders. *Journal of Learning Disabilities, 17,* 457-461.

McKim, B. J., Weissberg, R. D., Cowen, E. I., Gesten, I. L., & Rapkin, B. D. (1982). A comparison of the problem solving ability and adjustment of suburban and urban third-grade children. *American Journal of Community Psychology, 10,* 155-169.

Meyer, B. J. F. (1979). Organizational patterns in prose and their use in reading. In M. L. Kamil & A. J. Moe (Eds.), *Reading research: Studies and applications* (pp. 109-117). Clemson, SC: National Reading Conference.

Meyer, B. J. F. (1985). Prose analysis: Purposes, procedures, and problems. In B. K. Britton & J. Black (Eds.), *Understanding expository text: A theoretical and practical handbook for analyzing explanatory text.* Hillsdale, NJ: Lawrence Erlbaum Associates.

National Assessment of Educational Progress. (1985). *The reading report card: Trends in four national assessments.* Princeton, NJ: Educational Testing Service.

Nezu, A. M., & Ronan, G. F. (1988). Social problem solving as a moderator of stress-related depressive symptoms: A prospective analysis. *Journal of Counseling Psychology, 35,* 134-138.

Nickerson, R. S. (1989). On improving thinking through instruction. *Review of Research in Education, 15,* 3-57.

Nickerson, R. S., Perkins, D. N., & Smith, E. E. (1985). *The teaching of thinking.* Hillsdale, NJ: Lawrence Erlbaum Associates.

Oliva, A. H., & LaGreca, A. M. (1988). Children with learning disabilities: Social goals and strategies. *Journal of Learning Disabilities, 21,* 301-306.

Palincsar, A. S., & Brown, A. L. (1984). Reciprocal teaching of comprehension-fostering and comprehension-monitoring activities. *Cognition and Instruction, 1,* 117-175.

Pearl, R., Donahue, M., & Bryan, T. H. (1985). The development of tact: Children's strategies for delivering bad news. *Journal of Applied Developmental Psychology, 6,* 141-149.

Pearson, P. D., & Johnson, D. D. (1978). *Teaching reading comprehension.* New York: Holt, Rinehart & Winston.

Platt, J. J., Scura, W. C., & Hannon, J. R. (1973). Problem solving thinking of youthful incarcerated heroin addicts. *Journal of Community Psychology, 1,* 278-281.

Polson, P. G., & Jeffries, R. (1985). Instruction in general problem solving skills: An analysis of four approaches. In S. F. Chipman, J. W. Segal, & R. Glaser (Eds.), *Thinking and learning skills* (Vol. 1, pp. 417-452). Hillsdale, NJ: Lawrence Erlbaum Associates.

Raphael, T. E. (1984). Teaching learners about sources of information for answering comprehension questions. *Journal of Reading, 27,* 303-310.

Robin, A. L., Kent, R., O'Leary, K. D., Foster, S., & Prinz, R. (1977). An approach to teaching parents and adolescents problem solving communication skills: A preliminary report. *Behavior Therapy, 8,* 639-643.

Rubin, R. J. (1978). *Using bibliotherapy. A guide to theory and practice.* Arizona: Oryx Press.

Rumelhart, D. E. (1977). Understanding and summarizing brief stories. In D. LaBerge & S. J. Samuels (Eds.), *Basic processes in reading: Perception and comprehension* (pp. 265-303). Hillsdale, NJ: Lawrence Erlbaum Associates.

Ryan, E. B., Weed, K. A., & Short, E. J. (1986). Cognitive behavior modification: Promoting active, self-regulatory learning styles. In J. K. Torgesen & B. Y. L. Wong (Eds.), *Psychological and educational perspectives on learning disabilities* (pp. 367-397). Orlando, FL: Academic Press.

Schumaker, J. B., Deshler, D. D., & Ellis, E. S. (1986). Intervention issues related to the education of LD adolescents. In J. K. Torgesen & B. Y. L. Wong (Eds.), *Psychological and educational perspectives on learning disabilities* (pp. 329-365). New York: Academic Press.

Scribner, S. (1977). Modes of thinking and ways of speaking: Culture and logic reconsidered. In P. N. Johnson-Laird & P. C. Wason (Eds.), *Thinking* (pp. 483-500). Cambridge, England: Cambridge University Press.

Short, R. J., & Simeonsson, R. J. (1986). Social cognition and aggression in delinquent adolescent males. *Adolescence, 21,* 158-176.

Shure, M. B., & Spivack, G. (1978). *Problem solving techniques in child-rearing.* San Francisco: Jossey-Bass.

Singer, H., & Donlan, D. (1982). Active comprehension: Problem-solving schema with question generation for comprehension of complex short stories. *Reading Research Quarterly, 17,* 166-186.

Spiro, R. J. (1979). *Etiology of reading comprehension style.* (Tech. Rep. No. 124). Urbana, IL: University of Illinois, Center for the Study of Reading.

Spivak, G., & Shure, M. S. (1974). *Social adjustment of young children: A cognitive approach to solving real-life problems.* San Francisco: Jossey-Bass.

Spivak, G., & Shure, M. B. (1985). ICPS and beyond: Centripetal and centrifugal forces. *American Journal of Community Psychology, 13,* 226-243.

Stanovich, K. E. (1986). Cognitive processes and the reading problems of learning-disabled children: Evaluating the assumption of specificity. In J. K. Torgesen & B. Y. L. Wong

(Eds.), *Psychological and educational perspectives on learning disabilities* (pp. 87–131). Orlando, FL: Academic Press.

Statistical Abstracts of the U. S. A., 108th Edition. (1987). Washington, DC: U. S. National Center of Health Statistics.

Street, B. V. (1984). *Literacy in theory and practice.* Cambridge, England: Cambridge University Press.

Torgesen, J. K. (1980). Conceptual and educational implications of the use of efficient task strategies by learning disabled children. *Journal of Learning Disabilities, 13,* 364–371.

Urbain, E. S., & Kendall, P. C. (1980). Review of social–cognitive problem solving intervention with children. *Psychological Bulletin, 88,* 109–143.

Vaughn, S. R. (1987). TLC—Teaching, learning, and caring: Teaching interpersonal problem-solving skills to emotionally-disabled adolescents. *Pointer, 31,* 25–30.

Vaughn, S., & Hogan, A. (1990). Social competence and learning disabilities: A prospective study. In H. L. Swanson & B. K. Keough (Eds.), *Learning disabilities: Theoretical and research issues* (pp. 175–191). Hillsdale, NJ: Lawrence Erlbaum Associates.

Vaughn, S., & McIntosh, R. (1989). Interpersonal problem solving: A piece of the social competence puzzle for LD students. *Journal of Reading, Writing, and Learning Disabilities, 4,* 321–334.

Vygotsky, L. S. (1962). *Thought and language.* Cambridge, MA: MIT Press.

Williams, J. P. (1986). Teaching children to identify the main idea in expository texts. *Exceptional Children, 53,* 163–168.

Williams, J. P. (1988). *Teaching problem-solving skills to learning-disabled adolescents.* Final Report: Grant No. G008530043. U. S. Department of Education, Washington, DC.

Williams, J. P., & Ellsworth, N. J. (1990). Teaching learning-disabled adolescents to think critically using a problem-solving schema. *Exceptionality, 1,* 135–146.

Wong, B. Y. L. (1986). Problems and issues in the definition of learning disabilities. In J. K. Torgesen & B. Y. L. Wong (Eds.), *Psychological and educational perspectives on learning disabilities* (pp. 3–26). Orlando, FL: Academic Press.

Editors' Preface to Chapter 12

The following chapter describes an eight-lesson course module in the statistical logic of a certain class of decision problems: a recurring choice between two options (say to accept or reject an applicant), where preference depends on which of two unknown conditions holds (e.g., the applicant is or is not qualified) and there is diagnostic information available. The module calls for a good deal of mathematical sophistication, such as might be appropriate for an elective upper-class high school course.

The content of the course lies squarely within familiar statistical decision theory traditions, typified by Schlaifer (1969). The central paradigm is Bayesian updating, which specifies how personal probabilities for alternative hypotheses are revised in the light of imperfectly diagnostic evidence. The basic decision logic is the maximization of expected value. This depends on the probability of each hypothesis at the time a choice is to be made, and the value of each option in the event of either hypothesis. Primary attention is paid to the issue of assessing the required probabilities. Each hypothesis generates data according to a stable process on which sample observations are available, and these represent the evidence.

As suggested by the chapter title, the focus is on understanding *normative concepts* relevant to this class of decision problems. It does not attempt to address other aspects of solving a real decision problem, for example: the measurement and interpretation of utility; the subjective elicitation of probabilities; or the adaptation of a model to real world circumstances where the model does not exactly fit, which is invariably the case.

We present some suggestions on how the chapter might be used (see also author's introduction). The material is presented in such a way that it can serve as a self-contained teacher's guide. However, it will probably be most effective if embedded into host courses (or sequences of courses) with some coherent motivation. There are two types of host courses it could naturally fit into.

Use in a Decision Skills Program.   In a course intended to develop practical decision skills—the dominant theme of this book—this module could be taught after two introductory modules. The first would present the qualitative essence of "good" decision making and case-illustrate it, as in the ODYSSEY course (Adams & Feehrer, chap. 4 in this volume). The second would develop the basic quantitative paradigms of personalized decision analysis, such as expected utility and probabilistic inference, as in the DSC project (Laskey and Campbell, chap. 6 in this volume). The Swets module would then show how one variant of this paradigm can be developed mathematically, in a way that can enhance the logical soundness of a decision strategy. The motivation for this third module would need to be established through some introductory linking material.

It could be followed by a fourth "implementation" module which would integrate the Swets material into the decision-making framework introduced in the first two modules and apply its ideas to real problems. The four modules would then constitute a coherent introduction to applied decision analysis. Interested students could then branch out into either applied or mathematical sequel courses.

A danger with a course sequence like this is the possibility of disconcerting cognitive discontinuity for both students and teachers. The two suggested introductory modules, oriented towards enhancing real world decision skills, would only have a tiny statistical component, whereas the Swets module is dominated by statistical logic. The fourth implementation module would require another major shift in intellectual orientation and call for familiarity with real problem solving and cognitive aspects of eliciting input and interpreting output. Conversely, that last module would add little statistical content and so perhaps have little appeal for the statistically-oriented student or teacher.

Use in a Statistics Program.   An alternative pedagogical strategy, probably easier to accommodate institutionally in the present US educational system, would be to make the Swets module part of an unambiguously statistical course sequence. The total sequence could be constituted in a number of different ways. For example, the Swets module could be one of several demonstrations of the *potential* application of statistical concepts in the real world.

In any case the whole sequence would be taught by the math–statistics–computer faculty, and any cross-reference to a decision-making course would be optional. However, some interdisciplinary fusion is inevitable if this material is to contribute to practical decision making.

REFERENCE

Schlaifer, R. O. (1969). *Analysis of decisions under uncertainty*. New York: McGraw-Hill.

Chapter 12

Normative Decision Making

John A. Swets
Bolt Beranek and Newman Inc.
Cambridge, Massachusetts

INTRODUCTION

This chapter was first drafted as part of a teaching manual for a new high-school course called "Reasoning Under Uncertainty," viewed as an alternative to present courses on probability and statistics. The course was developed for a computer-supported environment, in which the teacher and class—and groups of, say, two to four students—use a computer as a tool for gathering, manipulating, and displaying data.

Emphasis in the course work is placed on visualization of processes (e.g., the approach of a distribution of sample means to a normal distribution as sample size or the number of samples increases); on linking multiple representations of a concept (e.g., representations of a distribution as a graph, equation, table of data, some summary statistics, and distribution-generating process); and on direct interaction of students with statistical objects (e.g., interactively moving a line on a scatter plot and seeing how a measure of the goodness of fit reflects the current position of the line). The course is described, along with field tests of some of it, by Roseberry and Rubin (1989, 1990).

This chapter describes a unit of the concluding one of six course modules. The modules, two in each of three parts of the course, were entitled as follows:

Part I. Discovering Similarities and Differences:
Module 1: Describing groups.

273

Module 2: Sampling from groups.
Part II. Answering Questions with Confidence:
Module 3: Making comparisons.
Module 4: Understanding relationships.
Part III. Coping with chance:
Module 5: Taking chances.
Module 6: Making choices.

Module 1 focuses on distributions and variability; 2, on sampling and reliability; 3, on statistical information and hypothesis testing; 4, on bivariate data and association; 5, on uncertainty and probability theory; and 6, on the roles of probabilities and utilities in choice. Another unit of Module 6 treated preferences; this one treats the choice of actions when the choice recurs frequently, each time based on a new observation or datum.

General Description

Throughout this module we consider how the theories of probability and statistics help one to make decisions under uncertainty. For the most part, the decisions are choices of one or another *action,* for example, to drive or take the bus. However, the theory and tools for making such action decisions are extensions of the theory and tools for making a statistical *inference,* for example, the choice between two hypotheses (say, a null hypothesis and the alternative hypothesis) and one of the later lessons in this module treats the parallels.

We consider the *probabilities* and the *utilities* of possible *decision outcomes.* Decision outcomes are more or less satisfactory and their utilities, as well as their probabilities, are effectively treated in a quantitative way. Various *decision rules* exist, to govern the choice of an action, that are based on information about the probabilities and utilities of the possible outcomes of the actions considered. The different rules use this information in different ways, and are more or less appropriate in different settings. Some of the more important rules depend on a quantity called the *expected value* of an outcome, which is defined as the probability of a given outcome multiplied by its utility. The main rule of this group is simply to choose the action whose possible outcomes, in total, have the largest expected value.

We emphasize in this module an important *class of decisions* in which decisions are made *repetitively,* always between the *same two alternative* actions, and each time after receiving some *evidence* that tends to tilt the decision toward one or the other action. The weather forecaster's decision to predict rain or no rain is one example. The college admission officer's decision to accept or reject a particular applicant is another. In general, these are *diagnostic* decisions.

Terms to be Introduced:

decision variable	prior probability
decision outcome	utilities (benefits, costs)

decision rule
optimal criterion
expected value
payoff

likelihood ratio
hypothesis testing
relative operating characteristic

LESSON 1: A DICE GAME ILLUSTRATIVE OF SOME COMMON DECISION PROBLEMS

In the early lessons of this module, we set up a dice game that students will play, in several variations, to illustrate the several factors in the problem of repetitive, two-alternative, diagnostic decisions. The students should be assured that later lessons will show the generality of the game's concepts and illustrate the practical importance of the class of decision situations that it represents.

In this first lesson, the students will learn about various *decision rules,* some rational and some not, and about the *optimal criterion* for implementing a rational decision rule.

Materials.   Two ordinary dice, and one unusual die, the latter having 3 spots on each of three sides and blanks on the other three sides.

Class Discussion.   Present to the students the first version of the dice game they will play. As in other versions of the game, three dice are thrown: the two ordinary dice and one unusual die. Here, the unusual die is one having 3 spots on each of three sides and blanks on the other three sides. One student is appointed to roll the dice.

After each throw, and before each decision, the remaining students will be told only the total number of spots showing on the three dice. They must then decide whether the unusual die showed a *3* or a *0*. For each trial, each student makes *journal entries* of (a) the total number of spots showing, (b) his/her choices, or *actions,* as "3" or "0", (c) the actual outcome as *3* or *0,* and (d) whether the action was correct or incorrect, that is, agreed or disagreed with the outcome. The students are told that they win an imaginary $1 whenever they are correct in either way—that is, they choose "3" when a *3* occurred or they choose "0" when a *0* occurred—and they lose an imaginary $1 whenever they are incorrect in either way—that is, they choose "3" when a *0* occurred, or "0" when a *3* occurred. (Note the denotation of a 3 or 0 italicized as the actual outcome and of a 3 or 0 in quotes as the choice or action.)

Class Activity.   Twenty-five trials of the game are played. Each student totals up his/her payoff, in plus or minus dollars. The students read off their respective payoffs and they are tallied on the board.

Class Discussion.   Choose a student with a low payoff and ask him to state how he arrived at his actions. The main possibilities are:

1. Use a consistent *decision rule,* based on a fixed *criterion number* of total spots showing—such that the criterion number of spots or more led to a "3" action and fewer spots than the criterion number led to a "0" action.
2. Use a consistent decision rule that reflects some other *policy,* for example, to choose "3" for the odd numbers and "0" for the even numbers.
3. Use some *variable rule,* perhaps based on a specific superstition.
4. Make a *random guess.*

Next choose a student with a payoff near the middle and solicit his basis for actions. Finally, choose a student with a high payoff and solicit his basis for actions.

Maybe it comes out appropriately with the data at hand and maybe not, but the idea is to develop the fact that the first possibility listed (decision rule) is *best* (most rational, and gives the highest payoff), and specifically, it is best when the appropriate, or *optimal,* number of spots is selected as the criterion number.

What opinions (or guesses) do students express about the *optimal criterion?* (They should enter their own opinions in their journals.) Can anyone explain why a particular number is the optimal number?

Homework.   Try to determine what the optimal criterion for this dice game is, and present a case for selecting that number.

LESSON 2: ANALYZING THE DICE GAME

This lesson proceeds through the analysis of the dice game as previously played. The students will assume varying roles in the analysis, depending upon how well they have done their homework. They will see how to determine various *relevant probabilities* and to show them as *histograms,* which will indicate the *optimal criterion* for the present version of the dice game.

Class Discussion.   Develop the idea that to choose the criterion number, one will want to know two distributions—the probability of each of the possible totals 2 through 12 when the third die shows a *0,* and the probability of each of the possible totals 5 through 15 when the third die shows a *3.*

Remind the students, if necessary, that they know from a previous module (on *probability theory*) how to set up a 6-by-6 matrix, as in Table 12.1, to determine the number of different ways in which each total 2 through 12

TABLE 12.1
Possible Throws When Third Die Shows 0

		Number of Spots Showing on First Die					
		1	2	3	4	5	6
	1	2	3	4	5	6	7
	2	3	4	5	6	7	8
Number of Spots	3	4	5	6	7	8	9
Showing on Second Die	4	5	6	7	8	9	10
	5	6	7	8	9	10	11
	6	7	8	9	10	11	12

can occur on two ordinary dice—relevant to trials on which the third die shows a *0*. That is, they can construct (on the board) a table as in Table 12.1. There we read along the positive diagonals and see that a *2* can occur in one way (*1,1* on the two dice), that a *3* can occur in two ways (*1,2* and *2,1*), and so on. There are 36 different kinds of throws possible, so the probability of a *2* is 1/36 (or .028), the probability of a *3* is 2/36 (.056), etc.

Help the students to see that determining the appropriate table for the trials on which the unusual die shows a *3* amounts merely to adding 3 to each cell entry in Table 12.1, as in Table 12.2. (Table 12.2 can also be constructed on the board, or perhaps having a handout containing Tables 12.1 and 12.2 is more efficient.)

With these tables in hand, one can proceed to list the probabilities of each total when a *0* showed, and then the probabilities of each total when a *3* showed, as in Table 12.3. Table 12.3 lists first the *number of ways* each total can occur given a *0* (Column 2) and given a *3* (Column 3), as well as the *probabilities* given a *0* (Column 4) and given a *3* (Column 5). (The remaining columns of Table 12.3 will be developed later.)

These probabilities are conveniently represented as two histograms, as in Fig. 12.1—the one to the left for a *0* and the one to the right for a *3*. (The quantity "likelihood ratio" at the top of the figure is developed later.) Ask

TABLE 12.2
Possible Throws When Third Die Shows 3

		Number of Spots Showing on First Die					
		1	2	3	4	5	6
	1	5	6	7	8	9	10
	2	6	7	8	9	10	11
Number of Spots	3	7	8	9	10	11	12
Showing on Second Die	4	8	9	10	11	12	13
	5	9	10	11	12	13	14
	6	10	11	12	13	14	15

TABLE 12.3
Probabilities of the Various Totals, the Likelihood Ratio,
and the ROC Coordinates

(1)	(2)	(3)	(4)	(5)	(6)	(7)	(8)
Sum of Three Dice	# Ways if 0	# Ways if 3	Prob. if 0	Prob. if 3	Likelihood Ratio	P(FP) ≥ Sum	P(TP) ≥ Sum
2	1	0	.028	.000	0	1.0	1.0
3	2	0	.056	.000	0	.972	1.0
4	3	0	.083	.000	0	.916	1.0
5	4	1	.111	.028	.25	.833	1.0
6	5	2	.139	.056	.40	.722	.972
7	6	3	.167	.083	.50	.583	.916
8	5	4	.139	.111	.80	.416	.833
9	4	5	.111	.139	1.25	.277	.722
10	3	6	.083	.167	2.00	.166	.583
11	2	5	.026	.139	2.50	.083	.416
12	1	4	.028	.111	4.00	.027	.277
13	0	3	.000	.083	∞	0	.166
14	0	2	.000	.056	∞	0	.083
15	0	1	.000	.028	∞	0	.027

the students: What do Table 12.3 and Fig. 12.1 tell us about the *optimal criterion* (*number*) in the dice game as played? They can see that totals of 9 or greater are more likely to occur when a *3* is thrown than when a *0* is thrown and that totals of 8 or less are more likely to occur when a *0* is thrown than when a *3* is thrown. If they think of the optimal criterion as 8.5, then they see that it occurs exactly in the middle of the pair of histo-

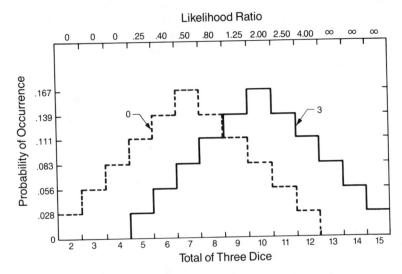

FIG. 12.1   Histograms of the two distributions in the dice game.

grams, that is, where the histograms "cross" each other. This result is intuitively proper, because this game is *symmetrical:* that is, (a) the chances of a *0* and a *3* are equal (at .5), and (b) the utilities are equal (at plus and minus $1). Tell the students that later they will learn how to analyze the game—that is, calculate the optimal criterion—when it is not symmetrical.

(Strictly speaking, we should use Bayes' Theorem to develop the probability of a *3* and of a *0* given each particular total—that is, the *inverse* or *posterior* probability—rather than stopping with the probability of each total given a *0* and a *3*—that is, the forward-going probability—as done here, but we shall finesse that complexity).

Homework. Any student who did not use the best decision rule and optimal criterion in the dice game played in Lesson 1 should go back to his journal and determine how much greater his payoff would have been if he had.

LESSON 3: VARIATIONS OF THE DICE GAME

This lesson analyzes the dice game further: first, when it is easier or harder, and, second, when the outcome probabilities and utilities vary. It develops the payoffs for games of varying difficulty with the help of the computer. It defines *prior probabilities* and it defines *utilities* as *benefits* or *costs*.

Class Discussion. Ask the students if they would rather play the dice game if the third die had 4 spots on each of three sides instead of 3. And why.

They can see that this new version of the game moves the two histograms further apart, so their decisions should be better and produce a higher payoff. For one thing the total 5 (as well as the totals 2, 3, 4) is now a sure sign of a *0*, and a new total, 16, is now a sure sign of a *4* (along with 13, 14, 15).

Ask what the optimal criterion is for this game. It appears that the right-hand histogram (in Fig. 12.1) moves one unit to the right, and the optimal criterion does also. It is 9.5 rather than 8.5. (So one says "4" for totals $\geq$ 10.) And ask what happens if the third die shows 2 spots on each of the three sides.

Class Activity. To see the effect of varying number of spots on each of three sides of the unusual die, the computer is set up to play the game six times—successively with 1, 2, . . . 6 spots showing on the third die. It gives each version of the game 1000 trials, using the optimal criterion for each version, and lists the payoff for each. The students can confirm that the payoff increases with increasing number of spots on the third die. They could list, or plot, these data in their journals.

Class Discussion.   Return to the earliest version of the game, with the sides of the unusual die showing 3 spots or none. Ask: What now if the third die shows 3 spots on four of its sides (rather than on three of its sides as before)? Does the optimal criterion change? In which direction? Why? Or, conversely, what if the unusual die shows 3 spots on just two of its sides?

It seems clear that the *chances* of a *0* and *3* showing will affect the optimal criterion—in that one would set a lower criterion if the chance of a *3* is greater and a higher criterion if the chance of a *3* is less. But how exactly will the chances affect the criterion? Note that it will be convenient to speak of the *prior probabilities* (meaning the chances before the fact) of a *0* and *3*.

One other factor will affect the optimal criterion, namely, the *utilities* of the decision outcomes. Ask how the optimal criterion would change if the utilities were set as follows (with the center dot meaning "and"):

$$0 \bullet \text{``0''} = 0 \text{ occurs and we say ``0''} = + \$1$$

$$0 \bullet \text{``3''} = 0 \text{ occurs and we say ``3''} = - \$1$$

$$3 \bullet \text{``3''} = 3 \text{ occurs and we say ``3''} = + \$5$$

$$3 \bullet \text{``0''} = 3 \text{ occurs and we say ``0''} = - \$5$$

Here it can be seen that it is more important to be correct when a *3* occurs. Hence, one will want to say "3" more often, and one will want to do so by setting a lower criterion number. But which number exactly? And note that we will want a higher criterion if it should be more important to be correct when a *0* occurs.

LESSON 4: A GENERAL FORMULA FOR THE OPTIMAL CRITERION

This lesson develops and exercises a general formula for calculating the optimal criterion, for any number of dots on sides of the unusual die and for any prior probabilities and utilities. New concepts and terms are the *expected value* of *outcomes* and *actions,* which are the bases for a general and important decision rule, and the *likelihood ratio,* a useful concept for all rational decision rules. We shall see that the expected values of outcomes determine an optimal criterion in terms of the likelihood ratio, which in turn, specifies the optimal criterion in terms of the particular *decision variable* at hand—here, the total number of spots showing.

Class Discussion. Now proceed to develop the general formula for calculating the optimal criterion. First define a quantity called the *expected value* of a *decision outcome*. It is the *prior probability* of that outcome multiplied by the *utility* of that outcome. For example, if the prior probability of a *3* is .5 and the utility of the outcome *3•"3"* is + $1, then the expected value of that outcome is .5 times $1, or $.5. Similarly, define the *expected value of an action*. This value is the total of the expected values of the possible outcomes of a given action. Thus, if the prior probability of the *3* outcome is .5, if the *cost* of the outcome *0•"3"* is − $1, and if the *benefit* of the outcome *3•"3"* is + $5, then the expected value of the "3" action is:

$$.5(- \$1) + .5(+ \$5)$$

$$= - \$.50 = \$2.50$$

$$= \$2.00$$

Now, establish the *decision rule* that one will say "3" whenever the expected value of that action is greater than the expected value of saying "0". That rule can be put into a formula by defining some symbols as follows:

Term	*Symbol*
probability	Pr
prior probabilities	Pr(*3*) and Pr(*0*)
outcome probabilities	Pr(*0•"0"*)
	Pr(*0•"3"*)
	Pr(*3•"3"*)
	Pr(*3•"0"*)
outcome utility	B(*0•"0"*)
(B stands for	C(*0•"3"*)
"benefit" and C	B(*3•"3"*)
stands for "cost")	C(*3•"0"*)
expected value	EV

The formula then is: Choose the action "3" whenever

$$[\text{Pr}(3•"3") \times \text{B}(3•"3")$$
$$+ \text{Pr}(0•"3") \times \text{C}(0•"3")]$$
$$> [\text{Pr}(0•"0") \times (0•"0")$$ (Formula 1)
$$+ \text{Pr}(3•"0") \times \text{C}(3•"0")],$$

that is, whenever EV("3") > & EV("0").

Now a new quantity must be defined to put that formula into a more convenient and useful form—one that will indicate the appropriate action for any number of spots showing on the three dice. This quantity is the *likelihood ratio,* denoted *LR.* The likelihood ratio is the ratio of two proba-

spots will show when a 3 occurs and the probability that a given total number of spots will show when a 0 occurs. Before proceeding with the new formula, go back to Table 12.3 and note that those probabilities are given in Columns 5 and 4 respectively. Note further that their ratio, LR, can be added to Table 12.3 as Column 6—thus showing the LR that corresponds to each total number of spots on the three dice. And note still further that the LR can be indicated for each value shown in Fig. 12.1 with the histograms, as arrayed along the top of Fig. 12.1.

After some algebra (not shown here) applied to Formula 1, one arrives at Formula 2:

Choose the action "3" whenever a total occurs such that its

$$LR > \frac{Pr(0)}{Pr(3)} \times \frac{B(0\bullet\text{"0"}) - C(0\bullet\text{"3"})}{B(3\bullet\text{"3"}) - C(3\bullet\text{"0"})}. \qquad \text{(Formula 2)}$$

(Note that the Cs are negative values, so there are two negatives making a positive in both numerator and denominator of the right hand term; hence B and C are simply added.)

For the dice game first described, Formula 2 indicates that the *optimal criterion* corresponds to a total number of spots such that for that number and larger numbers

$$LR > \frac{.5}{.5} \times \frac{1 + 1}{1 + 1} = 1.$$

And it can be seen in Table 12.3 and Fig. 12.1 that totals of 9 and greater have LR > 1, and one recalls that 9 (or 8.5) is the optimal criterion we selected earlier.

Homework.

1. Calculate the optimal criterion when there are *3* spots on four sides of the third die and *0* spots on the other two sides (leaving the benefits and costs at $1).

Answer:

$$LR > \frac{.33}{.67} \times \frac{1 + 1}{1 + 1} = .5$$

Implying, from Table 12.3 and/or Fig. 12.1, that the criterion number of spots is 6.

2. Calculate the optimal criterion for the same prior probabilities (.33 and .67), but with the asymmetrical benefits and costs shown before, that is:

$$0\bullet\text{"0"} = +\$1$$
$$0\bullet\text{"3"} = +\$1$$
$$3\bullet\text{"3"} = +\$5$$

$$3 \bullet \text{``0''} = +\$5$$

Answer:

$$LR > \frac{.33}{.67} \times \frac{1 + 1}{5 + 5} = .1$$

Implying, from Table 12.3 and/or Fig. 12.1, a criterion of 3.5 spots. Note here that one should choose action "3" unless 100% certain that a *0* occurred.

LESSON 5: THE PRACTICAL GENERALITY OF THE DICE-GAME ANALYSIS

This lesson shows that the dice game has the same structure as many practical decision problems, which may be termed "diagnostic problems." It introduces *continuous distributions* as alternatives to histograms, which are discussed later in relating this material to *statistical hypothesis testing*.

Class Discussion. Tell the students that today they will think about how decision problems like the dice game occur in practical settings, and come to see the relevance of their dice-game analysis.

Begin the discussion by reviewing and extending the decision problem as one in which the decision maker repetitively makes an *observation* and decides from which of two specified *distributions* of observations it came. In other language, the decision maker takes a *sample* and decides from which of two specified *populations* it came. In short, some *evidence* is acquired for each decision, and the evidence is taken as representing one or the other of the two defined alternatives. The decision is based partially on that evidence and partially on what general information the decision maker has in advance about the problem. In general, the decision maker is assumed to know: (a) the relative probabilities of occurrence of the two alternatives, that is, the probability that each population or distribution will be the source of the evidence on a given trial (their *prior probabilities*) as well as (b) the benefits of correct decisions and the costs of incorrect decisions.

Note again that there are two ways to be correct: selecting Alternative A when it actually occurs and selecting Alternative B when is actually occurs. Correspondingly, there are two ways to be wrong: selecting Alternative A when Alternative B actually occurs and selecting Alternative B when Alternative A actually occurs. Thus, there are six quantities to keep in mind: two prior probabilities, two benefits, and two costs. The members of each pair will often be different. For example, one way of being correct may be more beneficial than the other and one way of being wrong may be more costly than the other.

Such decision problems arise in what we may call "diagnostic settings." As an example, consider the physician who takes a count of white blood cells as evidence for or against an infection. He (she) uses that evidence in arriving at a choice of Alternative A (the patient has an infection) or Alternative B (the patient is free of infection). In other terms, he makes a "positive" (Alternative A) or "negative" (Alternative B) decision.

The physician may know that the prior probability of infection is high or low, depending on what else he has observed about the patient or knows about the incidence (recent occurrences) of that infection in the general population. He may believe that a "false positive" error, which may lead to another test or a prescription, is less costly than a "false negative" error, which may lead to no further action and the patient becoming sicker. On the other hand, he may prefer a false negative error to a false positive error, if, for example, the former leads to a review after a reasonable period and the latter leads directly to life-threatening surgery. Thus, he may vary the criterion he places on the count of white blood cells (the *decision variable*) according to these other, variable factors. If an infection is likely, or important to detect, he will set a lower criterion than otherwise.

Ask how many similar diagnostic problems the students can identify. There is the weather forecaster who reads the atmospheric conditions today and chooses between predictions of rain and no rain for the morrow. The librarian or library user reads the key words or other descriptors that accompany an article or book and decides whether or not it should be retrieved from the stacks as relevant to the information need at hand. The college admissions officer reads an SAT score or a high-school GPA and decides whether to accept or reject the applicant. A materials technician studies the ultrasound pattern created by an aircraft wing to determine whether or not the wing has an interior crack. A polygraph technician examines various electrical recordings from a suspect and decides whether or not the suspect is lying. The radiologist scans a chest x-ray to decide whether or not it shows a tumor. The stock broker reads the economic signs and decides to buy or sell. The IRS agent looks at certain features of tax returns and decides to audit them or not. And so on. It is clearly important that good decisions are made in these settings.

Next, formalize a representation of this decision problem for the general case. As in the dice game, one general idea is that the evidence, sample, or observation taken on each trial may be represented as a single number, one that lies along a *category scale* or a *continuum*. Thus, the radiologist may represent his evidence as a degree of confidence that he sees an indication of a tumor, say, on a 10-category scale. (This scale, ranging from 1 at low confidence to 10 at high confidence, might be construed as representing percent confidence, or probability, in steps of 10%, so that 80% to 90%, for example, corresponds to the ninth category.) In contrast, the physician measuring pressure in the eyeball to screen patients for glaucoma may do so

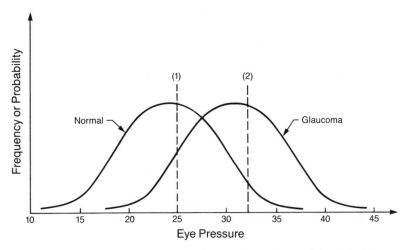

FIG. 12.2   Probabily distributions for two alternatives, and two illustrative decision criteria.

very finely, in very small units of pressure, so that he may use, in effect, about 100 categories. With that fine a scale, we ordinarily think of the numbers as lying along a *continuous* scale, rather than one with a few discrete *categories*. The distinction is that we shall represent the distributions of numbers differently: with few categories, we use *histograms*; with many categories, we use *continuous functions*. (The two representations will be seen to have pedagogical value: the students can themselves construct a histogram; the continuous distributions, as mentioned, can be related neatly to the testing of statistical hypotheses.)

Given a scale of evidence numbers, the second general idea in formalizing the problem (again as in the dice game) is that the distribution of numbers associated with one alternative will differ from that of the other. For glaucoma screening, when we plot the frequency of normal and abnormal patients at each pressure number, we will have something like the picture in Fig. 12.2. That is, patients who turn out actually to have glaucoma (as determined later by a more definitive test) tend to have higher eye pressures than those who don't. Which, of course, is why eye pressure is taken as a useful sign of glaucoma.

Still, eye pressure is not a perfectly reliable sign. The tails of both distributions go out to the extreme values measured, so any pressure number can arise either from a normal or an abnormal patient. Thus, uncertainty remains and the decision cannot always be correct. How should we make decisions in routine practice that will be as good as possible?

For example, how should physicians use eye-pressure measurements as evidence about a given patient in the decision about glaucoma? As in the dice game, rather than making the "positive" decision willy-nilly, they will want to choose some *criterion* amount of pressure and make the positive decision whenever (if and only if) that criterion is met or exceeded. The dotted line labelled (1) in Fig. 12.2 illustrates a decision criterion at 25 units of pressure. What pattern of decision correctness will result from that criterion? Let's see.

Recall for the students that the *proportion of area* under some portion of a distribution curve is equal to the *probability of occurrences* represented by that portion of the distribution. Figure 12.2 thus suggests that a decision criterion as 25 units will correctly classify about 90% of the abnormal population as having glaucoma (the area under the glaucoma distribution to the right of the criterion number). However, we see also that this particular criterion will incorrectly classify about 40% of the normal population as having glaucoma (the area under the distribution of normals to the right of the criterion number). When distributions overlap, some decisions will be wrong. What is needed, of course, is the best (optimal) balance between correct decisions and errors.

Assuming though that the eye-pressure test is the best simple test available, and is accurate enough for population screening, what criterion number should be used as the basis for routine decisions? Again, various *decision rules* are available. The physicians might base their rule entirely on the probability of a false positive decision (perhaps because they can handle only a certain number of patients in further tests). If they want to restrict that probability, say, to .05, what criterion would they use? A rough visual estimation from Fig. 12.2 suggests a criterion of about 32 units, shown as the dotted line labelled (2). (As we shall see later, this decision rule is often used in testing statistical hypotheses, as opposed to practical diagnostic problems—here, the statistical test would ascertain whether the glaucoma and normal populations differ significantly with respect to eye pressure.) What proportion of the glaucoma population, approximately, would be correctly classified under the criterion of 32 units?

As the student knows, a more comprehensive decision rule would explicitly take into account prior probabilities and benefits and costs, and would maximize the specific function of them (that is, their product) that is called the *expected value*. Then, roughly speaking, a relatively *lenient* criterion for a positive decision (say, at 25 units) would be better than a relatively *strict* criterion (say, at 32 units) for one set of prior probabilities and utilities— and poorer for some other set. In general, the student knows how prior probabilities will affect the optimal criterion and how benefits and costs will affect it.

The students should now be encouraged to think of and describe the other practical problems, one-by-one as cued by the teacher, in the terms of Fig. 12.2. For example, will the weather forecaster in the state of Washington be likely to use a lower criterion for predicting rain than the forecaster in Arizona? Why? (Prior probabilities.) Will the forecaster use a strict or lenient criterion for predicting a tornado or hurricane? Why? (Costs and benefits will dominate.) What will determine the library user's criterion? (Perhaps how many irrelevant documents one can tolerate receiving.) What determines the college admission officer's criterion? (Perhaps the number of places available.) What determines the criterion for deciding there is a crack in an aircraft wing? (The cost of missing a defective wing, relative to the cost of replacing a wing.) And so on.

Homework.

1. Do high-school students make any repetitive decisions of this kind? What might they be?

2. Does the baseball batter have a similar decision problem? How? Do the probabilities and utilities change during a time at bat?

3. Can the *expected-value decision rule* be used in cases where there are more than two actions, more than two decision outcomes for each action, outcomes that are more or less good but not necessarily right or wrong, and no new evidence on each trial? Construct some examples.

LESSON 6: OTHER DECISION SETTINGS AND OTHER DECISION RULES

This lesson picks up on the homework of Lesson 5, especially Assignment No. 3, to consider additional decision settings and additional decision rules.

Class Discussion. The homework of the previous lesson should be discussed in class for perhaps 15 minutes at the beginning of this lesson, in order to move toward the concepts to be introduced. The intent now is to go beyond the "diagnostic setting" to decision problems having more than two alternative actions, more than four decision outcomes, outcomes that are more or less good but not necessarily right or wrong, decisions made once rather than repetitively and made without additional evidence beyond the prior probabilities and utilities.

An illustrative problem meeting these specifications is given next, and five different decision rules are considered in connection with it. The specific problem and decision rules treated here are taken from Bross (1953). You may be able to devise a problem with content of greater interest to the students.

The problem is whether to drive one's car or take a bus to work (or school). Table 12.4 is taken as summarizing the relevant information, though it is admittedly simplified and arbitrary. The utilities are expressed in dollars, plus or minus, and note that the *cost of taking an action* is con-

TABLE 12.4
An Everyday Decision Problem (From Bross, 1953, p. 104).

ACTION	DRIVE CAR			TAKE BUS	
Cost of Action	-0.75			-0.30	
Outcomes	Arrive home early and without incident	Arrive home late due to traffic delays	Accident	Arrive home early and without incident	Arrive home late due to missed connections
Probability of Outcome	0.850	0.145	0.005	0.100	0.900
Utility of Outcome	0.00	-1.00	-50.00	0.00	-1.00

sidered here explicitly for the first time in this module. The probabilities for each action add to one.

Decision Rule No. 1. Consider only the most probable outcome for each action and their utilities. Choose the action for which the utility of the most probable outcome is greatest. This leads to:

Action:	Drive car	Take bus
Most Probable Outcome:	Arrive home early	Arrive home late
Utility:	-0.75	-1.30
Choice:	Drive car	

This rule emphasizes the probabilities and is appropriate when one outcome has a very high probability. It can be used when the utilities are not precisely known—indeed, when one has only a ranking of the utilities of the most probable outcomes. The next two rules focus on utilities: one optimistically and one pessimistically.

Decision Rule No. 2. Choose the action which *could* lead to the *most* favorable outcome.

Action:	Drive car	Take bus
Most Favorable Outcome:	Arrive home early	Arrive home early
Utility:	-0.75	-0.30
Choice:		Take bus

Decision Rule No. 3. Consider the *least* favorable outcome possible for each action. Of this set of least favorable outcomes one will be more favorable than the others. Take the action associated with this outcome.

TABLE 12.5
Probability Ranges (From Bross, 1953, p. 109)

ACTION	OUTCOME	PROBABILITY (RANGE)
Drive Car	Arrive home early without incident	0.80 -0.90
	Arrive home late because of traffic	0.10 -0.20
	Accident	0.003-0.007
Take Bus	Arrive home early without incident	0.05 -0.15
	Arrive home late because of connections	0.85 -0.95

Action:	Drive car	Take bus
Least Favorable Outcome:	Accident	Arrive home late
Utility:	− 50.75	− 1.30
Choice:		Take bus

Rules 2 and 3 did not require an estimate of probabilities. Purchasers of lottery tickets seem to be thinking along the lines of Rule 2. Rule 3 emphasizes security, and, specifically, the *control of losses*. Rule 4 following considers actions over a long period, as earlier in this module, and brings us again to the policy advanced in earlier lessons: *Maximize the expected value* (denoted EV).

Decision Rule No. 4. Choose the action that has the largest expected value.

Returning to Table 12.4, and multiplying the probability of each outcome by the corresponding utility, then adding up these products for all outcomes, gives − $1.145 as the EV of driving the car and − $1.20 as the EV of taking the bus. Driving shows a slight advantage, perhaps not meaning much, and the safest conclusion may be that the choice is nearly a toss-up.

The next and last rule is an attempt to combine the loss-control concept of Rule 3 and the expected-value concept of Rule 4, and applies when the probabilities are given as ranges rather than numbers. The probability ranges for the present problem are as in Table 12.5.

Decision Rule No. 5. Select the action associated with the largest of the least favorable expected values.

The least favorable outcome in driving is to have the highest probability of an accident (0.007) and the lowest probability of getting home early (0.80)—leaving the probability of arriving home late as 0.193. The EV is then:

$$(0.80)(0.00) + (0.193)(-1.00) + (0.007)(-50.00) - 0.75 = -1.293.$$

For the bus, the least favorable probabilities are 0.05 for getting home early and 0.95 for getting home late. The EV is then:

$$(0.50)(0.00) + (0.95)(-1.00) - 0.30 = -1.25.$$

A comparison of -1.293 and -1.25 according to Rule 5 indicates that the decision is still a close one, but now there is a slight edge for taking the bus.

We see that it is possible to use information about probabilities and utilities in different ways and come to different conclusions about the best action. It will be useful to consider the motivation behind Rules 4 and 5 particularly and the settings that led to them.

Rule 4 applies usually when a large number of similar decisions is made over a period of time and when moderate gains and losses are possible. In a business, for example, Rule 4 focuses attention on *long-run* profits.

Rule 5, or something like it, is appropriate when the idea of long-run profits breaks down. For example, a small business may have a choice of two deals, both of which require investment of the company's total capital. A profit is desired, but staying in business is important. This small business has to be careful or there will be no long run for it. The extreme loss-control rule (Rule 3) may be too pessimistic. An extension of Rule 5 is to *minimize the maximum risk*.

Thus, the choice between Rules 4 and 5 depends on how large a reserve one has. In a gambling game such as blackjack, the house can afford Rule 4. The player may prefer Rule 5, because survival—to be able to continue to play—is an issue for him.

Homework.   For each of the five decision rules, describe a decision problem in which the rule might apply.

LESSON 7: RELATED CONCEPTS IN
STATISTICAL INFERENCE

Most of the theory of statistical decision making discussed in this module comes from the theory of statistical inference. In this lesson, we merely touch upon a few of the relationships between the two theories.

Class Discussion.   Remind, or point out to, the students that a central problem in statistical inference (inferring significant differences, for example) is the "testing of statistical hypotheses," where two statistical hypotheses are defined by distributions as shown in Fig. 12.2. The left distribution is the null hypothesis, H_0, and the right distribution is the alternative hypothesis under test, H_1. H_0 might be the distribution of measures taken from a "control" group whereas H_1 might be the distribution of measures taken from an "experimental" group. One might ask: Is there a statistically significant difference between, say, the distribution means (where the means are the values of the decision variable—here, eye pressure—corresponding to the peaks of the distributions)? Now, what criterion would one tend to use for answering that question?

As we know, the common practice (mandated by the eminent statistician Ronald A. Fisher) is to use a decision rule, and specific criterion, that will yield a Type I (or false positive) error no more than 5% of the time. This decision rule focuses on "errors of commission" as being especially important in scientific inference and serves to limit them. While we might prefer an explicit consideration of *expected value* in each and every case, Fisher's criterion has stood the test of time rather well. It is as if the elements in the optimal expected-value decision rule tend to boil down to a likelihood ratio criterion that gives Fisher's 5% false positive criterion when "knowledge claims" in science are being *evaluated,* that is, when a knowledge claim is based on an inference that a given effect is likely to exist. However, a decision whether or not to *implement* a knowledge claim through some new procedure in practice—that is, an *action decision* rather than an *inference,* for example, about a new therapy in medicine—would benefit from a further consideration of probabilities and utilities.

To pursue this distinction between inference and action a bit further, we can note that Fisher believed that inferences drawn from a given experiment or sample should depend only on that experiment of sample—and, specifically, that prior data should play no role in such an inference. Action decisions, he believed, should be based on several experiments or samples, and on theories about large collections of data—and we might tend to agree. On the other hand, we can think of instances in which scientists are generally reluctant to base knowledge claims on single experiments and the 5% false positive criterion. An example comes from claims about parapsychological phenomena (extrasensory perception and the like) where it is often felt that the prior probabilities of such phenomena existing—based on what else we know scientifically about the physical world—are very low, and hence the 5% criterion is not stringent enough. Then again, advocates of paranormal phenomena may accept rather weak evidence for these phenomena because they believe that the value of inferring that they exist, if they really do, is very high: Such inferences, if compelling, would drastically change our ideas about present science and our universe. Maybe though, Fisher's scheme of things permits a compromise, a bow toward the importance of prior probabilities and utilities, in considering a 2% or 1% false positive criterion as reasonable options under certain conditions. Again, decision theorists would argue that probabilities and utilities should affect inferences in an explicit, quantitative way and not in some loose, almost qualitative way.

Moving on, one can see that the quality of statistical inferences about the significance of a difference between H_0 and H_1 will depend on the separation between those two distributions: As in the dice game, better decisions are made when the distributions are farther apart, that is, overlap less. Note for the students that one way to have the distributions "farther separated" would be to have their widths decrease, while their means remain the same. That is, to have their *variances* decrease, perhaps as measured by the *standard deviation*. In short, what is important in "separation," or "overlap," is the difference between the means divided by the standard deviation. That quantity is called "effect size" and denoted E in the evaluation literature, to describe the amount of effect of an experimental treatment in universal terms. Thus, $E = (M_A - M_B)/S.D._B$, where M_A is the mean of the distribution of measures taken for Alternative A (also H_1), M_B is the mean for Alternative B (also H_0) and $S.D._B$ is the standard deviation of Alternative B's measures (or H_0).

So *effect size* increases (for a constant difference between means) as the standard deviation decreases. And we know from the beginning of this course that the variance, or standard deviation, of a sampling distribution decreases with sample size. In fact, it decreases in proportion to the square root of the number of times the original sample size is multiplied (call that number T). So, for example, if we double the sample size, then T = 2, and the standard deviation decreases by $\sqrt{T}$ or 1.414; hence E increases by $\sqrt{T}$ or 1.414.

LESSON 8: SOME OTHER RELATIONSHIPS BETWEEN RELEVANT QUANTITIES IN DECISION MAKING

This lesson puts a nice cap on the material of Lessons 1 through 5, but may be omitted if it seems to be too much or too complex. The new concept is the *relative operating characteristic (ROC)*.

Class Discussion. It hasn't been mentioned before, but the students can notice that the *likelihood ratio*, for any given total of the three dice, is equal to the ratio of the heights of the histogram bars (in Fig. 12.1) at the given three-dice total. It was noted earlier that the various likelihood ratios calculated in Table 12.3 are also listed along the top of Fig. 12.1. And, further, that one can compute an optimal criterion number via the LR formula and proceed immediately to draw the optimal criterion line on the histogram in Fig. 12.2, without the intervention of Table 12.3. The same is true for continuous distributions, as in Fig. 12.2 (though one would have to make a scale on the ordinate of such a figure).

Drawing the criterion line on the distributions suggests that one can *evaluate* any criterion number by looking at the proportions of areas to the

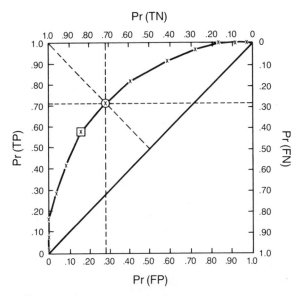

FIG. 12.3   The ROC for 0–3 dice game, showing the probabilities for the four types of decisions at each possible decision criterion.

right and left of the criterion line under each distribution. Those proportions, the student knows, give the probabilities that correspond to the four possible decision outcomes. Specifically, in Fig. 12.2, the area under the distribution of normals to the right of the criterion number is equal to the *conditional probability* of a "false positive" decision ("conditional" on the occurrence of a truly normal patient). The conditional probabilities of "true positive," "false negative," and "true negative" decisions are reflected in the other three proportions of areas, as demarcated by a criterion line. And those four probabilities together constitute a kind of "evaluation" of the criterion—that is, they indicate how good it is.

Another form of graph gives those four decision probabilities more directly. It is called a graph of the *relative operating characteristic*, or ROC (for reasons to be described), and scales the four probabilities on the four sides of the graph. Specifically, it plots the conditional probability of a true positive decision, here denoted Pr(TP), against the probability of a false positive decision, denoted Pr(FP), as the decision criterion is varied. Such a graph is shown in Fig. 12.3. Now note that the probability of a true negative decision, denoted Pr(TN), can be expressed as Pr(TN) = 1 − Pr(FP), because when a negative instance occurs, one says either "negative" or "positive" and is either right or wrong—so Pr(TN) + Pr(FP) = 1. So Pr(TN) can be shown across the top of the graph (with the scale running in the reverse direction). Similarly, the probability of a false negative decision is Pr(FN) = 1 − Pr(TP) and is shown at the right side of the graph. Thus, for any pair of distributions, the graph shows the various possible balances among the probabilities of the four possible decision outcomes—for all possible decision criteria.

Figure 12.3 shows the ROC for the 0–3 dice game as described earlier. The points (marked by an x) that are plotted there correspond to the probabilities listed in columns (7) and (8) of Table 12.3. They are the Pr(FP) and Pr(TP) pairs that correspond to a decision criterion at each possible sum of the three dice. Can the students say how columns 7 and 8 of Table 12.3 are calculated?

Thus, for example, the *symmetrical* criterion at 8.5 discussed earlier yields the point (x = .277, y = .722) as circled in Fig. 12.3. (We can see that this criterion is symmetrical, because its corresponding point lies along the negative (dashed) diagonal, for which the error probabilities, Pr(FP) and Pr(FN), are equal.) And we can see directly (looking at all four scales) that this criterion yields Pr(TP) = .722, Pr(FP) = .277, Pr(FN) = .277, and Pr(TN) = .722.

Functions relating Pr(TP) to Pr(FP) such as this are called relative operating characteristics because one can choose to "operate" at any point along the function (that is, choose any criterion) and the particular function one operates on is "characteristic" of the particular decision problem at hand—it represents the separation of the two distributions, or strictly, the value of E as defined in Lesson 6. (Less obvious and less important is the adjective "relative": It derives from the fact that the ROC shows the relationship between two OCs defined earlier in statistical theory.)

As another convenience in analyzing this decision problem, it happens that the *likelihood-ratio criterion* that yields a given point on the ROC graph *is equal to the slope of the ROC function* at that point. Thus, for example, the LR criterion that yields the circled point in Fig. 12.3 is 1.25, corresponding (in Table 12.3) to a sum of the three dice of 9 or greater. And the slope of the line connecting the circled point with the squared point is also 1.25. (Recall for the students that the slope is calculated by dividing Δy by Δx: here, working from Table 12.3, $\Delta y = .722 - .583 = .139$, and $\Delta x = .277 - .166 = .111$, and $.139/.111 = 1.25$.) For continuous distributions (as in Fig. 12.2), the ROC is a smooth line with constantly decreasing slope from lower left to upper right, and any particular LR is equal to the slope of a line tangent to the smooth curve at the point yielded by that LR criterion.

Class Activity. At this point, the students should exercise the appropriate software on the MAC, which serves to show several relationships graphically and dynamically. The continuous distributions of Fig. 12.2 appear at the upper left of the MAC screen and a blank ROC graph appears at the upper right. Now the student can use the mouse to move a decision criterion along the *decision variable* of Fig. 12.2 (from left to right, say) and see the corresponding ROC take form (from upper right to lower left of its

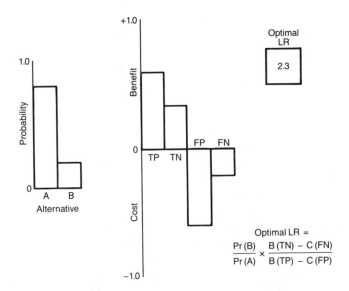

FIG. 12.4 Determining the optimal decision criterion by interacting with the MAC: bars representing prior probabilities, benefits and costs can be moved and simultaneously their values are reflected in the corresponding value of the optimal likelihood ratio.

graph). Then the student can indicate a decision criterion at any point on either figure (either along the decision variable of the distributions or on the ROC) and see the corresponding point on the other figure. Hence: (a) any given criterion for eye pressure (or whatever is the relevant decision variable on which the distributions are shown) can be evaluated by its decision probabilities (on the ROC graph), and (b) one can choose any balance of the four decision probabilities first (that is, any point on the ROC) and then see what eye pressure (or value of some other decision variable) to use as the corresponding decision criterion.

The elements of the optimal decision (prior probabilities, benefits, and costs) can be manipulated at the lower part of the screen, represented here as Fig. 12.4. At the left, when the student uses the mouse to raise the bar representing the prior probability of Alternative A, that is, $Pr(A)$, then $Pr(B)$ decreases, to maintain the relationship $Pr(B) = 1 - Pr(A)$. The student can set the various costs and benefits—of the four decision outcomes TP, TN, FP, and FN—to any values he (she) chooses. As she changes the prior probabilities and/or the benefits and costs: (a) the box labelled "optimal LR" gives that value, (b) the corresponding criterion line appears on the distributions, and (c) the corresponding ROC point is indicated by a line tangent to the ROC at that point.

Lastly, the student can move the distributions farther apart (or closer together), and make them narrow (or wider)—and see the ROC rise (or fall) appropriately—that is, rise toward the upper left corner, which represents perfect performance (E = ∞), or fall toward the diagonal line, which represents performance at a chance level (E = 0). Conversely, moving the ROC up and down will move the distributions farther apart or closer together, or change their variances (as desired). One can see, for example, how well a diagnostic test would have to separate the populations to give any desired error proportions.

Homework.

(1) Calculate and plot the ROCs for the 0–4 and 0–2 dice games (in which the number of spots on three sides of the unusual die are *4* and *2*, respectively). How much larger or smaller are the maximum payoffs in these games than in the 0–3 game (when the benefits and costs = ± $1? Method of solution: Determine probabilities of outcomes at the symmetrical criterion (LR = 1), add up benefits, and subtract costs.

(2) Determine the optimal operating points for each of the two ROCs of Assignment No. 1 at the symmetrical criterion (LR = 1). Would the optimal criterion or operating point differ (for equal prior probabilities) if B(*0*•"0") = + $1, C(*0*•"3") = − 5, B(*3*•"3") = + $1, and C(*3*•"0") = − $5?
Answer: No, because those Bs and Cs also give LR = 1.

(3) Determine the optimal operating points for each of the two ROCs of Assignment No. 1 for symmetrical (equal) Bs and Cs when the third die has spots (either *4* or *2*) on (a) four of its sides, (b) two of its sides.
Answer: The optimal operating point is one where the ROC slope is (a) .5, and (b) 2.0.

ACKNOWLEDGMENTS

This chapter was prepared with funding from the National Science Foundation under Grant No. MDR-8550103, but does not reflect the views of the foundation. The encouragement and advice of BBN colleague Raymond S. Nickerson is acknowledged with appreciation.

REFERENCES

Bross, I. D. J. (1953). *Design for decision.* New York: Macmillan.
Roseberry, A., & Rubin, A. (1989). Reasoning under uncertainty: Developing statistical reasoning. *Journal of Mathematical Behavior, 8,* 205–219.
Roseberry, A., & Rubin, A. (1990, Summer).Teaching statistical reasoning with computers. *Teaching Statistics, 12,*(2), 38–42.

Chapter **13**

Institutional Strategy for Teaching Decision Making in Schools

Vincent N. Campbell
Decision Systems, Inc.
Reston, VA

Kathryn B. Laskey
Decision Science Consortium, Inc.
Reston, VA

INTRODUCTION

This article has grown out of the authors' experience developing curriculum materials for teaching decision analysis at the intermediate level, training teachers in decision analysis, teaching decision analysis to middle-school students, and talking with teachers and school system officials about the opportunities and potential pitfalls associated with introducing decision analysis into schools. The article shares our insights regarding a strategy for building decision-skill learning into the school curriculum in ways that will, we think, be accepted by the school system, the teachers, the parents, and the community.

The remainder of this chapter discusses a set of four issues that must be addressed if a decision skills program is to be successfully implemented. The first issue is what to teach. This involves not just which decision making techniques to teach at what level, but also whether and how decision analysis is to be integrated with other coursework. The second issue is how to teach the material. Sound pedagogy is essential to the success of a program. The third issue is commitment from the teachers who would be implementing the approach. The final issue is parent and community support. The program could be scuttled if parents become angry and afraid that their children are being taught "wrong" values. Conversely, success will be enhanced if parents and the community see a clear benefit to their children.

CURRICULUM CONTENT

Integration into Existing Curriculum

Teachers and administrators we have talked to have strongly recommended integrating instruction in decision analysis into existing school courses, rather than proposing a new course, or even a large unit, on decision-making skills. This alleviates the necessity of finding a home for a new course in an already crowded curriculum. But integration will be successful only if it is perceived by teachers as being helpful to their main mission—teaching students chemistry, or biology, or health.

Decision skills may best be treated as a strand within each applicable course. For example, any course unit that has implications for important choices that people make could conclude with an exercise analyzing a typical decision in that domain. A short introductory module on the basic concepts of decision analysis could be an available option for students who have never had the strand in any course.

Strands could also vary in level of decision skills. Figure 13.1 shows a sequence of possible learning objectives. Early strands might be limited to Objective 1. Subsequent objectives could be added in later strands. Quantitative objectives (5–7) could be considered an optional strand for teachers who are comfortable with applying numbers in the analysis.

Integration into the regular curriculum poses a challenge to developers of decision-making materials. Material for examples and exercises must be developed for a variety of subject areas, though not necessarily all at once. This requires that the course developers include not just experts on decision analysis but also experts on the subject matter of diverse disciplines. But with this challenge comes an opportunity. We argue that integrating decision skills into the regular curriculum will enhance learning of both the decision skills and the course content. Decision analysis skills will be further reinforced if they are practiced in a number of different classes.

Practical Relevance to Students

Students need to be convinced of the practical value of learning decision-making skills. If the course is perceived as another academic curiosity with no real relevance, students will not retain or use what they have learned.

Conventional educational wisdom says that transfer to everyday situations is fostered by practice on problems similar to those that students will encounter in their lives. We suspect that decision analysis training will be more likely to transfer to everyday decisions if it is practiced on problems that students perceive as important, especially if these problems span different disciplines. We recommend that most of the cases or exercises on which students practice their skills be realistic, if not real, decisions. Realis-

Qualitative

1. From a description of a decision problem, identify:
   —The decision maker's *goals*.
   —The *options* available to the decision maker.
   —The possible *outcomes* that could occur if each option is chosen.
   —How *probable* each of the outcomes is.
2. Identify biases that can occur in thinking about the decision, and in collecting and evaluating data bearing on predictions. Recognize that the best decision might be different for different persons.
3. Use a decision making chart to structure a decision problem and organize information about goals, options, and outcomes. Given a decision problem, construct a decision making chart. Explain why some outcomes affect the decision more than others. Use the decision making chart as a focal point for discussing which choice is best and why people might differ.
4. Identify situations in which uncertainty affects our decision (i.e., when the decision would be different depending on which outcome happens). Identify sources of information about the uncertain outcome, and judge their credibility. Judge how our decision would change as the likelihood of the outcomes changes.

Quantitative

5. Use a number scale to compare the value of different options in terms of how they achieve the decision maker's goals. Assign numbers to the cells of the decision making chart so that the difference between scores of two options on each goal measures how strongly that difference matters for the decision. Check the number assignments by making cross-goal comparisons. Compute a total value score for an option. Use these scores to assist in making a decision.
6. Use numbers to describe how probable an uncertain outcome is. Use data to estimate probabilities. Use probability as an informal factor in decisions.
7. Multiply outcome probabilities and values to compute total expected value of an option. Use expected value as a guide to making a decision.

FIG. 13.1.   Major student objectives for decision skills strands.

tic problems are not only more interesting to students, they also introduce uncertainties, distracting elements, and confounded variables in diverse forms that students will eventually have to see through and interpret if they are to apply their skills to important problems in their own lives. Artificially simple exercises may be useful to clarify concepts and introduce techniques, but the problem content should evolve toward realism fairly soon.

These observations are also supported by teachers and by the research literature. Teachers reported to us that in seventh- and eighth-grade classes where they addressed decision making, a real and important decision sustains class involvement in decision making issues much better than a contrived problem. An actual instance of this was when the class addressed the decision facing a student whose friend talked to her about suicide and swore her to secrecy on the matter (identities were not revealed). If decision analysis is to be integrated into existing courses, the examples will naturally be drawn from the course content itself. For example, students in the civics class we taught analyzed the 1988 Presidential election. Not only did this engage students' interest, but it vividly illustrated, in a real-life situation, common decision making biases. Examples include single-issue voting, being influenced by attributes (such as party or personality) that would on reflection not be given such high weight, or refusing to change an entrenched opinion when given countervailing evidence.

Apart from greater interest and importance, a real problem tends to have the advantage that the students see the decision as a matter of opinion, and quite readily insert their own values and predictions into the situation. A "book" problem, on the other hand, is more likely to be seen merely as another school assignment or test, with the student's role being to find the correct answer known by the teacher. This traditional role is not as conducive to practicing decision making.

Beyond seeing the importance of the content of the decision exercises, students need to be convinced that the techniques they are being taught will help them make better decisions. An initial reaction of many students is that they do not need help making decisions: "I just do what seems right to me." Students need to be convinced that approaching decisions logically does not mean denying their emotions. The very foundation of decision analysis is the values and desires of the decision maker: Values are better served if one thinks logically about how best to achieve them. We have found it effective to create classroom demonstrations of common decision-making biases, to show students that they themselves are subject to these biases. Decision analysis can be presented as a framework for thinking about decisions in a way that is less subject to bias.

The general approach of connecting coursework to the community and the workplace is receiving increasing attention lately, and there have been encouraging reports about the success of such programs (cf., Goldberg, 1989). We strongly recommend a plan that leads students into practicing their growing decision skills on real decisions at home and in the community. These can be decisions that the students themselves implement, such as a neighborhood project, or they can act as surrogate decision makers for the town council or the school board. As surrogates, they may wish to present their analyses and conclusions to the authority actually making the decision.

INSTRUCTIONAL TECHNIQUES

The tools and teaching techniques need to be appropriate to the grade level and background of the students. This means not only creating adaptations of decision analysis as it is customarily taught at college or graduate level, but bringing in tools from outside decision theory itself.

Student-Directed Learning

Once the teacher has demonstrated a technique, students need to take the initiative in analyzing problems, either individually or in pairs or small groups. This may be true for many other educational objectives as well, but initiative and self-direction are at the very heart of making decisions well.

The advantage of self-directed practice probably derives partly from taking students out of the traditional passive role and putting them in charge of the decision. In earlier research on self-directed versus programmed instruction in elementary schools Campbell (1964, 1971; Campbell & Chapman, 1967), found that if students understood what they were trying to accomplish and were given supportive materials, they learned faster to solve problems if each student organized his own study than if all were given a fixed sequence of steps to follow.

Although some individual practice working through decisions is essential, either in class or at home, many of the advantages above may be obtained by having students work in pairs or small groups. Davidson (1979), for example, found that small group learning was especially valuable for inquiry and problem solving. The teachers on our team have recently completed in-service training on collaborative learning (Fairfax County Public Schools, 1988) and have applied it in the classroom. These teachers are convinced of the value of small groups as a learning mode. Having students work in pairs with students questioning and/or tutoring each other has also shown great promise. Levin, Glass, and Meister (1987) summarized evidence that peer tutoring is one of the most cost-effective educational innovations of recent decades.

The Decision Making Chart:
A Standard Framework

The objectives that we suggest for middle school level decision skills (Fig. 13.1) derive from various disciplines. Even within the primary source discipline, decision theory, different approaches such as multiattribute utility and probabilistic expected utility have evolved in parallel using somewhat different frameworks for teaching and analysis. Our students found this juxtaposition of paradigms to be confusing, as described by Laskey and Campbell (chapter 6). A single integrated analysis framework that encompasses all these concepts is needed. We propose the Decision Making Chart illustrated in Fig. 13.2 as a standard tool for learning formal decision analysis. We suggest that at first the chart be used for qualitative analysis of decision problems. Later, the same chart can be expanded to incorporate more complex aspects of a decision problem, such as numerical utilities and probabilistic expected utility.

The decision problem to which the Decision Making Chart is applied in Fig. 13.2 is taken from a high school chemistry course oriented toward community problems (American Chemical Society, 1988). Just before the town of Riverwood (fictional) is about to hold a fishing tournament, many dead fish are found downstream from the nearby dam that supplies the

Analysis of: __What to do about fish kill__

Goals:	Option: Wait and Watch	Option: Stop water use & cancel tournament
Maintain Public Health	Probably no effect - but small chance of deaths or serious illness	+ No public health danger
Keep good business climate	+ Small chance of serious long-term damage to town's reputation	Some businesses must close. Tourist businesses suffer serious losses. Minor damage to town's reputation.
Keep schools open	+ Schools remain open	Schools must close.
Avoid cost of trucked-in water	+ No water trucked in	Thousands of dollars
Preserve convenience (showers, pools, tap water, etc.)	+ Citizens are not inconvenienced	Citizens suffer great inconvenience

Summary and Recommendation:

The wait & watch option has only one possible negative, and that negative is unlikely. But it is a very serious effect if it happens - many people might die if the water is contaminated. Even though preliminary tests don't show anything wrong with the water, it does not seem worth risking the possibility. We have to sacrifice the positives - the business climate, the schools, the cost, and the convenience - to avoid risking a very bad outcome.

FIG. 13.2 Decision making chart.

town water. The cause of the fish kill is unknown, and preliminary tests have revealed no known toxins. The Mayor is faced with an immediate decision whether to stop water use until the cause is determined. This will, of course, entail cancelling the annual fishing tournament, which is a major source of revenues for the town's business community.

Figure 13.2 illustrates how students might use the chart for a basic qualitative analysis of the decision. Each row of the chart represents a goal or value attribute, and under each option the student enters a description of how the option is expected to affect that goal (the outcome).

We have found that students at the seventh- and eighth-grade levels readily grasp how to fill out the Decision Making Chart. An effective teaching strategy is to fill out one or two rows of the chart as a class discussion, after which students work cooperatively in small groups to finish the chart. We have found that the process of filling out the chart engages students' interest (if the decision problem is interesting). The chart is a useful framework for organizing their thoughts about the decision problem. To complete the chart, they need to examine both their values (to decide which goals are important enough to include in the analysis) and their knowledge about the problem (to make predictions of outcomes).

Although filling out the chart causes students to think critically about the decision problem, we have found that written justifications of the recommended decision often revert to simple statements of the main advantage of the recommended option. To reinforce a new way of thinking about making and justifying decisions, students need to practice writing justifications that mention the pros *and* cons of the chosen option, and describe why the pros outweigh the cons. Small group work can also be used effectively to counteract this tendency toward single-minded justifications. The process of group discussion encourages airing of different viewpoints. We recommend having the leader of a small group report to the class on the group's recommendation and the discussion that led to it, including any minority viewpoints or significant disadvantages to the option that was chosen.

One must take care not to convey to students the impression that the goal of instruction is to get them to make charts for all their decisions. An implicit objective is to be able to use the same concepts by more informal, heuristic methods. Most decisions encountered by students will be simple enough, with few enough factors to trade off, that informal methods will suffice. An example is the simple heuristic of going through the GOOP (thinking about goals, options, outcomes, and probabilities) before making a decision (see Laskey and Campbell, chap. 6 in this volume). This provides a positive method of thinking to minimize biases. Negative methods, such as asking people to avoid errors and biases, seldom succeed (Fischhoff, 1982).

The Decision Making Chart is a natural focus for addressing other objectives relating to decision making. Often there is uncertainty concerning the outcome of an option with respect to one of the goals (as is the case with the "Wait and Watch" option in Fig. 13.2). The chart helps students to identify these uncertainties, consider how they affect the decision, and set priorities for gathering additional information. As noted above, the chart can be expanded as a template for numerical computation of multiattribute utility and probabilistic expected utility.

Additional objectives might focus on particular goals that tend to be neglected by young people—especially goals involving the distant future and the welfare of others. One of the lessons we have developed examines social dilemmas, or problems in which self-interest conflicts with group welfare (e.g., recycling, not littering, paying taxes).

Generating new options is another important objective. Unstructured brainstorming is a common technique used for this purpose. Another approach is to use the Decision Making Chart as a focal point for discussion, explicitly attempting to change options so as to overcome their weaknesses, or to combine options to get the advantages of both.

TEACHER ACCEPTANCE

Perhaps the most important requirement for successful implementation of decision skills training is teacher acceptance. No innovation will succeed unless there is a group of enthusiastic teachers implementing it in their own classrooms and encouraging other teachers to join the bandwagon.

Three conditions are required if teachers are to accept and adopt a new methodology. First, they must be convinced of its value to students. We have found little resistance to the idea of teaching decision skills once arguments in its favor have been presented. Second, teachers must be convinced that teaching decision analysis will help them do their jobs better. A teacher is there to help students achieve the regular course objectives, and will reject any innovation that threatens to divert time and energy from this task. Finally, and probably most important, teachers must be convinced that they can learn and teach decision analysis.

Training in decision analysis should be targeted both to pre-service teacher education and in-service training. A course taught in the education department of a university can train pre-service teachers as well as provide continuing education credit for practicing teachers. An alternative for in-service education is school-based workshops. Offering some form of credit is important for motivating teachers to take the course.

Our approach to a course or set of workshops in decision analysis for teachers is based on the following assumptions:

1. Decision analysis is unfamiliar to most teachers and education majors, so the course must clearly show the advantages of learning such skills, and must very specifically illustrate materials and techniques that are likely to be effective.

2. If decision skills are to be integrated into the regular curriculum, as recommended, the contexts and decisions to which teachers apply them will be highly diverse. A programmed approach requiring a uniform sequence of steps is likely to seem inappropriate much of the time. Flexibility is required. The techniques learned must be easily adapted to a variety of contexts by the teacher.

Learning to apply decision skills will be an ongoing learning experience for the teachers as well as the students. It is not something that can be mastered quickly; competence in teaching decision skills will grow with practice, and will grow faster with access to advice from decision analytic experts and with frequent sharing of ideas among teachers.

Given these assumptions, we feel that a sensible course plan is as follows:

In-service teachers are encouraged to participate in teams of two or more from a given school, so that teachers can more readily share ideas during the first year or two of teaching decision skills.

The course is divided into two parts: learning decision analysis, and learning to teach decision analysis. A 2-week in-service workshop might be structured as follows. The first week consists of brief demonstrations and lengthy guided practice in using the Decision Making Chart in a variety of ways. Practice takes place mainly in the individual and small group modes.

We plan to develop several prototype exercises using the Decision Making Chart, each prototype emphasizing different decision skills, concepts, and objectives. Each prototype exercise will address a different decision problem. The complete set of prototypes is intended to provide teachers with a set of techniques sufficient for mastery of the objectives listed in Fig. 13.1. The prototypes are also intended as models that teachers can use to devise new decision problems matched to the content of their curriculum and the interests of the local community in which they teach.

Each time a new prototype representing some new objectives is introduced, teachers first work through the prototype following a fixed standard procedure that is expected to succeed with students as well. This provides a clear illustration of one good way to use the prototype. Some teachers may find it convenient simply to apply this model procedure in the classroom whenever it is appropriate. Many teachers will want to vary the procedure according to circumstances and incorporate their own ideas and techniques. Therefore, after the first pass through the uniform procedure, each group of teachers uses the prototype in a more creative fashion, first to analyze problems already structured in the format of the Decision Making Chart, and later to apply the Chart to new decision problems that they have to structure themselves. During this first week, underlying concepts and principles are summarized in 1 hour at the beginning, then elaborated briefly from time to time as they are needed to explain the rationale for particular analysis techniques or to correct errors.

The workshop begins with qualitative decision analysis (no numbers). This enables teachers to construct entirely qualitative lesson plans that achieve the qualitative objectives listed in Fig. 13.1. Later, teachers progress to numerical analysis, to appreciate the power it adds, and to have it as an option they may choose to use or not in the classroom.

In the second week the teachers plan lessons suited to their own curricula. Teachers having similar curriculum objectives can work together in small groups, or plan individually or a mixture of both. The workshop leaders circulate among the groups for most of the day helping and reviewing plans, and providing enhancement instruction as needed. The last hour in each day in the second week is reserved for joint idea sharing and discussion of difficulties and possible solutions by the whole workshop. It is expected that much of this time would be devoted to how to structure a particular new decision problem that a teacher wishes to address.

The teachers who have participated in our research have reviewed our draft materials for an initial prototype using the Decision Making Chart. They believe a workshop using this approach will give teachers the preparation they need in order to teach decision skills to their classes. Research under way and proposed will provide further evidence on the effectiveness of the workshop approach.

This same format could be applied to a semester-long university course. An advantage of an evening course for in-service teachers is that techniques could be tried out in the classroom, and teachers could report on their experiences at the next class session.

OUTREACH

Follow-up of Teachers.   We are currently developing a teacher workshop along the lines previously outlined, and expect to implement it within the next year or two. We expect to maintain contact with teachers who have attended workshops. Their degree of continuing involvement will be assessed, and their advice sought on how to maintain teacher enthusiasm. Teachers from the same district or area will be encouraged to meet monthly for in-service review and sharing conferences on teaching decision skills. Follow-up will help to identify which pedagogical tools are most effective, which learning objectives are best assimilated by students at different grade levels and from different backgrounds, and how the course can be improved for the future.

Outreach to Other Teachers.   Suppose teachers take workshops and apply the techniques successfully in their own classes. To what extent will they be able to help other teachers in their schools acquire the same capability? Is a workshop just a jump start toward this capability, which teachers could acquire more slowly but just as surely by informal sharing of ideas and materials among teachers? We suspect the answer will vary by objective. Helping students identify their goals, their options, and their biases may be easier to accomplish without formal training than helping students do a systematic analysis of a decision.

Outreach to Parents and Community.   If students are to apply their decision skills outside school (the ultimate objective), can parents, employers, and others in the larger community be engaged in helping students practice and implement these skills? At present there is little awareness in the community, or the schools, of even the notion of teaching decision skills, quite apart from issues of effectiveness. Parent orientation sessions are a beginning. Homework assignments that utilize parent support could help students relate what they learn to their lives, though issues of who decides what in a family may occasionally be thorny. Joint projects among schools, businesses, and other community agencies could extend the realm of implementation to real-life social decisions, with the students playing a role in the deliberations and analyses that precede such decisions.

District and State Programs. Finding a permanent place in the curriculum for decision making skills will depend on effective publication and dissemination of educational materials that include decision skill strands, and on adoption of these materials in the schools. Parent, community, and employer support will encourage local adoption. Wider adoption by large district and state curriculum officials will also depend upon favorable review by curriculum committees.

ACKNOWLEDGMENT

This work was supported by the National Institute of Child Health and Human Development under grant #2-R44-HD23071-02 to Decision Science Consortium, Inc.

REFERENCES

American Chemical Society. (1988). *ChemCom, Chemistry in the community*. Dubuque, Iowa: Kendall/Hunt Publishing Company.

Campbell, V. (1964). Self-direction and programmed instruction for five different types of learning objectives. *Psychology in the Schools, 1*, 348–359.

Campbell, V. (1971). Learner variables and learner control of instruction. In E. Rothkopf and P. Johnson (Eds.), *Verbal learning research and the technology of written instruction*. New York: Teachers College Press.

Campbell, V., & Chapman, M. (1967). Learner control vs. program control of instruction. *Psychology in the Schools, 4*, 121–130.

Davidson, N. (1979). Small group learning and teaching in mathematics. In S. Sharan et al., (Eds.) *Cooperation in education*. Provo, UT: Brigham Young University Press.

Fairfax County Public Schools. (1988). *Teacher research on student learning*. Report on research funded by a Fairfax County Public Schools Minority Achievement Grant. Reston, VA: Langston Hughes Intermediate School.

Fischoff, B. (1982). Debiasing. In D. Kahneman, P. Slovic, & A. Tversky (Eds.), *Judgment under uncertainty: Heuristics and biases*. Cambridge University Press.

Goldberg, D. (1989, August 6). Upward Bound Program Trains At-Risk Students, *Washington Post Education Review*.

Levin, H., Glass, G., & Meister, G. (1987). Cost-effectiveness of computer-assisted instruction. *Evaluation Review, II*(1), 50–72.

Chapter 14

Metaphors for Effective Thinking

Daniel D. Wheeler

University of Cincinnati

INTRODUCTION

All of the authors included in this book are committed to the idea that education can help people become more effective thinkers. We believe that appropriate instruction in school can help people become more effective in their everyday lives. We think that by focusing on decision making, educators can help adolescents make the transition to adult maturity.

Our work on decision making is part of a larger trend toward developing educational programs with general cognitive goals. Nickerson, Perkins, and Smith (1985), in their extensive survey of approaches to teaching thinking, found a wide variety of programs with diverse goals expressed in terms of reasoning, creativity, heuristics, and so forth. My goal in this chapter is to explore the diversity of interpretations of effective thinking in a way that links conceptualizations of decision making to other ways of understanding the situations facing adolescents. I will discuss four approaches, each of which embodies a metaphorical way of understanding situations in life. The dominant metaphorical frames for conceptualizing effective thinking have been problem solving and decision making. Two newer frames are design and improvisation.

I also hope to increase diversity in the ways we think about effective thinking. I see diversity as healthy. One way of looking at the issue is that we are teaching tools for thought. We would never expect one kind of hammer to be best for everyone. A carpenter's hammer has a claw for pulling nails. An auto mechanic's hammer substitutes a rounded end for shaping sheet metal. Even within the same field, expert mechanics may have different preferences for the feel of a hammer. Some may prefer wooden handles whereas others prefer steel or fiberglass epoxy—even if they cannot explain how the feel is different.

Looking at the World Through Metaphors

Lakoff and Johnson (1980, see also Lakoff, 1987) argued that people conceptualize the world using broad metaphors. These can be examined by analyzing the language we use to talk about the world. For instance, they claimed that our understanding of arguments is based on the conceptual metaphor *argument is war*. Our everyday expression about arguments show the underlying metaphor: "Your claims are indefensible." "He attacked every weak point in my argument." "His criticisms were right on target" (p. 4).

Some other culture might have a very different metaphor for arguments, such as an argument is a dance. In that culture discussions that begin with different points of view would have a very different form and feeling. The cooperative reaching of new positions would be emphasized by the dance metaphor rather than the winning or losing that we experience as a result of conceptualizing arguments as wars.

Lakoff and Johnson (1980, p. 5) said "The essence of metaphor is understanding and experiencing one kind of thing in terms of another." An argument is not really a war, but our understanding of wars and battles is used in the interpretation of arguments. There are often alternative metaphors that can be applied to a situation. Each metaphor highlights some aspects of the situation and hides others.

Metaphors can do more than help us understand and describe reality. C. Wheeler (1987) discussed the way metaphors actually create reality. When we use a set of metaphors to think about the world around us, we are creating the world within which we think and act. This metaphor of metaphors creates pluralistic realities within which no single world view is seen as the truth. For example, the idea that there is a single "objective" reality to which we can refer is itself a metaphor, a metaphor that creates a monotheistic world view.

It should be clear here that the concept of metaphor is not being used in the narrow literary sense, but in a wider (metaphorical) sense. Likewise, *monotheistic* is intended metaphorically to suggest belief in one view of truth, not to imply belief in a god.

The idea of objectivity itself is a metaphor in that it asserts that looking at all aspects of reality is like looking at a physical object. Our perspective can change so that we see different views from different angles, but the underlying object is considered to be always the same.

The metaphor of metaphors suggests that there are some things that can't be viewed like an object, such as the social relationships among a group of people. Each member of the group has an understanding of what is going on that is, at least partly, conceptualized metaphorically. But these different *views* (to use a term from the objectivity metaphor) are not independent of the reality, they are part of it. As the conceptions of the participants are part of the reality, at least this part of the reality is created by the conceptions of the participants.

Metaphors and Life's Experiences

Each person is embedded in a flow of life experiences. These are never a buzzing, blooming confusion; the flow is divided into events and situations using a conceptual system that is largely a part of one's culture. When something occurs, the category that it is placed in determines how it is interpreted and what kinds of actions are seen as possible responses.

Example: Jack (age 18) is sitting on a park bench when Jess (age 6, not previously known to Jack) rides by on a bicycle, skids at a turn in the gravel path, falls down in the grass, and starts to cry. There are several ways Jack might construe his experience. He may regard the event as one of life's little dramas to be observed, appreciated, and enjoyed. He could consider it an intrusion that shattered the peace and tranquillity of a quiet afternoon in the park. He might view it as a learning experience for Jess, who is learning about the dangers of loose gravel and about how to cope (alone) with minor pain and upset.

These ways of construing the event will probably not lead Jack to become involved. Other ways of construing the event would have a different outcome for Jack. He could interpret the crying as a cry for help rather than as just a response to pain and upset. He could see himself as the closest adult in a social system in which the closest adult has as substitute parent responsibility to help children in trouble.

If Jess is a girl, Jack would have another set of conceptual categories for construing the situation. Jess could be a damsel in distress just waiting to be rescued by a white knight. Or Jack could interpret crying girls as dangerous traps to be avoided.

All of these interpretations are metaphorical: The current situation is seen as like some other kind of situation. *Life's little dramas* suggests a stage play that is not real and that has some intended meaning to be interpreted. It also suggests that Jack is in the audience and should follow the cultural standards for good audience behavior. *Shattered peace* suggests that something has been broken into tiny pieces, probably beyond repair. The *closest adult* interpretation brings the parent role into play even though Jack has never seen the child before.

None of these interpretations is the *truth*. Nor are they mutually exclusive; Jack could interpret the situation in several ways at once. Each metaphor highlights some aspects of the situation and hides others. If Jack follows the parent metaphor and gives Jess a hug, the parent metaphor will hide from him the potentially sexual overtones of the act. These would have been highlighted by the damsel in distress metaphor.

Although none of the interpretations can be defended as the truth, there are principled reasons for urging some interpretations and not others. First, agreement about the interpretation helps people get along. If Jack and Jess both interpret the situation using a substitute parent metaphor they are more likely to act in ways consistent with each other's expectations and less likely to get into conflict. Second, interpretations can have strong value implications. We should be willing to argue vigorously against interpretations that conflict with our strongly held values. I, for instance, will challenge interpretations that reflect racist or sexist beliefs that conflict with my values about the equal worth of all people.

Encouraging Effective Thinking

One of the first steps in encouraging effective thinking is to get people to see more situations in which it is appropriate for them to take reflective action and in which what they do makes a difference in the outcome. There are two major metaphorical frames that have been used to encourage people to construe situations as opportunities for reflective action: the frame of problem solving and the frame of decision making. Opportunities for problem solving or decision making don't just occur, people have to interpret the stream of life as situations in which problem solving or decision making are appropriate.

Example: Chris is a junior in high school. She (or he) worked hard on the last essay for her English class. She went beyond what was required to gather information by talking to a neighbor who happened to be an expert on the topic and reading the book he suggested. But this took her longer than she expected and she was a week late handing in an essay that was only half as long as the assignment suggested. Today her teacher handed it back with a grade of F.

How could Chris interpret this situation? One interpretation is that life has just dealt Chris a joker. Her teacher (like most adults) just doesn't understand her. Life isn't fair and Chris will just have to put up with it. This framing of the situation allows Chris to accept the situation ("I don't care about grades anyway") or to get angry ("Damn the teacher!") but does not suggest that she needs to take any action.

An alternative for Chris is to interpret the situation as presenting a problem that needs to be solved. The problem-solving metaphor requires either that some aspect of the situation needs to be fixed (the problem) or that some goal needs to be achieved (the solution). There are a lot of ways Chris could construe this situation as a problem. Possible goals are (a) to get the grade changed, (b) to keep this situation from happening again in the future, or (c) to get back at the teacher.

The decision-making metaphor requires only that Chris conceptualize the situation as allowing alternative actions among which a choice can be made. There are plenty of actions that Chris could take, including (a) begging the teacher to change the grade, (b) planning ahead for the next assignment, or (c) slitting the teacher's tires.

I used to see the problem-solving and decision-making approaches as essentially the same. They both lead to similar formal analyses that take into account goals, values, choices, and consequences. In short, I didn't see them as metaphors with different consequences for the construction of reality. I now see the two approaches as highlighting different aspects of the situation. The problem-solving metaphor highlights the search for *one solution*. The decision-making metaphor highlights the *choice of alternatives*.

These do not exhaust the possibilities; there are other metaphors that lead to different ways of approaching the situation. Chris could think like an architect and design a plan for dealing with the situation. Or Chris could be like a jazz musician and improvise a response. The following sections explore these four metaphors.

THE METAPHOR OF PROBLEM SOLVING

What is problem solving from the point of view of the students to whom we are trying to teach effective thinking skills? The students are part of a wider culture within which they have learned something about what kinds of things are viewed as problems. They are also part of a school culture that provides its own examples of problems and problem solving. When we teach problem-solving strategies, the students' conceptions and key examples of problems may be enriched but not replaced.

It is difficult to appreciate any aspect of culture from within the culture. It is easier to appreciate our culture's metaphorical understanding of problems by contrasting it with an alternative conception. Lakoff and Johnson (1980) gave an example of an alternative that was provided by a foreign student's interpretation of a problem's *solution*: "which he took to be a large volume of liquid, bubbling and smoking, containing all your problems, either dissolved or in the form of precipitates, with catalysts constantly dissolving some problems (for the time being) and precipitating out others" (1980, p. 143). This is not the way our culture views problems, but it does suggest that some culture (maybe even our own in the future) could develop a very different understanding of problems.

The chemical metaphor is both beautiful and insightful. It gives us a view of problems as things that never disappear utterly and that cannot be solved once and for all. All of your problems are always present, only they may be dissolved and in solution, or they may be in solid form. The best you can hope for is to find a catalyst that will make one problem dissolve without making another one precipitate out. And since you do not have complete control over what goes into the solution, you are constantly finding old and new problems precipitating out and present problems dissolving, partly because of your efforts and partly despite anything you do. (Lakoff & Johnson, 1980, pp. 143–144)

This chemical metaphor contrasts with the *puzzle* metaphor that is more common in our society. Puzzles usually have a single solution. Once the answer is found, the puzzle is solved forever. Puzzles can't get worse or change character over time—the same answer always works.

Students have a lot of experience with problems as puzzles. In some grades they do homework problems in math and science practically every day. These problems almost always have one "correct" answer, usually defined as the one that is given in the back of the teacher's book. When they find the answer they are finished. In spite of our efforts to get students to check their answers, many students give answers that are unreasonable from a common sense point of view. They certainly don't view solutions to problems as something to be implemented and evaluated.

Another aspect of our cultural understanding of problems is that we *search* for solutions and *find* the answer. We think of solutions as something we will recognize when we stumble across them. When we can't find the answer we say that we are *stumped*. Apparently we plow the ground looking for answers and become stuck on the roots of an old tree stump.

There is considerable variation in our culture about what gets to be considered a problem. The current tendency, supported by some aspects of the movement towards teaching effective thinking, is to apply the metaphor broadly. We consider many aspects of our lives to be problems—aspects that in another time or place would not have been construed in the framework of problems.

There are also social class or socioeconomic differences. Within lower SES groups, aspects of life that middle class Americans label problems are more likely to be considered *troubles*. For instance, what I would call landlord *problems* is more likely to be called landlord *troubles* in a housing project. Although troubles can be overcome, the metaphor suggests that troubles are something to be endured. This way of construing the world encourages more passive acceptance of the conditions of life than active challenging of conditions and working for improvement.

The difference between troubles and problems is reflected in DeCharms' (1968) distinction *pawns* and *origins*. *Origins* are people who see themselves as capable of affecting their lives, of originating actions that make a difference in their lives. *Pawns* are people who believe that they have no power and that they are at the mercy of the external forces. DeCharms believes that we can teach people that they have power, that they can be origins just by acting as if they have power.

We try to teach people to be more effective thinkers by treating more aspects of their lives as possible occasions for problem solving. The implicit argument is very similar to that made by DeCharms: People have more power than they usually think they do. We can achieve more just by treating more aspects of our life as opportunities for achievement, in other words, as problems to be solved.

Attempts to teach problem solving to lower SES students may come across as unrealistic and condescending. Middle-class people can get away with challenges to authority and assertions of rights that would provoke retaliation against lower SES people. Middle-class people have far more access to knowledge and connections that may be essential in achieving their goals. The poor are often right that their troubles are to be endured rather than overcome. There are powerful structural constraints in our society that limit the opportunities for many people. Schools often function as sorting machines (Spring, 1989) that direct some kids towards the high status roles in our society and put blocks in the paths of others. Only a limited proportion can get through. If one child overcomes expectations and makes it into the high status track, some other child is kicked out. The image that school provides opportunities for everyone is a cruel myth that serves to blame the victim for failing to achieve.

Charges of cultural imperialism have also been leveled at educational efforts to instill white middle-class values in schools. The replacement of *troubles* with *problems* can be seen as an example of such cultural imperialism. It is not clear that one metaphor is better than the other—there is no culturally neutral position from which one could make such a judgment. To change metaphors changes what is highlighted and what is hidden—there are losses as well as gains in understanding. Furthermore, to organize education around the values of the middle class puts other students at an inherent disadvantage. Rather than helping them become more effective, it makes them more alienated from the school experience.

I agree that by teaching kids to view situations as problems we are changing culture. I also agree that we should have more understanding and respect for the diverse cultures of our students. But I don't agree with the argument that we should refrain from educational goals that imply cultural change. All cultures are changing all the time. There is nothing inherently wrong with trying to change culture. But viewing effective thinking in the context of culture makes it clear that deep changes are necessary. Lakoff and Johnson (1980) emphasized how difficult it is:

to change the metaphors we live by. It is one thing to be aware of the possibilities inherent in the CHEMICAL metaphor, but it is a very different and far more difficult thing to live by it. Each of us has, consciously or unconsciously, identified hundreds of problems, and we are constantly at work on solutions for many of them—via the PUZZLE metaphor. So much of our unconscious everyday activity is structured in terms of the PUZZLE metaphor that we could not possibly make a quick or easy change to the CHEMICAL metaphor on the basis of a conscious decision. (p. 145)

Note that Lakoff and Johnson are assuming that everyone is constantly facing many problems and has selected some for active work. This fits the way I feel about my life. I'm aware of lots of problems, like all the little things around my old house that need fixing. There are a few that I regard as active and I'm procrastinating on the rest.

The puzzle metaphor isn't true of people who construe life as filled with troubles rather than problems. An important goal of problem-solving approaches to effective thinking is to get people to apply the problem-solving metaphor more widely. The conception of something as a problem is the first step towards effective action.

Let's go back to Chris, who got an F on her last English paper. Assume that Chris was not a person who made extensive use of the problem-solving metaphor—she considered the F to be one of those troubles that occur in life. She thinks that the teacher was unfair in giving her paper an F for being short and late; he ignored the extra work she did and the quality of her ideas. But Chris was satisfied with what she had learned by writing the paper. And her image of the teacher was confirmed: He is a heartless bastard more concerned with rules and deadlines than with ideas and learning.

Suppose we were able to provide Chris with a course in effective thinking that emphasized a problem-solving approach. This would make it more likely that Chris would start looking for a solution to her *English-class problem*. The puzzle metaphor would lead her to seek a single action that would solve the problem. She might consider appealing the grade or resolving to be on time on the next assignment. The puzzle metaphor highlights the single actions that Chris could take. It hides more complex ways of responding that might have emerged over time as extended responses to her troubles in English class. It is hard to argue that either approach is better in principle.

The chemical metaphor would lead to other courses of action. It suggests that the F represents a potential problem that has always been present, but has just precipitated out. Maybe there is something that would encourage it to dissolve again. Maybe it will dissolve of its own accord. Whatever Chris does, it won't solve the problem permanently. She needs to consider how to keep it from precipitating out again in the future.

THE METAPHOR OF DECISION MAKING

The metaphorical frame of decision making emphasizes choice. The essential core of the concept of decision making is choosing or selecting among alternatives. When we attempt to teach effective thinking through decision making, the image our students have of a typical decision-making situation is one in which the choices are clear.

Often there are only two choices—either to do something or not to do it. We speak of being on the horns of a dilemma. The image for most people is a bull with two horns, or two possible choices. Very few people in our culture would think of a triceratops with three horns.

Once the choice is made, the decision making is over. Implementation and evaluation aren't normally thought of as part of the decision itself. We value people who are *decisive*, who can make a choice and move on without looking back over their shoulder.

Decisions also bring out conceptions of probability. Making a choice between the alternatives would be easy if we knew how the future was going to turn out. To the extent that our metaphors deny that the future can be predicted ("Life is a crapshoot."), they deny the possibility that making good decisions will be more effective in helping us reach our goals.

Each aspect of decision making that has been mentioned contrasts with the problem-solving metaphor. In typical problems, the choices are not clear. The solution to the problem is to find *one* good course of action, not to choose between two potentially good choices.

In problem solving you haven't solved the problem until you have achieved the goal and made the problem disappear. In decision making there is nothing to disappear. You are finished when you have picked one of the available options.

Problem solving seems to occur in a deterministic world. Considerations of probability rarely enter in. Decision making is often seen through a gambling metaphor. The best option is the one that gives you the best odds. Thinking about something as a decision highlights the probabilistic nature of the outcomes.

Let's consider Chris again. But this time imagine that Chris was inclined towards a decision-making view of life's challenges. He (I've changed gender to indicate that this is a generic case, equally applicable to both males and females) was very angry with the bad grade and wanted to take action to do something about it.

Chris followed the *horns of a dilemma* metaphor in conceptualizing the situation in terms of two alternatives: should he make a stink about it or should he swallow his pride and just sulk? These were the only two choices that he considered. He did think about different ways of making a stink, such as throwing a tantrum directly with the teacher or complaining about the teacher to the school principal. But these were not considered as separate alternatives to be evaluated; they were just examples of what he might do if he decided to make a stink about it.

Not only is Chris implicitly applying a decision-making metaphor to his situation, the major choice he is considering is conceptualized metaphorically. Chris may think that making a stink is the way to get his grade changed, but the *stink* metaphor carries the implication that the teacher's life will be made generally unpleasant by an unpleasant smell. And there are a lot of cultural metaphors ("an eye for an eye") suggesting that retaliation is appropriate quite apart from any objective it achieves.

In terms of a more formal sociolinguistic model, Chris may feel that it is necessary for him to respond to the challenge in order to *save face*. The F from the teacher was a major face threatening act. It asserts levels of power and distance that may be unacceptable to Chris. If he doesn't respond to the challenge he is accepting the teacher's implicit assertions about the relationship (Brown & Levinson, 1988).

Those of us who teach problem-solving or decision-making skills to students certainly hope that our students learn more sophisticated strategies than those implied by the simple metaphors of problem solving and decision making. In my work with Irving Janis on decision making (Wheeler & Janis, 1980), we used a five-stage model of decision making that was originally developed by Janis and Mann (1977). This broad model should keep students away from a simple *horns of a dilemma* conceptualization of decision situations.

Most of our work on decision making was completed before I began to use the conceptual framework of metaphors. But I have found that the metaphorical analysis adds to the five-stage model that we used. The five stages are:

1. Accepting the challenge
2. Searching for alternatives.
3. Evaluating alternatives.
4. Choosing and becoming committed.
5. Adhering to the decision.

The emphasis in the first stage is on getting people to respond to early warning signals (or signs of opportunity) before the situation develops into a major crisis. When they *accept the challenge* they have construed the situation as one in which active decision-making efforts are both appropriate and needed. The term *challenge* brings into play the metaphorical interpretation of being *tested* or *tried* and that one can either succeed or fail in meeting the challenge. We could have called the first stage *recognizing dangers and opportunities*. But we wanted to bring in the metaphorical implications of failure if the dangers or opportunities are not recognized.

In the second stage we use the metaphor of *searching* for alternatives. Searching is so commonly applied to ideas that it is hard to see it as a metaphorical extension of the concept of searching for objects in the physical world. But the language used to talk about the search for ideas shows that the spatial metaphor is right *under the surface*. New ideas are *uncovered* or *revealed*. *Digging deeper* helps to find them. In our chapter on this stage of decision making we tried to give students suggestions for more *places* to look for alternatives, such as asking for suggestions from friends or consulting experts.

In the third stage, evaluating alternatives, we use the metaphor of a *balance sheet*. We explain how a financial balance sheet gives an overall picture of the status of a company by showing how the income and expenditures balance. Likewise, a decision-making balance sheet allows the advantages and disadvantages of the alternatives to be *weighed* against one another. The students are asked to fill out a balance sheet for each alternative by listing both the tangible consequences and feelings of approval (or disapproval). They are also asked to consider the consequences for both themselves and for other important people in their lives. (See Mann, Harmoni, & Power, chap. 3 in this volume, as an example.)

The metaphor of a financial balance sheet might not appeal to some people, especially adolescents with no experience with businesses. So we suggested another metaphor that is much more familiar to adolescents: the *report card*. The same advantages and disadvantages that are listed in a balance sheet can be transformed into *grades* on a report card. Students have a familiar scale of "A B C D F" to use for their evaluations.

We call the fourth stage *choosing and becoming committed* to emphasize that choice is a process that takes time. We don't want students to take the balance sheet metaphor too literally by adding up the points and saying "That's it!'" to whatever alternative comes out on top. We advocate an *informed intuitive* approach. If a tentative decision doesn't feel right, more work is needed. The balance sheet may have left out some important considerations. Or the decision maker may need more time to become comfortable with the feelings that came out in the balance sheet.

Most people regard the making of a choice as the end of decision making. We add a fifth stage to emphasize that decision making cannot be regarded as successful unless the decision is implemented and adhered to. Setbacks are common, especially in decisions about the way in which one's life is to be lived. Temptations beckon when students try to change their study habits. The decision-making process should include the development of contingency plans for those setbacks that are likely to occur.

I taught a course several years ago for college freshmen and sophomores called "A Practicum in Thinking" that included a section on decision making along with problem solving and communication skills (Wheeler & Dember, 1979). The five-stage model was presented to the students, but the exercises emphasized the evaluation of alternatives. Students developed two balance sheets. The first was for a hypothetical decision about what kind of car to buy. After this practice exercise students prepared a balance sheet for their own real decision about a college major.

The students seemed to adopt the balance-sheet metaphor quite readily. Some of the students, especially those who were actually wrestling with the issue of selecting a major, said they benefited greatly. But in the course evaluation at the end of the quarter, the ratings for the balance-sheet exercises, although positive, were lower than the ratings for the other exercises in the course. I think a few students may have adopted the balance-sheet techniques, but I doubt that there was any lasting impact on most of the students.

Lakoff and Johnson's comments on the difficulties of changing metaphors (quoted earlier in the section on problem solving) suggest that I should not have expected students to adopt a new metaphor with just a couple exercises in class. Students can be made aware of the possibilities of balance sheets and they can be taught to apply the external structure of a balance sheet to decisions. But to adopt the balance sheet as a metaphor for decisions would mean that the student would think about decisions in a way that was inherently structured by the idea of an array of choices organized by a very abstract notion of a balance sheet. With this underlying structure, the action of making a specific external balance sheet becomes a very natural act for an important decision.

I don't know how to change the deep metaphors that structure our students' thinking. But I have two suggestions. First, I think high school is the time to try. I felt that with most of my college students it was probably too late. Second, we have the best chance when we catch students grappling with real decisions about their own lives. It may be better to work with students as they become concerned about decisions than to try to anticipate the need.

We should also encourage our students to adapt the strategies we suggest to their own ways of working. Perkins (1981) argued that in spite of evidence for the effectiveness of the SQ3R method of studying (Survey, Question, Read, Recite, Review), most people who are taught the method do not adopt it. But that does not mean that learning it is useless. People develop their own idiosyncratic strategies for studying—they figure out something they are comfortable with that seems to work for them. Bits and pieces of the SQ3R method may be incorporated into their repertoire of tools for studying that can be deployed when contextually appropriate.

THE METAPHOR OF DESIGN

Design has been promoted as a metaphor for effective thinking by a number of very different authors. Several years ago Koberg and Bagnall (1976) wrote an eclectic guide to problem solving and decision making that was tied together with the general theme of design. They stated in large type on the back cover "DESIGN IS a process of MAKING DREAMS come TRUE." They also use the metaphor of traveling through life and say that "The DESIGN PROCESS is a Problem-Solving JOURNEY" (p. 16).

Perkins (1986) proposed a major reconceptualization of the way we think about *knowledge*. As his title put it, he urged the metaphor of *Knowledge as Design*. For Perkins, "design refers to the human endeavor of shaping objects to purposes" (p. 1). He extended this idea to knowledge. Knowledge is not just information; it is created by humans to serve purposes.

At the end of his book, Perkins asked "What is the design that designs itself?" (p., 230). His answer is that humans are the only self-designing system we know about. We make plans and take actions with the deliberate purpose of changing ourselves. We decide to major in geology, to go on a diet, to learn to sail—all as part of a deliberate attempt to make ourselves different than we are now.

Perkins saw self-design as difficult, often more difficult than object design. We are limited by defensiveness and lack of perspective. We often need help, the help of a teacher. "A teacher, ideally conceived, is a designer who helps learners to design themselves" (p. 230).

Schön (1983, 1987) provided an extensive analysis of professional expertise using the metaphor of design. One of his key terms is *reflection-in-action*. Professionals can't just apply standard problem-solving techniques, they have to reflect on what happens and *design* a solution for the specific context.

Knowing-in-action is another key term. It is the "know-how we reveal in our intelligent action. . . . Our descriptions of knowledge-in-action are always *constructions*." (1987, p. 25) It is *tacit* (in Polanyi's [1967] sense) and cannot be described directly. Our know-how allows us to act without stopping to think, to solve problems, or to make decisions. We know what to do in the situation automatically.

Reflection-in-action occurs when our knowing-in-action is not enough. We hit a glitch and the standard routines won't get us through. Then we do a *stop-and-think*. Reflection can occur later or it can occur in a pause in the action.

Surprise is what triggers reflection-in-action. It can be either positive ("that's neat!") or negative ("oh no!"). The reflections lead to changes in our knowing-in-action. These changes may be applied either to the immediate situation or they may only show up much later.

Knowing-in-action is sometimes hard to tell from reflection-in-action. Knowing-in-action can adjust for changes in the situation. Performance is still knowing-in-action even when there are many adjustments to the specific situation or context. The feeling of surprise is what distinguishes the two. Schön's example is of a baseball pitcher. The professional pitcher makes many automatic adjustments, both major and minor, to the specific player at bat, to the context of the game, and to the conditions of the field. But occasionally the pitcher will be surprised. Maybe the batter unexpectedly swings at an outside pitch. This can trigger an episode of reflection-inaction during which the pitcher makes new adjustments to take advantage of the revised understandings resulting from the reflection-in-action.

Architects seem to be the prototypical designers in our culture. Schön based much of his analysis on detailed case studies of students in architecture school. Rowe (1987) provided similar case studies of the work of practicing architects.

One of the most obvious characteristics of architects' work is that they produce plans on paper before their designs are built. This is different from the popular conception of artistic design; painters and sculptors are usually seen as creating while working on the finished product.

The ability to plan on paper allows architects to work in what Schön (1987) called virtual worlds. Architects can try out their ideas in a virtual world without having to build real buildings. They can experiment with different designs and see how they come out before they commit themselves. This makes the experiments affordable—but it requires skills with the virtual world. Architects must be able to visualize something in the virtual world well enough so that they can make valid judgments about how the design would work in the real world.

Another aspect of architectural designs is that they deal with complex situations with many conflicting demands or constraints. The client begins with some clear requests (a house with four bedrooms) and many vague and possibly conflicting preferences (warm and cozy with a feeling of spaciousness). The site is never perfect. The sociopolitical context is important in dealing with environmental and zoning issues. Many of the constraints emerge during the design process; they are not evident at the beginning. It is impossible to set the goals at the beginning and then work in a linear fashion toward a solution.

In contrast to the emphasis in decision making on choosing among alternatives that have been worked out, architects rarely work out more than one alternative at a time. For instance, in designing a house for a specific site, there may be two reasonable choices for the position of the house and driveway on the lot. Rather than develop two plans and choose between them, the architect picks the one that seems intuitively more likely to lead to a good plan and then develops a design. Later he may run into problems: the elaborated design seems to have flaws. At that point the architect *backtracks* and throws away some of the design that has been completed. The backtracking may just go back a few steps or it may go all the way back to try the other way to position the house on the site. The choice the architect makes is between a developed design with known flaws and an undeveloped approach that may have the promise of leading to a better design.

Finally, no one ever thinks that there is a perfect design. In any situation there are probably many good designs that would work well. There are also many bad designs with serious flaws. Architects are satisfied to develop one plan that seems good.

Now it's time to pretend that Chris is a designer rather than a problem solver or decision maker. She (or he) needs to develop a design or plan to deal with having received an F on the essay that was late and shorter than the teacher specified.

The design metaphor may help Chris see the F as part of a larger context, not just as an isolated problem to be solved. The immediate context is the English class. Chris needs to consider her relationship to the English teacher, the interpretation of the teacher's intentions in giving the grade, the importance of this assignment, and the assignments that are yet to be completed for the course. Beyond the class itself, Chris needs to consider her plans for going to college, her relationships with her parents around the issue of grades, the effects on her friends, and her own self-concept.

Both the problem-solving and decision-making metaphors imply generation of multiple alternatives. In contrast, the design metaphor suggests that one plan is slowly elaborated into a complete structure. Chris may begin with the idea of apologizing to her teacher. Next she figures out a specific way to make the apology that includes a proposal to make up the assignment. But in her virtual world created by thinking about the plan she sees that the teacher probably won't think she is sincere. So she changes the plan to apologize in a different way.

So it goes. Chris slowly develops a detailed plan of action. At no point does she develop multiple alternatives to compare against one another. Rather, choices are made between the current elaborated plan and the hope of developing something better from a different starting point. For instance, Chris might discover after she develops the apology plan quite completely that she can't find a way to make the apology in a way consistent with her self-concept. At this point she rejects the apology plan and begins work on the details of another approach. This is the equivalent of an architect tearing up one set of preliminary drawings and beginning with a different approach.

THE METAPHOR OF IMPROVISATION

Schön (1987) used musical improvisation as an example of how knowing-in-action and reflection-in-action combine to produce effective performance. Each player in a jazz group responds with reflection-in-action to the surprises introduced by the others. The independent reflections lead the group in a consistent, coherent direction.

Sudnow (1978) provided a detailed first-person account of learning to play jazz piano. He was already reasonably good at basic piano playing from classical piano lessons. He described a major period of learning in which he was *going for the sounds.* He had progressed beyond his learning of scales, chords, songs, and other lower-level components of jazz piano. In going for the sounds, he was trying to make his music sound like what he heard on records or in the live performances of jazz pianists.

Later there was a major transition in his conceptualization of his playing. He called it *going for the jazz.* It was a different order of understanding. He likens the difference to that between an aphasic or foreigner and a 3-year-old child. Neither is a fully competent adult speaker of English, but the child has it together to say what she says. The higher order meaning is clearly in place and leads smoothly to what the child says. The foreigner may practice a phrase until it sounds smooth, but it is just an isolated phrase that is of little help when the foreigner wants to say something different.

Yinger (1987) made explicit use of the improvisation metaphor in an analysis of effective teachers. He reviewed research on several types of expert improvisation. In addition to Sudnow's work on jazz, Yinger discussed oral poetry, improvisational theatre, and everyday conversations as examples of improvisation.

Another aspect of Yinger's analysis is based on the notion of a language of practice. In order to be a practitioner (of anything) we need a language (in a broad sense) to think and talk about what we are doing. Yinger suggested that educators need something like the *pattern language* made explicit by Alexander, Ishikawa, and Silverstein (1977) for architecture. They described 253 patterns that occur across many architectural designs, such as *Entrance Transition* (pattern 112) and *Flexible Office Space* (146). For each pattern, they gave a general description of the pattern along with an analysis of what characterized successful examples of the pattern.

Patterns are not tied to a specific level of description. They ranged from global patterns appropriate to city planning, such as *Agricultural Valleys* (4) and *Industrial Ribbon* (42), to micro patterns for designing individual rooms in a house, such as *Corner Doors* (196) and *Filtered Light* (238). Part of the power of a pattern language is the flexibility it provides across levels of analysis.

Yinger (1987) applied this framework to the analysis of a good eighth-grade algebra teacher. The picture that emerges is that of a skilled improvisation based on patterns within patterns. "The teacher was cast as an actor in a three-way conversation between teacher, students, and problems." (p. 64) The teacher created (improvised) algebra problems for both himself and the students to work on. These fit the immediate context of the students' (mis)understanding in a way that preplanned problems could not. The fact that these were new problems for the teacher as well as the students meant that the work done by both in solving the problems was real.

The core of the improvisation metaphor is that experts have general patterns that they use to spin out smooth performances of complex actions. The patterns work at many levels, from the overall pattern of the whole to the tiny details at the micro level. The expert knows the patterns so well that they can be adapted to the immediate context. The patterns are not mere routines that can be run off in a fixed form whenever needed.

The metaphor of improvisation was applied by Yinger (1987) to the expert performance of a professional after considerable training and experience in teaching. But Yinger, and others, such as Dreyfus and Dreyfus (1986), consider all of us to be experts at our everyday skills, such as walking, talking, and driving. The metaphor of improvisation can easily be extended to our example of Chris. It would be nice if Chris were an expert improviser in the everyday task of coping with school.

The metaphor of improvisation suggests that Chris received the F because his improvised performance in response to the paper assignment in his English class was inadequate for his audience (the English teacher). He may have been trying to act like a mature, independent adult. But he was at the stage of *going for the sounds* (to use Sudnow's term) of independent adulthood.

Sometimes *sounding like* is enough. If you sound enough like a boss so that someone accepts you as the boss, then effectively you are the boss. But usually someone trying to sound like a boss just sounds bossy. There is a difference between sounding like and really being a boss. Chris may have thought that he was sounding maturely independent, but the teacher could tell that he didn't have his act together.

As Chris grows up he will discover that there is more to being an adult than just sounding adult. Then he will be able to *go for the jazz* of real maturity.

Looking at Chris through the eyes of improvisation suggests that the difference between successful students and unsuccessful students is not at the level of conscious decisions or deliberate problem solving. Rather the difference is at the nitty-gritty level of almost automatic actions.

Chris might benefit from thinking about the way he acts toward school as improvisation. Jazz musicians certainly work deliberately on their skill in improvisation. It would certainly move the focus away from what to do about the F on this assignment to the larger issue of how to act appropriately in responding to the demands of school.

The improvisation metaphor may also be useful to educators. How could we help Chris develop the skills necessary to improvise a better response to the demands of school? Are there some patterns or routines that we could teach Chris that he could use to assemble a successful performance? Yinger's analysis of teaching in terms of a pattern language suggests that we may be able to explicate some of the patterns in a way that will help students learn them. The multilevel nature of pattern languages may help bridge the gap between going for the sounds and going for the jazz.

De Bono's (1976) approach to teaching thinking skills could be considered in this light. His programs teach routines or exercises that are labelled so that they can be called up by the teacher or by the students themselves. For instance, he teaches students to *do a PMI*. PMI stands for *P*lus, *M*inus, *I*nteresting. To do a PMI means to consider the consequences of something and to categorize the consequences as positive, negative, or interesting. Once students have learned how to do a *PMI* the teacher can ask for a PMI on issues that come up in the classroom. As the students become skilled, the PMI becomes available to them as a routine that can be deployed in their improvised responses to the challenges of life.

CONCLUSIONS

It is my hope that the pluralistic metaphorical view presented here will help three groups of people: (a) those of us who are trying to teach decision-making skills, (b) our students, and (c) our critics. I'll take these in reverse order:

Rationality is not very popular in some quarters. Our critics claim that people don't want to (and shouldn't) become "problem solvers" and "decision makers." In other words, they don't feel that the problem-solving and decision-making metaphors should become the dominant frames through which people view life. The pluralistic metaphors should help our critics see that what they are often criticizing is the limited metaphor of decision making, which focuses primarily on the act of choice. We don't believe this is adequate any more than they do.

Even when they have been exposed to the full decision-making model, our critics (especially those in some of my classes) argue that the decision-making view is incomplete and limiting. Words like intuition and creativity are often heard. The metaphors of design and improvisation provide more scope for considerations of intuition and creativity. Acknowledging the wider view of effective thinking may help our critics accept the value of more formal decision analysis in appropriate circumstances.

For our students, the pluralistic metaphorical views encourage richer metacognitive analysis of themselves. The students might be encouraged to see themselves more different ways. Both the design and improvisation metaphors are based on experts. It takes long training to be good at either architecture or jazz. Students may be more willing to accept that it takes reflection and practice to become better at effective thinking.

For ourselves, the metaphors of design and improvisation can expand our conception of what we are doing when we teach decision making. Both architecture and jazz have educational traditions through which students learn to be experts. We may learn from these examples ways of helping our students become experts at designing and improvising a better life for themselves.

REFERENCES

Alexander, C., Ishikawa, S., & Silverstein, M. (1977). *A pattern language*. New York: Oxford University Press.

Brown, P., & Levinson, S. C. (1988). *Politeness: Some universals in language usage*. Cambridge, England: Cambridge University Press.

de Bono, E. (1976). *Teaching thinking*. London: Temple Smith.

DeCharms, R. (1968). *Personal causation*. New York: Academic Press.

Dreyfus, H. L., & Dreyfus, S. E. (1986). *Mind over machine*. New York: Free Press.

Janis, I. L., & Mann, L. (1977). *Decision making*. New York: Free Press.

Koberg, D., & Bagnall, J. (1976). *The universal traveler*. Los Altos, CA: William Kaufmann.

Lakoff, G. (1987). *Women, fire, and dangerous things*. Chicago: University of Chicago Press.

Lakoff, G., & Johnson, M. (1980). *Metaphors we live by*. Chicago: University of Chicago Press.

Nickerson, R. S., Perkins, D., & Smith, E. E. (1985). *The teaching of thinking*. Hillsdale, NJ: Lawrence Erlbaum Associates.

Perkins, D. (1981). *The mind's best work*. Cambridge, MA: Harvard University Press.

Perkins, D. (1986). *Knowledge as design*. Hillsdale, NJ: Lawrence Erlbaum Associates.

Polanyi, M. (1967). *The tacit dimension*. Garden City, NY: Doubleday.

Rowe, P. G. (1987). *Design thinking*. Cambridge, MA: MIT Press.

Schön, D. A. (1983). *The reflective practitioner*. New York: Basic Books.

Schön, D. A. (1987). *Educating the reflective practitioner*. San Francisco: Jossey-Bass.

Spreing, J. H. (1989). *The sorting machine revisited*. New York: Longman.

Sudnow, D. (1978). *Ways of the hand*. Cambridge, MA: Harvard University Press.

Wheeler, C. J. (1987). The magic of metaphor: A perspective on reality construction. *Metaphor and symbolic activity, 2*, 223–237.

Wheeler, D. D., & Dember, W. N. (Eds.). (1979). *A practicum in thinking*. Cincinnati: University of Cincinnati. (available from authors).

Wheeler, D. D., & Janis, I. L. (1980). *A practical guide for making decisions*. New York: Free Press.

Yinger, R. J. (1987, April). *By the seat of your pants: An inquiry into improvisation and teaching*. Paper presented at the annual meeting of the American Educational Research Association, Washington, DC.

Author Index

A

Abelson, R., 21, 28, *52*
Adams, M. J., 38, *52*, 79, 80, 81, 82, 83, 84, 91, *94*, 239, 240, *267*
Adelman, H., 70, *78*
Adsit, J. D., 47, *52*
Ajzen, I., 99, *117*
Alexander, C., 324, *327*
Alvermann, D. E., 237, 245, *267*
American Chemical Society, 301, *307*
Amsel, E., *52*, *56*
Anders, P. L., 242, *267*
Anderson, C. A., 107, *116*
Anderson, F., 74, *77*
Anderson, W. P., 238, *268*
Arbitman-Smith, R., 239, *267*
Argyle, M., 22, *52*
Arkes, H. R., 100, *116*
Ary, D. V., 31, *53*
Asarnow, J., 161, *182*
Asher, S. R., 46, *59*
Ashton, R. H., 187, *201*
Asnarow, R. F., 238, *268*
Au, K. H., 243, *267*

B

Baca, S., 28, *56*
Badgio, P., 98, 106, *117*
Bagnall, J., 320, *327*
Bailey, J. T., 186, *201*
Baker, E., 43, *53*
Baker, L., 254, *267*
Bandura, A., 22, 39, *52*, 169, *182*
Barclay, C. R., 106, *117*
Barclay, S., 208, *234*
Baron, J., 24, 29, *53*, 96, 98, 99, 100, 104, 106, *117*, *118*, 123, 124, *146*, 188, *201*, 237, *267*
Bassock, M., 51, *55*
Battjes, R. J., 34, *53*
Beck, D., 197, *201*
Bell, D., 23, *53*
Bell, C. S., 34, *53*
Belmont, J. M., 106, *116*
Benard, B., 161, *182*
Ben-Porat, Y., 28, *55*
Bereiter, C., 266, *267*
Beswick, G., 71, 72, 74, 75, *78*
Beun, B., 74, *77*
Beyth-Marom, R., 37, *52*, *53*, *201*
Bichler, E., 22, *58*

329

E

F

G

H

Subject Index